Boomers Away

The Nile at Aswan

Boomers Away

Travels at the Edge of the Comfort Zone

Donald Healey and Denise Healey

Granite Mountain Books, LLC
Prescott, Arizona

Copyright © 2012 Donald Healey and Denise Healey

All rights reserved. No portion of this book may be translated or reproduced in any form except brief extracts by a reviewer for the purpose of a review, without written permission of the copyright owners.

Published by: Granite Mountain Books, LLC
Prescott, AZ 86301

ISBN: 978-0-9857291-0-3
Library of Congress Control Number: 2012941169

Note from the Authors

Throughout this book we portray people from other countries and cultures speaking in broken or Pidgin English. At first glance this might appear demeaning or even racist. Let us assure you; it is not! An equal number of people that we encountered spoke English as their second, or third, or, fourth. . . language to embarrassing perfection. Broken English, however, is real and, thankfully, quite common. When our command of a local language was shaky or non-existent, there was almost always someone who spoke at least a smattering of English. Their English may have been broken, they may have been difficult for us to understand, but each effort left us impressed, and frequently very grateful.

CONTENTS

INTRODUCTION

As a wise Hobbit once said, "It's a dangerous business, going out your door. You step onto the road, and if you don't keep your feet, there's no knowing where you might be swept off to."

This book is a travelogue; not a sit on your couch with the remote in your hand kind of travelogue, but a true to life follow your heart travelogue. It doesn't involve shipwrecks among cannibals, petting the dental work of roving sharks, or base jumping from Alpine peaks. But don't be fooled, it is an adventure story; not extreme adventure reserved for an elite few, but genuine accessible adventure, the kind to which we can all aspire. It's about exotic places, unfamiliar customs, wonderful people, and exciting "new" foods. It's about living out of a suitcase and navigating through cultures that you've only seen on TV. It's about the million travel decisions that you make on your own. It's about 16 months, 5 continents, 18 countries, 108 cities, 6 rental cars, 7 motor scooters, 9 trains, 22 planes, 29 boats, 35 buses, 121 taxies and shuttles, 4 metros, 98 hotels, 353 restaurants, an elephant, and a bamboo raft!

Did you ever have the big travel dream? You know; the dream where you cast away your work-a-day life, stuff clothes into a duffle, and then set out to explore the world; a dream where you're a dashing mix of Indiana Jones, Phileas Fogg, and Dora the Explorer. That's what this book is about, a big wonderful dream.

My name is Don and in all fairness I admit that the big dream belonged to my wife Denise long before it ever belonged to me. She nudged and encouraged, pushed and cajoled, and eventually, holding hands, we stepped out of our door and onto the road.

We'd like you to come along and share our adventure. At worst, we'll keep you entertained. At best, maybe, just maybe, we'll inspire you to travel adventures of your own

Chapter 1

FIRST STEPS

Like many wonderful things in life, our journey began with daydreams. You might say that our travel adventures started with a twinkle in Denise's eye. A more tangible beginning arrived when we walked out onto a railroad platform and boarded our first train. In between those two events stretched oodles of preparation.

Daydreams about travel got us started, but it was action that turned our dreams into reality. The rest of this chapter (omitting lots of tedious detail) recaps how we readied ourselves to take our big plunge. If that sort of thing interests you; read on. On the other hand, if you want to head straight for a favorite country or an iconic sight? Go for it. This travelogue doesn't come with rules. You may want to read it from start to finish, but that's completely up to you. With independent travel the next decision is always your own. Hop around. Indulge yourself. We'll be there to meet you at the end.

For those of you still with us; we're not exactly sure when our dreams morphed into reality. Our planning probably began with a list of places that we both wanted to visit and a mutual distaste for long airplane flights. When we set those two parameters side by side it quickly became obvious that a bunch of there-and-back-again trips wouldn't fill our bill. If we were going to see the world, and at the same time avoid repetitive air travel, a "Grand Tour" was definitely in order.

Both of us love to travel and we're very fortunate to have done some of it in the past. When I was twelve (don't worry this doesn't get long winded), my father (a car salesman so it figures) had a stroke. Fortunately for our family, he recovered. While he was recuperating an uncle, who spent many years in Latin America, suggested that we keep our costs down by moving to Mexico. In what I deemed a gut wrenching abandonment of my entire life (tween angst) we left our home in California and moved to Guadalajara. The upshot of this forced change of perspective was that at a formative age I suddenly discovered that the United States doesn't hold an exclusive on wonderful sights, friendly people, and vibrant culture.

Denise comes from a career navy family. She spoke Japanese (long forgotten) before she spoke English and was often uprooted when her father was reassigned. Her home-base to home-base upbringing instilled a lifelong grass is greener attitude and fostered an inquisitive need to explore.

Luckily, we're kindred spirits. After we were married a couple of years (we just celebrated number thirty-seven), we headed off to Europe to expand our horizons. On a comfortable budget of $25 a day we spent five months bicycling through France, Italy, and Greece. In later years, we traveled through England, Spain, and assorted countries in Central America. Denise and I are both hooked on travel. We chipped around the edges of our addiction for a long time, but now we were ready for a big fix.

Like any serious addiction the reasons for our desire to travel are nuanced and multilayered. My own motivations are mostly straight forward. I love the rush of new experience. A bustling market alive with: bright colors, exotic smells, and excited sound, sets my dendrites to tingling. The majesty of a deserted beach or a line of rugged hills fills me with peace and wonder. A walk among the time-worn monuments of ancient man raises goose bumps on my arms. Even haggling with an overcharging taxi driver trumps any day sitting at home on the couch. I simply love to see and experience, and travel serves up a continuous smorgasbord of both.

Denise shares my basic drive to wanderlust, but her motivations go farther and deeper. She's an active seeker questioning and looking for experiences and interactions that focus and give added meaning to her life. Without getting all "Eat, Pray, Love," she's a spiritual traveler who opens herself to the mysteries along her path.

If you want to travel the world non-stop for a year or longer there are plenty of ways you can go about it. For one, you can chuck away everything, slip into sandals, stick a toothbrush into your pocket, depend on your wits, and apologies to Blanch Dubois, "the kindness of strangers." This method offers the distinct advantage that it requires little or no planning and further requires little or no finances. As a bonus, you're more or less assured of at least one hair rising adventure. Disadvantages to this mode of travel include: meals that are often dismal, couch surfing, dorms rooms, the occasional mattress colonized by bedbugs, border guards who aren't sure that you're the sort of tourist their country really needs; and not to be overlooked, the fact that you are more or less assured of at least one hair rising adventure.

Another option is to travel strictly first class. This method offers the advantages that your meals are mostly gourmet, your accommodations usually include a chocolate mint on your pillow, and you only visit the best and safest of places. Last but not least, you always have a guide or a translator standing resolutely at your side to insulate you from the vagaries of foreign travel. The disadvantages to this kind of travel include: first class hotels and restaurants that look pretty much the same the world over, visits to only the best and safest of places, and guides and translators who stand resolutely at your side and insulate you from the vagaries of foreign travel. Also, if you plan to be gone longer than two weeks whip out your Gold Card and hope that you have the credit limit of Midas.

Of course there's a whole continuum between these two extremes. We're not fond of bedbugs and we're certainly not rich, so one our earliest preparations was to make sure that we were both on the same page about the relative luxury, or lack thereof, that our journey would entail.

This is a good time to digress for a moment and talk about traveling companions and compatibility. Long-term travel requires a lot of decisions and unless you travel alone it also requires a lot of compromise. You hanker to spend all your time in museums or ogling ancient monuments. Your partner wants to spend all of "your" time sitting in smoky cafés or enjoying the olfactory pleasures of a local fish market. You want to seek out the local branch of KFC. Your traveling companion wants to eat off that questionable falafel cart on the corner. You want to take in a traditional ecstatic dance performance. Your partner wants to spend two hours chit-chatting with a smelly "holy man." You may have a problem. Travel companions need to talk about their expectations. Just because you get along well in every-day life or for two-weeks a year at that all-inclusive place in the Caribbean doesn't mean that you'll be compatible on the road. Long-term travel is a challenge. If you don't see eye to eye at home, don't expect an around the world trip to pull you closer.

Denise and I have a strong marriage. We enjoy traveling together and we each know what the other likes, dislikes, and expects. Just the same, we bicker. We argue. Occasionally we yell vile obscenities at each other. If you want to travel with someone, you need to be flexible and unlike the United States Congress you need to be willing to listen to your fellow traveler, appreciate their concerns, and occasionally give in to their whims. Yelling and obscenities aside, expectations are an ongoing conversation that you must never cut short. Try a short trip. It's always best to test the waters before you dive in head first.

Back to relative luxury; I'm a lucky guy! Denise is the sort of woman who likes foo-foo stuff but also loves camping and is willing, when push comes to shove, to rough it. The amount of luxury one requires on an extended trip has a direct impact on where you can travel and how much you're going to spend. If your budget is limited, and whose isn't, this becomes a huge consideration.

The "First World:" Western Europe, the United States, Australia, and so forth, is relatively expensive. The "Third and Fourth Worlds (4th is same stuff only cheaper and less developed):" Africa, parts of Asia, etc. are relatively cheap. This means that a budget that gets you: hostels, hot-plate Raman, and third-class overnight trains in the First World, may well get you three-star hotels, restaurant meals, and maybe a private driver in the Third World. For us, this was a no-brainer.

Third World travel places you up close and personal with poverty and its related miseries. It means that transport might be dusty, crowded, or non-existent. The only available accommodation can be a no-star place that's seen better days. Tap water is usually undrinkable. Requests for things you probably take for granted such as a washcloth or toilet paper (or even a toilet) might garner you looks of confused consternation. If you can accept these small challenges, Third World travel is hugely rewarding. In fact it is often much easier and more comfortable than you could manage on the same budget in the First World.

Once we seriously decided that we were going to take an extended trip around the world, we began to put our financial house in order. We had no idea how much our trip would cost, how long it would last, or even exactly where we wanted to go. What we did know was that it would be a vastly more expensive proposition than an annual two week vacation and that it would require a solid springboard from which to launch. Frugal to begin with; we saved. We paid off our mortgage and we eliminated our outstanding debt. Our plan, as scary (and flaky) as it might sound, was to sell our home; use a third of the proceeds to pay off our son's college loans, set aside another third for starting over, and travel the world until the last third was exhausted (or we were).

This scenario presented two challenges. First, we didn't know how much money we'd have to work with, and second, however much it was, it would eventually run out. These constraints together with our desire to make our trip last as long as possible, see as much of the world as possible, and enjoy ourselves to the fullest extent possible drove our luxury and destination decisions. This translated into a strategy to travel mostly in the Third World, spend most of our nights in high-end budget accommodations, eat our meals in modest restaurants, and occasionally splurge in a big way. We decided to thread a careful path between prudence and extravagance. We'd scrimp when we could, accept discomfort when unavoidable, and spend money with abandon when the experience required it. Like stones skipping across water we'd travel back and forth along the edge of the comfort zone.

Once we agreed that this was probably a workable scenario, we returned to our wish list of destinations. Happily, most of our must-sees were scattered across Third World locations; places that seemed to fit with our overall plan.

Our next big travel decision revolved around when to go. To our minds that meant weather; warm weather and lots of it. We threw about thirty potential destinations into a spreadsheet and plotted their seasons. When is it time for the monsoons? What are the months for the long-rains? When are the short-rains? When is it too windy, too dusty, or just plain too hot? When does winter begin? What day marks the start of cyclone season? Like Goldilocks testing porridge, we were looking for an experience that was just right. A little web research, a bit of color coding, and a pattern began to emerge. If we started our journey around New Years, spent a couple of months south of the border testing our travel skills, equipment, and luggage; then headed for Southern Europe and North Africa and kept more or less traveling to the east, we could bag an endless summer, or at least a satisfactory approximation.

Lest you get the impression that we planned a detailed itinerary; we didn't. What we did was throw together a rough, very rough, outline. We've met other around-the-world travelers who planned each and every step of their journey. Before they left home they arranged everything. They applied for all their visas, purchased all their transportation, and prepaid all their accommodations. A good travel agent can handle all those preparations and more. Getting an expert to do the heavy lifting may sound like a great idea, but it can, and often does, fall far short of an independent traveler's expectations. One of our fundamental decisions was that we'd go it "alone." This route risked reinventing the wheel, but it promised a wonderful learning experience that we couldn't pass up.

The big problem with long, detailed, completely prearranged trips is that they lack flexibility. This can be an enormous gotcha. What happens if you arrive in Katmandu, you love it and you want to stay, but your prepaid flight leaves tomorrow at 6 A.M? Well, the bottom line; you're up the creek. If you catch the flight, Katmandu sails away out the window and you always wonder what you missed. If you skip the flight, your itinerary crumbles like a house of cards, you're on your own, your deposits vaporize, and your costs go through the roof. Planning every day of a trip works fine when it's a two-week beach vacation. Do it for an extended trip and it's a ball and chain. It purchases you artificial peace of mind at the expense of lost opportunity and missed experience.

Sadly, in this Internet age reservations are a fact of life. No matter what; unless you walk to your destinations and sleep in a bedroll by the side of the road, sooner or later you have to make them. Many times you'll be forced to pay in advance and unfortunately, once such a reservation is accepted, it usually dictates how you use your time. We freely admit this reality but lament it just the same. To mitigate the impact of reservations on our schedule, we agreed to keep them to a minimum and try not to make them too far in advance.

Another reason we decided to "go it alone" is that it's all well and good for a travel agent to book you a round-trip flight and a resort package, it's another animal entirely for them to book you even a single month of travel that involves complicated connections between: hotels, trains, buses, ferries, taxis, and planes. On previous trips we'd encountered enough travelers with computer-print-out itineraries and fists full of vouchers to know that even professional travel plans can go awry.

You reach Katmandu only to discover that bus timetables have changed and that your next ride just rolled on without you. Or, maybe you arrive at your prepaid hotel to discover a bevy of noisy prostitutes decorating the lobby. You might, if you have cell service, and the time difference isn't working against you, be able to reach your travel agent by phone. No doubt, they'll commiserate with you about your predicament. They may even give you some good advice, but we seriously doubt they will be able to fix the situation as effectively as you can on your own.

If you deal with your own travel decisions day in and day out, annoyances like these are small bumps in the road. You missed your bus; no problem, you catch the next one. Your chosen hotel is a dive; there are three better ones just down the street. Independent travel builds confidence and self-reliance and that was a part of the journey we were seeking.

A part of the journey that we hoped to skip was government bureaucracy, but unfortunately like beggars and persistent touts bureaucracy is largely unavoidable. Strangely (to our minds at least), most governments take a zealous interest in who visits their country and how long they stay. This in turn gives rise to an inevitable need for passports and visas.

We were on our second set of passports, but we needed to renew them before we left. A passport is your number one essential travel document. Try to leave home without one and you'll probably find yourself standing at an airport check-in counter while a stern-faced employee refuses to issue you a boarding pass. A passport that's set to expire in a few months is almost as bad since many countries require several months of validity before they'll let you in.

We've never robbed our local A&P so our renewal was easy. All the info is available online, and the process is straight forward. If you give yourself plenty of time you can accomplish the whole transaction by regular mail; very cool!

With updated passports in hand, that were valid for the next 10 years, we should probably have turned our attention to visas. It's a tedious reality of travel that every country that you visit has its own unique bureaucratic hoops; hoops that you're required to negotiate before anyone invites you in. In the best cases, you fill out a couple of simple forms, either on a plane or as you walk across the border, and that's all there is to it. From there, things can go downhill rather quickly: paperwork increases to Byzantine levels, delays become the norm, and fees multiply like rabbits on Viagra. In the worst cases countries will only issue a visa if you visit as part of an organized tour or if you arrange your visa before you leave home. Fortunately, most countries love U.S. dollars and welcome American tourists with open arms; an attitude that works for us.

Still, since a little homework had the potential to save us big disappointments, we made a cursory check of who requires what. That's not to say that we applied for anything. Investigating visa requirements before you leave home is a good idea, but actually obtaining them is a little iffier. The problem is that visas often arrive with a shelf life; a limitation which poses significant scheduling problems. If you hold a visa that expires one year from date of issue and you plan to travel for 18 months, that visa is going to drive your travel decisions. If you hold half a dozen visas that all expire in 3 or 4 months, you've got a mess on your hands.

We didn't know exactly what countries we wanted to visit, so we just trusted our luck and researched entry requirements a month or two before we hit each border. This cavalier approach could easily have ended in fiasco, but fortunately for us, dumb luck sometimes works just well as thorough preparation.

Not knowing exactly where we intended to travel also played a role in our healthcare preparations. A lot of places exist in this world where sanitation takes a back-seat and exotic diseases slip behind the steering wheel. When you cross borders some countries require proof of certain vaccinations before they'll let you enter. This was stuff we needed to research and take care of at home. After some preliminary reading about conditions in the countries on our short list, we decided that a visit to a "travel doctor" was in order.

In case you don't know, a travel doctor is physician who specializes in travel-related health care: vaccinations, travel immunizations, prescriptions, health and safety education, so on and so forth. We found a likely one in our local yellow-pages, made an appointment, and headed on down. When we arrived a receptionist handed us clipboards and asked us to fill out the usual semi-obligatory health history forms. These were followed by forms where we were asked to write down our intended destination. You might see where this is going.

Travel clinics are not for the squeamish; listen to all the creepy disease warnings and health education, and you're almost as likely to bag your plans as you are to get any inoculations. The clinic we chose was used to dealing with people headed for three day safaris in Africa or seven day trips to Brazil. When we sauntered in with our plan to travel for a year or more, unsure of where we wanted to go, we threw a monkey wrench into the works. With his usual cookie-cutter recommendations in disarray our doctor scratched his head, hopped on the Internet, and thought a little harder than usual. In the end, he decided that a shotgun approach was the safest and stuck us like pin cushions. After a couple of hours, we walked out with: sore arms, yellow fever cards, emergency water purification kits, and a fist full of prescriptions; total cost $850.

As you might expect, the clinic prescribed a mountain of anti-malarial pills, and many months worth of tablets supposed to rescue us from traveler's diarrhea (yuck). This was a start but since Denise takes a couple of medications on a daily basis it was only the tip of our prescription iceberg.

Filling a prescription for a thirty-day supply of something is one sort of activity. Filling multiple prescriptions for a 16 month supply of the same medication is a whole different endeavor. We filled prescriptions at different pharmacies. We refilled 30-day prescriptions without using the originals. We requested "vacation" supplies. We spent hours on the phone with reluctant insurance companies and wrote them a stack of emails and letters. We filed appeals. We refused to take "no" for an answer and with dogged persistence we eventually gathered half a suitcase worth of meds.

At this point you might wonder why we bothered. Why didn't we just fill our prescriptions along the way as the need arose? Heck, the meds are probably even cheaper outside the U.S. In those early days of planning, the answer was paranoia. We worried that if we didn't take something with us we might not find it on the road. In hindsight, paranoia served us pretty well. In underdeveloped countries, you're lucky to find an aspirin, much less your pharmaceutical of choice. In places with better infrastructure, lots of medications are available, but it's a long-shot crapshoot whether yours is among them. In fully developed countries, they probably have your meds, but they won't honor your U.S. prescription. The bottom line is, if you need it; carry it with you!

Years ago, when we took our five month bicycle jaunt, our pre-trip logistics were crazy easy: get a copy of "Europe on $10 a Day," buy a couple of bicycles, put some clothes in a bag, pick up a stack of travelers checks, purchase seats on a Freddy Laker charter, move out of the apartment, and ask mom and dad to handle anything that pops up. This time around we were 50-somethings and there wasn't anyone to fill the "anything that pops up" role. Our family is small. Denise's mom was 85, our other parents are gone, and our son was busy with college. To make matters worse, we were now burdened with a modest 30-year collection of assets and normal business entanglements, all of which needed to be placed into a holding pattern.

Based on a modicum of soul-searching and an excess of head scratching, we decided that our best plan was to: dispose of or cancel everything that we didn't need, automate what we could, and handle whatever was left via the Internet. Easier said than done! We knew that despite our best efforts, "important" mail would still be sent to us via the U.S. Postal Service. Since we'd sold our home and needed a place for snail mail to go we trotted down to the local Post Office and rented a box. To our mind a P.O. Box was an easy and elegant solution. Our volume of mail would be small. We'd give the key to some trusted friend. From time to time they'd clean out the junk and they could email us about anything that actually mattered. What could be easier?

With the box in place we began to tell people about our new "address." That was when we discovered the flaw in our thinking. It was also when we discovered that insurance companies weren't the only intractable corporate entities with which we do business. Financial institutions don't like P.O. Boxes!

"Hi, we'd like you to change the billing address on our account."

"Certainly, do you have your account number? ... Okay and what's your new address?"

"It's P.O. Box..."

"I'm sorry; you can't use a P.O. Box."

"But, it's the only address we have."

"I'm sorry, but you have to give us a street address."

"We don't have a street address."

"Then I'm sorry, but we'll just have to use the address we have on file."

"But, we sold the place. We don't live there anymore!"

"I'm sorry; you have to have a street address."

"Really, you'd rather send our mail to someone else's house than use a P.O. Box?"

"I'm sorry; you have to have a street address!"

Some private P.O. Box services can disguise the fact that you use a box and that may have solved our problem. Unfortunately, it was an option we never thought to explore. After otherwise banging our heads against this bureaucratic wall to the point of absurdity, we gave up. We "moved in" with Denise's 85 year old mother and saddled her with the dubious pleasure of opening our mail.

We admit it, we're tempted to rant about our months of preparation, but since we promised to stay away from tedious detail here's a quick wrap up. We wrote notes on dry-erase boards, stuck up columns of post-its, and filled notebooks with our to-do lists. We researched hundreds of things: volunteer opportunities, how to catch a tramp steamer, travel insurance, international phone cards... We purchased "essential" equipment: silk sleep sacks, e-book readers, bathing suits... We reluctantly made reservations. We booked flights. We copied documents. At times the preparations felt overwhelming. At other times they felt endless. Still, we plodded along and slowly muddled through. Day by day our lists grew shorter and then one day to our pleasant surprise they were gone.

There were undoubtedly other preparations we could have made and a variety of things we could have done better, but sooner or later we had to stop planning and start traveling.

Chapter 2

MEXICO AND BELIZE

Day 1 - January 5 - Tuesday – San Diego, USA

Do you remember the feeling? You're eight years old; it's Christmas morning; presents are waiting under the tree. That's what we're channeling. Our planning is behind us. Our adventure begins; no more research; no more last minute purchases; no more obsessive compulsive luggage rechecks. An hour from now, Denise's sister takes us to the train station in Solana Beach. A few minutes later, we toss our bags onboard the romantically named "Pacific Sunliner," and then it's on to Union Station in Los Angeles.

L.A. might not leap to mind as an exotic first destination, but every journey begins somewhere. To ease into ours, we've decided to test our packing and planning skills with a two month "shakedown" trip into Mexico and Guatemala. Tonight we sleep at an airport hotel. Tomorrow, bright and early, we board Alaska Airlines flight 240 and then, with a whoosh and a roar, we're off to beautiful Quintana Roo.

Day 2 - January 6 - Wednesday – Akumal, Mexico

The moment you step through the doors of the Cancun airport humidity reaches for you with its strong sweaty fingers. Palm trees wave overhead and warm spicy air whispers of tropical secrets. *Ahhh, now this is more like it!*

After clearing customs and immigration, we ignored the crowd of taxi drivers and brochure waving hotel touts, zipped off our pant legs, and rolling bags behind us, trotted over to the nearby domestic terminal. Outside that terminal, we hopped onto a local ADO bus bound for Playa Del Carmen. ADO buses are modern and comfortable; they run about every 45 minutes, and at $9 per person they're a huge bargain when compared to taxis or private transfers.

Our last minute preparations bordered on hectic, so using a slight need to recharge our batteries as a convenient excuse, we've opted to spend our first week on familiar turf; a healthy dose of beach and sand before we jump into travel with both feet.

On past excursions to Quintana Roo (Yucatan Peninsula), we often spent a few nights in Playa Del Carmen. Back in the day, Playa was the quintessential poor man's paradise, a perfect blend of: appealing beaches, bargain accommodations, cheap eats, and laid back charm. Inevitably over the years the town (city) has grown. Playa still plays hard and offers oodles of fun, but this time around, we decided to blow on past.

The "Riviera Maya" expands by leaps and bounds. We know it's good for the local economy, but with each change a tiny wisp of local flavor seems to evaporate. With each tick of the clock the area moves a little closer to popular resorts everywhere else. Years ago, wandering down Playa's then dirt streets, we never imagined Wal-Marts and Sams Clubs, or that Highway 307, the main road down the coast, would ever expand to four lanes. Off-ramps and pedestrian overpasses (frequently ignored by the locals) have slowly replaced older glorieta (round-about) style cross streets and each year the highway inches closer to becoming a freeway.

Nostalgic whines aside, the Yucatan Peninsula is still one of our favorite go to destinations. When the ADO pulled into Playa's downtown station, we grabbed our bags, hailed a cab ($28) and rolled on for Akumal.

Located another 30 minutes farther south, Akumal languishes in something of a time warp. Nestled on its two bays, the enclave has grown more slowly (responsibly) than the rest of the coast. Along the Riviera Maya explosive change is unavoidable, but in Akumal its pace has been more sedate. Each year the community grows, a few new buildings appear, things gentrify, and prices climb, but so far Akumal manages to cling to its tropical Shangri-La roots.

Day 10 - January 14 - Thursday – Belize City, Belize

We devoted the past week to slowing down. If you're in the mood, there's a ton of engaging activities on offer in Quintana Roo. Activity wasn't what we had in mind. We were tapping into vacation mojo. Each day, we got up around 8 AM, wandered out to the beach, and plopped down in palapa-shaded chairs. Except for occasional snorkeling forays and the odd walk along the sand, we pretty much stayed put until dusk. Sure we moved the chairs as the sun went through its arc and of course we made beer runs to the little corner tiendita (store), but both were well worth the effort. Luckily we brought lots of sunscreen and our Kindle is packed with good reading material.

Akumal's Half-moon Bay is an excellent place to snorkel. Its waters are usually calm and clear, and its depths rarely reach above your head. Each time you slip on your mask and wiggle into your fins the bay presents you with something different. Large sea turtles are still abundant and if you're lucky they glide alongside you, squinting in apparent friendship. Even sitting on the shore you see their little heads poke above the water as they surface for air. Rays are also common, and it's amazing to watch the sea-bats as they "fly" silently through the water. Other large denizens include huge parrot fish, and the occasional barracuda. The coral in Half-moon Bay is varied, moderately healthy, and it hosts active schools of small brightly colored fish. Ogling the wiggleys is a brilliant way to pass an afternoon.

In the evenings we strolled down to happy hour at our favorite bar, The Buena Vida; a perfect place to sip bargain drinks and hobnob with: ex-pats, locals, and fellow travelers. After cocktails, the biggest decision of our day was where to eat.

Akumal is home an ever increasing number of restaurants. All offer good eating, but even with a shared main dish it's easy to drop $45 to $50 on your dinner. Several times we walked the mile or so to the "Akumal Pueblo," a service community located across the highway, where the food is just as tasty and they charge local instead of tourist prices; a whole roasted chicken with side dishes and fixings, 80 pesos ($6.67), yum!

By this morning we were recharged and lounged out, so with our base tans up to snuff, it was time to hit the road. "Collectivos" (shared taxi-vans) run up and down the Riviera Maya all day from Cancun to Tulum.

You just stand on the highway and wave your arm when you see an approaching van. Fifteen pesos ($1.25) will get you to almost anywhere on the route. From Akumal to Tulum is an easy hop, but this time we splurged for a regular taxi. We didn't want to drag our bags the mile or so out to the road and we needed to reach Tulum early because we didn't know the timetable for ADO express buses to Chetumal. As it worked out, it was a good move. Our taxi dropped us at the ADO terminal on the south end of town, and the next express was scheduled to depart about an hour later; just enough time to exchange some money and grab a delicious breakfast at, Don Cafetos, a long time favorite and Tulum institution.

Buses in Mexico are awesome. ADO (first-class) is totally modern, reclining airline style seats, bathroom, "in-flight" movies, air conditioning, etc. With one quick stop in the town of Felipe Carrillo Puerto, the trip from Tulum to Chetumal, on Mexico's southern border, took around four hours and cost only $14.40 per ticket.

At the bus terminal in Chetumal, we checked the time for the next express into Belize and then walked across the street to sample yummy tacos. Our wait wasn't long; after a bite to eat and a couple of refrescos (sodas) we were back on a bus. This time the line was "Premier" out of Belize. The coach was still "primera classe" but overall it was in its twilight years and shabbier than the ADO.

We pulled out on time and thirty minutes later arrived at the border. Our "new" bus featured an English speaking driver's helper who walked through and told everyone what to expect, which made the crossing a snap. On the Mexico side we got off, queued up at an immigration booth where our passports and visas were inspected, and paid a 200 peso ($16.13) per person exit fee. Next we reboarded the bus and passed through an extensive, fence enclosed, duty free zone where Belizeans (and Mexicans?) shop. On the Belize side of the zone, we climbed off the coach once again, collected our luggage, and passed through Belizean immigration and customs; equally easy

We've visited Belize before and it's a friendly vibrant country. Northern Belize is lush and green with a distinctive Latin over Caribbean feel and it makes a favorable first impression; Belize City, not so much. Most of the buildings in the small capital look drab and rundown. The streets are hot, dusty, and dirty. "Scenic" canals that flow through town are only a single step above open sewers. Overall Belize City exudes an unmistakable air of overcrowding and poverty.

Our bus dropped us at the main terminal which put us about a twenty minute walk from where we planned to stay. The sun was setting as we collected our bags, and one quick look at the area around terminal persuaded us that a cab was a better choice.

The hotel we picked for tonight is called the Belcove ($51.76). It fronts a small quiet street and its back faces a large, mostly clean, sea water canal. The Belcove is modest, almost a backpacker place. Its best feature is probably its proximity (about two blocks) to the water taxi dock; the spot in Belize City where you catch boats out to the cayes (islands) and tourist buses on into Guatemala. The area surrounding the hotel feels less intimidating than the bus terminal, but it's still pretty sketchy. We're sure that there are nice parts to Belize City, we just haven't seen 'em.

On a recommendation from the Belcove's helpful manager, we left our valuables locked in our room and walked several blocks to a corner restaurant called

Neri's. The streets here are dark and slightly ominous. People approach you and try to strike up conversations that will lead to a handout.

"Hello Big Man, where you going? Blah, blah, blah . . . ."

"I'm like Bob Marley. I sleep in the park. Blah, blah, blah . . . ."

"I'm dying of cancer. I need money to feed my children. Blah, blah, blah . . . ."

The cracked but relatively safe sidewalks in front of a nearby police station are littered with the sleeping homeless. Walks after dark in Belize City aren't for the faint of heart.

Dinner at Neri's ($12) went well; well that is, right up until the chili pepper. I ordered a local fish stew. The first bites were mouth-watering delicious, and then, without warning, I swallowed the hottest chili pepper, bar none, that has ever existed! I like spicy food, but we're talking Latin fever dream, nuclear meltdown hot! My eyes watered. My face turned red. My throat constricted. Sweat ran down my neck. I'm pretty sure steam whistled from my ears. For a few minutes it was touch and go whether I'd pull through. "Excuse me, kaff, gack, kaff, can I, gack, kaff, get another glass of water?" Denise enjoyed her meal. I may never taste again.

We're about to turn out the lights. Across the street, Rastas are holding a rooftop wake for someone's grandmother. The beat of Nyabingi drumming fills the night air. Tomorrow, we head for Flores on the shores of Lake Petén Itza in northeastern Guatemala and the start of a month long home-stay and Spanish immersion.

San Andrés, Guatemala

Chapter 3

GUATEMALA

Day 13 - January 17 - Sunday - San Andrés, Guatemala

We crawled out of bed this morning in Flores, a little worse for wear due to birthday overindulgence. Yesterday was my 58th. Although slow to get moving, we were excited; this was our day to head over to the "Eco-Escuela" in San Andrés. After a good breakfast at our hotel, we finished repacking and rolled our bags down to the lake. Behind another hotel, we met two administrators from the language school who'd motored across the water to pick us up.

After a pleasant twenty minute boat ride, we stepped ashore in San Andres. Our first impression (we haven't explored enough to form a second) is of an attractive small town clinging to a low hill overlooking the lake. The houses are mostly neat and well kept but extremely modest.

Our first stop was the school for orientation and semi-obligatory paperwork. After that, we were introduced to Isabel, the head of our host family. After smiles and handshaking all around Isabel led us to her home where we'll stay for the next month.

Isabel keeps her house clean and neat but it would certainly be considered a hovel in the U.S. Here in Guatemala it's home to a family of four, Isabel, her son Samuel, his wife Darling, and their almost three year old son Jack (pronounced "Yak"). As you enter the home, there's a small sitting area with a couch, two arm chairs, and a TV resting on an entertainment center type cabinet. Behind the chairs are curtains that lead to a small sleeping alcove and a storage area where Yak keeps his "car" and "burro" (toys). Separated from the sitting area by a low wall is the kitchen. Isabel has a propane stove, and nearby, a cold water sink. The water from the tap isn't potable so you have to treat it with bleach before drinking. There's a concrete counter space in the kitchen, but no cabinets. Immediately to the right of the kitchen is a dining area with a table and six chairs, a refrigerator, and doors to the three small bedrooms. Denise and I have been given the largest of the three and the family is going to share the other two. The walls of the house are a mixture of painted cinder block and concrete. The windows are wood-framed with shutters but lack both glass and screens. The roof is corrugated tin over open wooden rafters with six-inch gaps to the outside at the top of all the walls. Except for the front door which has a keyed lock, none of the other doors have knobs or store bought latches. Mostly, the doors are held shut with little hooks made from twisted bits of wire. The home's indoor plumbing is limited to a valveless "faucet" in the kitchen, which dribbles non-stop whenever intermittent city water is available.

Isabel's front door opens onto a steep narrow street, but step out her back door and you enter a small backyard dominated by a towering coconut palm. The home sits on a slope and the yard is an undersized patch of terrace with a rough "retaining" wall to one side and expansive views of the lake on the other. There's a cracked concrete walk, some ornamental greenery, and a few medicinal plants; nothing you'd call landscaping, but enough to soften the overall appearance. A single worn hammock (rapidly becoming our favorite spot and bone of contention) swings between a rafter of the house and a concrete fencepost. Walk under the palm tree and you come to the home's "bathroom."

The bathroom consists of a small cement block hut huddled against the back wall of the yard. The lean-to-like hut, visited by the occasional large green toad, is divided into two small stalls with gate-like wooden doors. One side houses a toilet and the other side a shower.

The toilet is plumbed but lacks consistent running water so, half the time, you flush it using a bucket. You fill your bucket from a 55 gallon trashcan that sits under the palm tree and is kept full for that purpose.

The shower is cold water only and consists of a headless half inch pipe attached to the roof. On most days there's only city water from morning until about 4 PM, so everyone showers in the middle of the day; not a drawback since our afternoons swelter and the cold water feels refreshing.

As for sinks, there's a freestanding concrete wash basin in the yard. This serves for everything from shaving and tooth brushing to hand laundry and yard watering. Lots of things in the house are older, slightly broken, and jury-rigged. All in all it's a far cry from what we in the U.S. take for granted.

At this point, we should mention that, as things go in this area, Isabel and her family are successful. Isabel now keeps house and hosts students from the school but she used to have her own dental lab. Also, she owns the house and the property on which it sits. Samuel, the son who lives at home, is in business in partnership with his older brother Johnny (pronounced "Yoni"). Johnny also lives in San Andres, but owns his own home. The two of them own two computer businesses in town. One, called "SkyNet," offers Internet access and well attended classes on computer use. The other, called "SkyVision," focuses on computer repair and technical support. Currently, they rent their locations, but they expect to eventually own them. Samuel works every day of the week, usually leaving the house before 7 AM and often not returning until 9 PM. Samuel's wife Darling attends a technical school where she's learning office skills.

In addition to her two sons, Isabel has a daughter, Thelma, who also lives in San Andres. Thelma lives with her husband Elmer and their son Jefferson, affectionately nicknamed "Gordo." Thelma and Elmer are both teachers, and, like Johnny, they also own their own home. Thelma teaches elementary school and Elmer teaches middle school.

Our picture of Isabel's family wouldn't be complete without at least a brief mention of their dog, Spot (pronounced, ess-Pot). We can't decide whether Spot is pitiful or just plain disgusting. He's 12 years old and there's nothing much to him but skin and bones. According to Isabel, he used to be bigger. As the story goes, a coconut from the big tree fell on his head, nearly killed him, and he's been scrawny ever since. In Spot's defense, we have to admit that his face does have a lopsided sort of grin. Since he's always looking hopefully at the door we assume that he gets fed; we just can't say exactly what. The only things we've actually seen him eat are a little bread, an orange, and his own poo. Spot seems to have a good disposition, but he looks mangy, has fleas, and he stinks. You definitely don't want him up wind. His vocal repertoire consists of a few half-hearted barks and assorted pig-like snorts and grunts. He also wheezes like an asthmatic and from time to time sneezes stringy snot onto anyone hapless enough to be standing nearby. *Good doggy!*

Day 18 - January 22 - Friday

We've completed our first week of classes and Denise and I are both pretty sure our heads are about to explode. At times we feel it's all falling into place, then at others we feel as though we're losing everything we already knew. We think, fingers firmly crossed, that we'll leave here speaking much better Spanish. We opted for morning classes and every weekday we have to be at the school by 8am. Fortunately, Isabel's house is less than half a block away so we can sleep in until around 7am.

When we get up; we go out back to the "bathroom" and then stand in the back yard washing faces, shaving, etc. About the time we finish, Isabel calls us in to breakfast. Most mornings we eat "mosh," sometimes with a little bread, sometimes with a banana. Mosh is a watery oatmeal-like dish made with milk. It's slightly sweet and from time to time Isabel flavors it with cinnamon sticks; think breakfast soup. I usually have a cup of hot instant coffee and on several days Isabel has made hot water with lemon juice for Denise. Today the coffee was lukewarm because the gas ran out in the middle of cooking.

Like the water and the gas, electric service is a little iffy in San Andrés and the other night it went out for several hours. It was a big outage since all of the other towns ringing the lake also went dark. In Isabel's house much of the electrical wiring is exposed, something you might have seen in the 1930's, with bits of extension cord spliced in here and there. The few switches in the house look about the same vintage and are so worn you can see the contacts spark when you turn them on and off. The wall sockets are all single, ungrounded, and loose. The one I'm using right now has a broken plate with the socket hanging out. The light in the outside bath has wires that dangle along the inside wall of the shower stall; splices covered by masking tape. *Hmmm, is that up to code?*

After breakfast, we walk up to the Eco-Escuela for our class. The school consists of just two rooms. It sits next door to the local police station and across the street from the burned out hulk of what used to be the school's much larger main building. The Eco-Escuela was originally built with funds from a U.S. NGO but by the time of the fire, a couple of years ago; it was independent and no longer receiving assistance. Without further outside funds the school has managed to continue classes but they've been unable to rebuild.

The Eco-Escuela was conceived as, and continues to be, an enterprise that allows locals to earn a living which doesn't harm the surrounding jungle ecosystem. The school is essentially a self-governing co-op that contributes to the livelihood of about thirty-five families. In an effort to spread the wealth as widely as possible within the community only one person per family is allowed to receive direct income from the school. Some of those, like Isabel, act as hosts and provide accommodations for students, others teach, act as administrators, or serve on the school's rotating board.

Before the fire, the building where classes are now held was the school's library. Both its rooms can safely be described as Spartan. The larger of the two has work areas for four or five students. Each work area consists of a small table with two chairs and a dry-erase board on an easel. There are a couple of bookshelves on one side of the room and a big stack of lumber on the other side (beats us, we haven't asked). The smaller room has an administrator's desk and another teaching table. There's also a water cooler that leaks if the bottle on top contains more than two of inches of water.

The number of students at any given time ranges from a couple to maybe a dozen. When we first arrived, there we only two others; a young woman from Austria, named Beatrix, and another young woman from Germany, named Anya. Beatrix has now moved on, and we've added two couples from Wisconsin.

All our instruction is one-on-one for four hours each day. Believe us when we say that someone equipped with a dry erase marker and a whiteboard can throw lots of information at you in four hours. The teachers only speak a few words of English, so no matter what your level of proficiency, 100% of your instruction is given in Spanish. That might sound difficult, but it is core to the immersion concept and the teachers are careful to tailor their program to meet your individual need.

My teacher's name is Brenda, she's half Maya-Itzae, always ready with a smile and a laugh, and has the patience of a Saint. Denise's teacher is Elga. She's petite, kind of modern, a bit of a jokester, and says "um huh" a lot. Brenda says "Ah ha." Denise and I think both sounds are delaying tactics meant to give confused students time to think.

The neat thing about instruction at the Eco-Escuela is that it's freeform. As your teacher gets to know you, they help you focus on areas where you need to improve, but at the same time they allow you to drive the process. This means that they provide you with formal instruction on basic grammar, tenses, etc. but at any time they are willing to segue into something else that interests you. You might be in the middle of a lecture on the uses of the Spanish Imperfect Tense and suddenly find the two of you discussing windmills or the difference between elk and moose. On Friday, Denise and I and our instructors spent two of our hours on a lakeside walk to the nearby village of San Jose.

Day 20 - January 24 - Sunday - San Jose, Guatemala

It's about 5 PM and we're again in San Jose; sitting in the pueblo's lakefront park, watching two women and their four kids scratch something onto a beautiful ornamental banana-like plant. The older of the two women is standing on her tip-toes working away with the sharp points of a pair of tweezers. It seems pretty destructive to us, but hey, other names are already there and it isn't our park. For that matter it isn't even our country.

After the "Vandals" left, we strolled over and to our chagrin saw that the woman had carved today's date along with "San Diego, California, Roz." Couldn't she have found something to deface at home?

Since there are no classes on the weekend, spoiled Americans that we are, we spent Saturday and most of Sunday in Flores indulging ourselves with hot showers and poolside beer. We ate breakfast with Isabel on Saturday morning, then packed a few things and walked up near the school to wait for a "microbus." The microbuses are mostly Toyota minivans and they swing by about every thirty minutes on a continuous circuit between

San Jose and Santa Elena. You know when one is about to arrive because the driver toots his horn and his assistant hangs out the window yelling, "Santa Eleeeeena, Santa Eleeeeeena." Each "bus" has three or four rows of seats behind the driver. As these fill with passengers, the assistant places additional wooden "seats" into the "aisle" so they can accommodate even more passengers. Once all the seats are full, they still might pick up a standing passenger or two. The fare for the thirty minute ride from San Andrés to Santa Elena is seven quetzales per person, about $0.84 each.

In Santa Elena, the microbus drops you near the "Mercado Viejo" or Old Market. This is a sprawling warren of stores and stalls selling everything from fruits and vegetables to clothing, leather goods, house wares, and clothing. We planned to do some shopping, but first, we wanted to get rid of our "weekend" pack. After squeezing out of the micro-bus, we hailed a "tuk-tuk" and headed for a hotel in Flores.

Tuk-tuks or "rotativos" are little three wheeled taxis. The driver sits in front and behind him there's a bench seat for two (or more) passengers. They race around everywhere trawling for fares and will take you to most locations for 5 quetzales ($0.63) per person.

Flores and Santa Elena are located side by side but they're miles apart in character. Santa Elena is a dusty, scruffy, and reputedly somewhat dangerous commercial center that sits on the shore of Lake Petén. Just across a bridge, located on an island, Flores is a small, attractive, safe, and relatively clean tourist center. We had our tuk-tuk drop us at an upscale ($57 per night) hotel called the Casona de la Isla, where we were soon ensconced in a room with a view. After a little "oohing" and "aahing" over the hot water and the air conditioner, we grabbed our shopping bag and made the sweltering walk back to the market. The day was really heating up and by the time we spent an hour purchasing miscellaneous necessities: a mirror, twenty-seven oranges, a melon and a pineapple, we were both red-faced and dripping.

In the scheme of things, being hot and sweaty worked out well, because it gave us an excuse to hang out by the hotel pool for the rest of the day and do "almost" nothing. The almost part is that we ate restaurant food (poolside), ordered multiple rounds of beer, and spent the afternoon drinking rum with three middle-aged Canadians: Dennis, Ray, and Mick. Mick occasionally tries to pass himself off as George Lucas and he looks enough like the auteur to make it fly. It was a good time, eh!

Sunday, we spent more quality time poolside and put away another restaurant meal before heading "home." Since the afternoon was hot, we splurged 125 quetzales ($15.06) for a private lancha (water taxi) to take us back across the lake to San Andrés. When we arrived, there were still a couple of hours before dark, so we walked the twenty minutes over to San Jose and finished our weekend studying in the pueblo's pleasant waterfront park.

Day 22 - January 26 - Tuesday - San Andrés, Guatemala

We mentioned our breakfasts of mosh, but we haven't said anything about our other daily meals. Everything Isabel cooks for us is tasty and nutritious, but lighter than our fare at home. "Almuerzo" or lunch is usually the largest meal of the day and also the most varied. Main courses change daily and have included: a "caldo de res," a thin beef soup that features a potato-like root vegetable called "payac," fried lake fish (heads and all), a thin fish soup flavored with a dark green-skinned squash called "juesquel" (sounds like whiskey), spaghetti, chicken, beef, and potato empanadas. Portions of expensive items like the chicken and the beef are small and served less frequently. One chicken leg apiece or a thin palm sized (Denise's palm, not mine) piece of meat is normal. Besides the main dish, lunch always includes a large quantity of delicious fresh handmade corn tortillas. If soup is the main course there's always a scoop or two of rice to toss in for bulk. Overall, meats, fresh fruits and vegetables are a little scarce and starchy carbs take center stage. The emphasis is on food that fills you up.

Like breakfast, "cena" (supper) is another meal that rarely changes. On most nights, it consists of tortillas, some bean porridge, and a scrambled egg or two. You spoon beans onto your tortilla, add a little egg, and munch away. From time to time Isabel adds either a dollop of thick cream or a smidgen of fresh cheese to liven things up.

Very little gets wasted, and food that isn't eaten often shows up at another meal or in another form: fried fish leads to fish soup, stewed chicken yields chicken broth to spoon onto your rice, and so on.

It doesn't feel as though were taking food out of anyone's mouth, but Isabel usually serves us separately, and if anything our hosts eat more modestly. So far, we've made a couple of trips to the market for apples, oranges, and other fruit to add to the family larder.

Day 23 - January 27 - Wednesday

So here we sit writing about food for a second day in a row. It might sound like we're fixated but that's not the case; today just happened to be a very good day on the culinary front. A vendor came by yesterday selling "bananos," so this morning we broke our fast with banano "pancakeys;" yum! The bananos also found their way into delicious banana and pineapple liquados (smoothies).

Later, during our morning class, we got wind that "Che," a kind of hanger-on from Belize by way of Chicago, was going to cook a Garifuna (descendents of African slaves brought to Belize) lunch for everybody. The school has a stove in the smaller room and Che whipped up his meal right there; distracting us with mouth-watering cooking aromas and throwing our studies into disarray. He boiled several pots of water and tossed in fresh squeezed coconut milk, plantains, broccoli, chicken, fish, garlic, spices and other delights. The end result was: delicious poached fish in sauce, chicken and vegetable curry, black beans with rice, and a killer homemade sauce conjured from tomatoes and jalapeños. Che cooked the whole feast just to be sociable. It must have worked because it certainly made us feel sociable.

Most students only attend class four hours per day, so the Eco-Escuela offers optional activities to help you fill your spare time. Some of the activities are free; others carry a small fee.

In the free category, we met with a local Mayan man who spoke to us about the history and culture of the nearby village of San Jose (the place with the nice lakefront park). Interesting stuff; the mostly full-blooded Maya Itzaes of San Jose are tidier than their immigrant neighbors and take more pride in their environment. In recent years, as immigrants poured in from other parts of Guatemala, the people of San Jose found themselves constantly picking up after the newcomers. In disgust, they eventually passed a local law which states that only persons of Maya Itzae descent are allowed to live in their pueblo. As a result of this unusual racial exclusion ordinance San Jose is attractive, has more amenities, and is noticeably cleaner than other nearby communities.

Another talk we attended was given by a man named Ramon who directs a nearby national park named, "Parque Naciónal Aristide y *something, something.*" About twenty-four years ago an airplane crashed in the jungle just outside San Andres killing everyone on board. Among those who lost their lives was the Venezuelan ambassador to Guatemala "Aristide *Something*" and his wife. When it occurred, the crash was big news and, as a gesture of goodwill to the Venezuelan people, the Guatemalan government declared the site a national memorial park. A flurry of activity ensued and a lovely modernist chapel was built, bronze and marble plaques were erected, and an eternal flame was lit. The park got off to a good start, but officialdom soon lost interest. The eternal flame guttered out, and the park slowly frittered away. Over the years, locals carted off the remains of the plane to sell for scrap, stole the plaques, and cut down the trees. Fires set on nearby cattle ranches swept through the site completing its destruction. Bats took roost in the chapel and the park was abandoned. Today a small conservation association is soliciting donations, planting trees and trying to breathe life back into the memorial as an eco-reserve.

On a different day, we visited the reserve with Ramon, saw the ongoing work firsthand, and volunteered for an hour or two raking leaves. The resurrection of the park is an interesting dream but sadly the road ahead of it is long and the destination by no means certain.

Another volunteer activity we joined was a clean-up of "Gringo Beach." This is a popular picnic spot on the lakefront that attracts local families every weekend for fun and relaxation. The place was a mess; literally carpeted with trash. We spent two or three hours picking up litter with our bare hands (*Oh, yuk!*) and stuffing it into plastic garbage bags. It was a big job, so luckily several members of a local youth soccer team also pitched in. When we quit working, the place wasn't exactly clean, but there was no question; the area looked better. The following Sunday afternoon we walked past the beach and it had reverted to a landfill. *Oh well, it's the thought that counts.*

Activities on offer for a fee have included visits to local caves, a zoo, and fishing on the lake. So far we've passed on everything. It's not that we're indifferent. Well okay, we'll admit that we're indifferent about the caves. It's more about the money. All the activities carry a fixed price; say 200 quetzales ($25). If eight people go it costs 25 Q a piece. If two go it costs 100 Q each. Since we're currently the only morning students and everyone else is afternoon, there's no one with whom to share the cost. The amounts aren't high, but neither is our interest. We've opted to wait and see if we can go for less.

Day 24 - January 28 - Thursday

Rain off and on today

Day 25 - January 29 - Friday

The sun is out again. It's a little before 10 AM and were sitting in Isabel's back yard. The folks from Wisconsin take off today. We agreed to let them have our morning spot so that they can leave at noon and still get in a final class. The result is that we're off to a lazy start. Breakfast was a banano and melon smoothie, some sweet bread, and a couple of oranges. Denise's neck is stiff and sore this morning so after breakfast she sagged out in the rickety rebar "lawn chair." I'm sitting nearby pecking at the computer and trying to stay upwind from Spot.

Later in the day, we returned from a walk to find that Isabel had prepared a traditional medicine poultice for Denise's stiff neck. She'd picked rubbery palm-of-your-hand sized leaves from a plant in the yard that she calls, "Hoja de Aire" (air leaf). Next, she heated the selected leaves, salted them on one side, and then rolled them into tubes with the salt to the inside. To use them, you unroll a leaf and place the salty side against whatever is sore. The leaves are moist and sort of stick wherever you place them. When they dry, after about ten minutes, you take them off. Denise reported that they felt warm at first and then cooled; a naturopathic Icy-Hot if you will. She's not sure the leaves did much, but at least they felt good.

Day 28 - February 1 - Monday

Saturday and Sunday we were back in Flores for another Gringo weekend and the Casona de la Isla gave us a local's rate without asking. *I guess we're becoming regulars.*

Saturday started with the sound of chopping; outside the back window, palm fronds littered the yard and more were falling from the sky. The immediate cause of the leafy downpour was "Don" (honorific, not name) Beto. Don Beto is a diminutive 48-year-old Mayan guy who was perched in the top of Isabel's magnificent coconut palm energetically hacking away with a machete. It seems that Samuel has been after Isabel for some time to have the tree removed. Ever since Spot got bopped with the coco, he's been worried that someone else will walk to the toilet at the wrong moment and get a green bowling ball on the noggin. Working without a ladder, a net, or even a safety rope, Don Beto was whacking from the top down in what appeared a Lilliputian effort.

After breakfast, an enjoyable rice dish that suspiciously resembled mosh, we grabbed our overnight bag and walked up to the police station to catch a mini-bus to Santa Elena. Last time we hopped a van; it eventually filled its seats and even added one or two standing passengers. Silly us, we thought that was capacity. This trip we discovered that it is entirely possible to cram thirty people into a fifteen passenger Kia mini-van! Remember all those clowns that come pouring out of the little circus car, well they have nothing on the average Guatemalan on the way to market.

Our weekend was low-key. We managed an hour of pool time but then the rain blew in and that was that. We're talking serious tropical rain, the kind that falls in warm sheets, splatters on tin roofs, and gushes from eaves and downspouts. The kind that turns gutters into small rushing rivers. It was a rain that came in long roaring showers separated by silent dripping breaks. We sat out the showers, read and studied, and took advantage of the breaks for quick walks and restaurant meals.

When it came time to head home, we let a "taxista" talk us into taking his (nice dry) cab back to San Andres. It cost us more than the micro-bus, but it was less than last week's boat.

When we arrived back at Isabel's, most of the palm tree lay in the alley out front. While we'd idled, Don Beto had spent two full days whittling it down and dragging it through the house (no other access to yard). Sunday evening he was still at it, having swapped his machete for an axe, he was toiling in the rain in his shorts chipping away at the remaining stump. We suspect that the whole job would have taken 45 minutes with a chainsaw.

The tree's demise yielded seventy-five large cocos that Don Beto took away to sell for "helados;" chill 'em, poke a hole, stick in a straw, and yum. Isabel kept another thirty or so for their milk. When we asked her why she'd felled her valuable tree instead of putting up a safety net, a look of horror flitted across her face. *Oops! That idea was two days late and a couple of quetzales short.*

It's 8:30 PM and we're sitting on our bed listening to rain patter on the roof as it competes with the dueling hymn-singing congregations of nearby evangelical churches. There are several churches within earshot and each one tries to out sing its neighbor. What they lack in talent they more than make up for with enthusiasm. "Hey Denise, It might be time to close the shutters."

Day 30 - February 3 - Wednesday

Yesterday, for the second day in a row, there was no running water. Two days is longer than usual, but since there was still water in the trashcan, everyone took it in stride. Today, the water came back on in the morning and was gone again by noon. Oh well, the wash basin refilled, so we'll probably "shower" with a bucket.

In the afternoon we visited to a local "curandera" (folk healer) to learn about medicinal plants. We met Ernesto, the school's administrator, and he led us to the curandera's house. Doña Nanda, as she's known locally (who by the way is Ernesto's aunt) has practiced traditional medicine for the past twenty-five years. She in turn learned her trade from an uncle in Belize who started her off with a notebook of essential rituals. She holds "office" twice a day in her living room, once for a couple of hours in the morning, and then again for a couple more in the evening. Her patients are local people suffering from a variety of minor complaints ranging from colicky babies and colds, to heat exhaustion and urinary problems. Doña Nanda treats those she can using a mix of herbal remedies and ritual, and turns away those she can't help. She told us that just that morning a woman brought in her daughter for treatment, but since the child was plainly suffering from an intestinal infection, she'd urged the woman to go to a hospital.

Many of the poor and uneducated are afraid to seek professional medical help so ethical curanderas like Doña Nanda fill the gap. The efficacy of her cures depends on the application of medicinal plants, prayer and ritual, and on the faith of the patient.

Some of the treatments that she described seemed reasonable; others, not so much. In the later category was one where she takes a lime and the fresh egg of a free range hen (store bought won't work) and holds them both in her hand. She pours "aguardiente," white lightening, over them in the sign of the cross and then with the proper prayers passes them over the patient's body.

We can't remember exactly what the ritual is intended to cure but if fever is involved, at the end of the treatment, the egg is broken into a glass of cool water to "draw out the heat." The treatment is normally repeated once a day for seven days. If after four days the patient isn't improved, the treatments must be continued for a total of nine days. We checked with our insurance carrier to see if it's a covered procedure, but they haven't returned our call.

Denise just stuck her head in and said that we'd better shower fast because the water's back on.

For dinner tonight Isabel served "bollos" (pronounced "bo-yos"). These are a local variation on the tamale. They're made with a corn dough to which is added tomatoes, onions, oil, spices, and beans. Balls of the dough are wrapped around bits of chicken, placed in banana leaves, and then individually steamed. The resulting bollos are both tasty and filling; which is a good thing because Isabel made lots of them and they'll be on our menu for several days.

We can now expound a bit more on Spot's diet; today we saw him eating cantaloupe rinds.

Day 33 - February 6 - Saturday - Flores, Guatemala

It's a soft overcast evening and we're sitting in the Las Terrazas Bar of the Hotel Casona De La Isla. Another week has slipped by and, yes, we're in Flores again.

Our week flew, but it was a little tough on Denise because she's still having problems with her neck that make her uncomfortable. The tables here in Guatemala tend to be high and the chairs a little low and we spend a lot of time each day, hunched over writing.

On Thursday, we participated in another fun extra curricular activity. We met Ernesto and "Cush," the school's "lanchero" (boatman), at the lake front and then took his boat across the lake to a little island called Peténcito; home to a small private museum.

The museum leans toward weird and dusty in the way that small private attractions often do, but that doesn't detract from its appeal. It features two collections, both of which were mostly assembled by the owner's father. One is an excellent collection of Classic and Pre-classic Mayan artifacts retrieved from nearby digs. There's a little bit of everything from beautiful painted bowls and vases, to skulls with inlaid teeth, to roller stamps for making temporary tattoos, to huge lance points. The wild part was that the owner kept pulling things out of his cases and handing them to us for inspection. "Here, hold this." We're talking delicate artifacts dating to 300BC!

The other collection is totally different but just as engrossing in a crazy mad scientist sort of way. In addition to being a Mayaphile, the guy's father was also an early radio and electronics fanatic, who was fascinated with Nicolas Tesla. Half the little museum is filled with weird science, Tesla coils like you've seen in a hundred old monster movies, old radios, strange meters, and questionable medical devices. At one point the owner said, "Hey, look at this, it's an old X-Ray generator!" He flicked out his hand, flipped a switch, and four sparking electrodes came to life throwing off, "zap, crackle," comic book suitable, flashes of deep purple light. *Holy crap! I hope the people we jumped behind are thick enough to save us.*

When we finished with the museum and its questionable wonders, we motored over to another part of the lake where we visited a wildlife rehabilitation refuge, called "ARCAS" (Asociación de Rescate y Conservación de Vida Silvestre, Wildlife Rescue and Conservation Association). The goal of the refuge is to rehabilitate wild animals which are confiscated by the authorities from black marketeers and illegal hunters. At any given time ARCAS shelters close to 1,000 animals ranging from parrots and wild pigs to ocelots and jaguars. Unfortunately, the animals on display to the public (that's us) are only those that for one reason or another can never be re-released into the wild. Visualize old, aggressive, disagreeable, aging spider monkeys that aren't afraid of people, parrots that would rather speak Spanish than squawk, and three legged ocelots, and you'll get the picture.

On Friday I had class in the morning, but Denise's maestro (teacher) needed to take her son to the doctor and couldn't show until afternoon. By 1 PM it felt way too hot to study and Denise decided to play hooky so that we could get in an extra "gringo" night in Flores. We both studied hard all week and felt a little burnt, so the allure of a swimming pool, good restaurants, and a bathroom that's both private and handy was just too good to pass up.

On the way over we discovered that KIA vans have nothing over Toyotas. And, despite the KIA's impressive loading capability; it's also quite possible to squeeze twenty-four people into a twelve-passenger Toyota. Of course, when the baby in front of you vomits, it helps if you're wearing sturdy closed-toe shoes. The Mayan lady seated next to us was barefoot. *Ick!*

Day 36 - February 9 - Tuesday - San Andrés, Guatemala

Today was a pleasant busy day full of activity. In the morning we went to class as usual but then we decided to do something different. Another of the students, Martin, had arranged to go to an elementary school and perform music for the kids. Martin is from Ireland and he performs traditional Irish songs on his concertina. No one really wanted to study, so, teachers and all, we tramped up to the elementary school to watch Martin do his thing. The kids at the school were delighted by Martin's visit and either listened attentively or clapped along with his jigs. For our part, we got a big kick out of tagging along from class to class; sharing the children's' excitement and enjoying their shy happy smiles.

By the time we returned to our own classroom, we'd frittered away most of the morning and we decided to bag the rest of the day's Spanish lesson. Instead of studying, Denise and I played chef. None of our teachers had ever tasted macaroni and cheese (no kidding), so we arranged to whip up a platoon-sized batch for everyone's lunch. We made the sauce last night in Isabel's kitchen, while she took careful notes, and when it was ready, tossed it in the fridge. All we needed to do at the school was cook up the noodles, reheat the sauce, drain, mix, and eat.

The meal was a big hit. The students liked it because it was comfort food from home and the locals enjoyed it because it was "exotic" and foreign. When we dished up the first bowls, our teachers cracked up laughing and half seriously kept asking, "Where are the tortillas?" Everyone ate seconds (or thirds) and one teacher shyly asked if she could take a plate home for her family to try. Luckily, we made a huge pot, so we still managed to take leftovers back to our host family where it was again received with genuine excitement. Isabel even took the final scoops over to her daughter Thelma's house so they could also get in on the gringo cuisine.

Somewhere between spoons of mac and cheese we learned that, after lunch Ernesto, the school's administrator, was headed out with Cush in his motor launch to pick up new students in Flores. The result was that for the price of a couple of beers we scored an almost free boat ride across the lake. It couldn't have worked out better if we'd planned it. We needed to go to Flores to arrange a visit to a Mayan archaeological site called Yax'Ha and since the day had turned hot we were so not looking forward to another crowded mini-bus.

After our jaunt across the lake, we returned to San Andrés and headed up to our new favorite spot, the Hotel Benjamin. The hotel is a simple unpretentious place whose big draw, besides cold beers, is a beautiful covered terrace that looks out over Lake Petén Itza and the surrounding hills.

It was an almost perfect evening. I was enjoying a slight buzz, Latin music was playing softly on the radio, and the sky was a beautiful dark blue. Across the background of indigo drifted a flotilla of puffy multi-hued clouds heavy with rain. It was the sort of dusk that people paint.

That night was supposed to wrap up with a lakeside "fogata" (bonfire), but when everyone showed up at Ernesto's house it began to rain. Since water and fire don't mix, we all hung out on a dry front porch, swapped stories, and sipped beers and "magic water" (white lightening). Cush, who's a bit of a character, sang and played his harmonica and Martin squeezed away on his concertina. By the time the rain let up enough to walk home, nobody missed the fire.

Day 39 - February 12 - Friday

Today was our last day at the Eco-Escuela which was probably a good thing because both of our brains are close to saturation. It feels like we grew a bunch of new dendrites, but it also feels like they didn't grow fast enough to keep up with the inflow of information. Denise and I each took around 90 pages of handwritten notes. I purchased two new pens before our trip and used them both up. She went through mechanical pencil leads like they were going out of style. *Arrrgh! Writer's cramp!* We think that we learned a lot, but now it's up to us to put it to use.

We definitely got our money's worth. The cost of one-on-one instruction and the home stay combined was a stunningly low $40 per day for both of us; that was: four hours per day of one-on-one instruction, lodging, and three meals a day, plus free optional activities. Eco-Escuela rocks!

Interesting segue about wages; in this part of Guatemala a highly skilled stone mason earns about $8 per day, his skilled assistant earns maybe $6, and an unskilled laborer earns around $4.

After our last class, we returned "home," ate, did last minute packing, and said our goodbyes. Over lunch, Isabel who is a sweet and very religious person did a little last minute proselytizing. When we first arrived, she'd invited us to go with her and her family to their evangelical church. After we politely declined she never mentioned religion again except to thank the lord for pretty much everything, "Gracias a Dios!" which makes a lot of sense, if you're so inclined. While we ate, she told us that we're great people and what a blessing it was to have us in her home. She then handed us two fire and brimstone religious tracts and earnestly reminded us that no matter how good our hearts, unless we accept Jesus Christ as our personal savior that we're sliding down hot well-greased rails straight for Hell. We thanked Isabel for her concern and assured her we'd give her pamphlets serious consideration.

A final word about "ess-Pot;" on that last day, we walked out to the bathroom to find him eating kibble! We were totally gobsmacked; it must have been his birthday or something.

Day 41 - February 14 - Sunday - Flores, Guatemala

Yesterday was our tour to Yax'Ha. We enjoyed every minute of our Eco-Escuela experience, but after a month in one place we were ready for new adventures. The Yax'Ha trip was a good beginning.

After a couple of false starts, our tour operator pulled together the five people he needed for the trip to run: ourselves, a couple from Minnesota, and a woman from Norway traveling by herself. We all met at 10:30 AM outside the Café Arqueologíco in Flores and hopped into a private mini bus. The late start was great because it let us sleep in and it was also timed to let us catch the sunset. After a drive of a little over an hour and a half, we arrived at La Blanca, the first stop on our itinerary.

La Blanca is the mostly unexcavated ruin of a post-classic Maya city which was home to around 10,000 people. It's a neat site to tramp around. With only minimal restoration in place, you can easily see how such work proceeds, and how it's slowly revealing La Blanca's secrets. If you've never seen unexcavated Mayan buildings and temples, they look like ordinary tree covered hills. The only hint that something amazing lies hidden beneath is that the hills rise too abruptly from the surrounding earth.

After leaving La Blanca, we drove another twenty minutes to a small rural pueblo where we stopped at a tidy ranchito so a local woman could prepare us lunch. Our meal of stewed beef, rice, tortillas, and horchata (a beverage made from: ground almonds, sugar, cinnamon, and vanilla), was served up under a small thatched ramada in her front yard. While we ate; inquisitive pigs, chickens, and dogs all wandered past. The animals were closely watched by two small grandchildren whose job it was to shoo away anything that wandered too close. The little girl, the oldest of the pair, did most of the shooing, using a combination of stern commands and judiciously chucked stones.

After lunch our hostess invited us to step into her home and take a tour of her kitchen. Her "stove" consisted of a wooden table that was covered with a bed of clay. At one end, the clay rose up to form two shallow fire boxes into which could be placed a couple of sticks of wood. On top sat a large round, slightly concave metal disk. The disk, or "comal," could be moved from one "burner" to the other and served as the stove's cooking surface. Outside the house there was also a large clay beehive-oven in which the woman baked bread and sweets that she offers for sale. The yard was pleasant, the surroundings fascinating, and the food tasty; the lunch stop added an unexpected bonus to our outing.

When we left the ranchito, we drove about forty minutes until we reached Yax'Ha. Yax'Ha is the third largest archaeological site in Guatemala (behind Tikal and El Mirador). Again, much of it is unexcavated, but it's as interesting for what you don't see as for what you do. We walked through flat jungle areas, once great causeways, now overgrown and surrounded by mysterious towering mounds. It's an easy place to visualize the great and vibrant city that was. Maybe more so than any ruin we've ever visited, Yax'Ha feels like, not just a religious center, but a city where people lived their daily lives.

Yax'Ha is impressive, but it's not heavily visited; except for a handful of others we had the city to ourselves. We saw howler and spider monkeys in the trees and for a time a wild fox shadowed our footsteps. At sunset we climbed Yax'Ha's highest pyramid, and far above the forest canopy, watched as the glowing orange orb sank slowly behind distant hills. *Awesome day!*

Majahual, Mexico

Chapter 4

MEXICO Redo

Day 44 - February 17 – Wednesday – Calderitas, Mexico

Whew doggy! Yesterday was one hell of a long day! We'd decided that it was time to say our goodbyes to Guatemala and head back to Mexico. We'd also decided to skip a second night in Belize City and make a long eight-hour run straight back to Chetumal. We got up around 5:30, ate an early breakfast at our hotel, and then rolled with our luggage to catch a shuttle from "Grupo San Juan."

When the bus arrived at our meeting point, ninety percent of its seats were already taken by tourists who'd boarded at earlier stops. Our roller bags got lashed on the roof, my CPAP got shoved behind our feet, and Denise and I squeezed side-by-side in a "double" seat that was clearly designed for only three butt-cheeks. About twenty minutes later, two more passengers boarded the shuttle and one of them sat next to the person in front of us.

"Hey, you can't sit here. There's only room for one."

"I'm sorry, but the bus is full. There's nowhere else!"

For the next two hours they rode in disgruntled silence, four butt-cheeks squeezed into a space meant for three. Meanwhile, I stretched my left leg into the aisle and squirmed to keep my own ass from falling asleep.

At the Guatemala Belize border, things improved; well, at least a little. We got off the bus with our luggage, paid a $5 Guatemalan exit tax (only charged to those of us with U.S. passports, *Hmmmm...*), and then walked over into Belize. On the Belize side about half-a-dozen of our fellow passengers shifted to another shuttle headed for Belize City. The now vacant extra seats made the rest of the trip more or less tolerable. I went to the back of the bus and Denise had the "double seat" to her self.

About two hours from the Mexican border we pulled over for our only other stop of the day, a potty break. *Gracias a Dios!* The spot we pulled off the road was a private restroom concession perched on the banks of the Orange River. As we all clambered off the bus, a young man rushed out to collect his restroom fees. The charge to use the "facilities" was one Belizean dollar ($0.50). Unfortunately, the people on the bus didn't have any. Most of us were carrying: U.S. dollars, Mexican pesos, and a few leftover quetzales. We were in transit. *Why would anyone want Belize dollars?* While passengers hopped around looking pinched. The young entrepreneur glared at everyone and steadfastly refused to accept anything but his own national currency! With the toilet negotiations at an impasse and anxious people beginning to scout the nearby bushes, a Guatemalan gentleman stepped forward and offered to pay everyone's potty charge; eternal gratitude earned; international crisis averted.

Next stop was Belize border control where, to the anger of several people, everyone had to pay another $15

U.S. per person exit tax. We took the fleecing in stride. After all, we'd been in their country for at least three hours.

We already held our Mexican tourist visas so crossing that side of the border was a breeze, and it was also free of further charges. At this point however, things got interesting. Our plan was to spend a restful night at the Hotel Santa Teresa near the Chetumal bus station, and the following day head on to Tulum.

After our shuttle crossed into Mexico our driver pulled it into a side street and waited for everyone to re-board. We passengers had to disembark on the Belize side and cross the border on foot carrying our luggage. This seems to be a routine border ritual, but it's weird because if you look like a tourist (of a certain age or income) they just wave you on through; no x-rays, no inspections; no anything. *Go figure?* On the side street where our bus was parked, another bus was also waiting. The two drivers chatted and then ours wandered back. "Hey, that bus is going to Tulum in five minutes and he has a few seats available. I'm going on to our designated drop off, but if anyone is interested, you can hop off here and go with him straight to Tulum."

Denise and I looked at each other, "Heck yes, why not? We'll get to Tulum by 7 PM, and wake up right where we want to be." The price was right, so we hurriedly and switched buses.

The "new" bus was fast and comfortable; nevertheless, when we reached our destination, three hours later, both of us were: hungry, stiff, and tired. As we climbed off in Tulum, I suddenly realized to our mutual horror that I wasn't carrying my CPAP. We'd left $2,000 worth of equipment that I can't do without, shoved under the seat of a Guatemalan shuttle!

I asked the driver of the bus we were on if he had a contact number for the other driver or at least a number for Grupo San Juan; no luck. "Your only hope Señor is to go back to Chetumal and try to catch him at 5:30 AM at the ADO bus station before he heads back to Flores."

Well, screw that! Trusting in authority, we hailed a taxi and for 30 pesos ($2.50 U.S.) had it take us to the town police station. Although Tulum is a major tourist destination, none of the police at the station spoke any English. With the aid of our newly immersed Spanish, we explained what had happened and asked if someone could help us contact the Grupo San Juan driver. The officers were friendly, made a call to their counterparts in Chetumal, and initiated some bureaucracy. After a twenty minute wait, they asked for our cell phone number and said they would call us if the "case" broke. We were then sent on our way with a stern admonition to contact the Chetumal police in the morning and follow-up about the "Tulum suitcase thing."

Well, screw that! Twenty minutes later we were outside a gas station convenience store waiting while our taxista bought a caffeine-rich coke to fortify him for the three hour, $100 US, nighttime, drive back to Chetumal! When we finally rolled in around midnight, it turned out that our driver and his assistant (he'd brought a friend to keep him awake on the drive back) didn't know their way around town. We had to give him directions to get him to the ADO station.

To make a long exhausting story short, we ended up in the same bus station hotel where we originally intended to stay. I managed about four hours of sleep (or sleep apnea as the case may be), met the Grupo San Juan bus at 5 AM, and *(Gracias a Dios!)* managed to retrieve my CPAP. *Okay, let's not do that again! From now on we count bags every time we move!*

We were (surprise, surprise) pooped today so instead of heading to Tulum, we went to the nearby beach area of Calderitas, booked a room with a view, and kicked back. Stuff that doesn't kill you makes you stronger!

Day 50 - February 23 - Tuesday - Akumal, Mexico

If this is Tuesday, it must be Akumal! We're up to day 50 of our shakedown trip and another week has whizzed by. While we were in Calderitas we took a quick side excursion to the small but interesting archeological site of Oxtankha. Buses don't make the run so we negotiated with a taxista to drive us out and wait while we walked around. The round trip cost us about $20 which wasn't a rip-off but was still a little high. Taxistas aren't stupid; they know when they have you over a barrel. If you want to go, you have to pay. *Oh well, if we're going to have fun, we can't pinch our pennies until they scream.*

At this point we changed our plans. Instead of heading on to Tulum, we hopped a slow bus to Majahual. Majahual is a cruise ship port on the southern cost of Quintana Roo; a tropical destination that's usually touted as the "Costa Maya." We'd stopped there in the past and weren't overly impressed, but since that visit a hurricane had whisked most of the town off to OZ. According to scuttlebutt, the rebuilt Majahual was now the "in place," so we decided to give it another chance.

The biggest visible changes were: an improved beach, a nice ocean side "Malecon" (cement boardwalk), and more concrete buildings. We liked it a little better, but it's still a spot that borders on bizarre. Majahual is a tropical paradise whose whole reason for being is to separate cruise ship passengers from the contents of their pockets. When a ship is in port, the place hops with noisy beach bars, restaurants, craft stores, people giving massages under the palms, braiding hair, and touts offering pretty much any tourist activity that you can conjure. When the ship blows it's "all aboard" whistle, everything instantly disappears: chairs are stacked, metal shutters are drawn, and 95% of the town closes up. At that point, except for a few expats and strays like us, you have a closed-for-business paradise to yourself.

We stayed a couple of nights in a cute comfortable little place called Cabanas del Doctor; a throw-back accommodation where you can still rent a clean, thatched roof, cold water hut for $37 per night. We stayed at the same place on our first visit and amazingly it only cost us $2 more this time around; that despite the fact that they rebuilt after the hurricane. We enjoyed ourselves and might have stayed longer, but unfortunately the weather didn't cooperate. There's really nothing to do in Majahual except lie on the beach and that doesn't work when it's drizzling and the wind is howling.

Back on another bus, we once again rolled into Tulum, where, after a bit of running around, we managed to locate a reasonably priced rental car. Buses are great but for the next few days we wanted to be masters of our own schedule. We stuck our bags in the trunk, rolled up the windows, cranked up the AC, and set our sights on Valladolid.

Well actually, we wasted some time driving around Tulum's beach area. The weather had improved and, if we found reasonable lodging, we thought we might stay a night or two. Not! The days of reasonable beachfront lodging in Tulum are long gone. The once idyllic area is now a solid string of shoulder-to-shoulder resorts catering to upscale hipsters who want to "rough it" while having their chakras aligned. The least expensive place we checked was $176 US per night, a spot where we'd stayed only three years ago for $65!

We ended up at the Hotel Meson del Marque in Valladolid where prices are still Old Mexico ($57). The Meson del Marque is an upscale colonial hotel that sits right on the town's colonial square. The core building dates from the seventeenth century, with high ceilings, open beams, and beautiful tile work. The original courtyard houses a fine restaurant and behind it are: a swimming pool, gardens, and contemporary guest rooms with all the amenities. After a long hot day, the pool was glorious.

On Sunday, we drove out to Rio Lagartos. This was the main reason that we rented the car. Rio lies on the Gulf of Mexico about 110KM from Valladolid and bus connections are slow. The attraction is the Ria (yep different spelling) Lagartos Biosphere. You hook up with a boat guide and then spend three hours or so zooming through mangrove lined channels, looking for wildlife. We were lucky and in addition to the pelicans, ospreys, cormorants, and bright pink flamingos, we saw several toothy crocodiles basking in all their prehistoric glory.

As a zany collateral activity we stopped at some salt flats to float in pools which have such a high saline content that it's impossible to sink. It felt pretty bizarre. And speaking of bizarre, after the float we covered ourselves with "white clay;" a "natural Mayan beauty treatment that will take five years off you." We're a little too late for the full benefit, but it was fun wiping mud on each other. We think the guides just get a kick of seeing tourists smear themselves with flamingo poo.

We finished the evening standing on the fourth floor veranda of our hotel watching the stars come out. As we stood there gazing up, something huge swept across the sky. We were at a total loss as to what we were seeing. It looked like one of those asteroid chunks that fall roaring to earth in disaster movies and crush hapless yellow cabs in New York. The only thing wrong with that scenario was that the object was clearly moving too slowly. On the other hand it was moving way too fast to be an airplane. A single huge contrail of dark smoke stretched behind the object and instead of lights its head seemed to be glowing. We were both like, "Yeah, that's awesome!" So what was it Google? Welcome home space shuttle Endeavour!

Day 51 - February 24 - Wednesday

Yesterday we arrived in Akumal at around one in the afternoon. It was warm and partly sunny, but large puddles clued us in that the rain had just stopped. Denise sprinted straight for the beach while I drove back to Tulum to drop off the rental car. A quick drive and a collectivo ride later, I rejoined her on the sand (well actually on the lounge chairs). We stocked up on snacks and rum before we left Valladolid, so well accoutered we spent the rest of the afternoon refreshing our tans. When the sun finally slipped away, we flip-flopped down to the Buena Vida for happy hour at their "swing bar" and a light dinner on the beach.

Today, the rain is back. It's overcast and cloudy, but it isn't cold, or even cool, so we really don't mind. We wouldn't want every day to be like this but so far it's been fun to just hang out in our room. The waters of the bay are so still and calm that we can stand at our windows, or out on our balcony, and watch the rays and turtles swimming along the shore. *Ah sigh!* On the other hand, we think we might be a little bummed if we were part of the 70 person wedding party that has traveled down here for a ceremony on the beach. It's not raining right at the moment but somehow we doubt this is what the bride had in mind.

Day 53 - February 26 - Friday

Yesterday was warm, beautiful, and still, so we spent it on the beach (what else?). As afternoon rolled around, we popped a couple of Leons. Leon is Yucatan's best dark beer and you can't get it in the U.S. Well, those two bottles led to two more, and those two led to a couple of rum drinks that would have sported little umbrellas if we'd had any. In due course, Denise announced that she needed to use the bathroom, and headed back to our room. After she got back, it was my turn to answer nature's call.

"The maid's cleaning our room right now. You might want to wait."

That wasn't in the cards, so I walked up the outside stairs to the fourth floor, and headed straight for our open door. As advertised, the maid's mops and buckets were sitting out front and the little Maya lady herself was washing our dishes. I said a quick "Hola," and bee-lined it for the bathroom. When I was finished, I washed up and headed for the fridge to grab another couple of cold ones. When I opened the door, I was like, *What's all this crap, and holy cow, where's our beer?*

As I stood there looking befuddled, the maid quietly asked, "¿Señor, es esta su habitación?" (Sir, is this your room?) *Oh Lord! I just peed in someone else's newly clean bathroom and then tried to rob their refrigerator!*

I managed a couple of stammered excuses (in barely intelligible Spanish) and beat a quick sheepish retreat. Back at the beach, Denise laughed herself silly.

"What a dunce! I'm going to have to keep an eye on you!"

"Hey, the rooms look alike and they're right next to each other. You said the maid was in there cleaning. It could have happened to anyone."

"Sure dodo head, anything you say!"

I was thrown off balance by my blunder, but not so flustered that I didn't stop in the right room and snag our next round of beers. Anyway, we cracked those bad boys and passed the rest of the afternoon without further incident.

Around 5 PM we decided to leave the beach, freshen up a little, and then head over to the Buena Vida. When we got back to our room (the right one), Denise walked into the bedroom.

"Hey, why'd you mess up the swans and the paper flowers?'

"What, swans?"

"You know the ones the maid made on our bed with the towels."

"I didn't touch anything. The maid didn't make any swans."

"I saw them. They were right there when I used the bathroom . . . Oh God!" We looked at each other for about two seconds and then laughed ourselves into tears. The maid must have thought we were nuts. *Ah demon rum!*

Day 56 - March 1 - Monday

Our shakedown trip is winding down. We fly back to San Diego on Wednesday so we're making the most of our last couple of beach days. Well, Denise is making the most of them; I'm fighting a cold. Not what I would have chosen for a wrap up but what can you do. Ni modo!

Port of Call, Nassau, Bahamas

Chapter 5

ACROSS THE ATLANTIC

Day 98 - April 12 - Monday - San Diego, USA

One week left until we resume our big adventure! All things considered, our south of the border shakedown added up to a rousing success. We reacquainted ourselves with the pace and uncertainties of independent travel. We vetted our equipment and best of all we learned something and thoroughly enjoyed ourselves. Back in San Diego we acted on what we learned, tweaked our plans, and spent the past month making our final preparations before we re-launch. The big enchilada lies just ahead.

Once again to-do lists have dominated our waking hours. We paid our annual taxes (sadly, travel is no escape); finalized a COBRA health insurance arrangement (in hindsight it was a huge waste of money), and purchased short term travel insurance of the sort that reimburses you for foreign medical bills and flies you home if you have the incredibly bad luck to be scraped off the sidewalk by an errant bus or fall prey to a tsetse fly (also probably a waste of money). We took advantage of the lifetime warrantee on Denise's Osprey travel pack, which had developed a small hole, and at the same time discovered that mine (North Face) didn't carry any warranty because we bought it on-sale at an outlet store; caveat emptor!

We purchased: a second book-reader (Kindle) which if you're interested is an awesome way to carry a "sack full" of pleasure novels and an ever growing "stack" of travel guides, a couple of tiny mobile surge protectors, a "Packsafe Travelsafe 100" which is a steel-mesh lined sack that may or may not protect your valuables, but makes you feel better than just stuffing them under your mattress. We added to our wardrobes and bought packing cubes to organize our goodies. We squirreled away extra reading glasses and Velcro ties and we used Western Union to send a deposit to an Arabic immersion school in Morocco (gluttons for punishment).

Now, we're eager to be on our way and there's little to do except wait. In lieu of a long flight we've opted to begin our journey with a long Atlantic cruise from Galveston to Barcelona. Antsy or not, reservations hold our starter pistol.

Day 104 - April 18 - Sunday - Galveston, USA

Our trip from San Diego to Texas was uneventful; a crowded mostly boring flight to Houston (God I hate flying). We followed the flight with a shuttle to the "luxurious," $39 per night, Knight's Inn in the exciting, hold your breath, suburb of Humble. The first day of our around-the-world odyssey finished with an "exotic gourmet" dinner at Denny's.

"You can't miss the Denny's; it's just past the gas station and the adult novelties store."

Oh well, no complaints; you get what you pay for.

Today started out with a twist. We took a hotel shuttle back to the airport where we were supposed to meet a pre-paid bus that would take us on to Galveston. When we arrived at the airport, a large bus was sitting outside at the curb loading passengers and luggage. Both the people climbing aboard and the bags going underneath were festooned with Royal Caribbean tags and stickers. I walked over and asked the driver if the bus belonged to Galveston Limousine Service.

"No," replied the driver, "but if you're headed to The Voyager of the Seas, hop on."

"Huh? We already paid Galveston Limo."

"Who cares, all these buses are going to the same place!"

"So, your company won't charge us?" The driver rolled his eyes and told me to toss our luggage underneath.

Meanwhile, Denise called Galveston Limo, "No, it's not our bus! Ours will be there in a little while. If you don't wait, you won't get your $100 back!" Denise had a serious lack of enthusiasm for our change of plans, but by then our bags were locked away and I was dragging her to a seat. "Hey, this bus is here, the driver said it was okay, why not?" She was pretty sure that we were being shanghaied and that I was flushing the money we'd already paid. As it turned out the driver was right; all those buses go to the same place.

Anyway, we're onboard the ship now and ready to set sail for destinations unknown; actually we know where we're headed, but mystery always adds spice. The sea-facing wall of our stateroom is all glass and opens onto a compact private balcony featuring two chairs and a small table. Dolphins are playing beside the ship. Is that a good omen?

Day 109 - April 23 - Friday - Mid-Atlantic

Today is day six of our transoceanic crossing and, this morning while we worked out on the stair-steppers in the gym, a small exhausted bird with a yellow chest sat on the deck quivering and sheltering from the twenty-eight mile per hour wind. Our last port of call was Nassau in the Bahamas and since then we've sailed a thousand miles into the Atlantic. How this little guy ended up in the middle of the ocean at the same spot is a good question. If he's smart, he's found himself a cozy corner somewhere to stowaway and eat leftover pool service until we hit the Azores.

The color of the sunlit water is an impossible blue that stretches to the horizon in all directions. Every time I stare over the rail, I find myself thinking of Columbus and his three tiny wooden ships. The Pinta was only three times as long as our stateroom barely more than twice as wide!

Because of the ash cloud spewed forth by that Icelandic volcano with the unpronounceable (and for that matter unspellable) name and the subsequent cancellation of many airline flights, about 400 passengers from Europe, failed to make our cruise. It wouldn't have mattered to us except that now we're seated at a table for ten with six of the chairs empty. Fortunately, the other two chairs are filled by a pretty interesting couple (hope they feel the same). Bob, a retired teacher (military schools abroad), is 80 years old. His wife Chris, 48, is East German; with a PHD in agricultural biology. They met over twenty years ago when they were both tourists in an Eastern Block country. Chris was standing with a map in hand and Bob asked her if he could take a look. It was love at first sight. When the Wall came down (remember the Iron Curtain, etc. etc.?) and Chris was able to travel, they were married. Afterwards, they lived in South Korea and Italy for a number of years and traveled extensively. They now live in the hill country of Texas, north of San Antonio. In other words they have a lot of good stories. We think that there'll be plenty of quality talk to fill our mealtimes so we're going to stick with the empty chairs. Besides, we like our waiter; Hennery, an Indonesian ex-punk-rocker from Jakarta.

Day 118 - May 2 - Sunday - Barcelona, Spain

We've arrived in Barcelona and I haven't been keeping up our journal. While the days aboard the Voyager of the Seas slipped by, we walked around in a haze. Nearly every day at noon, the ship's clocks were set forward by one hour. One minute it was 11:59 AM and the next it was 1:00 PM! There were nine time changes in all and by about the fourth we were deep into semi-permanent "jet-lag." An hour a day may not seem like much, but it whipped us both. Most days we hardly did anything except lay by the pool and work on our politically incorrect tans (fortunately the weather was good). When we felt the urge to be active, we took dance classes (Meringue, Cha-cha, Waltz, Fox Trot ...), went to the gym, or walked miles around the deck (eating doesn't really count as an activity).

Occasionally, we suffered lapses in better judgment. Denise, and a smiling cruise director with ulterior motives, egged me into the "Mr. Sexxy Legs" contest, where all the contestants were encouraged to act like fools. I won the most athletic legs contest (which gives you a picture of my dignity and the other contestants' physical condition).

Denise took a stab at the climbing wall, but after three valiant attempts failed to reach the summit. "My arms would start to ache and I just didn't feel I had the strength to reach up and pull myself to the next level." She was going to try again, but (luckily) we were busy in port for the rest of the trip. She says that she'd like to give it a go on land without the ship rocking back and forth. I suspect the urge will disappear along with her "jet-lag."

Most of our crossing was smooth, but we did encounter three sea days when ocean waves were around 45 feet! Neither of us minded the slight rocking except that our balcony door began to hammer like a cartoon woodpecker on a steel telephone pole. After a day or so of constant "pecking," we complained and were offered a couple of other rooms. Neither seemed as nice as where we already were, so we manned up and slept with ear plugs until the seas calmed. Royal Caribbean gave us a 15% credit off a future cruise for our inconvenience. Who knows, maybe we'll use it to get back home.

Cruise ships are floating hotels that remind us of Las Vegas casinos except with larger buffets, less smoke, and cheesier entertainment. The first night it was a weird Circ d'Soleil wannabe couple that performed acrobatic feats. For their finale, the man held the woman above his head with one hand while she spun around on his arm doing the splits or something. Other nights were filled with a virtual cornucopia of the mostly forgettable; a so-so Elton John tribute, a fifties group "The Original Drifters" that may or may not have included any original Drifters, show tune extravaganzas, a reasonably funny comedian, crooners, another Circ wannabe acrobat, a juggler, and a guy who dressed up like Zorro, played piano, and cracked a whip. Yeah, that's what I'm talking about! That's entertainment!

Denise tried her luck at Bingo twice. She really wanted to win the big snowball round which was worth $6,300. I thought it sounded like a good idea too, but sadly it wasn't in the cards (or ping pong balls).

Besides the Bahamas on our third day out of Galveston, we made three other ports: Ponta Delgada in the Azores on day ten, and Málaga and Cartagena in Spain on days thirteen and fourteen. There wasn't much to do in Ponta Delgada and it rained during our visit. We weren't fazed however; we were just happy to be ashore and didn't care. The island is pretty and most of the buildings and streets are made from black and white tiled volcanic rock. In Málaga we toured the city's Picasso museum and also the artist's birth home. Neither of us are huge Picasso fans, but we still found the stops appealing and entertaining. Later, we ran into Bob and Chris and quaffed a beer at a sidewalk café. Leaving them to people watch, we capped our Málaga visit with a climb up to the Alcazaba, an interesting Moorish fortress set on top of a steep hill.

The next day in Cartagena, we again wandered. It's a nice city with a lot to see ranging from ancient Carthaginian and Roman ruins to beautiful "Modernisme," Catalan Art Nouveau, buildings. We finished with another hill top walk that offered great views over the city and port.

Barcelona, Spain

Chapter 6

SPAIN

Day 124 - May 8 - Saturday

The past week has flown by and already it's our last night in Barcelona. Once again we've been doing instead of writing. When we left the cruise ship (feeling like beached whales, courtesy of tasty food 24/7 and an inherent lack of willpower), we climbed aboard a port shuttle. For two Euros each, the bus took us several kilometers to a towering monument to Columbus which anchors the foot of Barcelona's most famous pedestrian drag, La Rambla. From the shuttle stop it was only about a block to the nearest metro station. Trailing our roller bags, we popped underground and rode the train seven stops to a station in the vicinity of a hotel that we reserved off the web. Another four blocks of walking and we were greeting the receptionist.

Our room is Spartan but adequate. Its furnishings consist of: a bed, a wardrobe with three hangers, two shelves, and a small safe; two little wall mounted night stands, a tiny wall mounted fold down table, and one folding chair; everything geared for compact efficiency. The bathroom is almost as cramped as the one onboard the ship but lacks any shelves or hooks on which to stow our stuff. The best things about the room are the in-room safe and the neat view out the window.

Directly across the street stands a splendid un-restored Modernisme home. It's a building that you can stare at for a long time. Its walls are thick and in most places curves dominate straight lines. A tower rises above it. Rich details vie for attention and the floral inspired wrought-iron that frames its windows and gardens is a pleasure to behold. Sadly, the building is frittering away from lack of maintenance. According to our hotel receptionist, it's owned by a couple of old biddies who refuse to sell it to the city and they either can't or won't fix it up themselves. Barcelona has tagged the house as "historic," so that it can't be altered, but that didn't happen until after the old ladies sold one of its towers which was torn down and taken somewhere else. Now the city is waiting for them to croak so that it can take over and renovate.

On our first day in Barcelona, we arrived at our hotel around 10:30 AM. Since our room wasn't available until 1 PM we left our bags with reception and walked around. First we checked out, Plaza Lesseps, the area near our hotel, scoping out eateries, bakeries, markets, and other "essential" establishments. Next, we hopped back on the metro and returned to Plaza Catalunya, Barcelona's main square. It was a beautiful, sunny day. From the plaza, we strolled down La Rambla people watching: a little girl chasing pigeons, yellow-clad sanitation workers sweeping the streets, couples walking arm-in-arm, and street performers plying their trade. We picked up some maps, drank in the atmosphere, and relaxed with steaming cups of rich black coffee. Later, we walked up the Passeig de Grácia (another main drag) for a quick peak at the outside of two of Antoni Gaudi's most famous Modernisme buildings; the Casa Batlló and the Casa Milá. Gaudi's architecture takes our breath away with curving lines and organic exuberance it's as if he's tapped into a direct line to Mother Nature.

At that point, I sort of ran out of steam. I think the rum shots that Chris egged Hennery to pour at our last shipboard dinner might have somehow been involved. At any rate we headed back for our hotel. Along the way, we decided on an alfresco dinner; picked up an apple and a sandwich and ate a picnic in nearby Parc Turó del Putxet.

Prices in Spain, especially Barcelona, are spendy. The minimum entrance fee that we encountered for museums and the like was 2.50 Euros each. That's only about $4 U.S. which might not seem like a lot, but when you are charged everywhere and some of the more popular attractions cost as much as 16.50€ per person, it quickly adds up. Most of our dinners ranged from $50 to $80 U.S. and we thought it was a score when we found a "budget" buffet lunch for $15 each (there was a line waiting to get in). The city is clean and lively and exudes a great vibe. If you can afford it, Barcelona is probably a great place to live. As tourists, watching our budget, a week felt just about right.

We filled every day with great sightseeing. We wandered the city's Gothic quarter. We visited everything from another Picasso museum (which we admit was pretty cool), to underground Roman ruins that underlie some of the city's medieval buildings, to an eclectic shoe museum. We toured jewels of modernisme architecture including the Palau de Musica, Gaudi's Sagrada Familia, and casas Batlló and Milá. We explored Parc Guell, tested the city's street cuisine, and zipped hither and thither on the Metro. We stumbled onto a street fair, tables piled high with: giant wheels of cheese, mountains of savory sausage, and huge baskets of crusty bread.

We even managed to squeeze in a long day trip by train to Figueres to visit the Salvador Dali museum and theater. It's a wonderful place, but how do you describe the surreal? If you're a Dali fan these are exciting must-sees; you just gotta go! If you're a quibbler; two hours each way waxes a little tedious.

Day 125 - May 9 - Sunday - Benicassim, Spain

Headed out today; we packed the night before so after we got up, we made a few OCD checks of our room, and then said goodbye to the Hostal Puxtet. For the next leg of our journey we arranged a rental car. Our pick-up location was at the Sants Estacio train station which luckily is also a stop on the green L3 Metro line. We wheeled our bags a few blocks to the nearby Lesseps stop and then went underground for the short ride.

Our car is a "Skoda." I know; we'd never heard of it either. Our best guess is that it's the illegitimate love child of a Mini-Cooper and a Rav4. It's a stick shift and exhibits the handling characteristics of a dry leaf in a stiff autumn breeze. Cruise control is for wussys.

Exiting the heart of the city proved a little hectic, but Sunday traffic was light and most of the streets are well signed. We zipped down boulevards, whizzed through round-abouts, took all the right turns, and eventually reached the Autopista where I felt comfortable enough to ease my death grip on the steering wheel. After that, our drive was smooth sailing; smooth with the annoying exception of repeated $10 highway tolls charged about every sixty miles. The freeway swept us through countryside that was pleasant if maybe a tad monotonous. Despite the tolls we stuck with it to put distance between ourselves and Barcelona. Three hours later, we'd filled our quota for quality car time and called it a day in Benicassim.

Benicassim is a small town on the coast that was already a popular beach resort by the late 1800's. These days it's a little sleepy and makes a good low-key layover. By the time we found accommodations and got settled our stomachs were growling for lunch. The receptionist at our hotel recommended a place called Jota's and it turned out to be a killer recommendation.

We each ordered the 15 € ($20) fixed price, multi-course "Menu del Día." Our meal started with wine accompanied by olives, peanuts, and pork rinds (hey, they were good). At the same time, we were served, several delicious croquets (deep fried mashed potatoes with small pieces of ham inside). For her first course Denise went with a mushroom crepe. I tried an appetizer plate (entremeses) of ham, cheese, boiled egg, salad and pate. For our mains; Denise ate a yummy filet of sole with a light breading, lemon butter sauce, mushrooms and crispy shoe-string fries. I tucked into paella, rice with chicken and all kinds of seafood: mussels, calamari, clams, shrimp, and fish. For deserts we chose almond flan and tiramisu. All this was followed by tiny cups of rich coffee and finally by shot glasses and a bottle of apple aperitif. The service was good and the food was better; best meal in Spain so far.

After lunch, we walked out of the restaurant to be greeted by rain splattering in the street. Since our coats and umbrellas were back at the hotel, the weather gave us an excuse to indulge our lazy side. We scuttled straight back to our room and enjoyed a late afternoon siesta. Later the sky cleared and we walked along the town's beachfront promenade and, together with other Sunday strollers, enjoyed the sunset.

In case you're curious; this time of year the sun in Benicassim sets around 9:30pm! Most stores close between 12:30 PM and 4:30 PM, and then reopen until 9:00 or 9:30 PM. The exceptions are restaurants, many of which don't open for dinner until 8:00 PM or even later.

Day 126 - May 10 - Monday - Torrevieja, Spain

Driving today tested our patience! Our new consensus is that many of Spain's freeway exit signs are at least moderately confusing. They tended to tell you where you are only when you're already abreast of your chosen off ramp. Of course by then it's much too late to swerve over from the left-hand lane and pull off. If you do manage to exit, more times than not, you find yourself dumped you into a Byzantine labyrinth of side streets miles from the named location.

Denise wanted to hike up a Gibraltaresque rock called Peñon de Ifach that juts into the sky located near another beach resort named Calpe. The spelling of place names in this part of Spain change, depending on whether you're Castilian, Catalan, or Valencian and to make things interesting Spain uses them interchangeably on its road signs. Anyway, we rolled down the Autopista paying one toll after another, trying to figure out where to get off for Calpe (or maybe Calp, who knows?)

To make a tedious story shorter, we eventually found the exit but then spent forty-five minutes driving narrow corkscrew streets looking for a hotel recommended in our guide book. Before we finally located the place, we had to park, bicker, and search on foot. For our efforts we were presented with a hand written sign that told us that the hotel was shut tight for the off season and suggested that we, “Call *blah blah blah* for information.” By then, we were hungry and tired so Denise suggested that we drive to the Gibralteresque rock and have a picnic. Afterwards, maybe we'd do the hike. Following another white knuckle search we ended up in a dirt parking lot. There was nothing about the spot that even vaguely suggested picnic and the trail-head was far away up the hill. Plan C was to find a bench at the beach and eat our picnic. By the time we accomplished that objective it was almost 4 PM. Faced with the rapidly dwindling day, we bagged the whole hike/Calpe idea and moved on to plan D; keep rolling until we find somewhere we like better.

The best cultural experience of the day: “Highway Hookers” along the N340. Passing through a semi-rural area (speed limit about 40mph), we noticed a young attractive woman in a short dress (we're talking at the crotch short) standing on the side of the road. It looked like she was trying to hitchhike. A few minutes later we passed another young woman also in a sexy dress, heels etc. and also standing on the side of the road. In all, we passed 6 or 7 similarly dressed women. Spaced singly, about a mile or so apart, they were prostitutes, working the truck and commuter traffic. A couple even sat in plastic chairs while they waited for business to pick up. We Googled it. It's not legal, just blatant.

We ended our day in Torrevieja another beach resort (go figure) where we found a decent hotel, called the Cano. Tired of driving and with reasonably priced accommodation in hand we decided to settle in and spend the next day lounging and boardwalk strolling. The Cano is situated about six blocks from the beach and our third floor room has a little balcony with two chairs and a table. We drank poor man's sangria; cheap wine mixed with diet gaseosa (7-Up), and enjoyed our view over the street. Later we walked down to the beach area front and shared a beer with chicken & beef kabobs, rice and pita bread for 9€ ($11.74).

Day 129 - May 13 - Thursday - Mojacar, Spain

It's about 6:30 in the evening, the sun is shining, the sky is blue, and I'm sitting on the small tile ocean-view balcony of our $52/night hotel in Mojacar. Denise is in the tub taking a long soaky bath. Today was and is a good day. Mojacar is a small beach resort on the coast of Andalucía. All the buildings are white and the Mediterranean is turquoise blue.

We rolled in here yesterday evening after another long tiring day in the car. We had planned to go to a town called "Cabo de Gata" on the edge of a large nature reserve; unfortunately the place sucked. The natural area we could see from the road was ho-hum and the supposed good stuff was all: "leave your rental car," *in this isolated spot to be stripped and vandalized,* "and then hike 14 kilometers to the spectacular rugged cliff or hidden beach." When we arrived in "Cabo de Gata" it was more like "Caca de Gato." Off season, the resort community felt as though the beautiful people left and tossed their keys in the ocean. Most of the buildings were shuttered. The food and lodging that was available looked limited and unappealing. After driving around a bit, we again decided to bag it (fortunately we're flexible) and backtrack to our number two choice, Mojacar.

Big difference! It's off season here too, but instead of rolling up the streets, they just charge a little less.

Our hotel is the nicest place we've stayed so far, and breakfast is included in their terrace café, just across from the beach. After eating our toast, butter, jam, coffee, and orange juice, we crossed the street and walked along the shore discussing the merits of the chairs provided by the various beach bars. Next, we hopped a local bus for the short ride to Mojocar Pueblo. Mojacar has two parts. There's Playa Mojocar (where we're staying). It consists of about seven kilometers of small hotels, bars, and restaurants that run along stretches of sandy beach. In the hills, behind and above, perches Mojacar Pueblo; it's an older town with narrow winding pedestrian streets, whitewashed walls, and a completely Mediterranean vibe. We spent couple of hours exploring its tight alleyways. Some led to magnificent views, others to dead ends, all of them painted white and trimmed with flowers; nice place to get lost.

When we exhausted the pueblo's sights, we walked (exercise) back to our hotel, picked up a quiche and a goat's cheese empanada and ate a picnic on our balcony. We finished the afternoon with two beers and three hours on the beach reading and watching the Mediterranean lap the shore. I'm not sure what the evening has in store, but my wine glass is empty and Denise is out of the tub.

Day 131 - May 15 - Saturday - Algeciras, Spain

This is our last full day in Spain. We're in the port city of Algeciras where tomorrow we'll board a ferry for the forty-five minute ride to Morocco. Algeciras is mostly industrial and uninteresting so we're using our final day to get in some last minute quality pool time. We could easily spend longer in Spain, but we think we'll wait to come back when the Euro is a little weaker. Our maximum budget for Spain was $200 per day, but including our transportation costs: trains, car, gas, tolls, etc. we finished with only $23 to spare.

Chapter 7

MOROCCO

Day 132 - May 16 - Sunday - Tetouan, Morocco

Showered, packed, snarfed breakfast at the hotel, and caught a taxi to the passenger port where we boarded our ferry. The crossing was excellent. The ferry was clean, fast, and modern and they threw in complimentary coffee and croissants with our ticket. We sat on the fantail for the short trip and enjoyed great views of Gibraltar the whole way (the rock looms over Algeciras harbor). Almost before we knew it, we'd passed a Pillars of Hercules statue and entered the port of Cueta.

Cueta is a Spanish ruled enclave, so although we'd arrived in North Africa, we were still technically on Spanish soil. As we left the ferry terminal, a driver from the Dar Loughat language school met us holding up a "Donald Y Denise" sign. Mouhasine, who spoke mostly Spanish, was our driver for the forty-five minute trip from Cueta to Tetouan (pop 320,000). He helped us through the border (passport control, between Spain and Morocco etc), then showed us where to find the school and dropped us at our hotel. Unfortunately, since we're a couple and Morocco is a Muslim country, we can't do a home stay.

We settled into our room at the Panorama Vista, a hotel that more than lives up to its name with dramatic views of the Rif Mountains. Our room is simple, but bright and pleasing with a small balcony. The hotel is also well located, about three blocks from our language school and the main pedestrian thoroughfare, and another couple of blocks from the medina.

After we rested, we went out and wandered around to scope things out. It was Sunday evening and the streets were filled with the kind of crowds we normally only encounter at the Eugene Celebration (turns out it's normal most evenings). Vendors were hawking their wares, families were strolling, and men in robes and women in head scarves hurried hither and thither. Cafes line the streets and their outside tables are packed with men, smoking, drinking tea and coffee and watching the world go by. Men outnumber women on the street about five to one and it feels a little weird. Everything is exotic but not overwhelming. We just heard our first call to prayer, awesome.

Day 133 - May 17 - Monday

Now we know why they call them "foreign" languages. You've heard the phrase, "it's Greek to me." Forget Greek; Arabic is a maniacal Rubic's cube. Today was our first day of class and we're still waiting to see if our heads will explode. We know we said the same about our Spanish immersion in Guatemala but this time we really mean it! As absolute beginners, we were placed in a class by ourselves for two hours in the morning and again for another two hours in the afternoon. Our teacher is named Ishmael and almost 100% of our instruction is in Arabic. The only time we hear another language is when he gives us the translation of an Arabic word that we've already repeated several times. Usually he just holds up a picture. I might also add that when he does translate a word it's as often into Spanish or French as it is into English. Did you know that each Arabic letter has nine different sounds that are each written differently? And, that each of those nine different forms is written differently depending on whether it appears at the start, middle, or end of a word? We didn't! It's absolutely amazing that in a class where everything sounds like gibberish Ishmael is still managing to teach us stuff (not that we're going to remember it with our sieve-like brains). The guy is awesome! If we don't learn Arabic, at the very least we'll be wicked deadly at charades.

Day 134 - May 18 - Tuesday

We're up to ten letters and at the end of each class our brains are mush.

Day 135 - May 19 - Wednesday

Fifteen letters! Did we mention that Arabic is written and read from right to left? It feels like we're using our workbooks from the back to the front. Denise is fighting a cold so we ate "harira," tomato soup, for dinner. Two bowls in a nearby café set us back a whopping $0.96.

Day 136 - May 20 - Thursday

"Arrggh!" That's a sound of frustration not Arabic, although we suspect it could be a sound that we haven't covered yet. We're up to twenty something letters and, oh by the way, half of them are ruled by the sun and half by the moon and pronunciation varies further depending on whether they are sun letters or moon letters, *Arrggh!* We better get back to studying. Thank god Denise and I are the only students at our level. At least this way we only look like idiots to each other (and of course Ishmael).

Day 137 - May 21 - Friday

We made it through our first week of class and all twenty-eight (maybe 29) letters of the Arabic alphabet and our heads are still intact. It's going to take a lot of rote memorization before we can readily identify each one and possibly vocal cord surgery before we can actually say them. The good part is we're making some progress. The bad part is that we're learning Modern Standard Arabic (MSA) which isn't actually spoken in Morocco, or anywhere else for that matter. It's used everywhere in the Arab world (including Morocco) for TV, newspapers, and reading the Quran, but different countries use different spoken dialects; some close to MSA, others pretty far removed. An educated person from say Saudi Arabia would have no problem discussing world events with an educated Moroccan (using MSA) but he might have a hard time talking to a shopkeeper or ordering lunch. We've been jumping our communication hurdles with a mix of Spanish, French (both widely spoken here), English, and our few words of Arabic.

Day 138 - May 22 - Saturday

There's no class today, so we both slept in. We've been busy since we hit Tetouan and it felt good to wake up with nothing we had to do. After a lazy start, we wandered downstairs for breakfast. Breakfast is included with our room so were getting to be regulars. Everyday it's the same, but it is way better than the typical included breakfast in Spain. In Spain it's a coffee and a croissant 'or' toast and jam. Here we each get a large glass of fresh squeezed orange juice, a coffee with milk and sugar, a yogurt, several breads including croissants and pastries, and butter and jam. There's just enough variety in the breads and yogurt flavors to keep things interesting.

This is good point to mention that Morocco is cheap, which is also a nice break from Spain. Dinner: drinks, soup, salad, shared entre, tea, and shared dessert; can be eaten at a spiffy upscale restaurant with ambience and good service for about $20. If you go to a neighborhood café, you can get plenty of soup and couscous for two people for $5 or less.

After breakfast, we headed over to Tetouan's medina. "Medina" in Arabic means city but most tourists and their guidebooks use it to refer to old walled-in areas of narrow winding streets (no cars) that have remained relatively unchanged for hundreds of years. Tetouan's medina is a World Heritage Site. The best way to visit these sprawling mazes is just to wander about, soaking in the sights and sounds, and inevitably becoming lost. We held off our visit until today so we'd have plenty of time and no deadlines. Just to the right of a royal palace, where the king resides several months each year, lies Bab er Rouah, the Wind Gate. That's where we ducked into the medina. Just inside the gate lies a souk (market) that specializes in gold jewelry, where small jewelry stores, one after another, line the street, their windows bright with baubles. From there the streets wind through one souk after another: the fish market, the clothes market, the cheese market, the furniture market, the shoe market, and so on.

One of the coolest things we saw was a pair of tailors sewing traditional robes. They were seated in a small stall each working on a garment. Outside the stall were two small machines each with eight long threads attached to a bicycle chain type mechanism. The threads stretched from the machines seven to ten feet to where the tailors were seated. Working at near sewing machine speed, each man would make a manual stitch with a hand needle and in the process pick up four of the eight threads. At that point, the chains would change the position of the eights threads relative to each other and then the process would repeat. It's hard to explain, but neat to watch. The eight threads weren't on spools. Instead, the chain machines rode on little wheels, and as the threads were used up, the tailors pulled the machines closer and closer until it was time for new threads. The results were seams and embroidery that looked as though they'd been done with a serger.

Watching a woman buy a chicken was another cultural experience. A bunch of them were caged at the front of the vendor's stall. The woman pointed to one, and the chicken guy pulled it out and sat it on a scale. "No, that one's too big," or something similar in Arabic, who knows? The guy picked a smaller one and set it on the scale, "Yep, just right." From the scale, the bird was flopped onto a counter where a quick "thunk" separated it from its head. The chicken guy then held it neck down over a sink and drained the blood.

"Ooh, fresh," said Denise. The woman smiled and drew her finger across her neck.

Other stalls held cobblers at work, carpenters with their chisels and mallets creating furniture, or tables piled to overflowing with mounds of multicolored olives and dates. We ended up lost a couple of times but always managed to find our way back to a main drag.

People here are nice and if they see you looking around, they'll happily point you in the right direction. That's the upside. The downside is that every other person who talks to you is a tout who tries to attach themselves to you and lead you into a buying situation: restaurant, spices, leather, you name it. They all have a good working command of Spanish, English, and French and each and every one of them has a line.

"I'm a student trying to learn blah, blah, blah..." "You're lucky! Today only is special Berber market blah, blah, blah..." "My family runs an arts and crafts school, blah, blah, blah..." We don't want to be rude, so when someone speaks to us, we tend to answer. Unfortunately, nine times out of ten it's the wrong move. To be honest, the touts here are persistent, but not overwhelming. If you politely repeat "Laa Shukran" (no thank you) and walk away they usually give up and leave you alone. So far we've only been snookered once. An ersatz restaurant "owner," while discussing the merits of "his" establishment, managed to walk us into his spice store for an on the spot sales pitch; live and learn. Touts are supposedly worse in other cities so it's probably good practice.

We wrapped-up our medina visit with a stop at a simple ethnographic museum and lunch at a "palace" restaurant. The museum was interesting but the lunch was a bit of a letdown. The Unnamed Guidebook describes the place as a "classic Moroccan experience" with entertainment, and "endless plates of food," located in a "superb setting." In fairness, the place was nice inside. The food on the other hand was utterly forgettable: a bowl of tomato soup, a mountain of mushy couscous, grilled rabbit-pellet-sized chunks of meat (four each), a shared 12oz bottle of water, several tasteless cookies, and some lukewarm mint tea. The service was non-existent, and the entertainment was only so-so. Also, we were pointedly told to tip. Since the total for the meal with tips (waitress, dancer, musicians) only came to $23.33 we can't bitch too much; really a joint geared to group tours. On our way out of the medina, we bought a big bag of assorted homemade candy for 20 dirham ($2.30), that helped balance the scale.

Cultural tidbit - Napkins – often non-existent and where available they're usually small stiff triangles of hard smooth tissue paper. We tend to leave all our meals with fingers that are sticky or greasy or both.

Day 147 - May 31 - Monday

Tetouan is a city of busy streets, fountains, presidential palaces, royal portraits, Moorish minarets, whitewashed walls, and Spanish balconies; it's also a city of contrasts. We walk down one street and late model Mercedes taxis line the curb from one corner to the next. We walk down another street and it sways to the clip-clop rhythm of a string of laden pack horses or of a Berber tribesman on his pony. A traditional water vendor with plastic jugs wrapped in cooling fresh-cut grasses sells refreshment by the glass while two steps away a rakish youth in sunglasses hawks the latest hip-hop CD. A businessman in a western suit and tie hurries along with his briefcase. In the other direction a man in a long robe, skullcap, and sandals pushes his wheelbarrow full of oranges. There's a lot to see and experience in Tetouan, but we feel that two weeks has allowed us enough time to take the city's pulse. We've wandered all the streets near our hotel, worn a path to neighborhood pastry shops, and learned to find our way back and forth through the winding alleys of the medina. We've also exhausted nearby restaurant possibilities.

It's strange; sweets and pastries in Morocco are awesome, but otherwise eating is a tad mundane. It's not that most of the food here isn't delicious; it is! It's more a case of limited selection. Several small cafes line every city block but they all seem to offer exactly the same menu. The centerpiece is grilled Panini sandwiches with a variety of fillings and French fries (if you get it to go, they cram the fries inside the sandwich), pita type sandwiches with the same fillings, or burger type sandwiches with the same fillings. Some places spice things up with pizza and lasagna. It's all fresh and well prepared but any way you slice it, it's still pretty much fast food. Soup is also a staple on the menus at both cafes and restaurants. It varies from place to place, but we encountered only one kind. It's a tasty tomato base with some noodles and a little meat, called "harira." Sometimes you see it by name, but more often than not the menu just says "soup" (or the French or Spanish equivalent). In fancier restaurants menus offer couscous served with vegetables, chicken, meat (other than chicken), or some combination of the three. "Tanjines" are essentially the same ingredients cooked in a special terracotta pot without the couscous, but with a sauce and the added option of fish. Finally, you can get all the same stuff grilled. All restaurants give you bread and olives and they usually serve the same two or three salads. Would I like some cheese to go with this whine? Yes absolutely, but not the flavorless white goat stuff that garnishes salads and frequently appears at breakfast. God, could I be a bigger whiner?

Our two weeks of Arabic instruction ruled! We're years of study from speaking the language, but seeing as we started from zero, we've learned a surprising amount. We can both (with a little luck) recognize the letters of the alphabet and sound out Arabic words on signs (although we usually have no idea what they mean). We've also just about mastered a few travel essentials like: please, thank you, where is the bathroom, and may I have the bill please, etc. Now the real trick is to use everything that we learned before it fades into the confusing background clatter of our journey.

Since Tetouan now feels familiar and we've crammed our heads with as much Arabic as they can hold at one seating, we've decided to move on. Yesterday we purchased bus tickets for Chefchaouen a small town situated about an hour and a half away in the Rif Mountains (supposed kif/hashish capital of Morocco); only about another hour and we head out.

Went down to pay our bill and got a bit of a shock. The amount was what we were quoted (in fact a little less), but when I handed over our credit card the desk clerk responded, "I'm sorry sir the credit card machine is broken. You can pay cash. That will be 4,350 dirham please (about $508)."

"When we made our reservation we were assured that you took credit cards. We don't have 4,350 dirham."

"They told you that? The machine is broken for some time. You can use ATM just next door." So, I schlepped next door and maxed out the ATM; its limit was 4,000 dirham, dug in my wallet and scrapped together the rest. We've since learned that it is fairly common here to be told that a place accepts credit cards only to later learn that they only deal in cash. It's also common to be told that a place has Wi-Fi, when in many cases "had" Wi-Fi is more on target.

Day 149 - June 2 - Wednesday - Chefchaouen, Morocco

We've been in Chefchaouen for three sweltering days. This town, like so many in Morocco, is split into two parts, the old medina, crammed with history and atmosphere, and the "Ville Nouvelle," all the newer mostly uninteresting stuff. We're staying in the medina which is a bit touristy but also sort of magical. The walls of its narrow winding alleys are washed in blinding whites and deep soothing blues. The blues are what make the town special. They seem to hold in cool air, deepen the shade, and make you feel as though you're wading through pools of clear water. Adding drama to character, the medina sprawls across a rugged hillside that snuggles tightly against craggy rock peaks of the Rif Mountains.

We're situated in a cute little hotel called Dar Antonio that's run by a friendly helpful guy named Isham. The Dar (house) is located at the shaded bottom of a tight blue alley that refreshes every time you descend it. The hotel has seven small rooms with two shared bathrooms, all arranged on three floors around a tiny central courtyard. Our room, nicely decorated in ethnic funk, is on the second floor next to a small terrace patio (and a bathroom).

The old city is small, and we easily took in its sights in a couple of days. We started by enjoying the twists and turns of the medina. I think by the time we leave Morocco we'll be well and truly medina'd out. So far (at least) they're still engaging. Yes, we've seen similar sights in local markets in Mexico and Guatemala, but the tight alleys and ancient walls of the medinas somehow give the souks a flavor all their own.

Our second day, we walked through the old medina wall at "Bab Ain" (the Spring Gate) and took an energetic uphill trek to an old Spanish mosque with expansive views of the town and surrounding valley. The walk gave us some much needed exercise and also served up fun glimpses of rural life: Berber women firing up a beehive bread oven; goat and sheep herders tending their animals; people walking to town loaded with goods; and women hand washing carpets and clothes in the river. The Spring Gate" gets its name from the fact that the river at its feet gushes from the rock of the mountain only about 100 yards upstream.

The best thing to do in Chefchaouen is sit in a café in the medina's main square and people watch. The food is still usual fare, but the people-watching is first-rate. There's also a nice old Kasbah (kind of a fort) on the square that was good for a short visit.

The town is hosting some sort of world agriculture conference and the second night of our stay they feted the delegates with an ethnic music concert. The affair which took place inside the Kasbah was private, but lying in our room we were still carried away by the wafting strains of its Arabian Nights melodies.

We only planned to stay in Chefchaouen for two nights but we've been dickering with a tour agent named, Abdesalam, and the haggling took longer than we expected. The school in Tetouan hooked us up with the guy and suggested that he might help us plan the rest of our time in Morocco. "Very good, very professional." Since he also got a nod in The Unnamed Guidebook, and reservations (and touts) here in Chefchaouen are reputed to be a hassle we decided to give him a whirl. He made an overpriced proposal. We said "No," and suggested a different plan. Addesalam said he would work that up. "Let me run the numbers (paraphrased)." Later an associate delivered a second overpriced proposal. We countered with what we thought the deal should really cost (based on web rack rates). They said they couldn't meet our price so we thanked them for their time and bought a couple of CTM bus tickets for Fes. Footloose and reservation free, we leave tomorrow at 9:30 AM.

Day 151 - June 4 - Friday - Fes, Morocco

The bus trip to Fes was interesting and mostly comfortable. The air-conditioning on our Tetouan bus was MIA so we were a little leery of the four hours to Fes. Luckily, it wasn't a CTM "feature."

The countryside reminded us strongly of dry agricultural areas of California; stretches of land on the edges of the central valley and the Sierras with similar plants, landforms, and colors. Just about the time you start thinking, *Yeah, I've seen all this*, you spot people harvesting hay by hand, overloaded donkeys, or a cluster of Berber tents. Then you realize that what look to be Manzanitas are really olive trees.

About half way through the trip our bus driver pulled into a roadside café for lunch and a welcome restroom stop. If you ignore the Turkish toilets, the restroom part was straight forward. The lunch part left us scratching our heads. The café only served drinks.

Outside was a small butcher shop with a row of hanging carcasses that dripped blood onto the porch. Goats or sheep; without their skin and heads, it was hard to tell. A few steps away sat a barbeque operation where a couple of guys in chefs' coats were grilling cuts of meat over coals and serving them to waiting customers. We edged up to the counter and licked our chops, but the cooks ignored us. After a couple of minutes, a sympathetic woman saw our confusion and waded in to help. It turns out that you must select and buy your meat from the butcher shop; then you carry it over and pay the barbecue guys about $0.50 to cook it for you. We thanked the woman for her help and tucked into "sandwiches," juicy grilled sheep (or goat?) patties mixed with mint and other spices, stuffed into thick wedges of crusty bread; delicious.

When we arrived at the bus station in Fes, we were approached by a tout asking if we needed a taxi. I said, "Sure," and asked how much to take us to a hotel we'd selected.

He came back with, "50 dirham" ($5.83) which seemed a little high but I thought *what the heck* and agreed. When we got outside, it turned out that his car was a beat-up private mini-van rather than a licensed "petite taxi."

"Whoa, I think we want a regular taxi."

"All the same price, we'll take you to the hotel."

"I don't know."

"The taxis are between shifts right now."

"I don't know."

"My family needs to eat too." We tossed our bags in the back and amid a few misgivings climbed inside. When the doors closed and it turned out there weren't any side windows, Denise got the "we're being shanghaied look." Then the van's driver, "is OK is my brother," turned the ignition, "rurrr... rurrrrrr... rurr," nada, zip.

When he called some people over to push him, we both shouted "Laa, Laa!" "No, No!" in Arabic and hopped out. The regular taxi to the hotel cost us 20 dirham.

Day 152 - June 5 - Saturday

Our first choice, Hotel Batha, was full-up, but they recommended another just around the corner called the Hotel Bab Boujloud (cheap, clean, air conditioned). It takes its name from the huge medina gate that's only fifty yards away.

When you step through that gate, you enter a labyrinth; the largest city on the face of the earth without cars. Everyone carries cell phones and there are cyber-cafes and stalls selling designer jeans, but it still feels like something out of a distant past. Over 9,000 narrow streets and alleys, some no wider than hallways, wind their way through dim canyons created by the walls of ancient buildings. The main streets are lined with shops selling fruits, chickens, rabbits, clothing, carpets, books, trinkets, turtles, leather goods, shoes, perfumes, spices, baked goods, and everything else you can imagine. Shopkeepers sit or stand encouraging you to step inside while crowds of people move along shopping, chatting, laughing, and living their lives. Mixed in with the crowds are occasional donkeys, horses, mules, tiny tractors and handcarts whose drivers shout "Balak! Balak!" (lookout!) as they hurry to deliver everything from propane to soda pop

Yesterday, we decided to splurge and spend $25 to hire a guide. We'd already walked the medina on our own, but the navigation is confusing and some of the best sights lie hidden at the end of those dim unmarked hallway wide streets. It's also hard to find your way to the good stuff without fending off touts. Anyway, we thought we'd get more out of the experience with a fun, licensed, English speaking guide, someone with a ready smile and a good sense of humor, who could tell us the important bits and answer our questions. "Saaid," our official guide (23 years experience, arranged by Hotel Batha), was none of those. He was an unintelligible turd hoarder with the personality of a stump. He mumbled, smoked every chance he got, barely smiled, and his command of English was so poor he couldn't understand our questions. All Americans were "rich." All Koreans were "cheap." Algerians, "Phtooie, I spit in their general direction (paraphrased)." On the plus side, he did take us to everything we wanted to see. You get a full day for $25, but when he asked about what we wanted to do after lunch, we thanked him for his "excellent commentary" and beat a hasty retreat.

All of the city's monumental walls, and there are a lot of them, surrounding: the medina, palaces, gardens, and kasbahs are pocked with regularly spaced square holes. Inside the holes live swallows, thousands of swallows, and each evening as the sun sets, the birds emerge to whirl in a crazy ballet and mingle their sharp cries with the calls to prayer that echo from the city's minarets. Fes is all about hustle and bustle and its birds are sauce for the experience.

Cats are also out in abundance. Not because of the birds; Moroccans just seem to like and tolerate them. Felines large and small hang out everywhere; not just in Fes but throughout the country. We're not talking crazy cat-lady quantities, but Morocco definitely lacks a spay-and-neuter program. Cats sleep in shops, sit wistfully in front of meat markets, and troll food places looking for handouts. One evening at dinner three joined us at our table. One just sat there. Another cried the whole meal, ignoring our attempts to shoo it away. The third tried to jump on the table from time to time; business as usual at the restaurant that didn't warrant a second glance from our waiters. Some Moroccan cats seem scruffy and they're all a little lean, but in general they look reasonably healthy.

We finished our stay in Fes with a great cultural immersion. Each year the city hosts a festival of sacred world music, and as luck would have it, it started while we were here. There's a pay venue that features $300 per seat tickets and international performers, but there are also free performances at various locations throughout the city. Tonight was the first big free show and it took place in a huge plaza just around the corner from our hotel. What a trip! The music was Moroccan, sort of syncopated, undoubtedly Islamic, maybe folk, hard to describe. Twelve or more guys were playing percussion, flutes, and weird six-foot trumpets, fronted by a vocalist who sang in a sort of chant. The sound was exotic and slightly hypnotic, but the enthusiastic crowd was the real show.

A couple of thousand mostly young men (almost no women except foreigners) were grooving and rocking out like they were at a sold-out AC/DC show. They danced holding hands (no women), shimmied, jumped up and down, sang along (knew all the lyrics), waved their arms and shirts, and tossed people into the air. To our foreign ears the music seemed totally wrong, but if the singer had suddenly told everyone to hold up their lighters it wouldn't have seemed out of place.

Day 154 - June 7 - Monday - Merzuga, Morocco

Following Fes, we decided to head out and visit sand dunes at the edge of the Sahara. It's possible to get there using public transport but it involves second class buses or an eight hour overnight ride. After tossing it around, we decided it was time to rent another car. A quick jump online and we had one scheduled for a week. Yesterday after breakfast, we took a grand taxi (150 dirham set rate $17.50) from our hotel out to the Fes airport and picked up our car. The taxi ride was slightly expensive, but a downtown pickup would have included the joys of city driving in Fes, a pleasure that we felt was best avoided.

Almost immediately upon leaving the airport we fell into a Moroccan speed trap; a sudden shift from 100km per hour to 60km per hour followed by three cops under an olive tree with a radar gun. They don't chase after you; they just wave you to the side of the road. The cop addressed us in French to which we replied that we didn't speak French.

"You know in English what mean, "trop vitesse?"

"Uh, too fast?"

Still speaking in French, "Oui, too fast; speed 60 km you go 72." *Ok, so we were doing 42mph in a 36mph zone, how bad can that be?* "You pay fine, 40 Euros." *$50 crap!*

We both rolled our eyes and groaned. "You're not serious? Please, we don't have much money."

Still in French, "Are you working here or just tourists?"

"Tourists."

Switching to English, "You like Barack Obama?"

"Oh, yes! He's a really good man."

"George Bush?"

"Phtooie, we spit in his general direction (paraphrased)."

"Ok, you go, be careful."

"Thank you, thank you!" Who says it doesn't pay to be a liberal?

After that, it was clear sailing; what an awesome drive. From Fes, our road ran up into the mountains of the High Atlas passing through evergreen forests, rocky alpine meadows, and the faux Swiss village of Ifrane. That was pretty good scenery, but the best came later in the day when we passed back down into arid territory and drove through the gorge of the Ziz River. The gorge was only a few miles long but it was like passing through the bottom of a mini Grand Canyon; colorful canyon walls, tablelands, and twisted faces of sculpted rock. Every curve offers a different spectacular view. Along the bottom of the gorge ran the Ziz, its banks covered with palm trees, mud walled towns, and ancient citadels.

About seven in the evening we rolled into Dar El Janoub, a Kasbah style hotel on the edge of a sea of sand.

Day 155 - June 8 - Tuesday

Tonight will be our third night here; the place is amazing. Dar El Janoub is a modest resort with a restaurant and seventeen rooms set inside thick mud covered walls that surround a sparkling central pool. Our room is large, high ceilinged, dark, and comfortable; with air conditioning when we need it. To one side of the Dar the land is flat, rocky, and barren. To the other, undulating mountains of sand roll away into the distance. At sunrise and sunset (too hot at other times) we can pull open the shutters of our big window and watch the play of shadow and color on the dunes.

Yesterday, the wind gusted all afternoon, blowing light sand that coated everything, worked its way under our door, hid the dunes from sight, and forced us inside for dinner.

Today, the air is once again still and clear so we walked for an hour in the sand before eating breakfast on the patio. It's hard to express the eerie majesty of the shifting dunes. They make you feel insignificant but at the same time they touch and refresh your soul.

Right now it's a little after 3pm; we're hanging by the pool and the wind is starting to kick up. Between the stillness, the power of the dunes, the swaying palm trees, and the occasional line of camels in the distance, Merzouga is a true natural wonder.

Making our stay even better, everyone on the staff of the hotel is friendly and helpful from the desk clerk, Rashid, to our waiters, Aziz and Achmed. And, believe it or not, we're the Dar's only guests!

Day 156 - June 9 - Wednesday

Rubbed sleep from my eyes and stumbled out of our room; greeted by another beautiful desert day. A fierce white sun already glares down from the east, but a light morning breeze carries a lingering hint of night. Birds fill the trees. Denise is still asleep. I sit by the pool shooing a small cat that keeps jumping on my lap; walking on my keyboard.

Day 157 - June 10 - Thurs - Ait Ben Haddou, Morocco

Once I finally got the cat hair off my shirt (had to use tape), we ate a slow breakfast on the terrace and then took our last good look at the sea of sand. Another day in Merzouga could have been nice but as it might have led to a touristy camel ride. We decided it was time to move on.

During the last two days, we've seen stunningly beautiful country. Our drive carried us through heat scorched desert landscapes reminiscent of the arid American West; expansive vistas, isolated towns, Nature at her best. Time and again, the scenery reminded Denise of her tours to Arizona and Utah. Your mind easily makes the substitution, but the impression slips away as you pass through oasis palmeraies; splashes of verdant palm-frond-green; life that suddenly erupts in the middle of nowhere. The land here was once trampled by the tracks of ancient caravans; a crossroads where gold and slaves flowed from the Sahara and fortunes were made and lost; all long ago but with a little imagination, hints of the grandeur remain.

Our first stop was Rissani a small once strategic town where the Alawite dynasty that today governs Morocco (remember ruled by a king) launched their first battles of conquest. The town sits in a palmeraie where the River (Oued) Ziz disappears quietly into the sand. We followed a twenty-one kilometer, mostly bumpy dirt, "Circuit Touristique" that skirts Rissani and winds past crumbling castle-like mud and straw "ksar" (multi-family homes), "ksour" (villages composed of groups of ksar), and the scant remains of the fabled city of Sijilmassa. We also visited Ksar Oulad Abdelhalim a huge rambling desert palace; once home to outcast members of the royal family. Its imposing ruins now house a small museum. We were its only visitors.

As we moved beyond Rissani, we drove across barren gravel strewn plains and passed through other small dusty former caravan towns; all of them fascinating. Loaded donkeys and horse carts share the road with cars and trucks and veiled women trudge along under heavy bundles. It's strange to imagine your life moving at the pace of a plodding animal. Camels (dromedary – one hump) and herds of goats graze on the sparse desert vegetation.

At one point our road passed through a region where dozens of hand dug wells spread away into the distance; some with hoists for raising water others without, but all of them scattered about like so many giant white ant hills. Near the wells the land was parched clay, treeless, and empty. Enterprising Berbers had pitched a couple of roadside tents, arranged some items to sell, and posted signs proclaiming the area a "Rest Stop."

We finished our first day out from Merzouga sitting by a hotel pool in the Todra Gorge listening to bird song and the welcome sound of running water. The gorge which lies just a few kilometers off the main road is sort of a small version of Utah's Zion. Surrounded by desert, increasingly steep rock walls shelter a refreshing green canyon, a small river, houses, and gardens. A few miles beyond our hotel, the canyon walls draw together and the pavement ends. We would have liked to linger in the area and do some hiking, but flight reservations now drive our schedule.

Our next day was incredible. From the Todra Gorge, we struck out for another natural wonder, the Dades Gorge. Visiting this second gorge entailed an out and back drive of about thirty miles each way; an unfolding kaleidoscope of: shear canyon walls, hairpin turns, stupefying views, and fantastic weathered rocks. A couple of driving hours in second gear; bar none; it was one of the most scenic drives either of us has ever taken.

We stopped for lunch at a modest, newish looking, hotel with two or three rooms and a bright one-room glass-enclosed restaurant that perched on the edge of a cliff. We were the restaurant's only guests and the staff seemed surprised that anyone had actually stopped. Their menu listed the usual options but all they really had in the kitchen were plain omelets (no cheese), soup, and mint tea. The small dining hall was decorated in pastel desert tones with rugs and bits of ethnic funk. The views were incredible.

Back on the main road, we rolled through more desert landscape. Towns here are the color of the earth and their buildings, both old and new, blend seamlessly into the landscape.

Later in the day we passed through the city of Ourzazate, modern and dusty. Ourzazate has aspirations to be a tourist Mecca but holds little of interest other than its film studios. According to our guidebook there are several; all of them vying for the attention of directors filming arid sagas. We didn't stop, but from the highway we spotted siege towers and the walls of old Jerusalem; the leftover set from "City of Heaven" (the crusader epic with Orlando Bloom).

About twenty kilometers further on, we reached the UNESCO world heritage site of Ait Ben Haddou. Ait Ben Haddou's claim to fame is its well preserved (and restored) ksour. From the windows of our little guesthouse room, we looked out across a nearly dry river at a city that stepped right out of "Ali Babba and the Forty Thieves." Perched on a hillside and topped by a fortified granary, the huge ancient castle of mud has served as a backdrop for movies ranging from "Gladiator" to "Jewel of the Nile." With few residents and few people moving about, Ait Ben Haddou is quiet and mysterious. Wandering its deserted alleys is like stepping back in time. No coincidence they filmed "Jesus of Nazareth" here. With each step you felt as though just around the corner you might bump into one of his apostles. The Unnamed Guidebook carps that the city has seen too much restoration, but we didn't get that hit at all. For us, it was a high point.

Day 161 - June 14 - Monday - Marrakech, Morocco

Today is our last full day in Morocco. Tomorrow we fly to Istanbul. The drive from Ait Ben Haddou was again spectacular. With the exception of the two gorges and a stretch out to Merzouga our route followed major primary highways. You'd never have guessed it if you didn't know. With only two lanes, light traffic and no shoulders, it all felt off the beaten track. From the desert, our road switch-backed slowly over the Southern High Atlas mountains, arid landscape again giving way to refreshing alpine meadows, grazing goats, and evergreen forests. Clouds clung to the mountain tops and we even passed through an area wet from recent rain.

About ten kilometers out from our goal the road abruptly forked and signs on both forks pointed in opposite directions. They both read "Marrakech." Since our map was worthless, we turned around and drove back a couple of hundred meters to where two traffic cops stood by the side of the road. Using half-remembered high-school French I told them that we wanted to reach the airport and asked them if we should go right or left? Of course they both pointed in opposite directions. An earnest discussion followed in Arabic with one cop eventually deferring to the other (outranked?). "Take the right fork." We think they were bored because they then proceeded to give us detailed directions in two part French harmony. When I pulled out a small pad to jot some notes, they insisted on drawing a map. One cop started it and the other finished. The first drew so big that the second guy had to squeeze his part (the bulk of the map) down so small it was barely legible. We thanked them and drove away. Wonder of wonders the directions were pretty good. They wound us here and there through the center of the city but eventually we reached the airport with a minimum of hassle.

After we dropped our rental car, the Europcar guy hooked us up with a buddy to drive us to our hotel for 100 dirham (about $12). Since this was lower than the going taxi rate we took the offer. Fortunately, the guy walked us to the hotel's entrance. We're pretty sure that we'd never have found the place on our own. From where we left the car we walked a couple of hundred yards and then ducked into an unmarked alley that twisted and turned. At times the lane narrowed to almost shoulder width. At other times it seemed about to dead end. When we finally stopped before our hotel's low medieval door, it was unmarked except for a small street number "40."

Called, "Chouia Chouia," our lodging is a "riad," a home lovingly converted into a welcoming bed and breakfast. We spent the first two nights in a room in their "annex" across the alley, and are spending our last two in a third floor "suite" in their main building. The first room featured a "sunken" platform bed and was painted brightly in shades of yellow. The suite features a sitting area and cooling shades of blue. Both rooms are decorated with sculpted concrete (I keep banging my head on low arches), Berber rugs, wood, and ethnic accents and fabrics that make us wish for curly-toed slippers. Breakfasts are served on a rooftop terrace and there's a small plunge pool in the main building ($64/night).

We're both glad that we finished our stay in Morocco with Marrakech. It's far and away the touristiest spot we visited; an assault on our senses that might have warped our perspective if we'd seen it first. We made semi-obligatory rounds of all the museums, but the heart of Marrakech is the Djema El-Fna a large central plaza that's a never ending sideshow. Trinket shops and restaurants line its edges. In its center are rows of wheeled carts where vendors sell fresh squeezed orange juice for about $0.30 a glass, stands loaded with dates and nuts, water vendors in traditional costume, monkey handlers, street musicians, snake charmers, women who think your need henna art, and tourists; lots of tourists.

In the evening other carts come rushing into the square loaded with the equipment for dozens of impromptu restaurants that quickly spring up to create a culinary labyrinth. Finished with their daily work, crowds of locals join the mix along with games of chance: three card Monte, fishing for bottles of coke, try your hand at golf putting; acrobats, more musicians, and more tourists. On our second night, a fancy stage was set up and they held live boxing matches (go figure). All in all, Djema El-Fna is a little weird, a little contrived, a little less exotic than it sounds, and an experience not to be missed.

If you're looking for a walk on the wild side in Marrakech, you can always cross a street. In the medina you still see handcarts and plodding donkeys, but here in Marrakech rushing bicycles, motorcycles, and scooters add danger to the mix. Sometimes tooting their horns or ringing bells, they weave at fairly high speed through the dense ambling crowds. Even in congested narrow alleys you need to pay close attention so that you don't get clipped. Pedestrians emphatically do not have the right of way in Marrakech. Crossing main thoroughfares, you wait at the curb until there is a gap in traffic or until enough people are present so that a driver thinks twice before running you all down. Once you're in the crosswalk, you're still fair game and cars and motorcycles will try to roar through any open gap.

Marrakech's other big attraction beside the Djema El-Fna is its "souks." These, like other markets that we've visited, are located in a nearly incomprehensible warren of narrow streets. The big difference here is that instead of selling to locals, the shops are mainly aimed at tourists: carpets, metalwork, leather goods, souvenirs, etc. If you're a shopper, beware, you could get lost in the souks forever. "Dutch, German, where you from? Come see my shop, just looking, no obligation."

Shopkeepers are aware of the natural gregariousness of Americans and they use it to their advantage. If someone speaks to us in a friendly manner it's a genetic hardship for us to keep our mouths shut and walk brusquely away. At Ait Ben Haddou a guy chatted us up, pointed out a few sights, and told us that he'd rented props to "Gladiator." "Yeah, I rented them a what-cha-ma-call-it. Do you know what means, what-cha-ma-call-it?" "Uh, no." "Here let me show you." Next thing we knew, we'd somehow ended up in his shop and he was pitching his wares.

In Marrakech, Denise encouraged me to keep an open mind. "If we never speak to any of these people we're going to miss out on cultural experiences." As you might guess, we got taken. "Hey, you Americans? I'm not selling anything. Don't be so skeptical, I just want to practice my English. I tried to go America but I was how you say, 'swindled?' I was married to German woman. I don't sell anything. I'm a healer, you know Reiki? You, know Reflexology? Here, come in my booth, I want to show you letters. "Why you so skeptical?"

"I'm sorry, but every time we talk with a shopkeeper, it starts out about friendship and communication and ends up about us buying something."

"You hurt me. This is not about money, I'm a healer."

Next thing we knew, we'd somehow ended up in his shop. Twenty minutes later Denise was lying on a bench getting her pressure points poked and had received an unrequested diagnosis and massage. This was followed by the friendly healer's holistic prescription: "drink two liters of water a day, eat lentils twice a week for two months, break wind frequently, and have sex (wink, wink) four times a week."

"Ok, that will be 950 dirham please (over $100)."

"Say what?" I guess it was about the money after all. After a brief and slightly heated negotiation we settled on 250 dirham; still a rip-off, but cultural experience doesn't come cheap. Oh well, live and learn; at least our encounter didn't completely "souk" (bad pun).

Don usually writes about our adventures while I (Denise) contribute and critique. Now, it's one of those times when I need to put my own spin on the action. It's true that our interlude with the "healer" ended with him demanding money from us, but as I told Don, we don't have room to buy things and carry them with us (and shipping anything home is a hassle). I feel that expenses like this are a necessary and essential part of our journey. It's part of why we travel. It's like paying for entertainment. Don understands my point of view, but that didn't keep him from grinding his teeth. I probably won't get him into another trinket shop for the rest of our trip. Just the same the "healer" was sort of fun and only half full of hot air. Later that night we filled part of his prescription: two liters of water and "wink, wink."

Since I'm on a roll, I think that I'll go ahead and tell you about what I did with my last full day in Morocco. I decided to leave Don at the riad and check off another Moroccan must-do on my own; visit a "hammam." Here, the local people go to public bathhouses. Men go during certain hours and women at other times. Not knowing much about the protocol for hammams and not speaking Darija, I was too chicken to try a public one all by myself. In the end, I opted for the next best experience. I made myself an appointment at a salon that offered a private hammam package: gommage (peeling with traditional black soap), Moroccan massage, traditional pedicure and manicure (which were what I really needed). The manicure and pedicure were done at the same time by two women both named Marrian. They massaged the special black soap into my cuticles and soaked my hands and feet in warm water with dried rose pedals. Except for using orangewood sticks to push back my cuticles, the manicure was pretty normal.

The "Marrian" doing my feet really liked the small white flowers that had been painted on my big toenails by a Vietnamese nail tech in San Diego. After she applied my French polish, she attempted to paint new flowers with her orangewood stick. When she finished, she proudly showed me the results. Squinting, I put on my glasses. *Not bad for a first attempt with no brush, kind of looks like a flower.* "Shookran, shookran, merci," I smiled.

While I waited for my polish to dry and a hammam bath to become available, a French woman came in and sat down next to me for a pedicure. Thankfully, she spoke some English and was able to help translate some of what the women at the salon were trying to tell me. We starting visiting and I found out that she'd lived in Morocco for about two years and owned a reflexology business. We also discovered we were only two days apart in age; this earned me a kiss, kiss on each side of the cheek. Women came in and took their scarves off and relaxed in the absence of men, it was nice to spend a little girl time.

After a long wait, I was finally called to the hammam. I stripped down and a woman took me into a small tiled room and had me sit on a tile bench. First she poured hot water over me and rubbed me all over with the black soap. Once I was all soaped up, I was left alone in the "hot room" for five minutes for the soap to work its magic. Once my pores were open, the woman returned and rinsed me off with more hot water from copper buckets. Next, she pointed to a marble slab massage table and I crawled up, trying really hard not to slide right back off. Once I was on the slab, she worked me over from head to toe with a scrubby mitt and then rinsed me with a phone shower. Next she massaged me all over with some type of henna and rinsed me again. Finally, she shampooed and rinsed my hair and, squeaky clean, took me into another room where mint tea, a bathrobe, and a fainting couch all awaited. After that, they left me to sleep.

About 20 minutes later, I was ready to go and using sign language I asked if I could get dressed. At that point, they asked if I wanted brushing, pointing to my hair. Since I'd already been there three hours and wanted to get back to the hotel and Don, I said, "No thanks." I bought a small bottle of lotion, and tipped each woman. The whole experience came to about $55; a budget buster, but more good entertainment and worth every penny.

Tomorrow, on to Turkey...

Beehive House, Harran, Turkey

Chapter 8

TURKEY

Day 169 - June 22 - Tuesday - Istanbul, Turkey

We landed in Istanbul nine days ago flying in from Marrakech via Madrid. The layover in Madrid was short, our Iberia stewardesses fed us a passable no-pork-guaranteed meal, and other than arriving in Turkey at midnight, it was a most excellent flight.

For some inexplicable reason whenever we try to book flights online they either arrive in the wee hours (direct and cheap) or they arrive during the day but take three times as long and cost three times as much. We keep searching for that mythical flight that's direct, cheap, and arrives while the sun still shines, but like the equally mythical unicorn it eludes us. Anyway, we pre-booked seven nights at a hotel in Istanbul's Sultanahmet district (old town) and as part of the deal they threw in a free airport transfer. Arriving in the middle of the night, not speaking a word of Turkish, a driver holding up a sign with your name on it looks pretty good.

Our first reaction to our third-floor digs at the Dara Hotel was, "Holy crap! This is the size of a walk-in closet!"

"Are you sure it's the right room? It looked bigger online." After sleeping on it, we decided that stepping over our luggage for a week was no big deal. The room was clean and bright, there was plenty of hot water in the tiny shower, and the views out its windows were the stuff of travel brochures. Old Istanbul spread away in the distance and immediately across a cobbled street, we looked out over the minaret, garden, and lead covered domes of a medieval mosque. Five times a day its muezzin called the faithful to prayer and each call was a live performance as entrancing as it was exotic. We heard calls to prayer everyday in Morocco, but this guy across the street was something special. Farther away, beyond the mosque, we could see a ferry port and ships moving about on the Bosporus.

On the hotel's fourth floor there's a terrace, with even better views, where every day an included Turkish breakfast buffet is served between 8:00 and 11:00; yogurt, boiled eggs, dried figs, olives, breads, cheeses, dried apricots, cold cooked peppers, cold sautéed eggplant slices, fresh cherries, strawberries, melon, baloney, orange juice, tea, coffee, cereal, and a few things we're forgetting. The buffet doesn't change, but there's enough variety that it never got old. Tables are arranged under canopies and gulls wheel overhead squabbling and laughing while you eat.

Considering that we just picked a place off the web, the Dara Hotel was a lucky choice. Our room, despite the fisheye-lens marketing, was comfortable, and the hotel staff and the food were top notch. Amenities aside, it was the Dara's unexpectedly great location that made our stay.

The hotel is situated right in the heart of Sultanahmet only a couple of minutes walk from all of

Istanbul's best and most iconic sights. A short two block stroll put us at one end of the ancient Roman hippodrome next to a column where racing chariots once made their careening turns. Fifty yards further stands a hieroglyph covered obelisk, dedicated to the greatness of Tutmoses III, stolen from Egypt and erected on its present site in 396 A.D. Walk along another block and you stand in front of the domes and six soaring minarets of the famous seventeenth century Blue Mosque; a living house of worship that rivals those in Mecca. Turn 180 degrees and across a fountain you're facing the castle-like Hagia Sophia considered to be the greatest church in Christendom and the Muslim world; beyond that, sits the world famous Tokapi Palace.

We spent a full week in the city and it went by in a blink. Old Istanbul is magical. Each morning we got up, ate a leisurely breakfast, walked out the lobby door about 10:30, and didn't return to the hotel until after 6:00 P.M. Except for short lunches we spent 100% of our time seeing the sights, and take our word for it there are a lot of them! Istanbul suffers from a near embarrassment of cultural wonders. In addition to the places we already mentioned, we visited the Istanbul Archaeological Museum, The Museum of Islamic Art, an underground Byzantine cistern the size of two football fields, the Grand Bazaar, and the Spice Market. Some of the sights, like the Tokapi Palace and the archaeological museum, required hours to just breeze through.

Highlights were, Alexander's Tomb a huge stunningly beautiful carved marble sarcophagus from 400 B.C.; graffiti scratched into a marble rail inside the Hagia Sophia, "Halvdan was here," carved by a Viking before the year 900A.D.; crazy ice cream sellers who attract customers by juggling their product like fifty pound blobs of silly putty; people watching; chestnuts from a street vendor; a guard in the Blue Mosque telling a male tourist (not me) to cover his legs and cross them; people watching (again because it was that good); lentil soup and puffy bread at a restaurant called Doy Doy.

Day 171 - June 24 - Thursday - Goreme, Turkey

We left Istanbul day before yesterday on the "Meram Expressi" an overnight sleeper train bound for Konya. It wasn't the Orient Express (or much of an express at all for that matter) but it was still pretty neat. After a last day of sightseeing, we picked up our luggage from the Dara at 5:00 P.M. and walked about ten minutes to where we caught Istanbul's urban rail tramway. A clickty-clackty fifteen minute ride and we disembarked at the Karakoy ferry dock where a boat was just loading. On board the ferry we crossed the Bosporus from Europe into Asia and arrived at Istanbul's imposing Haydarpasa train station. Conveniently, the stone-walled station, a 19th century landmark, has its own dock and you can almost walk off your ferry and into the waiting room.

The Meram Expressi was already at the siding when we arrived and we were able to board about forty minutes later. Our sleeper compartment featured a large window, big comfortable seats, a work desk, a fridge, two fold down bunks (Denise got the upper), and a sink. About the time we stowed our gear, the train rolled out of the station and it was all more clickty-clack from there.

Attractive European countryside rolled by while we ate a light meal in the dining car of soup and jalapeno salad (so hot that I had to pick out the peppers). After dinner we got ready for bed and turned in. In the morning the sun streamed in our window and the country sailing by had become the "Midwest" with fields of wheat that roll away into the distance.

Our train departed Istanbul on time, but after that its schedule went right out the window. We were supposed to arrive in Konya at 8:39 AM. By 9:30, we were still an hour away. About that time a Canadian woman who was in the next car walked by our open door. "Hey, has your conductor talked to you? Ours said something to us about some problem with the tracks. I think everyone has to get off at the next stop and take a bus." *Hum, okay that's an interesting news item!* Our steward wasn't anywhere nearby so I started wandering forward. I didn't find the conductors until I reached the dining car (other end of train). Three of them were having a smoke, ours was asleep. One of the smokers nudged him, "Pssst, this guy wants something." "Is the train going all the way to Konya? Is there a problem with the tracks?" "Konya yes bus, one hour." *Okay dokay.*

A little way down the tracks the train came to a stop and everyone clambered off, some passengers on one side, some on the other. We handed down our bags and followed others from our car toward a waiting bus. As our stuff was being thrown underneath, we looked around and noticed that a bunch of people were missing. "What happened to the rest of the people?" "Where are the Canadians?" We took our seats, all the while wondering if there was more than one bus and if this one was headed in the right direction (ours). When the driver closed the doors and pulled out, I tapped a man in front of me and asked "Konya evet (yes)?" He looked at me, "Konya" and pointed out the front window.

Things couldn't have worked out better. On the way to Konya's train station our bus passed near the town Otogar (bus station) and the driver asked if anyone wanted off. We didn't understand the question but I heard him say, "otogar" so we both waved our hands. As he pulled over, another bus also drove up and deposited the Canadians. We rolled our bags a hundred yards and saved ourselves an expensive cross town taxi.

At the bus station with dozens of competing counters, we were quickly directed to a line that ran to Goreme. Twenty minutes after that we were riding in air conditioned comfort. Can you believe it, the bus had an onboard steward and twice during our three hour ride he pushed a tiny drink cart down the isle serving free coffee, tea, and soft drinks? Before each service he passed through the bus with napkins and a bottle of hand sanitizer. Yeah, match that Greyhound!

Day 172 - June 25 - Friday

Wow, we've landed in a really cool place. According to The Unnamed Guidebook, "Goreme is the archetypal travelers' utopia: a beatific village where the surreal surroundings spread a fat smile on everyone's face." I can't say it better. The town sits at the base of eroded sandstone cliffs whose fantastic weathered faces are peppered with rough hewn cave houses and pigeon keeps. Dotted throughout the area are even more fantastic "fairy chimneys," towering hoodoos of stone, likewise carved into homes and hotels. Radiating out from the village are a series of sinuous white canyons with hiking trails, panoramic viewpoints and rock hewn ninth and tenth century churches. At the Flintstone's Cave Hotel our Jacuzzi equipped cave room looks out on Nature's own magic kingdom. All the place needs is Hobbits.

Day 174 - June 27 - Sunday

Tonight is our fifth night in Goreme. Since we've been here, we've gone hiking in Pigeon Valley, climbed to the top of Ulchisar Castle, a natural rock citadel that's the highest point in Cappadocia, toured the Goreme Open Air Museum with its collection of thousand year-old frescoed cave churches, descended four stories into the claustrophobic underground city of Derinkuyu where third century Christians led bomb-shelter lives to escape Roman persecution, lunched by a river while hiking in the Ihlara valley, scrambled through the huge rock-hewn remains of the Selime Monastery, lounged by the pool, swilled ice cold Efes beers, and tucked away one good meal after another. Between its laid back vibe and wealth of stuff to do, Goreme is a hard act to follow.

Day 177 - June 30 - Wed - Eastern Cappadocia, Turkey

Right now, we're riding in a small bus (Mustafa is driving) headed back to Cappadocia on the last leg of a whirlwind three-day, 1,640 kilometer, tour to Eastern Anatolia and Western Mesopotamia. We set out from Goreme the day before yesterday with twelve like-minded tourists, our driver, and our guide Asim (pronounced "Awesome"). With everybody's luggage stowed in back, Mustafa put pedal to metal and eastward we bombed. This was blitzkrieg tourism with most of the "good stuff" a long day's drive away.

The countryside that scrolled by our windows once again looked like California's swarthy Turkish stunt double. "Just pull the camera back a little and no one will know the difference." I don't remember fields of tobacco or groves of figs and pistachios in California, but if you squint just a little...

Our first stop was the Sultan Han “caravansari,” a fortress like structure built in the 1230’s as part of a series of way stations along the “silk road” to China. High defensive walls surround a compound that once provided overnight accommodation and protection to merchant caravans bringing valuable trade goods from the East. In return for a ten percent cut, the Seljuk Empire allowed merchants three days room and board at each outpost and provided the caravans with an armed escort (sort of an early insurance policy).

After we left the caravansari, we rolled until we reached a town called Goksun where we grabbed lunch at a roadside café. Our only other “real” stop came about an hour later in Kahramanmaras where we sampled what our tour flyer and guide described as “the most delicious ice cream in all Turkey.” Well maybe; pungent goat milk ice cream topped with grated pistachios eaten with a fork is definitely something we don’t get everyday. It could be that like “salgam suyu,” chilled beet juice mixed with vinegar, it’s an acquired taste. Anyway, throw in a few potty breaks and nine hours of driving and it gets you from Goreme to the slopes of Mount Nemrut.

We over-nighted at the Hotel Euphrat, a pleasant place with simple rooms and great views, located about ten kilometers below the mountain’s summit. The next morning, no strike that, in the middle of the night (3 AM!) we all crawled out of bed. Under a full moon, we drove to the end of the road and then hiked up an ever climbing rocky path. Just before sunrise we reached the sprawling if unimaginatively named East Platform. One of two monumental temples that crown Mount Nemrut, it was built in 300 BC by King Antiochus I Epiphanes, a man of considerable ego who considered himself a buddy of Hercules and a lesser god in his own right. Ahead of us to the east squatted a low stepped platform oriented toward the rising sun; to our left raised the monumental torsos of Zeus, Apollo, Fortuna, and other gods seated on ancient thrones of stone. The heads (about 6 feet tall) of the gods, weathered and cracked, lie at their feet, tossed down by the shifting earth. Behind the silent statues, the whole top of the mountain is a huge manmade tumulus of tiny stones protecting the last resting place of Antiochus down through the ages.

The drive from Goreme to Nemrut Dagi was long and tiring. Our 3AM wake-up bordered on insanity and the morning was see-your-breath cold. When, as they had for thousands of years, the first rays of the sun struck the enigmatic faces of the patiently waiting gods none of it mattered. Antiochus built his temple to reflect his vision of strength and grandeur and after millennia his crumbling ruins still wow the masses. After watching shadowed purple cloaks of the surrounding mountains lighten and fall away before the questing oranges, reds, and yellows of the rising sun, we moved on.

A path leads around Nemrut's tumulus summit and walking slowly we soon reached the, also "creatively" named, West Platform. This second level plaza also features crumbled architecture, monumental heads, and top-of-the-world views. Its scale is smaller and it lacks the morning curtain call of its fraternal twin, but the West Platform still fires the imagination. When the creativity of other human beings has the power to reach out and touch us across the ages, it is perhaps as close as we can ever come to immortality.

With the sun fully up, the old gods returned to their vigil and we scrambled back down our now visible trail. A short ride in the van, quick showers, and breakfast, all followed, and then we hit the road for a day jammed-packed with first-rate sightseeing.

Part way down the mountain, we stopped and took another short hike to visit the remains of ancient Commagene, the 80 BC capital of Arsameia. Most traces of Arsameia are long gone, but a cave temple dedicated to Mithras and a large impressive steale of king Mithridates shaking hands with the god Hercules remain. Near to the steale there's another cave temple with a long Greek inscription describing the founding of the city. It was strange to pause amidst the rocks, trees, and scrub brush of that empty mountainside and realize that we stood in the heart of a once populous city.

Following Commagene, we visited a graceful Seljuk bridge over the river Nymphaios, an impressive second century Roman bridge, built to honor the Emperor Septimus Severus, and the tomb of Karakus another barren tumulus mound fronted by a solitary column and a weathered stone eagle. Next, we made a brief foray into the modern era and stopped to ogle the massive Ataturk Dam, once the largest construction project in the world. After the dam, it was back to the past as we crossed the Euphrates River, entered Mesopotamia, and headed for the ancient town of Harran.

Harran, which sits on a dry windswept plain within sight of the Syrian border, is one of the oldest continuously inhabited places on earth. Inside its crumbling walls huddles a community that dates from 1,900 BC and is mentioned in the Bible's Book of Genesis. Many of the structures that exist today are mud-and-straw brick beehive houses, a style that reaches back into distant antiquity. Seen from a mound at the town's center, Harran is modest place; a small rural village that wouldn't warrant much attention except for its unique architecture and the palpable presence of age that drapes around it like a dusty cloak. It's a place where you feel the weight of unseen history.

The beehive houses are fascinating and fortunately one of them was fitted out as an ethnic museum/gift shop which meant we could poke around inside. High cone shaped roofs gave the rooms a pleasant airy feel and the thick mud walls kept out the desert heat. It looked like it would make a home.

Outside, enterprising locals had erected a small covered seating area where they sold cold drinks and tiny cups of molasses thick coffee. They only had two cups, so if you wanted coffee you had to wait until someone else finished. The waiter would ask if you were done, then simply take the cup, add a little more coffee, and hand it to the next person (saved on cleanup). Backtracking from Harran, we returned to Sanliurfu where we would spend our second night.

There's a lot of overlap between Christianity, Judaism, and Islam, and the prophet Abraham is an important figure that gets kudos from all three. Long ago Sanliurfu was called Urfu and long before that it was simply Ur. Well, just so happens that Abraham's old stomping ground was also called Ur. There was another Ur farther east, but fifty-fifty odds were good enough for Sanliurfu to lay claim to the prophet. According to the Quran, Abraham righteously destroyed some false idols and was cast into a fire for his effort. Allah, seeing his servant's plight, saved him by changing the fire into water and the flames into fish. Today, in a park-like setting, you can visit a pool of fat happy sacred carp (the flames), a spring that gushes from the spot where Abraham fell, and a holy cave where he may or may not have been born. Of course we headed right over.

Aside from unplanned excitement when a small girl fell into the carp pond and was rescued by bystanders, the most interesting of Abraham's "slept-heres" was his spring. Set back in a cave, the fount is a Muslim holy site. Two doors lead into the cave's interior, one for men and the other for women. Inside the approach to the spring is divided so that neither gender can see the other. To enter the cave you must first remove your shoes and women must completely cover their heads, arms, and legs. Inside the reverence is palpable. Devout people pray, pour the holy water over their heads, drink it, and put it into containers to carry away as a cure-all. Our visit only lasted a few minutes but it was a real cultural eye-opener.

Next, we explored the local bazaar, a good one with an interesting coppersmiths' alley, sipped tea under a shady tree, wrapped up day two, and headed for our hotel.

With the addition of lunch, a minor sight or three, and bathroom stops; pillow to pillow, we spent eighteen hours constantly on the go. Take those eighteen hours, add them to a previous nine hour day cooped up in a small bus, toss in a bunch of total strangers, and you might have had a recipe for tourist Hell. Fortunately, our mix turned out to be a recipe for Turkish delight.

Everything we saw was unusual and interesting and our group clicked together right from the get go. We were an international hodge-podge: ourselves; three silly American gals about thirty, "confident professional women"; Beto a handsome, long-haired, pierced, grad student from Mexico City; a quiet young Japanese couple on their honeymoon, who only spoke Japanese; a

Turkish guy who lives in Germany, he used to own a kebap shop, but now he plans to study engineering; a cute Turkish gal who lives in Switzerland; two camera toting Chinese guys from Hong Kong; and Sylvan, a Frenchman who has worked for twelve years with Doctors Without Borders. Independent travelers one and all, everyone was outgoing and fun, and brimming with stories to tell. English (luckily for us) was the group's lingua Franca and the time flew. Denise especially enjoyed getting in some quality "girl time" with the Americans.

I'd be falling down on the job if I didn't again mention our driver Mustafa and our guide Asim. Mustafa was flat-out excellent. He drove safely and confidently for hour after hour keeping to a schedule that would have killed most bus drivers in the U.S. And Asim; well Asim really was awesome. He was the exact opposite of our turd roller from Fes. He was fun, organized, knew everything, told good stories, and shared cultural tidbits; conducting his running commentary in both fluent English and Japanese (he also speaks Arabic, Turkish, and French).

Today, we slept in. Instead of a 3:00 AM wake up, we were allowed to snooze until 5:45! An hour later we'd eaten breakfast and were back on the road for the long haul back to Cappadocia. When we left Sanliurfu, Beto and the Turkish gal stayed behind to catch flights to other destinations. Gradually, throughout the day we shed other companions until now, on the last part of our drive, there are only four of us left.

Today's highlights were a stop in the town of Birecik for a (yawn yawn) visit to a bald-ibis (birds) breeding facility (120 up from the near extinction level of 7); a chance to stick a toe into the Euphrates River (Hey, it was the Euphrates and we wiped with alcohol afterwards); and a stop in Gaziantep to see the world's second largest collection of Roman mosaics. The mosaic museum was a jaw-dropper featuring dozens of second century room sized floor mosaics across which cavorted gods, goddesses, and assorted mythological creatures.

Stretched out across two seats, nibbling cookies and sipping beet juice (I don't think I'm going to be a fan), there's only another 240 kilometers to go.

Day 181 - July 3 - Sunday - Konya, Turkey

Well, we finally pried ourselves loose from the Flintstones Cave Hotel in Goreme. We originally arrived there planning to spend only three nights, but lingered for two more while we relaxed and waited for our Mount Nemrut tour. With its enchanted location, excellent pool, and friendly attentive staff (special kudos to Mehemet and Durmush), it was an easy hotel to like. In fact, we enjoyed Flintstone's so much that we risked a Rip Van Winkle and stayed for another three nights after our return from Nemrut. By the time we eventually convinced ourselves to leave, we'd been guests so long that the hotel tossed in our last night for free.

Several daily buses run between Goreme and Konya so we decided on one at 9:30 AM; not too early, not too late. We passed through Konya, the buckle on Turkey's Islamic Bible belt, on our way from Istanbul, but this time we decided to stop for the night so that we could visit the city's Mevlana Museum, a shrine and tomb for Celaleddin Rumi the thirteenth century mystic philosopher whose followers came to be called the Mevlevi or the order of whirling Dervishes. Serendipitously, it turned out that every Saturday the

Dervishes hold a Sema (religious ceremony) that is open to the public. Adding icing to our cake, entrance was free. Throw in the fact that UNESCO lists the Dervish sema as a "masterpiece of the oral and intangible heritage of humanity," and we couldn't pass it up. From about 9 PM until 10 PM we watched the Dervishes whirl, an ordered choreography that was also a trancelike communion with God. Despite an amphitheater setting and a large crowd of spectators (mostly reverent Turks), it was a moving and thoroughly entertaining experience.

On a side note, we went to see the Dervishes with Bianca and Guillerme an early thirties couple from Brazil. We bumped into them waiting for the Konya bus and it turned out that they we're also on an around the world trip. Guillerme had been on the road fourteen months and Bianca been traveling for eight. They were both lots of fun and we made good use of the contact, picking their brains about places they'd already visited: Africa, India, Myanmar, etc... The people you meet along the way are half the journey, and when it comes to information, nothing beats firsthand.

Day 181 - July 4 - Sunday - Side, Turkey

Yesterday was a travel day. Around 9 AM we said goodbye to the Otel Usulan (a nice, clean, shared bathroom, $32 per night place) and rolled our bags down the street. A ten minute walk took us to Konya city center where we caught an urban tram (light rail) for a seven kilometer ride out to the otogar.

At the bus station, with an hour to kill, we walked over to an outside café for breakfast. When we sat down, we came face to face with our first untranslated Turkish menu. The only items we recognized with any certainty were cay (tea) and Nescafe (self-explanatory). After squinting for a while, Denise decided to play it safe and go with the tea. I ordered "kahvalti" which looks sort of like the word for coffee (kahva). I didn't know for sure what it would be, but we'd seen another similar word which meant breakfast so I figured what the hell. The worst that could happen was that I'd find myself eating a $5 goat scrotum kebap at 10:00 AM. When our order arrived, it was an anticlimax: small tea for Denise, large tea for me, sliced tomato, sliced cucumber, sliced baloney, cheese, olives, a boiled egg, jam, butter, honey, Nutella, and bread; in other words your basic Turkish breakfast. We really need to bone up on the language.

The bus ride from Konya dished up another "match that Greyhound" moment when shortly after boarding the steward made his rounds and served everyone ice cream! The seats were comfy and each one was equipped with its own mini-TV. There were about a dozen satellite channels and if you couldn't be bothered to look out your window you could tune to a channel with a driver's eye view of the road ahead. We stuck to the window view. From Konya the road climbed over a beautiful mountain pass (great rock formations and evergreen forest) before dropping down to the Mediterranean coast.

Our lunch stop was a little iffy because neither our driver nor our steward spoke any English. We pulled into a roadside rest with WC's, a café restaurant, and a market, and everyone piled off. That told us that the stop was either lunch or a five minute toilet break. Denise tried to ask the steward by pointing to her watch but only received a smile and an airy wave of the hand which still left us wondering. Rather than take a chance we used the bathrooms and then headed for the market where we grabbed cookies and a dry ready-made cheese sandwich. As we stepped out the door we noticed that a couple of young guys were washing the bus. Okay, maybe we're not leaving right away.

Denise stepped into the café and tried to discover what was on their menu and whether we had time to order anything. Her conversation was degenerating into confused looks on both sides when she spotted a woman sitting by a large griddle making egg-sized balls of dough.

She pointed, "What's that?" "Gozleme." *Alright, we're in business!* "Gozleme" is a word we both recognized. It's a sort of filled Turkish tortilla or crepe. "Can we get it to go?"

"Yes, meat or cheese?" We sat at a table and watched the woman roll out one of the dough balls until it was paper thin and at least two feet around. She sprinkled the flattened dough with cheese and herbs, folded it in half, and tossed it onto the griddle. Another woman then tended the snack as it puffed up and exuded a delicious enticing aroma. Our waiter had just finished cutting and wrapping the hot cheesy treat when the call came to get back on the bus. As we climbed on board, Denise turned to me, "You can have the sandwich."

When we purchased our bus tickets in Konya we told the agent that we wanted to go to the town of "Side" (pronounced See-day). "No, no Side, you go Manavgat then mini-bus." Manavgat is just a long stone's throw, well actually a seven kilometer throw, from Side, but since The Unnamed Guidebook said that regular shuttles link the two town bus stations, everything looked good.

On arrival at the Manavgat otogar, we were told, "No! No Side, you mini-bus (downtown) Manavgat, then other bus Side." *Great! So there are no "regular shuttles!"* The only way to reach Side was to catch a local city bus to the center of Manavgat and then try to snag a transfer from there. Dragging our bags, we left the otogar and walked out to the street. Then it hit us! We had no idea which side of the street to stand on. Buses were running along both sides but downtown Manavgat could have been in either direction. Nearby, on the otogar side, there was a bus stop and a guy standing at the curb waiting; a bus stop but no signage.

"Excuse me, do you speak English?"

"No, little."

"Bus Side?"

"Side?"

"Yes, Side."

"You go Side?"

"Yes, Side." At that point, he stuck two fingers into his mouth and whistled loudly at a passing car. The car made a quick u-turn and pulled up at the bus stop. A brief conversation in Turkish ensued, and a moment later the driver had his trunk open and was rearranging groceries to make room for our bags. The guy who'd whistled jumped into the front seat and we climbed in back.

"Side?
Where Side?"

"Hotel Conny's," looks of confusion, "Otogar."

"Otogar?"

"Yes." Ten minutes later we were in Side and our "guides" were asking shop keepers for the location of Hotel Conny's. Since that didn't produce any immediate results, they shrugged and dropped us across from the otogar. We thanked them both and I gave the driver 15 TL ($9.64 which he was reluctant to accept) for his trouble. Denise thinks the two guys were buddies and that the guy at the bus stop was waiting for his friend to pick him up. I'm not so sure they even knew each other. Did the driver take the first guy back to his bus stop? Who knows? Whatever the deal, it saved us a bunch of hassle.

Day 183 - July 6 - Tuesday

Conny's is a pleasant boutique hotel run by a friendly outgoing Dutch couple named Ad and Conny (natch). It features a nice pool, a bar with occasional live music, and a restaurant that's so good that we're going to eat there for a third night in a row. Tonight at 9:30 the bar is hosting a World Cup Soccer party so expats can gather to watch a finals match between Holland and Uruguay. They have the place heavily decorated with orange flags and balloons and expect a crowd of maybe two hundred.

Ad and Conny opened their successful hotel six years ago; Side is a packed-to-the-gills party tourist destination, and strangely, we're the very first Americans they've ever had as guests! It's weird, Side crawls with Europeans of every flavor, its beaches are lined with rows of chairs and umbrellas; bars, hotels, and restaurants crowd its streets; faux booze-cruise "pirate ships" ply its waters; para-sails fill its skies; and we are regularly met with surprise and consternation when we tell people that we're Americans. In the words of one tout, "Americans; what are you doing here?" We laughingly say to each other that we're going to start telling people that we got on the wrong bus.

Day 184 - July 7 - Wednesday

The soccer party was a kick (excuse the pun) and the turnout exceeded expectations. You need to picture two hundred and seventy Dutch soccer fans all decked out in orange; orange shirts, giant orange hands, funny orange hats, orange clogs, orange trumpets, the occasional milk maid outfit, and lots of beer. As "New Worlders" we were secretly rooting for Uruguay, but to the wild joy of the crowd, Holland carried the match three to two. Holland's second goal was a tricky shot off the head of Robben (or was it Schnieder?) that took the wind out of Uruguay's game. Naturally the orange victory led to an excess of exuberance and the loud singing of Dutch victory songs. We didn't roll into bed until after midnight. Next Sunday, we'll be long gone but, they'll do it all over again.

We're going to spend one more day here in Side. Denise is feeling a little blah so we figure another day by the pool or at the beach is a better prospect than a possibly long day of shuttle buses and otogars.

Despite an overblown tourist scene, Side is a pretty good stop. The town has been inhabited since around 600 BC and has the Roman and Hellenistic ruins to prove it. As you wander its main road you pass ancient fountains, monumental gates, colonnaded markets, and a 2nd century AD amphitheater that is one of the largest Roman ruins in this part of the world. If you continue through Side's touristy carnival streets lined with: bars, boutiques, souvenir stands, and touts encouraging you to stop for a drink, you eventually arrive at the sea dramatically framed by temples to Apollo and Athena. It's an odd sloppy mix of impressive antiquity and modern kitsch but it sort of works.

Day 186 - July 9 - Friday - Olympos, Turkey

Yesterday, we shook the sand of Side from our sandals, zipped on the (shudder) pant legs, and headed for our next destination, the laid back post-hippie hang-out of Olympos. After breakfast, Ad gave us a lift back to the Manavgat otogar. When we walked up to a counter and said we wanted to go to Antalya (transfer point for Olympos) we were rushed outside and immediately placed on a bus that was already pulling out. *Yeah high-five, only 9:30 AM and already we were on the move!* We congratulated ourselves on our good luck and settled back to enjoy what we expected to be a quick ride. A few minutes later the bus headed into downtown Manavgat and began trawling for passengers. *Crap, no expresses to Antalya!* We stopped at almost every corner and pretty much anywhere else anyone wanted to get on or off. Two hours and only 38 miles later, we rolled into the Antalya otogar. That was just the start of our milk run.

In Antalya we were pointed to a mini-bus where we sat while its driver tried to scare up other passengers. About twenty minutes later he hit his tipping point and we set off on another sporadic journey. Another two and a half hours later, we found ourselves standing outside a cliff-top café at the Olympos turnoff. The café serves as a makeshift bus stop and another van waited in its parking lot to take passengers the last few miles down the mountain. Waited is the key word. After its driver tossed our bags in back, we munched gozleme, drank tea, looked at the view, and twiddled our thumbs, while another forty minutes slipped past.

Oh well, no schedules to keep and we weren't in a hurry. The last hour of the drive was beautiful and reminded us of motoring through Big Sur country in

California: evergreens, scrub brush, meadows, and rugged mountains that plunge down to the sea. Of course it's a warm Mediterranean sea rather than a dark cold Pacific.

Present day Olympos is a collection of budget backpacker dorms, tree houses, and bungalows that sit snugly tucked into a rocky gorge close to where it spills into the Med. A dirt road winds through the middle; pine trees and orange trees shading the shoulder to shoulder pansiyons (Turkish word), bars, and restaurants. Robinson Crusoe meets Swiss Family Robinson is the predominant theme and everything exudes a kickback Sierras summer camp feel. At the end of the road, just before a pebbly beach, a small river flows through the Olympos of yesterday; a collection of ruined vine and tree covered Roman tombs, walls, aqueducts, and temples which date from the first century B.C. Olympos is a very cool spot.

Faced with a daunting choice of accommodations we based our selection on economics. A business card from Flintstones snagged us a 10% discount and we registered at the Turkmen Treehouses. "Treehouses" sound romantic but, they're mostly dark windowless, bathroom-less, hovels that bake when it's hot. We went for the "deluxe" room; wood paneled, en-suite facilities, plenty of windows, our own third floor balcony, and AC; not a bad deal at $64 including breakfast and dinner.

Day 187 - July 10 - Saturday

We spent yesterday exploring the Roman ruins and baking on the beach; not exactly your tough day. The Brazilian couple that we met in Goreme is here also so after dinner we wandered down to their pansiyon (called Deep Green) and sat shooting the breeze until one in the morning.

Olympos has a kind of funky Shangri La thing going and strangely it feels like we're on vacation from our trip. We only plan to hang here one more night but clearly it's a place that people have trouble leaving. As one sign reads, "I came, I saw, I stayed, and stayed, and stayed, and ..."

Day 188 - July 11 - Sunday

The Internet was working yesterday so we spent the morning Jonesing for plane tickets. As things now stand, we leave Turkey on June 30th and fly to Nairobi Kenya. Naturally we arrive there at 1 AM. Oh crap, more planning! If there's any downside to our "go where the wind blows" mode of travel, it's laying out the details of our next leg. Both of us like to live in the moment and figuring out where to stay two weeks down the road does not fill the bill. After the plane ticket we should have focused on a hotel. After all, who wants to arrive in Nairobi at 1 AM without a plan? Instead we went back to the beach. It was a little rocky getting in and out of the water, but it beat the heck out of surfing the Internet.

We finished the day with a "Flame Tour." Around 9:30 PM we climbed into a mini-bus and took a forty minute ride over to Cirali in the next canyon. Cirali is the hopping off point for visits to the mystical Chimaera. Chimaera, the son of Typhon, was part goat and part lion, with a dash of fire breathing dragon thrown in for good measure. Sometime before the second century B.C. he was killed by the hero Bellerophon (mounted on the winged horse Pegasus; of course). Where the Chimaera fell to earth a cluster of flames still spontaneously blaze from the ground. Cool beans!

After the mini-bus ride, we hiked for another twenty minutes in the dark. A hillside path carried us steadily upward and then, sure enough, random jets of flame spouting from the ground. At first glance the 30 or 40 flares look like nothing so much as a cluster of small glowing campfires. Then it hits you, the flames rise from the bare rock! They appear to dance and burn without fuel and they've been doing it for more than two thousand years! No wonder the ancient Olympians devoutly worshipped Hephaestus, the god of fire.

Day 193 - July 16 - Friday - Fethiye, Turkey

Wow, and another excellent five days slip by like nothing. The morning after our visit to the mysterious (obligatory descriptive) Chimaera, we climbed on another mini-bus, for a one and a half hour trip to Demre. Demre's main attractions are some nice Lycian tombs and an ancient church where Ole Saint Nick once preached (Santa Claus! Hey, there was a statue and everything). The real reason for the ride, however, was to get us down to Kale harbor where we boarded a gullet (wooden yacht) for a four-day and three-night blue water motor cruise to Fethiye.

Now that was serious relaxation! Our boat could accommodate sixteen people plus a crew of three. Fortunately, there were only eight of us passengers. Sixteen would have felt crowded and uncomfortable, but eight was awesome and exclusive. Sean and Carmen were from Canada, and Tim, Jess, Miri, and Justine were all from the land down under. Much to Tim's delight, Jess even had a tube of Vegemite to prove it.

Urzai, Mustafa, and Dahli were our crew. Miri and Justine thought that they were a little too touchy (Turkish Muslim guys and nearly naked European women, ouch). And, I'll be the first to admit that when Justine got stung on her rather nice ass by a jellyfish, the captain may have been a little too thorough with his application of salve. Otherwise, the crew was a blast. I might add that Justine also received the sobriquet, "Jellybum."

Each couple (Miri and Justine, "we're not Lesbians," just pals since age four) had their own tiny cabin with a private bathroom. The cabins were adequate for stashing gear and changing clothes, but too hot and stuffy for comfortable sleeping. To escape the heat, most people, including Denise, camped out on deck. Rather than make what I considered an embarrassing spectacle of myself with my whirring CPAP and "Snorkel Boy" headgear, I sweltered inside.

The crew did all the sailing (motoring) and cooking, while us passengers worked on our "rest fatigue."

I got a little seasick our second morning; green around the gills but no barf (too much info), but that soon passed and it was a wonderfully idyllic four days. We anchored in pretty bays at night and during the day visited exotic sounding places like "The Sunken City," "Pirates' Cave," and "Butterfly Valley." The truth of the cruise was that the sights were a little overhyped but with the laid back vibe, occasional beer, and frequent swimming we didn't care. Besides, where else do rowboats pull up and sell you Nutella filled gozleme and over-priced ice cream?

Denise is clearly the poster child for "tanorexia" but even she got enough sun that when our cruise ended in Fethiye she spent the next two days hiding in the shade; tanned and happy, everyone had a blast.

Day 194 - July 17 - Saturday - Pamukkale, Turkey

Fethiye is a pleasant albeit sweltering harbor town that caters to the needs and wants of upscale yacht types and summer renters. Near the docks is a sort of malecon lined with cafes and small park spaces. Across the coastal road, shady pedestrian streets filled with touristy bars, restaurants, clothing stores, jewelry shops, and souvenir stands fan out away from the water. Farther inland the town turns hot, commercial, and mostly uninteresting. Behind the whole, rise cliffs whose rock faces are dotted with carved Lycian tombs, a Roman amphitheater that's seen better times, and the crumbled remains of a crusader fortress.

We lounged about Fethiye for a couple of days recovering our land legs while we decided where to go next. Theoretically, we were hanging out in our air conditioned room surfing the Web. Unfortunately the Internet service was intermittent and the air conditioner was on the fritz (we got a discount). So with the days both hot and humid, we spent most of our time sprawled by the hotel pool.

We also downed the occasional gin and tonic; one of which deserves a special mention. Anna, the hotel's regular bartender (all Turkish backpacker places seem to have an Australian "Sheila" or two as temporary help) had the afternoon off and one of the hotel's male Turkish employees was filling in. When I ordered two gin and tonics a quick look of confusion flitted across his face. As a good Muslim, he was used to popping the occasional beer for his guests, but my request for mixed drinks nudged him into unknown territory (cue Rod Serling music). He placed two tall highball glasses on the bar and took a bottle of local gin off the shelf. "*Hmmm, how much should I use?*" Not sure on proportions, he decided to err on the side of generosity and emptied the bottle into the two glasses, filling them each about two thirds full of straight gin. "Sorry, I'm out of local gin. Is it okay, if I use the Imported?"

"Uh, no, I think that's fine like it is." Next, he added a wedge of lemon, a splash of tonic, and a straw to each glass. A couple of small ice cubes completed the mix but the drinks were still about an inch below the lips of their glasses.

"Hmm, are you sure you wouldn't like some more gin?"

"Uh, yeah sure, why not, okay." Denise and I both got hammered; ah there's nothing quite like celebrating cultural differences.

We admit that we were unabashed slugs during our time in Fethiye, but nevertheless we did manage a couple of forays into town. Our first night ashore we went out to dinner with our "V-GO" shipmates at the local fish market; a totally enjoyable experience; once the restaurant assembled a fan and aimed it in our direction. The fish market is a rectangle of small stalls that sit in the middle of a larger square surrounded by restaurants. You browse the fresh-caught fish and make your selection. We went together with Sean and bought: a sea bass, a slab of salmon, and three fourths of a kilo of shrimp. Once you have your fish in hand you head for the restaurants all of which vie to cook your purchase. For about $3.50 per person they grill your seafood with spices and sauce and then serve it up along with salad, fancy bread, and water melon; lip smacking good!

Our second night, we discovered that our own hotel, The V-Go Levant, served a variety of excellent grilled dinners: chicken, lamb, fish, etc. with plenty of tasty sides all for only $6.50. After that, it was strictly "dinner in."

Our other major Fethiye exploration was a long hot morning walk to take a closer look at the city's Lycian tombs. The effort was well worth it if a little strange on two counts. The first was that when you reach the base of the cliffs where the tombs are located, there's a fence and a ticket booth that charges $6 per person to approach them. The weird part is that the tombs are empty and there's nothing to see except their facades; and ... you can see the facades just fine from outside the fence. I'm not sure who pays the entrance fee, but it wasn't us.

Our second bit of weirdness came putt-putting along as we followed posted signs pointing to a second set of tombs. A middle-aged guy riding by on a motor scooter stopped and asked us if we needed directions. "No thanks, we're just walking to the tombs."

"Yes, yes tombs very good; that way."

We said "Thank you" and continued walking. He rode on up the hill. As we neared the tombs, we passed him again parking his motor scooter. "Tombs that way, very nice." As we followed the signs, he walked ahead and pointed at a couple of the tombs. "See, very old, chip, chip."

"Okay great, thanks, see you later."

Hand out, "Tip!" *Tip, you're shitting me!* The guy had glommed onto us and had only been there maybe three minutes. "Tip, tip!"

"No, we didn't bring any money. No tip!" He watched disgusted as we walked away. *Bad guide! No Donut!*

Turkey is an easy friendly place in which to travel, but once you're firmly on the tourist route the locals make a bit more effort to get into your pockets. We had a great bus ride from Fethiye to Pamukkale; comfortable bus, beautiful mountain scenery, and interesting rural towns, but it also ended with a bad behavior moment. About a half hour from Pamukkale we reached the end of our bus' line in Denizli. Since our tickets were "Fethiye to Pamukkale" our bus steward walked us over to a dolmus (mini-bus) that could take us the rest of the way and paid the driver our fares (we both saw him hand over the money). As we drove along, our driver kept picking up people until the 19 passenger van was carrying 27. Evidently there's a legal limit because each time he spotted a "polis" car he told all the standing people to duck down! When we arrived in Pamukkale, the driver helped us with our luggage and then asked us to pay our fares. "No, we already paid."

"You Pay!"

"No;" followed by lots of angry yelling in Turkish. "We saw the steward give you the money. Look here's our ticket!" He tore up the ticket and there was more yelling on both sides. Finally, the ruckus drew an older man out of a bus company office who invited us all inside. The old man sat down behind a desk and then our driver began to yell at him! The long suffering old guy listened patiently, but when the harangue showed no signs of abating, he caved and paid the driver a second time just to be rid of him.

Some other tourists who were on the bus paid double to avoid the hassle. The amount wasn't much, but the price was clearly posted in the bus and if the driver always gets double he'll just keep ripping people off.

Day 196 - July 19 - Monday

After we thanked the old guy at the bus company, and surreptitiously flipped off the dolmus driver, we wheeled our bags across the street and into the welcoming lobby of the Atremis Yoruk Hotel. The Artemis caters to backpackers and small groups and is pleasant enough that we ended up staying three nights: big pool, decent Turkish breakfast, air conditioning that doesn't blow on you, Internet (well not so much), and free tea and coffee all day. There was also a free Turkish bath that we didn't use because the weather felt too hot.

Yesterday, we spent our morning wandering Pamukkale's famous travertine pools and poking around the remains of the ancient Roman city of Hierapolis. A couple of blocks up from our hotel, steep hillsides rise from the edge of town to a surrounding plateau. From end to end, the slopes are shrouded in surreal layers of travertine. Pamukkale means "Cotton Castle" and at first glance, the travertine looks for all the world like a puffy blanket of snow. The pools and terraces are reminiscent of Mammoth Hot Springs in Yellowstone Park, but unlike Mammoth the lime rich waters at Pamukkale are mostly cool.

We paid an entrance fee, shucked off our sandals (all shoes are prohibited) and began a quarter mile barefoot walk up the travertine to the plateau. There are two other entrances on top where tour buses deposit their hordes, but the barefoot route is way more fun. The path underfoot is a continuous sheet of rough white marble with tiny wavelike ridges. Milky white sole-deep water ripples downward from the plateau, so for much of the walk you wade. As you climb you pass large travertine coated pools (man made) where tourists can bathe without damaging the more fragile natural pools. Only a glance and you can see why ancients thought Pamukkale's waters might be the cure for what ails you.

At the top of the travertine, wait the ruins of Hierapolis (they've waited for a long time). We slipped our sandals back on and spent a couple of sun baked hours walking the remnants of its once marbled, paved, and colonnaded streets. Most tour buses make a bee line for the site's two main attractions, its large many tiered theatre and "the ancient pool" where for an additional $17 per person you can take a warm dip among broken marble columns (we passed). Elsewhere, the day's heat kept the crowds away and we had much of the city almost to ourselves.

Denise and I are both more intrigued by mysteries of the ancient Maya, but the scale and artistry of Roman public works still never fails to impress. In Hierapolis we saw the remains of streets underlain by sewers and water systems; fragments of ruined temples, monumental arches, and great fountains; and alongside these lay more mundane ruins like latrines, graves, and public baths. Everywhere underfoot sit chunks of carved marble and the whole place evoked images of a living and once vibrant city.

One of our favorite bits was the "Plutonium," a tunnel (now sealed against foolhardy tourists of low IQ) that according to Roman priests led straight to the underworld. This was easily believed, as poison gas bubbled (still bubbles) from a spring at the tunnel's end. To prove their claim, priests regularly tossed birds and small animals into the tunnel where they quickly succumbed; ipso facto a gateway to Hell. Neat!

Day 200 - July 23 - Friday - Selcuk, Turkey

After Pamukkale, we headed for the super-star Roman city of Ephesus. We're now locked on the "tourist track" and Ephesus is next on the "must-see" list. We caught a tourist bus outside the Atremis Yoruk and "luxuriated" in our narrow seats while it made a more or less direct four hour run to Selcuk (Ephesus). This time riding on a bus that was willing to stop anywhere worked in our favor. Instead of going all the way in, we asked our driver to drop us about a kilometer out of town at a backpacker hostel called Attila's Getaway.

We're not only on the tourist trail; we're also on the hostel trail. Yeah, they mostly cater to young backpackers; and okay, we're often their oldest guests; and yes, they always show us their most expensive room; but hey, they're lots of fun and they're a bargain! Attila's is located in a nice rural setting and its buildings wrap around a swimming pool and a relaxing shady courtyard. There's plenty of comfortable seating ranging from large plump cushions to plastic lounge chairs and a friendly outdoor bar. Dinner and breakfast are served alfresco in front of the bar with great views over the surrounding countryside. Our double room with private bath, AC (whenever there's power), free Internet (whenever there's power & signal), and breakfast and dinner set us back $53 per night.

On our first full day at Attila's, we caught the "carpet guy's" free shuttle to Ephesus. He picks you up at the hostel and drives you right up to the site's entrance. After you're dropped you off, you're given a couple of hours for sightseeing and then he picks you up again at a different entrance; all "free" of charge. The catch is that on the way back to the hostel you have the "opportunity" to stop for free tea and an "educational" presentation at a Seljuk carpet shop. It was tough, but we marshaled our willpower and managed to return to our room without buying a rug (or a kilim, or a hanging, or a bedspread, or a table runner, or a pillow case, or...).

With a constant stream of cruise ship buses rolling in and out, Ephesus itself was a scrum of tourists. The only good thing about so many people tramping about is that it helps you visualize the ruin as a living city. Denise and I thought that they needed to make everyone change into togas at the gate.

Ephesus is another of those places, and we're starting to think that there are a lot of them, where Rome springs to life among remains-of-this and chunks-of-that. In spite overexposure the ancient city still thrills and mostly lives up to its hype.

We thought that the most interesting section of Ephesus was an area called "The Terrace Houses." For an additional (natch) $10 per person we got to walk through a large covered area where there is ongoing research and restoration of a number of upscale Roman homes. The interiors feature frescos, mosaics, and fountains and give you a pretty good feel for the life of a well-to-do family circa 100 A.D.

Many of the terrace house rooms were once paneled in marble, but over time roofs and walls collapsed and the sheets shattered. Today, fragments of marble are slowly being reassembled; the world's largest jigsaw puzzle.

On our second day at Attila's we walked into Selcuk (about 35 minutes) to visit a local city museum which houses many of Ephesus' best finds. The museum is small but its collection is impressive and we were glad we made the effort; mostly marble statuary, with some gold, and glass items tossed in for variety. A folding bronze (patio?) chair and table were especially cool. We have to admit that we were totally sucked in by the marble stuff. The idea of someone 2,200 years ago sitting down with a mallet and a few hand tools to carve amazing life size statues day in and day out just blows our minds.

We spent two more lazy days at Attila's while we tried to organize hotels in Istanbul and Nairobi. Hotels all over Turkey have Wi-Fi Internet access so you'd expect that researching destinations and making reservations should be a snap. The reality is that it's almost always a trying experience. Either the hotel's access point is down, or the Internet service provider is down, or the power is down, or the connection only works in the lobby if you stand on your head. Attilla's had good access points, but the ISP and power kept failing. It was really hot in the area; so we suspect that AC use kept overloading the grid. At any rate we managed five minutes online here and three minutes online there and eventually we wrangled a pair of reservations. With a bit of luck there should be someone waiting at the airport in Nairobi with a sign when we land at 2AM.

When the Internet wasn't up or when we just got sick of it, which was often, we hung out by the pool, sampled the wares of Attila's bar and chatted up other travelers. Hostels are great places to gather information. Because they are budget accommodations they tend to attract people who want to stretch their money. Some of the guests are just on the cheap, but a surprising number are frugal because they're long term travelers. Like us, a lot of them have been on the road for months and frequently they've just returned from somewhere we plan to visit. Everyone is eager to share their adventure, so we constantly trawl for good hotels, convenient transportation, hot tips, and more "must sees." At Attila's we spent quite a while talking with a pair of personable guys from Belgium. The two of them were teachers on summer vacation; they'd just returned from Egypt and Jordan, and luckily for us they were chock-full of good suggestions.

Interestingly, the majority of foreign travelers we've encountered in Turkey are young Aussies and Kiwis; which is kind of weird when you consider that the primary historical link between the countries is the Aussies' and Kiwis' disastrous World War I defeat at Gallipoli.

We ended up four nights at Attila's; it may have been the cold beer and the good conversation, but it might also have been the mash potatoes on barbeque night.

Day 204 - July 27 - Tuesday - Gokceada Island, Turkey

Leaving Ephesus we made our way slowly back to Istanbul. First, we caught a lift from the hostel to Selcuk's otogar where we purchased tickets for an hour and a half hop to the next big town called, Izimir. It was market day in Selcuk so we killed thirty minutes before our bus left "window" shopping the stalls. I bought a macramé bracelet for a buck; Denise bought pretzel sticks and cashews.

Once we reached Izimir, we were directed to another ticket counter where we arrived just in time to grab seats for an onward bus to Eceabat (our planned destination). There was a little confusion at the counter because none of the eight people behind it spoke more than a word or two of English. After a moment we were handed a cell phone (evidently someone had used their lifeline) and in broken English we were told that we would have to change seats.

"Huh? Same bus?"

"Yes, yes same bus."

"OK, good." With the problem apparently solved, we hurried outside tossed our bags into a waiting bus, and ran for the "tuvalet" (toilet) while the bus held its departure.

The day before, we tried to buy tickets on a direct bus from Ephesus only to discover that it was already sold out (high season, duh). With our connections up in the air, we'd sweated our transportation ever since. As it turned out, we left Selcuk at a better time, had a shorter trip, and better yet, arrived in Eceabat before dark. Strangely, we were never asked to change seats, go figure.

Except for a few scenic coastal sections, most of the long drive was blasé moré. The best bit came at the end of the ride when our bus went seaborne. Eceabat sits on the Gallipoli Peninsula on the European side of the Dardanelles Strait, so in Cannakkale the bus drove onto a car ferry for a thirty minute crossing from Asia back into Europe. While we were on the water our bags were unloaded from the bus and when we docked we simply rolled them off the ferry and walked across the street into town.

Eceabat, a jumping off spot for the Gallipoli battlefields, was only an overnight stop for us, but it was still entertaining. We stayed in a nice modern offbeat hotel called "Crowded House," wandered the town's patriotic WWI exhibits (heroic statues and cheesy dioramas), and ate an enjoyable dinner at a restaurant named after a famous Turkish general.

Since we just mentioned Eceabat's history exhibits, this is probably a point to also mention the Turkish propensity for direct translation. Everywhere we've visited in the country we've encountered informative signage, pamphlets, and brochures that are written in both Turkish and English. We can only assume the Turkish versions make sense. The English appears to have been generated verbatim from an online translator and often approaches incomprehensibility. "Good knowledge the reading will confer for applicable outcome." Say what?

The following morning we caught a dolmus that carried us across the peninsula by way of "Battlefield Park" (you know, Gallipoli, ANZACs, pre-"Road Warrior" movie with Mel Gibson) to the dock at Kabatepe. From there we boarded another ferry for the ninety minute boat ride to Gokceada, the bigger of Turkey's only two inhabited islands. A highlight of the crossing came when a scarved and bundled tween-age Muslim girl walked past Denise, skirted and tank-topped, and made the kiss-kiss tsk-tsk sound at her. A rough translation of which is; "I disapprove of your outfit you disgusting foreign harlot." Denise took it in stride.

Gokceada Island was a welcome change. It's scenic and pastoral and, for a Mediterranean island, pleasantly underdeveloped. It's still a tourist destination but most of the tourists are Turkish weekenders from Istanbul. That gives the island a completely different vibe from the foreign tourist trail that we've been following. English is spoken less on Gokceada than anywhere else we've visited in Turkey. At one point, as we walked up to an information kiosk, a grumpy Australian guy seated on the steps looked up at us with resigned disgust and said, "Don't even bother mate. They don't speak a word of

English." It didn't matter. We used sign language; crude but effective, and enjoyed every stumbling interaction.

Tomorrow at 6AM we hop a direct bus back to Istanbul for our last two nights in Turkey.

Chapter 9

KENYA

Day 208 - July 31 - Saturday - Nairobi, Kenya

Whew, pretty tired today; yesterday was long with a capital "L." Checkout at the Hotel Dara arrived at noon but our flight to Nairobi wasn't scheduled until 6:45 PM. With several of hours to kill, we left our bags in the lobby and wandered aimlessly around Old Istanbul; buy a postcard here, a stamp there, tokens for the tram. We eyed the Turkish delight, but decided that we'd already eaten enough. That and a little thumb twiddling brought us to 2:30. We walked back to the Dara, collected our bags, and then rolled them about a quarter mile (cobbles are the worst) to a tram stop. Boarding the streetcar, actually a short four or five car electric train, we rode it to the end of the line. Next, we rolled and carried our bags to an above ground metro station where we caught a commuter train to the airport; total cost for an hour's travel about $4.50.

At the airport, we checked in and then headed over to the "duty free." Back when our trip was still in the planning stages, we rationalized that rather than buy a new camera, we'd just take along our old one; less expense and less to worry about. Of course the old one has been dying on us ever since. With the prospect of African safaris ahead, it was almost a sure bet that the first lion we saw would cause it to die entirely. We shopped around for a replacement in Istanbul but suffered from sticker shock when we heard the prices. According to other travelers, Turkey imposes some kind of tax that jacks up the price of electronic items. Consequently, we found ourselves shopping old model cameras that cost twice as much as we'd need to pay at home. We were about to give up when someone suggested duty free at the airport; hey great idea! We looked at cameras on the net (good connection at the Dara) and wrote down a large list of brands and models that were highly rated and in our price range. Naturally, when we got to the duty free none of them were on offer. We bit the bullet and bought an overpriced (twice US price) Canon we know nothing about, with a warranty that's only good in Turkey. Moral; buy the new camera before you leave home and take the old one along as a back-up.

After eating some equally overpriced airport food, we headed for our gate. A last look at a nearby departures board and we learned that instead of gate 206 we were now leaving from gate 307. Gate 307, located on a sublevel at the far end of the airport, is where they send you if your plane isn't going to leave anywhere near its scheduled time and they don't want passengers on other flights to see your distress. By hiding you away, Turkish Airlines is able to maintain the illusion that its flights are on time. As we sat by Gate 307 we watched the board for our flight read, "Now Boarding," and then, "Last Call." About an hour later we finally climbed onto a bus that took us out to the plane. Our Nairobi arrival shifted from 1:30 AM (bad enough) to 3:00 AM.

Despite our grousing about the delay, we have to admit that the flight was good, and the level of service outstanding. First stewardesses came through the plane handing out earphones for the free movies; next a beverage service with real hazelnuts. After that, came a delicious full dinner with free booze. I snarfed the red wine; Denise went for a gin and tonic. These services were followed by more beverages and, last but not least, a fancy little zippered pouch containing complimentary: slippers, an eye-mask, and earplugs! Regardless of the amenities, both of us slept like crap and staggered off the plane groggy and exhausted.

Our introduction to Kenya was an hour long wait to be processed through immigration. When we finally shuffled to the head of our line the process went fairly quickly. Thankfully, after we retrieved our bags we found a patient cabby holding up a sign with our name. Another twenty minutes hurtling through the dark and we were pulling the mosquito netting around our bed at the Khweza Bed and Breakfast.

Day 179 - July 2 - Friday

First impressions; Nairobi is huge, bustling, and definitely impoverished. Our bed and breakfast is pleasant and clean with a few crafty artistic touches that add to its charm. The staff is helpful and friendly and the hotel kitchen, when it's sporadically open, serves up food that's tasty and filling. Walk past the doorman/guard, step through the metal gated front door, and outside you're in an area that by U.S. standards feels poor and rundown. The streets are broken, pot holed, and dusty. Litter collects everywhere and everything you see appears in need of paint and repair. From the B&B's nice rooftop terrace you look out over dirty modern buildings interspersed with cardboard slums and dirt streets slippery with mud. The street behind the Khweza is clogged with burning trash. People are everywhere. Small shabby stores line the street and vendors sell used clothes from rows of tables at the nearby intersection. Traffic races by; aged brightly colored buses of all shapes and sizes, their drivers jockeying for position amid a surging chaos of cars, trucks, carts, and pedestrians. As we watched, one bus even charged up the edge of a dirt median strip in the wrong direction. A dirty haze hangs in the air.

We went out yesterday and walked a few blocks. According to our hotel's front desk, the area is reasonably safe as long as it is daylight and you don't flash any valuables. We took off our gold wedding bands. Strange place; you don't actually feel unsafe; on the other hand everything is so alien that you don't feel you can confidently read your surroundings. You're also wary when you read hotel reviews (not ours) and their big selling point is that, "Guests can safely leave the hotel and take a walk to the Village Market (an upscale shopping center) next door." We have to admit that it's also given us a new appreciation for what it must feel like to be Black in a lily white city like Eugene, Oregon. We've driven into the center of town a couple of times and have yet to see a white face on the street.

The parts of Nairobi that we've seen appear only marginally worse off than say Belize City, but it's definitely not what we'd call a hot tourist destination. Sadly, it's a place you fly into and arrange a safari before moving on to someplace else. We booked ours with "Big Time Safari, LTD;" one of two outfits to whom we talked. Big Time's office is downtown, near city hall, on the seventh floor of a high-rise office building. The surrounding area is better than our hotel's locale but their building still has guards at the entrance and also on their floor. Big Time's one-room office has an iron gated door that they must buzz you through and the men's room at the end of the hall doesn't have any paper or seats on the toilets. A couple of doors away, a "super market" of modest convenience store size features a pair of assault rifle armed security guards dressed in full combat gear. Tomorrow at 8:15 AM we set off with a guide for the Masai Mara, Kenya's share of the world famous Serengeti.

Day 211 - August 3 - Tuesday - Masai Mara, Kenya

We arrived at the border of the Masai Mara Game Reserve yesterday afternoon following an interesting five hour drive from Nairobi; an hour and a half of good road, an hour and half of badly potholed road, an hour of dirt, and a couple of brief stops. Big Time Safari picked us up at our B&B in the morning and took us to their office where we made our final payment and met two of our safari companions, Jan and Bert (our age, interesting) from Tasmania, Australia. The four of us then bundled into a mini-van.

"This man (driver) will take you to meet your guide in Narok (about 160 km away)." "Sorry for the change of plan. After you meet your guide in Narok everything will be as discussed." *Okay, since now they have all our money, that doesn't sound like a propitious start.*

We left Nairobi in a light rain and headed for Narok. At about kilometer sixty we drove out of the mist and reached the top of the breathtaking Rift Valley Escarpment. This was a planned fifteen minute stop where we were supposed to stretch, take pictures and enjoy the panorama. The views were great, but we bombed right on past, no stop, and no pictures. *Okay, that's not good either.*

Further down the road, just short of Narok, we pulled into the "Longonot Transfer Hotel" parking lot. Our guide, Patrick, was waiting with his safari van (pretty much the same Toyota mini-van except the roof pops up) and two more companions, Julio from Guatemala and Melanie from France. *I guess we're back on track.*

Driving on into Narok with Patrick now behind the wheel, we stopped for a good lunch at the "Mara Golden Spoon." The Golden Spoon is an enclosed compound that features an outdoor buffet, picnic tables, restrooms, and of course souvenir opportunities. The restaurant caters to the safari trade and its parking lot was packed with other mini-vans.

After lunch Denise and I struck up a conversation with two trinket vendors who were working the crowd. After the usual pleasantries, one of them asked, "How much do people earn in America?"

"Minimum wage is around seven dollars"

"Seven dollars every day?"

"No, per hour," the two young vendors exchanged looks of shock.

"Seven dollars each hour; if I could go to America I'd be a rich man in a month!"

"Well, it sounds like a lot, but it really isn't. In America things are much more expensive. For instance, it sometimes costs us as much as $300 a month to heat our home and food is also expensive; a single banana may cost you 75 cents."

"Yes, but you are rich." We tried to explain more about the relative cost of living between our two countries, but we don't think they bought it. We walked away and left them scheming how to reach America.

Back on the road we settled in and enjoyed the scenery. Much of this country moves on foot and people-watching along the highway shoulder is world class. We also passed our time reading business names. Lots of businesses, large ramshackles to small hovels, along the highway sport fancy names; names that raise a smile, but that frequently seem at odds with appearances: "Ripe Banana Mini-Café," "Honey Pot Pub," "Stadium Mattress" (a hotel), "Alpha Shiloh Barber Shop," and our own personal favorite, the "Butchery Leisure Hotel."

Shortly after lunch we stopped again and picked up a fifth companion, Emily, a friendly young teacher from Boston. Big Time Safari told us there would only be six people total in our van. *Hmmm.* Our first impression of Patrick was that he seemed uncommunicative and a bit surly, so by the time we reached the reserve we were both a little concerned about our choice of safari companies.

Then... we went on our first game drive and suddenly it was like having a bit part in a live action version of "The Lion King." Oh my God! We knew we were going to see wild animals in Africa. We were ready. We've been to zoos. We've even been to the San Diego Wild Animal Park and seen the animals in their "natural" habitat. What we weren't ready for were thousands (yes that's thousands!) of zebras and wildebeests; hundreds and hundreds (maybe thousands) of gazelles, impala, and antelope; lions and more lions, a pride of twelve, other lions with their kill, and still other lions with their cubs; big elephants, medium elephants, little elephants, baby elephants; herds of giraffe; bunches of hippos; cheetahs, cheetahs with their cubs; warthogs; ostriches, ostriches sitting on their eggs; vultures, mongooses, crocodiles, and more wildebeests. Yeah there are that many of them!

Day 213 - August 5 - Thursday

At this point we've made a total of four game drives in the Mara. We went out our first evening for about three hours, spent a full ten hours the second day, and on day three we went on a morning drive from 7 AM until 1:30 PM. Today we went out again in the morning from 6:30 AM until 8:30 AM. Each drive was different and totally amazing; wildlife everywhere; more cheetahs, more lions, more giraffes, then suddenly a reclusive leopard, or a grazing herd of Cape buffalo, or a strolling hippo, or a couple of grooming baboons. We even watched a lioness stalk and charge a group of warthogs! And the backdrop to all this Animal Planet activity; landscapes that are simply stunning; flat acacia studded plains, rolling hills of golden windblown grass, narrow green river courses lined with leafy palms, dust devils, and sunsets that take your breath away. Stand under an improbable "sausage" tree, stare a full grown lion in the face, gaze across an empty savannah at the Zen-like spectacle of a lone acacia tree; the power of the Mara overwhelms us.

As if the overabundance of nature isn't enough, there are also the iconic Masai people themselves. Tall, stately, and friendly, they live around the edge of the reserve, leading lives that appear to make only small concessions to the modern world. In the Mara it's still possible to see a young Masai warrior wrapped in a brightly colored blanket, a sword-like knife strapped to his waist, a spear and staff in hand, prodding his cattle across a dusty road. Young boys herd goats. Women dressed in robes of electric yellow, red, purple, and blue; with necklaces and marriage bands at their ankles carry heavy plastic water jugs from the river. Men just as brightly dressed as the women go about their business with pierced ears and a staff in their hand. The fact that they may have a cell phone tucked in the folds of their robe does little to detract from the imagery. Many of the scenes you encounter make you feel as if you've just stepped off a steam train wearing a pith helmet.

While visiting the Masai Mara we stayed in a mid-range "tented" camp. The park charges high fees to sleep inside its boundaries so except for a few luxury outfits, which ours isn't, most safari companies set up shop just outside the "fence." Our accommodation consisted of a canvas walk-in tent that's pitched on a concrete slab. Over the tent is a second roof of thatch that provides a sort of porch and shades the tent from the hot sun. Inside the floor is covered by a piece of linoleum and there are two wood-frame beds with mosquito nets. The back door of the tent opens into a concrete bathroom with a toilet, sink, and shower; all very (very) basic.

The camp is used by several safari companies so the number of people it hosts varies from day to day. During our three nights it probably ranged between eight and thirty. There's a kitchen and an open covered seating area near the tents and all meals are buffet style. The food is nothing special, but like all our Kenya meals so far, it's tasty and filling. Portions tend to be large (especially the serve yourself variety) and what's on offer is heavy on starch. Most of it sort of falls into the realm of "comfort food." A typical meal includes: potatoes mashed or roasted, spaghetti or macaroni noodles, stewed chicken, beef, or fish (with more potatoes), some kind of cooked cabbage, cooked lentils, white rice, bread, some kind of cooked vegetables, and watermelon for dessert. If we don't want to gain weight were going to need to watch our eating.

Day 214 - August 6 - Fri - Lake Nakuru & Nairobi, Kenya

At this point we're riding with a totally different safari company. On our second day in the Mara, our guide Patrick introduced us to Gabriel, a guide with "Planet Adventure Safaris" and told us that from then on we'd be riding with him.

"I'm going back to Nairobi to pick up another group, since you're going on to Lake Nakuru, Gabriel will take you. Just call him 'Soy'." *Say what?* The next day, scratching our heads, we climbed into Soy's van along with Jackie and Helen, a couple of nice English gals, who actually were clients of Planet Adventure Safaris. On the good side, Jackie and Helen were fun and with only four people there was plenty of room in the van. On the downside Soy's van was a little more beat up, rattled a little more, and didn't have a CB radio.

The lack of a radio meant that we couldn't take advantage of the chatter between other guides, "Hey, hurry over here. I just spotted two hippos doing handsprings." Instead, Soy's drives were old school. He cruised slowly along isolated tracks, pausing quietly from time to time to see if something would poke its head out of the brush. In the long haul his way was just as satisfying (we saw a leopard that we might otherwise have missed), but initially we were like, *What the hell? Didn't we pay for a van with a radio?*

Yesterday, after our morning game drive, we left the Masai Mara and headed toward the national park at Lake Nakuru. It was another long drive; an hour of dirt, an hour and a half of potholes, another lunch at the "Mara Golden Spoon," more potholes, another stop at the "Longonot Transfer Hotel" (while we waited for someone from Soy's company to bring him something?), and another hour and a half of good road.

When we arrived in Nakuru town, Soy informed us that Jackie and Helen would be staying at one hotel and we would be at another. Theirs had a bell hop in a red coat; ours had a guard in a paramilitary uniform with a Billy club. (The Chester Hotel turned out to be a decent overnight with a good restaurant and super helpful staff.) As we were about to climb into the elevator, Soy says; "Tomorrow breakfast at seven, then I'll pick you up or maybe a different guide." *Say what?!!* After a little interrogation we learned that a new guide from Big Time Safari was going to collect us in the morning, maybe..., unless he didn't show, in which case Soy would probably be back. *No, not good, too iffy!* We told Soy, that we understood, but that he still needed to meet us at breakfast at 7 AM to make the handoff, and say goodbye (i.e. you'll show up if you expect to get your tip).

Next morning, we ate breakfast and then waited...and waited...and waited. Finally, at about nine, I went up to our room and Denise went to the lobby of the hotel to keep a lookout and work on blood pressure issues. A few minutes later, the phone in the room rang. "Soy's just pulling up with the girls. Come on down."

When I reached the lobby, Denise was standing in front of the hotel squinting down the street. "He pulled up but while I was calling you, he just backed up and drove off."

According to our hotel security guy, "He's probably just turning around," *that doesn't make any sense*, "or maybe gas," *okay that's possible*, "He'll be right back."

We went back into the lobby and sat down with our stuff and waited...and waited...and waited. I was in denial.

"He'll be back or maybe he heard from the other guy who's on his way. Someone's bound to show." After about twenty minutes, Denise had had enough and asked the hotel manager to call Big Time Safari and find out what was going on.

After a few minutes on the phone, the manager waved us over. "They can't reach Soy," *who doesn't work for them!* "If he's already on the Nakuru game drive he might not have any cell service. They'll call back after they reach him." Another twenty minutes; the phone rings and the hotel manager tells us that a van from Big Time is on the way. So the upshot was that Soy didn't see us out front, an hour after he was supposed to meet us, so he just drove off. A Big Time group that was headed in a different direction just happened to be at Lake Nakuru. The Nairobi office told that guide to catch Soy, shove his own people in Soy's Planet Adventure Safaris van so that they could continue their game drive, and then bomb back to Nakuru to scoop us from the lobby of the Chester Hotel. Hey, if you want independent travel you gotta be flexible!

Finally on the move, we were hurried into Lake Nakuru Park and given a quick game drive by our new guide.

"Hi, I'm Denise, what's your name?"

"My name's Patrick."

"Funny, our first guide was named Patrick too."

"Simon, my name is Simon." *Whatever!*

After seeing about a million flamingos, very cool, and a number of White Rhinos, even better, we caught up with Soy at the "Baboon Cliff Lookout." Everybody switched back to their respective vans (we guess) and once again we rolled out with Jackie and Helen. Soy finished our game drive (add Black Rhinos to the list), drove us back to Nairobi, and dropped us at our respective destinations. His tip was somewhat diminished. Not surprisingly, Big Time Safari didn't ask us to fill out their customer satisfaction survey; great animals, adequate lodging, shitty logistics.

Day 216 - August 8 - Sunday - Nairobi, Kenya

Tonight is our third night back in Nairobi. This time were staying at the Hotel Meridian a theoretically upscale place nearer to city center. Were paying 62% more per night, $92 vs. $55, but we liked the Khweza better. The Meridian looks like it was built in the 1970's and never updated; heavy dark wood, shabby gold bedspreads, and cheesy lobby mirrors. We could have splurged an extra $30 for a nicer room but we're too cheap. On the other hand, although the hotel is blah, the area is undeniably better. You still can't walk around after dark, but during the day it feels pretty normal.

We spent all day yesterday arranging for another safari (different company), this time a two night luxury trip (for our anniversary) to Amboseli National Park.

Today, we visited the National Museum, where we hung out with "Turkana Boy," or at least his remains; a 1.6 million year old hominid who's probably a distant relative. Another distant and more famous relative, "Lucy," was there too! With luck, tomorrow we'll finalize our safari, leave Nairobi's dusty streets behind, and once again head for the wild kingdom.

Day 219 - August 11 - Wed - Amboseli Park, Kenya

Today is our 36th wedding anniversary so we're celebrating with a two nights and three day upscale safari (big splurge) at Amboseli National Park. We climbed out of bed this morning and as we walked to breakfast, we were treated to the sight of elephants grazing in the distance; cool beans! While our safari to Masai Mara hovered around the top of the budget category, this one is reaching for the low rung of the luxury experience.

On Tuesday morning, Ali Zololo, our private driver picked us up at our Nairobi hotel in a like-new customized Land Rover. We were supposed to hit the road at 7 AM (Ali was there at 6:45), but didn't make our departure until almost an hour later.

In accordance with their stern posted warnings, we'd placed all our valuables in one of the hotel's safe deposit boxes. Just like a bank, each box requires two keys, one held by the hotel guest, secured against careless loss by a $50 USD deposit, and a second key held by the hotel. When we got ready to leave, we learned that the hotel's only key was kept safely in the manager's pocket and that he didn't arrive at work until about 8AM! *Okay, good to know.* Thank god we weren't trying to catch a 4 AM flight.

Because of our delayed start, we were treated to an unplanned opportunity to experience Nairobi's rush hour traffic. Not an experience that makes our recommended hit list; we were both glad that neither of us was behind the wheel. It took about forty-five minutes for Ali to escape the surging tangle. After that we made a brief stop at the entrance to Nairobi National Park on the edge of the city so that Ali could load our Amboseli park fees onto his Kenya Wildlife Service (KWS) "smart card." Since most park entrances are isolated, many don't risk accepting cash. All fees must be paid with a preloaded KWS credit card.

After that it was smooth sailing and we headed southeast along the Nairobi-Mombasa Highway. Two hours of good tarmac and one potty stop later (always at a curio stand); we turned off the pavement and bombed down a wash-boarded dirt road to the Amboseli's Iremito Gate. Masai women with shaved heads, dangly earrings, elaborate necklaces, and rows of bracelets, sit under a large cactus. Wrapped in brightly colored fabrics, water jugs at hand, they're hard at work on beaded trinkets. Through an isolated concrete arch, and we were into the park proper.

While Ali steps inside a guard station to have his paperwork reviewed, we wait in the Land Rover and try to ignore the attentions of a pair of persistent vendors. Denise buys a beaded leather bracelet. I fain disinterest. At that juncture one of the vendors takes a liking to my sunglasses and offers a trade. "Here, you take all this stuff I made and you give me your glasses" (paraphrased). Now this was a tempting offer because his carvings were pretty cool and my shades we cheapies. I couldn't do it.

"Here, you take the glasses. They're a gift." This might have been an anticipated outcome, but I figured he needed my sunglasses more than I needed his carvings.

Amboseli is an area of vast hazy primordial vistas; on one side sits the snowcapped bulk of Mount Kilimanjaro, usually obscured by dust and clouds, and rolling away from its slopes stretch vast plains of dry savannah grassland and harsh alkali hardpan. Near the park's center you encounter the concentrated marshy remains of the previous rainy season.

Like the Masai Mara, Amboseli is an Animal Planet smorgasbord. Its resident wildebeests and zebras don't walk about in gigantic migratory herds, but you see them at every turn along with all the other usual suspects: gazelles, impalas, giraffes, lions, hippos, baboons, monkey's and elephants. Elephants are the big (excuse the pun) stars of the Amboseli show. The park is home to 10,000 of the slow moving giants. Lines of them march across the dusty plains. Solitary bulls stand sentinel in the distance. Family groups cool off in the marsh, roll in the mud, or kick up dry tuffs of grass on the savannah. Babies nuzzle for attention. Sweethearts intertwine their trunks. Indifferent to camera toting tourists and our safari vehicles the elephants move majestically with a grace that belies their size; absolutely amazing! Other great animal sights were a pair of tree climbing lion cubs and a spotted hyena den with ugly grinning adults and wrinkled nearly hairless youngsters that kept scrambling in and out of a hole in the ground.

Our accommodation in Amboseli is the Serena Lodge; a far cry from our tented camp in the Masai Mara. The lodge sits right in the middle of the park. "Don't feed or encourage the monkeys. They are unpredictable!" We didn't feed them, but it was hard not to give them a little encouragement, especially when they were having energetic sex on our patio. There are alarm-buttons scattered around the grounds that you can press if large animals breach the lodge perimeter. At night, the rest of the food chain is kept at bay by an electric fence. *Ooh scary!* The grounds are nicely landscaped and all the accents are safari chic right down to a few Maasai warriors waiting strategically for Kodak moments. Our room is done in earthy colors with pictures of wildebeests and hyenas painted on its walls. The swimming pool is ice cold and the restaurant's buffet food (full-board) is top notch. Attentive staff are everywhere and it's my guess that if we'd come a couple of years earlier they were probably calling all the guests "Bwana." Now, what did I do with my Louis Vitton pith helmet?

Lake Manyara, Tanzania

Chapter 10

TANZANIA

Day 220 - August 12 - Thursday – Moshi, Tanzania

We gobbled our last Serena buffet breakfast at 6:30 this morning so that we could be on the road by 7:00. We were headed to the Kenya/Tanzania border and the plan was that we'd link up with an onward shuttle that originated in Nairobi. Some time had passed since Ali had last driven the dirt road from Amboseli to the border town of Namanga and he was concerned about reaching there in time to make our connection. By all accounts the road was in terrible shape and he expected several hours of slow rough driving before we hit tarmac. Ali was a good guide, but he missed the boat on this one. The road was terrible, but the going wasn't slow. In many places people had simply stopped using the road and drove on the shoulder which was in much better shape. By 8:30 we'd reached Namanga.

It was good that we arrived at the border in plenty of time to catch our shuttle, but Namanga isn't exactly a tourist destination. It's a grotty, slightly interesting, wide spot in the road where trucks and buses queue up to cross the frontier. Roadside businesses cater to the needs of the drivers: used auto parts, gas, and cheap eats; while locals try to hawk curios to bus passengers; and people in private safari vehicles. Naturally our shuttle ran late, so we were able to enjoy the sights of Namanga for a full three hours. Oh well, it wasn't like we needed to be anywhere.

To keep the wait from being a total bust, we used some of the time to wade through border bureaucracy. On the Kenyan side we waited in a line to get stamped out of the country. With that complete, we walked across the no-man's land into Tanzania where we filled out four immigration forms and then stood in another line. After we reached the front of that line, and paid our $100 per person (*Ouch!*) entrance fees, we stood in another line while they took our passports somewhere to be photocopied; evidently a major process. Finally, with everything in proper bureaucratic order, we walked back into Kenya to wait for the "Impala Shuttle."

It was a long wait. With nothing to do, we sat in the Land Rover as the day warmed and two hours slithered past. We dripped sweat and fidgeted. Ali nervously and repeatedly checked his watch. He was anxious to get back to Nairobi and we were hot (excusable pun) to be on our way. When our shuttle eventually rolled into Namanga it was about an hour behind schedule. On the good side, the driver was expecting us and our two pre-booked seats were empty and waiting. To make sure that the seats were available, we were forced to purchase them before we left Nairobi and also to pay for the unused Nairobi to Namanga segment so that they'd remain empty. I got to sit in the front seat across from the driver; great view. Denise got to sit near the back; good conversation, but smelly bus fumes.

With the border crossing behind us, we headed into Tanzania. For the first couple of hours we drove through the rain shadow of Mount Kilimanjaro; a dry dusty waterless region of sparse population and thorny grey acacia trees. Here and there lone Masai walked slowly driving their cattle. Elsewhere, small groups trudged along carrying empty plastic jugs headed toward some distant well or sump. The highway was broken and potholed and any sections that weren't, were completely torn up for reconstruction. We suspect it's a permanent condition. The upshot was that most of the driving was along bumpy dirt tracts that parallel the "real" road.

As we moved out of Kilimanjaro's rain shadow suddenly everything changed. The landscape lurched from harsh and unforgiving to green, lush, and tropical. The tarmac improved, and fields of corn, coffee, and bananas lined the road. A little further along, we entered the large commercial city of Arusha. We thought about staying there, but after consideration opted to ride another hour into Moshi, a city that's smaller and a little less hectic.

Day 226 - August 18 - Wednesday

When we first dreamed of an around the world trip, part of Denise's vision always included the idea that somewhere along our way we'd find an opportunity to participate in volunteer work. While on safari in Kenya, we met other travelers who told us how much they'd enjoyed the town of Moshi in Tanzania. Reading up on Moshi in the Unnamed Guidebook, Denise came across a blurb about a volunteer organization that sounded like it might fill the bill. The organization, called "Footprint 2 Afrika," is involved in a variety of community projects and also runs a hostel where you can stay while volunteering. She sent them an email and they wrote back saying that they'd love to meet with us and that we should give them a call when we hit town.

On arrival in Moshi we decided to walk out to their hostel; drop in and get an unannounced impression. "Hostel Hoff" was easy to locate and it only took us twenty minutes to walk there from our hotel (The Kilimanjaro Crane). Sara, the woman who ran the hostel, wasn't in so we chatted with Christine, a volunteer who was sitting in the hostel's common room working on her computer. Christine was from Montana and she'd been in Moshi volunteering for the past couple of weeks. She still had two weeks to go. She shared what she was working on and seemed frustrated because there was so much to do and so little support. Meanwhile another volunteer from NYC wandered in. She said that she'd walked out to the school where she was volunteering, a half hour walk, only to find the school's gate locked. She waited outside with some of the children coloring and playing games. After a time, a teacher came to the gate and told them that there was no school today and that they should all go home; no explanation. The volunteer walked back to the hostel. Another young woman came in and also joined the conversation. Despite their frustrations, all three seemed excited about their overall experience.

At this point, Sara, the NGO's administrator, showed up and told us rather briskly that she was full up and that she didn't need any help. A little taken aback by her attitude, Denise told her that she'd emailed ahead of time and that "Johnson" had invited us out to the hostel.

"Yes, we've had this problem before. The Unnamed Guidebook made a mistake. We are 'Path to Africa' NOT 'Footprint 2 Africa!'" *Huh?* Christine then asked Sara why we couldn't help her with her projects. "No. Another volunteer is coming in two weeks and they've already been in touch."

"Okay, if you don't have anything for us can you tell us about Footprint 2 Afrika and where they're located?"

"I don't want to say anything about them because I live in the same town. I don't want any problems." *Double huh?* We asked if she could suggest any other organizations that could use our help and after a little further prodding she gave us a couple of phone numbers. *Okay, that was weird.*

Later, while Google-ing volunteer opportunities in Moshi, Denise came across another NGO, "Heart to Africa." She again sent off an email and shortly received a nice response from Monika, their director. Monika said that she was currently out of the country, but gave us a local phone number for Beverly, a volunteer who was running things in her absence. A short hotel-toll call later (our cell chips don't work in Tanzania) and Beverly invited us to meet with her at a local bakery the next day. Sort of like going out for coffee on a first date; it was an interesting meeting. Beverly was a newly retired teacher from Georgia who'd been here for a month teaching English in Heart to Africa's school for adults.

The school teaches English, business, and computers to thirty-seven adults for two semesters per year; each term six months long. Classes are Mon through Thurs from 9 AM to noon. Each Friday the school's volunteers visit the homes of two of their students so that they can better understand their living situations and needs. The NGO also runs a daycare (same location) from 2-4 PM, free for children of their students and other neighborhood kids. After sharing her stories and telling us about the organization, Beverly walked us from the bakery out to the house (volunteer hostel) and school.

The operation appeared beautifully run. We entered the front gate (everything here is gated) and found a nice garden, a three bedroom house, four classrooms and a small daycare center. The house/hostel was very clean. Each room had a bunk bed, and there was one bathroom, a nice sized kitchen, dining area and a common area; much neater and more professional looking that the first place we visited. The modest sized classrooms are furnished with nice long tables that serve as desks and benches for seats. There was a personal laundry area for the volunteers and the grounds were nicely maintained. The cost to stay at the house is $300US/per person/week with dinner provided daily and one hundred percent of this fee funnels back to the program.

We were enthusiastic about what we saw. Unfortunately Heart to Africa didn't have any full time slots for additional volunteers. Beverly saw our disappointment and suggested that if we hung around Moshi for a couple of weeks they might have a few odds and ends for us; maybe some painting or cleaning, but nothing consistent. Volunteering was going to be a little tougher than we thought.

Another big bugaboo if you want to volunteer in Tanzania is that you have to apply for a "Class C Visa;" a task that is probably better accomplished before you leave home. The visa requires a copy of your passport, a copy of the page in your passport showing where they stamped your entry into Tanzania, six passport sized photos, a job/work/life experience sort of resume, and a copy of your diploma or some kind of document showing a record of your highest level of education (oops didn't bring those), and last but definitely not least $120US.

The crazy thing is that Tanzanian bureaucracy is so bad that some volunteers who apply don't receive their Class C Visas until they're finished with their stint, ready to leave the country, or already gone. Even crazier, immigration spot checks places where volunteers work and occasionally hauls someone in if their paperwork isn't in order. At a minimum, you have to show them the receipt that shows you started the process, i.e. paid the money.

The day after our visit to Heart to Afrika, Sadock Johnson, "Call me Johnson," from Footprint 2 Africa (the real one) picked us up at our hotel and took us out on a full day circuit of some of the organizations with which he's involved. First, we toured his hostel which has three units that each contains bunk beds, bathrooms, kitchens and common areas. I believe the internet listed the cost here at $21US per person per night with breakfast and dinner included. We didn't ask if we could stay because the hostel was a ways out of town and, at $50 per night, we prefer the privacy and convenience of our hotel.

At the hostel, we were joined by John, a science teacher from San Francisco, who arrived in town the night before. After being shown around the hostel, Johnson loaded the three of us into his Land Cruiser and we began a search to find the volunteer opportunity that would suit us best.

We started at "YOLK for Success." Yolk is a private training center that's essentially a formal high school completion program where adults, 18 to 40's, pay a fee to prepare for an annual test they must pass to receive their diplomas.

As the center's English teacher explained the process that students must go through to graduate and possibly qualify for college, our eyes went wide. First, they have to take all their subjects in English! Most of the people in Tanzania speak a tribal language first and are then taught Kiswahili in primary school (if they attend). When they are old enough, with or without having learned Kiswahili, they are advanced to secondary school and suddenly every subject, except Kiswahili, is taught *exclusively* in English. Most students, and many teachers, barely speak English, but to advance to the next level of schooling they are forced to prepare for a standardized exam that is only offered in English! The test is also offered only once a year so if a student fails, and most do, they must wait a whole twelve months before they can retest. Even more ludicrous, the exam, which covers five or six subjects, is graded by the government and all the student learns is whether they passed or failed. They receive no clue as to which of the subjects caused them problems so the poor student is left with no recourse but to review everything!

In classrooms at YOLK over 100 students (only one teacher) sit copying notes off the blackboard. Blackboards in all the schools we visited yesterday contained outlines of subject matter that looked like it was copied directly from an obtuse textbook; a moldy dry pedantic obtuse textbook. Speaking of books ten to twenty students frequently share one copy! Every blackboard outline that we read was written in English that was so complex that neither of us was sure that we really understood what was chalked up there. It boggles the mind.

Imagine, sitting in a class with over one hundred other students. There is only one teacher and you must share your aged textbook with at least ten other students. You are trying to learn a complicated subject in a third language that you barely speak! Now imagine that you have to take a three hour exam in that third language and that if you fail you will be held back for a year before you can try again; absolutely unbelievable!

Students that do pass can move on to their next level. According to what we were told, if you want to go to college the only way to get in is if you know someone or have lots of money. We can only guess how many adults meet these criteria, as many students at private schools like YOLK are turned away at the gates each day because they haven't paid their fees.

After touring the YOLK classrooms we loaded back into our vehicle, driven by Johnson's partner Emerson, and headed out to a rural public school. Oh my God! This was a government "supported" school. According to what we were told, the only support the government actually provides are salaries for an administrator and a couple of teachers, or maybe only one, we weren't clear. The school has four useable classrooms and serves over 250 students. Bathroom facilities consist of a row of pit toilets for the students, girls on one side of a wall, boys on the other, and two enclosed stalls for the staff. The only running water is a single spigot outside of one of the classrooms.

Just past the classrooms and latrines there is an outdoor "kitchen" where one cook prepares a single meal each day for the students; ugali, a thick dough-like mass of corn mush served with bean sauce gravy. We were told by the administrator that ugali is such a staple that for most of their lives many of the students have eaten little else. It's the only dish the school prepares because giving the students "anything different could upset their digestion." When we walked up, the cook was boiling the day's ugali over an open wood fire in a huge, oil drum size, pot set precariously atop three large rocks. It looked like an accident waiting to happen. A second pot filled with bean gruel sat atop three more rocks and bubbled over a smaller fire. Throw in a pair of wooden stirring paddles and that was the extent of the school's kitchen. No plates, no utensils, no cartons of milk; none of the everyday things we as first-worlders take for granted.

Students at the government school arrive daily at 8 AM and don't eat their meal until around 3:30 PM. The classrooms are incomplete. Concrete walls, dirty, no window glass, dirt floors, wooden desks with rickety chairs and a wall section painted black for the blackboard (same complex English outlines). The roof was corrugated metal. There wasn't any electricity at the school. There also weren't enough teachers; maybe two fulltime and a few part-timers that don't always show up because they don't always get paid.

Shocking as it may seem, based on the quality of their service, public schools in Tanzania aren't free. Students or their families are expected to pony up around 22,000 shillings a year. That's only about $15 USD, but for many it's beyond their means.

Unlike the private continuation schools such as YOLK, at the government schools unpaid students are still allowed to attend. Except for donations from the impoverished local community, student fees are the school's only resource. Without the fees and donations the school doesn't have money to cover its meager expenses but nonetheless the government still requires it to service any students who show up.

Another serious problem is that primary schools are supposed to teach younger students how to speak English so that by the time they get to secondary school they're already proficient. Unfortunately many teachers at rural primary schools barely speak English themselves and they're not allowed to hold a student back. Ready or not, they're required to pass students to the secondary school where law requires that all instruction take place in English.

The administrator at the public school invited any interested students who felt they spoke adequate English to join us in a classroom for a conversation. About 25 to 30 older students showed up. They were mostly very shy, dressed in uniforms, some with large holes in their sweaters. After a couple of minutes it became obvious that, although light-years beyond our grasp of Kiswahili, their command of English was extremely limited. Based on our "conversation" Denise and I both doubt that they could understand the complex math and history that we'd seen written on the school's blackboards. When encouraged by the administrator, they haltingly told us about their hopes and aspirations. They were the same as kids anywhere. One outspoken young man wanted to be a politician, another wanted to be a truck driver. A girl in a tattered sweater who wanted to be a homemaker, told us tearfully about the embarrassment of not being able to pay her fees. It's a humbling experience to realize just how fortunate we are simply because of an accident of birth.

After saying our goodbyes, we returned to Moshi for lunch. Following lunch, we proceeded to a private preschool, called "The Kilimanjaro Children's Foundation," which focuses on the teaching of English to young children between three and six years old. Their class size was around 60 children to one teacher and they were currently being assisted by two volunteers from Ireland. As the students progress in their English they're moved into a second and third classroom for further study. The school's facilities were reasonably nice because initially a church group from Illinois came down and helped to build and supply it. The foundation school also serves a daily meal but like the rural school they're in need of a kitchen and cooking is done outside over a wood fire. This school was free to children who lived in the surrounding slum.

By now it was getting late in the afternoon and Johnson wanted to squeeze in one more school before we finished our day. This last school was similar to the first that we visited in the morning. It was an informal continuation school, but their goal was more to help tutor students in their subjects rather than simply prepare them for the government exams. The students here squeezed into a couple of small classrooms for their lessons with overflow sitting in the courtyard outside. In the afternoons students were allowed to use the outside areas for independent study. Deo, the school's administrator, suggested that if we were interested we could come to the school between 2 and 4 PM and help individual students with questions or English; kind of like study hall tutors.

The day was an eye-opening experience and we can't thank Johnson from Footprint 2 Africa enough. Without so much as a hint about compensation, he picked us up, drove us around, footed the bill for gas, and patiently educated us. By the time we arrived back at our hotel at 6 PM we were both overwhelmed by the depth and extent of the need that we'd encountered. The need is so vast that we aren't even sure where we could begin. Denise had an expectation that, organizations would have a permanent person in charge of ongoing efforts and that we'd just be able to walk in and they would put us to use. On the ground, it feels like if you really want to make a difference here you'd need to plan carefully and then to come ready to lead a particular project and guide it from start to completion. You'd need to develop a plan, raise funds, buy supplies, etc. etc. etc. Sadly, it feels as though many projects barely make a scratch. Volunteers start something, but then they leave and there's little or no follow through.

Christine the first volunteer we mentioned was working on a project with some young Tanzanian women, ages 14 to 19, who were madly sewing rather crudely made dresses and coin purses to sell in a new retail shop they were about to open. Startup money was coming from an NGO grant. Everyone was excited, their shop was being painted, and they were trying to sew sufficient inventory for their grand opening. Unfortunately, no one had spent any time figuring out overhead so they had no idea how much they needed to charge for their product to turn a profit. Worse yet, this endeavor doesn't make any sense in a town where a significant number of experienced tailors and seamstresses, possibly hundreds, already line up along the sidewalks sewing anything from nice handbags and dresses to men's dress suits. At Hostel Hoff, the volunteer from NYC had shown us a beautiful dress; she'd purchased the fabric in one shop and then had one of these street seamstresses fit and sew it for her. Total cost for her new dress was $18 including the hand batik fabric! There was no way the young women's products were even close to this quality. As another volunteer put it while holding up a completed handbag, "This stuff is crap!" At a minimum the young women in the program needed sewing lessons and business management assistance. Instead, Christine was helping them word a request for another grant.

A corner coffee shop and cafe next door to the about-to-open retail dress shop was also run by the same group of young girls. We decided to order some lunch and so contribute a smidgen to their business. The entire menu on the blackboard consisted of offerings prepared with either rice or beans or both: rice & beans, beans & chicken, fish and rice etc, etc. We went up to the counter.

"Hello, we'd like an order of rice and beans please."

"Sorry, no rice or beans," said the bored looking girl behind the counter, also no offer of an alternative.

"Oh, okay, thank you, maybe we'll try tomorrow." Things that make you go, *Hmmmm?*

Out of the organizations we've been exposed to so far the one that appears the most well managed is "Heart to Africa." Tomorrow we've been invited to come to one of their morning classes where they debate topics in English to practice their public speaking. Monika, the administrator, is scheduled to return on Tuesday next week and they may be able to use us to help fix up and clean a marketing space for a co-op they're helping to organize.

Now we're left to digest all that we've seen and decide if there's a way we can involve ourselves and make a meaningful (non-cash) contribution. At the very least yesterday opened our eyes to the struggle of obtaining an education in Tanzania; an education that students hope will lead them to a brighter economic future.

Day 233 - August 25 - Wednesday

Since our volunteer idea didn't grow wings, we did what all Muzunga, the Swahili equivalent of "gringo" which probably translates loosely to "crazy white folk," do. We went on another safari. This time, we'd decided to visit Tarangire National Park, Lake Manyara, and Norongoro Crater; all big attractions on the "northern safari circuit."

Our luxury Amboseli trip was big fun, but for a couple of cheapos, the price difference didn't cut it. We can't complain about great lodging; just the same, you go on safari for the animals and the landscapes, not the thread count of your sheets. To book a luxury safari you can walk into pretty much any upscale travel agency, there actually are a few, and plunk down your money. To purchase a good budget safari, you need to comparison shop.

The trick is to find a good budget agency without picking up a tout. If you walk into a safari office with a tout in tow, you've just increased the price. It's not easy to blend in Africa. First of all you're white; then there's the zip off pants, the shoulder bag, and the water bottle. Everything about you screams tourist which is synonymous with "walking wallet." Touts in Moshi don't overwhelm, but spend forty-five minutes on the street and you're almost assured of being approached. "Jambo! Hello Papa! Hello Mama! Where you from? Oh, very nice! You want safari? My brother/cousin/uncle/family... blah blah blah. Come visit our factory/museum/cultural center... blah blah blah." Avoiding too much eye contact, waving them politely away, and repeating, "Hapana, hapana asante," (no, no thank you) will usually extricate you in fairly short order. If a tout is particularly insistent, you can do like we did and duck into a café until the "pugasi" (tick) goes away. Touts are thickest near safari offices so we took a couple of exploratory walks to identify locations before diving straight inside.

Jan and Bert who we safaried with in Masai Mara had a satisfactory experience with an outfit called Spoonbill so we tried them first; small, dark, shabby office in a rundown building with a gal who couldn't tell us much beyond the price; *Okay, not them.* Next came Mauly Tours with a nice modern office and tours at twice the price. After Mauly, we tried KiliCrane Travel at our own hotel. All the woman at their desk could tell us was the price!

"Yes, but what's the itinerary?"

"After you pay, you'll get all the details." *Say what?!!* "I need $200 deposit right now so I can make arrangements." She was surprised and confused when we didn't immediately reach into our pockets and hand her $200. A few minutes after we thanked her and left, she called our room and asked if we could come back down. Denise went back. "You understand I need the deposit right now to arrange?" *Yes, great idea! Let's give you $200 with absolutely no idea what we're buying.* She still couldn't fathom our reluctance.

After that, we walked over to the Kindoroko Hotel where we'd noticed a flyer posted by someone looking for safari companions. We were ushered into the hotel's attached tour office.

"Yes, there is a safari you can join."

"Can you tell us about it?"

"Yes," then nothing.

"Uh, how many people are already going?"

"Hmmm," the guy makes a quick phone call and hangs up, "Three people."

"Where are they from?" He makes another phone call.

"A couple from Germany and one man from England"

"What is the itinerary and what's the cost?" At this point, we learn that the guy in the office is a bench warmer and that the girl who "knows" is out to lunch.

"You wait. She'll be here at 2 PM." *Hmmm, hour and a half, we don't think so.*

"No worries, we'll come back."

Leaving the Kindoroko, we headed to another local outfit called Kessy Brothers. We decided to try them because they've dotted Moshi with small advertising signs, strategically placed near other agencies.

The mention of signs calls for a brief segue. In Tanzania, if you want to erect a permanent sign, you have to pay a government tax. If you fail to pay, an inspector comes around and spray-paints your sign with a big red "X." The result is that half the advertising you see is readable but splashed with red. As far as we can tell there's no follow-up; the X'ed sign seems to stay put and we assume the offender still never pays. Who knows? Kessy's signs weren't X'ed so at least we knew they weren't scofflaws.

Kessy Brother's office is small, bustling, and unlike most of the competition, staffed by people who know their product and can give a clear explanation of what they offer. Their safari price for two guests was fair but still more than we wanted to pay. Since we weren't on a schedule, we gave them our names and said to contact us if they could group us with another two or three people sometime in the next few days.

When 2 o'clock approached, we returned to the Kindoroko. The "safari agent" wasn't back from lunch but the others interested in the tour were waiting in the hotel lobby. Mike and Stephie from Germany had posted the flyer and Paul from England had been their first response. They had a 2 PM appointment with the agent; so while we waited for her to show we sat around and got acquainted. By the time she arrived, an hour late, we'd all decided that we were compatible and that we could make a good safari group. Back in the tour office, she explained the safari in something less than desired detail.

"Okay, so this picture is of the room we'll be staying in at the lodge?"

"It's the deluxe room that you'll get if it's available."

"Are there three deluxe rooms?" The agent makes a vague inaudible response. "So if a deluxe room is not available, what room do we get?"

"Another room"

"Do you have a picture of it?"

"No, you need to decide in half hour if you want to go and give me deposit." *Hmmm this seems familiar.*

Her final price for the three day two night tour was $80 per person higher than Kessy's price for five people so with our new companions in tow we headed back to their office. Seraphin at Kessy's was delighted to see us (naturally) and again went over everything in thorough detail. They brought round their safari vehicle so that we could inspect it, introduced us to our guide, Kent, the youngest Kessy brother, introduced us to our camp cook, George, and agreed to forego full payment until they picked us up the next morning. When they mentioned that they provided free water, something everyone else charges for, and also free beers with dinner, we all signed on the dotted line. Seraphin said that Kent would pick us up at 5AM.

The Kessys like to get an early start so that you have plenty of time for the first day's game drive. After a hasty confab we all agreed that we wouldn't feel slighted if we slept in and started at six.

The next morning bright and early Kent was waiting in front of our hotel with the Land Rover and the fixings for coffee and tea. We stopped briefly to pick up box lunches, gathered Mike, Stephie, and Paul at their hotel, and set out for adventure. Truth be told, we set out for Arusha, but it's hard not to call it an adventure when you're in a vintage Land Rover, rolling through an exotic country, and you're on your way to safari. Just driving down the road here is heady stuff; the people with their bundles, the roadside stands and markets, the hustle and flow of towns, everything is interesting.

Passing through Arusha, we stopped so that Mike could visit an ATM. Earlier, before Kent arrived; Mike suffered a major tourist nightmare. He walked to a closed bank across the street from his Moshi hotel and used their ATM to withdraw cash. He inserted his card and asked for the maximum of 400,000 shillings, $270 USD. The ATM whirred; then it whirred again. It returned the card and then it spit out a receipt showing that he'd received the 400,000 shillings; only problem, no cash! Mike was not a happy camper. To make a long story short, the ATM in Arusha worked and back in Moshi, Seraphin went to the bank when it opened and straightened everything out. Now that's good service!

Safaris are definitely not "seen one, seen them all" experiences. Some of the cast might be the same and some of the sets might look familiar, but each new park we visit is its own unique performance. The first thing that catches your attention about Tarangire is its "baobab" studded landscape. The baobab tree is alien, strange, and wonderful. Back when the world was young, God became so angry with the mighty baobab that he pulled it up by its roots and replanted it upside down. What God plants stays planted, and to this very day the baobab tree grows with its roots in the air. Probably not true, but one look and you can see where someone got the idea. The trees are huge and, yep, they do look like they're growing upside down.

Beyond the baobabs, there were: elephants, giraffes living and dead, baboons, mongoose (mongeese?), wildebeest, gazelles, dik diks, birds, warthogs, and termites (have I left anyone out?); every creature posed against backdrops that couldn't exist anywhere but Africa. With a short break for a picnic lunch, we spent six hours driving slowly along bumpy dirt roads hanging out of the Rover's pop-up top actively looking for game. We didn't spot the leopard we all visualized, but every moment was fun.

Around 4 o'clock, we reluctantly left Tarangire, which by the way means "animal river," and headed for "Twiga Camp" our overnight spot located conveniently close to both Lake Manyara and the Norongoro Crater. Twiga is sort of like a platypus; a little of this, a little of that; an odd mix, but one that still manages to scuttle along. To start off, it's a lodge with deluxe and standard en-suite rooms (we didn't get the deluxe rooms but at least we knew what to expect), a bar, a pool, and a restaurant where no one seems to eat. Beyond that, there's a shared shower block, an open area where camping safaris and overland groups pitch their tents, and an outdoor kitchen where George and other safari chefs work their magic.

When we arrived George had a table set for us and met us with coffee, tea, and popcorn; a little strange but it worked. Later after we washed up (you get absolutely filthy on game drives) he produced a meal that was both delicious and presented with flare. By the time he brought out our "free" beers we were all so sated and tired that we opted to "save them for tomorrow."

On day two we ate breakfast at 6:30 AM so that we could get an early start at Norongoro. As we were finishing, Kent walked up to the table.

"I have to get the fan belt on the Land Rover changed. I'll be back in about thirty minutes."

As he drove away, I turned to Denise, "Fan belt, I don't know; that sounds more like a bad water pump."

An hour later, Mike was getting a little concerned. "Kent said he'd be just outside the gate. I'm going out and see if I can find out what's up." After a short reconnaissance Mike reported back, "Kent had to send for a new water pump. He's gone for the "rescue" vehicle and will be here in a few minutes."

This is where shopping our safari paid off. When we asked, "What happens if we break down?" most operators said, "The driver will fix the problem (*yeah sure*)." Or "We'll send out another vehicle (*from Moshi five or more hours*)." Or, "Uh, our vehicle is well maintained. There won't be any problems. Hakuna matata (*right*)." When we asked Kessy Brothers, they told us that they always keep a spare vehicle at Lake Manyara just in case. After another few minutes, Kent rolled up in a nice Toyota safari van and we were off.

Based on our experiences so far, Land Rover's and mini-vans with pop-up roofs are the only way to go and "comfy" bucket-seats handily beat benches. Before we arrived in Africa, we considered an "overland" truck tour.

A younger friend had gone on one a year or two before and it seemed a good possibility. Overland trucks are heavy-duty rigs with a bus-like space mounted behind the driver's cabin. The trucks carry kitchen and camping gear and the passengers share communal cooking and other responsibilities. After we saw the trucks lumber about the National Parks and we watched people crawl into their small tents, we were glad we gave them a pass. If you like groups the trucks might provide decent point-to-point transportation, but on safari, Rovers and vans still get our nod. You have enough companions with you for comradeship but not enough for a crowd. You get to drive around with the top up and the wind in your hair. None of the seats face backward and, especially in the Masi Mara, you can get up close and personal with the animals.

The drive from Twiga Camp into the Norongoro Crater was a real nail biter and we don't think any of us wished that we'd gotten the earlier start or that we were riding in a larger vehicle. Once we reached the park and left the pavement, we entered a dense fog. The blowing grey stuff mixed with the ever present road dust and, presto-change-o, just like that everything outside our windows turned to shadows and phantasms; "gorillas in the mist anyone?" As we crawled along the twisting narrow road, those of us seated in back only saw well enough to suspect that shear drops lurked just around each bend. We crossed our fingers and hoped that Kent, leaning forward in his seat, could see more. He kept the wipers working, but the sludge of dirt and fog worked harder. From time to time he had to stop, hop out, and splash water on the windshield. Just to make things interesting, random huge trucks or "chicken" buses occasionally hurtled out of the gloom, forcing us to the shoulder.

When you get right down to it, our drive was probably safe and short. At the time however it felt long and maybe a little scary. I think all of us were somewhat relieved when we eventually crested the crater's rim. Suddenly, most of the fog was above us and spread out below lay the surreal world of the crater floor.

Norongoro Crater is just what it sounds like. It's the caldera of an enormous dormant volcano. The volcano's towering walls completely encircle the place creating an isolated ecosystem, a sunken island cut off from the surrounding world. It's possible for animals to climb in and out, but the walls are so shear that most of the wildlife which has wandered in over the millennia has chosen to stay. The way down was so steep and so deeply buried in dust, that we were glad for the dry season and four-wheel drive.

Game driving the crater floor was another magical experience. First, we spotted a loping jackal. That was followed shortly by a sleeping cheetah. A little farther along, we caught sight of a rarely seen serval cat and a group of gazelle. Next came elephants, lions, a black rhino (really more of a long-way off black speck), and lots of hippos.

The fog was long gone when we stopped for lunch by a beautiful lake, Kent advised that we eat it the van. "It is better. The birds will try to steal your food." Trusting out guide's expertise we stayed inside and watched with envy as other safari goers settled down for a picnic in the grass. Moments later they were squealing and scuttling for their vehicles as large aggressive hawk-like birds called "black kites" swooped down and grabbed for their lunches. The worst we had to contend with were chattering sparrow types that lined the opening of our pop-up and jostled for position while they waited for us to drop something. None of them darted inside, but Alfred Hitchcock definitely came to mind.

After lunch it was on to wildebeest, hyena, giraffe, water buffalo, and baboons. It's hard to fully describe the safari experience and do it justice. With so much wonder at every turn, you simply run out of superlatives. When time came to leave the crater; we climbed out via another steep road which lifted us from savannah up through tropical forest, treating us to a slideshow of incredible views. Back at Twiga camp, George was waiting with another coffee service and another delicious dinner. This may not be luxury but it sure works for us.

The next morning, the Land Rover was back and we made an early start for a half day game drive at Lake Manyara. The focal point of that excursion was the "hippo pond" a marshy estuary of the lake that plays host to its namesakes along with large herds of zebra and wildebeest; all of them standing around in front of thousands of pelicans and flamingos. It was the kind of scene that just makes you stand there with your mouth hanging open. Off to one side was a dead bloated (is that an oxymoron?) hippo that had probably died in a mating fight. Man, talk about your roadkill; almost as impressive dead as alive!

At length we tore ourselves away from the pond and crawled back into the Land Rover. As we pulled away, another guide hailed Kent. "Hey dude, I think you're getting a flat (or at least the Swahili equivalent)." Kent hopped out and sure enough; time for a tire change. The Rover's oversize jack proved recalcitrant and pretty soon every guide at the pond along with a couple of male Muzunga were gathered around making suggestions. It was a guy thing, but having changed my share of tires I was content to go back to hippo watching while others swapped testosterone. Once the jack was working and Kent borrowed a suitable wrench the fix went quickly. Denise and I were secretly glad the Rover carries two spares.

More buffalo, a herd of giraffe, and a troop of baboons and we were on our way back to Twiga for lunch. A long sleepy drive later we pulled up in front of Kessy Brothers Moshi office and our last African safari was over. What a terrific experience! Kent was a friendly and knowledgeable guide, George was a friendly and skilled cook, our companions were fun, and the price was reasonable. On a final note, the Kessys were concerned that we might be upset, which we weren't, over the mechanical problems, so they invited us back the next day for free beers and T-shirts; couldn't pass them up.

Day 237 - August 29 - Sunday

Last Tuesday when we arrived back at the Kilimanjaro Crane Hotel, their Internet was unavailable. The hotel buys connection time from a local ISP and then sells it to its guests by the hour or in 24 hour blocks. When you ask for a Wi-Fi connection the receptionist reverently scrutinizes a piece of notebook paper that lists temporary IDs and passwords. After careful examination, they give you one and then it's duly marked off the sheet. The technical problem; they'd issued all the codes. To get new ones, someone needed to call their ISP (a couple of blocks away). After that the ISP needed to deliver a new list or someone from the hotel had to go over and pick it up. This was a major problem requiring several phone calls, repeated discussions among employees, and of course consultations with supervisors.

The Hotel ran out of codes before we left on our safari and it took them until Friday to get new ones; almost a week. Meanwhile, we chomped at the bit and waited to book airline reservations to Zanzibar and Egypt and make other time sensitive arrangements. Ultimately, we walked into a local airline office and bought the Zanzibar flight directly. "Poli Poli," as the African's say; "slowly, slowly." In other words, "chill, take it easy;" good advice since there's really nothing else you can do. We spent a week longer in Moshi than we wanted, but tomorrow we fly to Zanzibar; on the move again.

Day 242 - September 3 - Friday - Zanzibar, Tanzania

Denise is on a "dahow," outrigger canoe, snorkeling trip to the local reef with a family from Holland and I'm relaxing on the beach with a beer. I was going to go along on the reef trip but the boatman was an hour late, hakuna matata. By the time he sailed up, I was well into a, "been there done that" mood. Today is our fourth full day on Zanzibar and it will be our fifth night at the Kilima Kidogo (Little Hill) Guesthouse. As usual, the island's power is out.

Before we arrived, our plan was to spend five nights on the east side of the island at the Kilima Kidogo in Paje; then head north for another five nights in a town called Nungwei. After that, we figured that we'd spend our last few island nights in Stone Town. Stone Town is the old section of Zanzibar's main city (also called Zanzibar) where we hope to catch the end of Ramadan celebrations (Zanzibar is 97% Muslim). As things stand, we just asked Kilima Kidogo for a couple more nights and may skip the north end of the island completely.

We'd like to see more of Zanzibar, but there are compelling factors in play. First, the Kilima Kidogo is a really nice place. No, we're talking really nice! It sits right on the Indian Ocean, surrounded by palm trees, and fronts a beach of white flour-fine sand. The guesthouse's main building is a spacious, tropical, single-storey home, with a comfortable living room/common area, a kitchen, and deluxe accommodations on each side. The airy living room opens on to the idyllic beachfront and a couple of yards away waits an inviting thatched-roof sand-floored bar. Behind the main building sits a separate wing of "budget" rooms, where we're staying. The inexpensive rooms are small and simple, but clean, attractive, and pleasantly decorated.

A second factor that's urging us stay put is money. Zanzibar feels expensive! Except for sand floored backpacker places and lodges that are a one-mile walk from anywhere else, rooms run about 30% more than on the mainland. Rates for mid-range and above accommodations average $80 or more per night. In that sense Kilima Kidogo is a great deal as we're only paying $60 with an included breakfast.

Food is a similar story. At backpacker and local beach cafes prices are a third higher than the mainland, while at our lodge and other upscale joints the prices are triple! Guess where we're eating? Okay, we'll admit that the costs are reasonable for a beach resort in paradise, but it's still a little hard to swallow when the value feels weak. In Africa in general and Zanzibar in particular food and accommodation are adequate but what we've received for our dollar suffers by comparison to Turkey and Morocco. Oh God, we're spoiled!

We could probably find a place in Nungwei that's at least as reasonable as the Kilima Kidogo, but we're not sure it's worth the effort. Paje is rated as one of Zanzibar's two best beaches and the range of island transportation leaves a lot to be desired. At one end are private taxi's which get you places quickly, but aren't cheap. A forty-five minute ride from the airport, arranged by the guesthouse, cost us $45. At the other extreme are large trucks with benches in back, local versions of the mainland dalla-dallas that carry passengers chicken bus fashion. A ride from Stone Town to Paje in one of these takes a couple of hours but only costs $1.50. Spoiled tourists that we are; indeterminate schedules, the crush of humanity they squeeze in, and luggage hassles have pretty much taken dalla-dallas off our island exploration plate. Somewhere in the middle are shared tourist vans that you need to book in advance. Who knows? At this point it's easier to just sit on the beach with a rum and coke (I finished the beer) and watch the tide roll in and out.

Denise came back well chilled but thoroughly enjoyed the snorkeling. I guess I'll have to lever myself up and try it before we leave. Wrapped in a damp towel, she was Jonesing for a hot shower, but with the power out, the generator spluttering, and the pump not pumping, it didn't happen. She settled for a bottled water sponge bath which got rid of a little of the sea scum but didn't do much to warm her up.

Later, after she quit looking blue, we walked fifteen minutes up the beach to eat dinner at "Teddy's Place." Teddy's is a backpacker "resort" that rents out four or five sand floor shared-bath "bandas," windowless thatched huts, for about $20 a night. The accommodations are a little basic for our taste, but the place exudes a good vibe and features a decent bar and restaurant.

Teddy's compound is surrounded by a six foot high crenellated concrete wall that makes it look a little like an old fort. When you approach from the beach, you climb in via a rickety wooden stile (ladder). As we clambered over, we spied Paul, who shared our Norongoro safari, lounging on a beach bed. He rolled in the night before from Stone Town and was shooting the breeze with an Aussie named, Ben. Naturally the reunion called for drinks so after a quick tour of Paul's banda we adjourned, in the best colonial tradition, to the bar for "Waka Wakas," gin and tonics made with local Konyagi gin.

Friday was Teddy's "Ramadan Dinner" night, which meant they serve an all you care to eat buffet of local dishes for under $7 per person. Great deal! There were big bowls of all sorts of yummy stuff: cassava root cooked with coconut milk, coconut beans, calamari and octopus, brown rice, baked bananas, vegetable sauce, grilled fish, and sweets like light donut holes with syrup. I filled my plate once and was too full to make a second pass.

After dinner we risked the "shudder" dark fifteen minute beach walk back to our guesthouse. Everywhere you go in Africa you're told not to walk around after dark and at a certain point it just gets really old. The sand was bright, the stars were out, and we walked quickly.

Day 243 - September 4 - Saturday - Paje, Zanzibar

Yesterday, Dena, the owner of Kilima Kidogo, offered us the opportunity to change rooms to a second floor unit with a sea view. Since the price is the same, we naturally agreed. We suspect that Dena hopes the view will make us stay put. Unfortunately, the power outage (back on for the moment) did something to the guest-house water system. At the moment we have a sea view but we don't have a toilet or a shower that works. When we reported the problem, Dena sent the "maintenance" guy up to check. He turned on our sink and since it dribbled he assured us that the problem was temporary and that in a few minutes everything would be fine. Ten hours later the sink is now up to a strong dribble but the shower and toilet are still missing in action. Oh well, hakuna matata, we'll see what today brings. We may have to forego the view in favor of running water.

Power outages and their related inconveniences occur regularly on Zanzibar, but lest you get the wrong impression, we're not complaining. We were told that one recent outage left the island without power for several months so we consider ourselves lucky. When the lights go dark, the locals take it in stride and at the guesthouse Dena turns it into an opportunity for fun, pulls out kerosene lanterns, and invites the guests to gather around a dining table in the main building for socializing and cards. Dena taught us to play several games and we taught everyone "Bastard" that we learned on our gullet cruise in Turkey.

Day 245 - September 6 - Monday

The power came back, the toilet got fixed, the shower got hot, the view got the nod, and we told Dena that we're going to stay until the 9th. One lazy beach day is running easily into the next and "why bother" seems our operative phrase. Included breakfasts are served in the beach bar until 10 AM which means that we're able to linger in bed. There's plenty of coffee and each day a slightly different variation of fresh fruit, juice, eggs, and bread with butter and jam. Some days the eggs are scrambled other days they're done as Spanish omelets, or poached; your choice. Bread is always the cook's choice and ranges from local crepes to Johnny cakes or fry bread. Denise is trying to teach the other guests that peanut butter goes with everything.

After breakfast we usually spend a couple of hours working on our long term travel plans. I'm scoping out options for Egypt, we fly to Cairo on the 15th, and Denise is reading about India. It would be nice to skip this sort of planning and just travel by the seat of our pants, but so far a modicum of foreknowledge has kept our hassles to a minimum. We also learned early on that we don't know diddly-squat about most of the places that we want to see. Holding a vague notion that you want to visit "Siwa Oasis" is one thing. Actually getting there is totally different.

I like to work in our room under the fan; kind of a Key Largo vibe. Denise opts for a beach bed on the sand. By noon our brains approach saturation, so I join her under the palms and we whip out the novels. Some mindless reading, some politically incorrect tanning, a couple of beers, a stroll along the shore and we've frittered away another perfectly good afternoon.

Yesterday was "Swahili buffet" night at Teddy's so we hooked up with Paul for another tasty local spread. It was also his last night before flying back to England which again called for Waka Wakas in the bar and another starry walk on the beach. Hey, it's not a vacation, it's a lifestyle! Tomorrow is Denise's birthday, the big 58, and Dena has promised us meals on the house. The price works so I suppose we'll dine in. Oops, time for my malaria pill!

Day 249 - September 10 - Friday

It's still on the sleepy side of 8AM. Our fan lop, lop, lops lazy overhead circles and soft yellow light filters through the curtains. The surf is busy. It murmurs and growls while early birds squabble over worms filling the air with tropical screeches. We were supposed to wake up in Stone Town today. Instead we're starting day twelve at Kilima Kidogo. We had every intention of moving on. Fortunately, at the last minute we came to our senses, cancelled our taxi, and opted in favor of two more nights of sand and sea. There's nothing much on our agenda and this is an excellent place to watch it happen. The demands here are limited to paying our bill and making it to breakfast before 10AM. So far, we've managed both.

Day 250 - September 11 - Saturday

There's a new moon right now and the tides here in Paje are running from one extreme to another. When the tide is in, there's not much beach. You can dive into the water and be swimming twenty-five feet from the shore line. When the tide is out, it's as if the ocean drained away. Yesterday after breakfast, we walked out to the reef. We headed straight out from the guesthouse, just kept walking for almost forty minutes, and the water never rose above our knees!

Most of the reef coral is dead and sand covered, but there's still a lot to see. Its tide pools and its shallows hide sponges, urchins of all sizes (you have to wear shoes), sea cucumbers, shells, small schools of fish, and the occasional snake. Starfish are plentiful and decorate the sea floor in panoply of shapes and sizes from small spindly brittle stars to solid plate-sized pentagons. Their colors run the gamut, from vivid scarlet to bright yellow and from royal blue to deep sea green. Some stars wear their colors like a solid cloak; others appear as though a child drizzled them with cake frosting and electric sprinkles.

The reef is also home to octopi and lobster, both of which are heavily fished by the locals. Everyday, when the tide is low, men walk the exposed reef with sharpened sticks poking and prodding into holes. Others take their stick and a mask and dive the shallow waters. We never spied an octopus at large but every man we saw seemed to carry a net bag containing four or five that he'd caught; tentacles trailing out the bottom. Lobsters are less common, but we did see a fellow snag one and proudly hold up his catch. He was excited by his success, but we also think he was eyeing us for a quick sale. Why carry a lobster all the way back to the beach if a Muzunga will buy it from you right here in the water? We congratulated him on his luck and politely declined.

When the tide turns, the sea returns quickly, rushing back in fast flowing currents. Declining a canoe offer, we waded, waist deep before we regained the shore.

Later in the afternoon, Dena, the guesthouse owner, organized a trip in a dalla-dalla to a nearby peninsula to watch the sunset; nice and companionable.

Day 251 - September 12 - Sun - Stone Town, Zanzibar

After we finally peeled ourselves away from Paje, we got back on plan and spent our last two nights on Zanzibar in its capital of Stone Town. Extra time lazed away at the beach turned out to be time well used because the city doesn't offer all that much. Guide books wax loquacious about Stone Town's Arabic heritage and its narrow atmospheric streets, but compared to the souks and winding alleys of Morocco it's pretty tame.

Our first night in town was "Eid el-Fitr," the end of Ramadan celebration, which didn't quite live up to our expectations. Ah, there go those darn expectations again. Lots of people were out and about, dressed in their best outfits, crowded around impromptu food stalls, filling the town's waterfront park to capacity, but overall it was a very subdued affair. Imagine a small town 4th of July celebration with no music, no parades, no events, no street performers, no speeches, no fireworks, and no booze and you have a rough idea of the evening. People-watching, on the other hand, was excellent.

During the day we wandered around hitting the recommended highlights: the main market with its stacks of fruits and vegetables, crowds of vendors, and stinky fish stalls; the natural history museum, now a dilapidated empty shell; and the "House of Wonders," the old presidential palace, so called because, when first built, its electric lights and cage elevator were wonders to the populace. Today, it's a wonder that it doesn't collapse from neglect.

Travel is all about the sights, the people, and the unexpected experiences. Most of the unexpected experiences are pleasant, but every once in a while you encounter one that stretches toward the far edge of disagreeable. Ever since we hit Africa, with one or two exceptions, our beds have been tucked beneath mosquito nets. We've also been taking daily anti-malaria pills. Several popular pills act as a prophylaxis against malaria, but before we left home we'd settled on

Doxycycline. Our travel doctor felt that, given the widespread resistance to other drugs, Doxycycline was the best all round choice for our trip. For our part, we liked the drug's apparently lower incidence of side effects. And that folks brings us to the far edge of disagreeable.

The other day, while sunning at the beach, Denise mentioned that her fingernails and toenails felt like they were burning. She was wearing sunscreen and her skin felt normal for a tanorexic, so she rubbed an extra dab of sunscreen on her nails, and shrugged off the sensation. The next morning, to her shock, she discovered what appeared to be bleeding under her thumbnails. The rest of her fingernails and toenails were also red and some looked as though they might be starting to separate from their nail beds. *What the Hell???*

Internet self-diagnosis: "photo-onycholysis," a loosening or separation of a fingernail or toenail from its nail bed that results from exposure to sunlight. It turns out (*who knew?*) that our nail beds contain less melanin than the rest of our skin and are less protected from sunlight. *Okay, but why now?* Well, it also turns out that one of Doxycycline's relatively few side effects is increased photosensitivity. In this characteristic it's not alone. When it comes to increased photosensitivity lots of drugs hop into the pool: NSAIDS, antibiotics, and sulfonamides, to name just a few. Denise takes a daily anti-inflammatory. Throw in the Doxycycline, pop a couple of naproxen for an achy back, and voila, the perfect nail bed storm!

With only three Africa days remaining, Denise has stopped taking her Doxycycline and our fingers are firmly crossed that her nails don't make like autumn leaves and scatter on the ground.

Day 253 - Sept 14 - Tues - Dar es Salaam, Tanzania

Yesterday evening, we took the "fast" ferry from Zanzibar here to Dar es Salaam on the mainland. The crossing was passably rough (I took Dramamine) and anything but fast. We were supposed to leave Stone Town at 3:30 PM but it was an hour later before the crew finished loading cargo and actually cast off. The trip was advertised to take 90 minutes. At the onset we pounded along at a good clip, then something happened (broke?) and we came to a complete stop. After bobbing around for a few minutes we started forward again, but now at a lazy crawl. Instead of 90 minutes, the crossing stretched into four full hours!

Adding insult to injury; we could have avoided the whole Dramamine experience and flown at no cost! When we purchased our airplane tickets from Moshi to Zanzibar, we told our ticket agent that we wanted to go to the island, but we didn't mention Dar es Salaam. Later, talking with our friend Paul we discovered that his ticket on the same flight and at the same price from the same agent included a multi-day layover in Zanzibar and then allowed him to continue on to the capital. Oh well, live and learn.

When our fast ferry finally tied up in Dar it was well after dark; not a wander around after dark kind of city. Walking off the gangway we were met by a scrum of taxi touts looking for fares. Rather than go it on our own, we gave one of them the nod and let him lead us toward his car. Before climbing in we negotiated 10,000 TSH to take us to the "Keys Hotel."

"Why you want to go to Keys Hotel?"

"We have a reservation."

"Okay." The Keys was a sister hotel to one we'd visited in Moshi. The Keys in Moshi was nice and web photos of the one in Dar looked equally good; simple rooms, dining area, conference center. Not!

When our taxi pulled up front, we were both like, "Where's the hotel?"

"Right there!" "Right there," was just past a gaggle of hookers and wanta-be drunks obscuring the entrance. I waited in the "lobby" with our taxi tout and our luggage while Denise checked out a room. Her verdict was a big thumbs down. The room was clean enough, but the overall environment was just too rough.

"Okay, what hotel do you recommend?" Our taxi guys wound us through the dark streets of Dar, full of the same vaguely disquieting nighttime hustle and bustle as Nairobi, and eventually delivered us to the "Valley View Hotel" in a quieter neighborhood. The Valley View was a good steer. The hotel is basic but features TV, mosquito nets, and a decent restaurant, all of which I fully appreciated when I woke up this morning with a bad head cold. Because I feel crummy, we spent our last day in Tanzania hovelled in our room doing a lot of nothing.

Sekhmet, Karnak, Egypt

Chapter 11

EGYPT

Day 254 - September 15 - Wednesday - Cairo, Egypt

At 4 AM today a taxi picked us up and ferried us out to Julius Nyere International for our 6:15 Egypt Air departure. The flight was smooth (tasteless meal) and landed us in Cairo a little before noon. When we cleared customs and immigration there was once again a taxi guy holding up a sign with our name (that's the bomb). Thirty minutes later we were in the heart of old downtown Cairo taking a creaky, slightly scary, elevator to the twelfth floor and the lobby of Hotel Osiris.

Day 255 - September 16 - Thursday

If you stay in a twelfth floor hotel room with a balcony the first thing you notice about Cairo is its rooftops. They're filthy, buried with rubble, no telling how it got there, and covered by a sickly growth of dirty satellite dishes; fields of high-tech toadstools that stretch to the horizon.

The second thing you notice is traffic noise; a low roar that surges continually from the streets below.

Roads are congested bedlams. At all hours of the day and night drivers of cars, trucks, taxis, buses, and animal drawn carts join in a chaotic dance, purposefully ignoring signals and lanes. Egyptians probably didn't invent the car horn, but they are undoubtedly among its most enthusiastic devotees. It's a good thing we've learned to sleep with earplugs.

After our included hotel breakfast: toast, butter, jam, spreadable cheese, yogurt, a crepe with syrup, orange juice, and coffee, we struck out in search of the Consular Services branch office of the India Embassy. India is our next stop after Egypt and, unlike the other countries that we've visited; India requires that all tourists obtain a visa before their arrival. Lucky for us, this is doable in Cairo.

Finding addresses in Cairo is a little tricky. Street signs are limited to major thoroughfares and even those are hit and miss. Address numbers are essentially nonexistent and you're lucky to see one per block. "Sharia Talaat Harb," where the consular office is located, is a big street near our hotel so we managed to get that far with a minimum of confusion. From there, we just sort of felt our way along looking for clues. We saw two addresses in about a seven block stretch so at least we knew we were headed in the right direction. After that we spied the "Metro Cinema" which we knew was close to the office. Since street numbers are rare, many printed addresses include a reference to a nearby recognizable landmark, i.e. "near Metro Cinema." Just the same, we would have walked right past the consular office if Denise hadn't spotted a small dusty flag drooping above a second story window.

The building that houses the office is typical of Old Cairo. The façade dates from an earlier period and might be considered stylish if it wasn't encrusted with decades of grit and grime. The entrance hall is dingy and fly-specked; the floors are dirty with a bit of trash strewn here and there. A well worn stairway leads upward wrapping around a rickety caged elevator. A few older ramshackle signs advertise tenants; among them is a small tarnished plaque that proudly announces that the Indian Embassy is on the second floor. Eschewing the elevator we headed up.

Our visa application process started out straight-forward; fill out a couple of forms, pay application fees, and show our passports. Then things got sticky.

"Where will you enter India?"

"We're going to fly from Amman Jordan to Dehli." *Well, maybe, unless we change our minds.*

"And, where will you leave India?"

"We'll fly from Bangalore to Bangkok." *Or whatever, unless something better comes along.*

"May I see copies of your flight reservations?" *Say what!!?* It turns out that India is a stickler for making sure that you're only there for a visit. We tried to talk our way past the requirement by proving that we had adequate financial resources and no reason to outstay our welcome, but to no avail; no tickets, no visa! "Don't worry, just come back on Tuesday with copies of your tickets and 750 Egyptian pounds ($133 US) and you can pick up your visa, no problems."

Crap! Back to the hotel to surf the Internet for flights to and from India; which would be a heck of a lot easier if we held even a vague idea of when we want to get there and how long we want to stay.

Day 256 - September 17 - Friday

We changed hotels today. We booked the Hotel Osiris on the web but they could only accommodate us for six of the seven nights we wanted. Since it's a clean place with a decent breakfast and a good location, we decided to take all the nights they could give us and find a different hotel for the one night when they're full. Nabil, the owner at Osiris, recommended the "Cosmopolitan" and offered to book us a room for only $75. Since the Unnamed Guidebook describes the place as Spanish Inquisition style with mysteriously spotted carpets and surly service at $55 per night, we thanked Nabil for his offer and winged it. A little wandering around and we ferreted out the nearby City View Hotel with great views overlooking El-Tahrir Square one of Cairo's main intersections; $60 per night with a good restaurant.

After we checked in at the City View, we spent the rest of the day at the Museum of Egyptian Antiquities located only a stone's throw away. Wow, what a place; we think you have to describe it as the world's best crappy museum! The collection is wonderful and incredible and it fills the building's every nook and cranny. Unfortunately, most of it is housed in displays that look like they were assembled for a 1939 high school science project. Think about the dustiest, most cluttered, small town museum that you've ever visited. The Cairo museum is just the same writ large. There's no air conditioning and it swelters. Old wooden cases are crammed to bursting. Sunlight glares on things that it shouldn't. Many items are unlabeled; others are labeled with torn scraps of notebook paper on which something has been scribbled in pen or pencil. It's absolutely mind blowing.

We saw a few new cases being installed that looked like they'd come from Costco or Cases'R'Us. You can only hope that Egypt's grand plans for a new museum near Giza will eventually bear fruit.

Highlights of the museum were the exhibition of treasure from Tut's tomb, nicely displayed, and the Royal Mummy Rooms. The mummies carried an extra $20 per person admission charge but it was well worth it to get access to the museum's only two rooms with AC. If you visit on a hot day, save the mummies for last!

Day 257 - September 18 - Saturday

Back at the Hotel Osiris, we spent half of today huddled in our room struggling with our Egypt itinerary. We arrived in Egypt with a loose plan, but due to India's ticket-in-hand visa requirement, we suddenly found ourselves needing to know *exactly* when to move on. After a lot of "what if's" and "start-over's" we compromised on a date and spent the rest of the day huddled in the room surfing an intermittent Internet connection in search of reasonably priced tickets; Ah the romance of world travel!

Day 258 - September 19 - Sunday

We went into full on tourist mode today and set out to see Egypt's number one sight, the pyramids. I don't think there's anyone in Cairo who doesn't sell day tours to the pyramids. To keep things simple, we booked ours with Nabil; private air-conditioned mini-van, driver, English speaking guide, admission to Giza, Saqqara, and Dashur, and a full lunch. We managed to scare up a gal from the U.S. named Ronique to share the cost so it worked out to $65 per person. You can get to the pyramids on your own, but it's a hassle, especially if you want to visit Saqqara and Dashur which are somewhat isolated.

The Great Pyramid of Khufu, Cheops, lives up to its hype as one of the wonders of the ancient world. Sure it's right on the edge of Cairo, but for us that only added to its mystery. A heavy haze, probably permanent smog, hung over the city. Instead of an urban wasteland, what we glimpsed past The Great Pyramid was a shadowy mirage of some mythical distant future; cool beans.

Our guide counseled that we should go to the Giza Plateau first to beat the crowds. He was right. For a short time after we arrived we were able to enjoy the pyramids of Khufu, Khafre, and Menkaure, minus the semi-permanent blanket of humanity that surges at their base.

It's probably been said a bazillion times, but now it's our turn; the Giza plateau is an awe inspiring place. First off, the pyramids are big. No! We mean really big. Khufu stands over 250 feet high and weighs in at around six million tons! Then, there's their age. How often do you see a structure that's over 4,500 years old? Then, there are the alignments; each pyramid aligned perfectly with the next, and each of their bases aligned with the cardinal points (I checked with my compass)! And the desert; what about the desert? It stretches away on three sides desolate and empty. Oh yeah, and the camels; they're there mostly for tourists to ride, but the sight of the pyramids backed by the desert with camels trudging in the distance; that's a hard act to follow!

"Okay, if you're ready, we go now to see the Sphinx." *Holy Amun Ra Batman! We forgot The Sphinx was even here.* Ronique wanted to ride a camel (expensive and uncomfortable), so while she headed over on her "ship of the desert," we hopped in the van and did it the easy way. As we neared the big guy, we sent the van on ahead so that we could walk the remaining distance and immerse ourselves in the full overawing impact. Even after a million pictures, we weren't really sure what to expect.

Our first glimpse of The Sphinx was sort of like an in-person glimpse of Arnold Schwarzenegger. "Gee, I though he would be bigger." As we walked closer and the road dropped lower, it approaches from above and behind, we realized the analogy doesn't work; The Sphinx is huge! We Googled it. It's "the largest monolith statue in the world, 241 ft long, 20 ft wide and 66.34 ft high. We stood there staring for a long time. Despite being too close to the city, KFC is just across the street, The Sphinx still manages to exude an undeniable air of mystery and of time without beginning or end.

After The Sphinx, we reunited with Ronique, climbed into the van and headed off for a close encounter with a papyrus shop. Guides get a commission on anything you buy, so whenever you organize a tour in Egypt you have to specify that you aren't interested in: papyrus, onyx, or traditional markets, etc, etc. If you don't, instead of sightseeing you spend most of your time learning about high pressure sales techniques. Since this was our first guided tour, we figured, *What the heck, you can't visit Egypt without at least one papyrus shop.* Actually, it wasn't too bad. They served us Egyptian tea while a salesman demonstrated how papyrus paper is made. Sort of interesting; basically the plant is a reed. You slice off thin slices, lay them in a crisscross pattern, whack them a few times with a mallet, and let them dry. After the demo we were each given a slip of paper on which we were told to note the item numbers of the "art" we wished to purchase. Then we were turned loose to browse. Although all the papyrus art was pharaoh themed, most of it had the questionable appeal of velvet paintings. The stuff that didn't look cheesy was ridiculously priced. "We can ship!" After a second cup of tea and about fifteen minutes of polite looking, Ronique bought something. I didn't see her purchase before she rolled it up, but I thought maybe an Elvis or those kids with the big eyes. Later, Denise told me it was ducks. We opted for a $0.88 bookmark; good purchase.

Next, we headed off for the huge necropolis of Saqqara, burial ground for ancient Memphis. A half hour south of Giza, in a seven kilometer stretch of desert, lay the dusty tombs of Old Kingdom pharaohs, their families, and other notables. The big (really? another pun) attraction here is the Step Pyramid of Zoser. Dated to 2,650 BC Imhotep's imposing creation is one of the world's earliest stone monuments. It stands at one end of a vast funeral complex and its six massive steps rise to a height of sixty meters. Surrounded by a 1,645 meter long paneled limestone wall, it's darn impressive.

Saqqara is an archaeological site with lots of appeal and Zoser's pyramid is just the start. Our favorite sight was the "Mastaba of Ti," sitting below ground level it is Saqqara's most elaborate and highly decorated tomb. It's owner was a 5th century bureaucrat nicknamed, "Ti the Rich," and its walls are painted with detailed scenes of daily life: people fishing, preparing food, working the land, dancing, building boats, trading, herding cattle, etc.; really neat stuff.

We finished our Saqqara visit with a 25 meter scramble down a steep three foot square shaft that descends into the Pyramid of Teti; not for the claustrophobic. At the bottom of the shaft sits Teti's huge basalt sarcophagus which, according to our guide, is Egypt's oldest example of a sarcophagus with inscriptions.

This is a good point to digress and talk about photography. Picture taking, with or without, flash is prohibited inside pretty much all of Egypt's tombs and museums and even some outside locations. Why exactly is anybody's guess, maybe to keep a stranglehold on marketable imagery. Who knows? At any rate, for most guards and caretakers, the restriction represents an economic opportunity not to be missed. When we reached the bottom of Teti's shaft, a galabiya and headscarf clad watchman was right behind us. Holding his finger up to his lips (secrecy, silence) and looking furtively back up the tunnel. "You, picture here. Good! Madam, Sir, you there, camera good picture. Shsssh!" The idea is that you're supposed to hand him your camera. He'll snap a couple of prohibited out of focus photos of you standing in front of the sarcophagus or whatever, and then you'll show your appreciation for the broken rules by giving him baksheesh (tip/bribe). This is a scenario that repeats itself with tiresome frequency throughout Egypt; which is not to say that we didn't snap a few pictures here and there.

The last stop on our day tour was Dashur. Dashur is situated another ten kilometers south and features two more impressive pyramids, the oddly shaped Bent Pyramid, a result of poor engineering, and the world's oldest true pyramid, the Red Pyramid. Here again we did the Indiana Jones thing and scrambled down into the tomb. One of the big pluses to Saqqara and Dashur is that they are less visited than Giza. Instead of rubbing shoulders with thousands, we often had rooms and plazas all to our lonesome. Believe us; that's a very cool thing when you crawl down a 190 foot ladder-steep, one meter square, shaft into the heart of a pyramid.

The interior of the Red Pyramid is awesome. At the bottom of the tunnel we found ourselves in the first of two antechambers with thirty-six foot high corbelled ceilings. In the second chamber a two storey scaffolding-like stair leads to the burial chamber itself with an even more incredible forty-five foot high ceiling. By the time we were ready to leave, other tourists were climbing down the shaft; but for a while, it was just us, the graffiti of 19th century explorers, and the ghost of Sneferu.

Day 259 - September 20 - Monday

This morning we took a long walk to visit the quirky Gayer-Anderson Museum. The museum was the home of a British officer who between 1935 and 1942 restored two adjoining 16th century houses and then filled them with antiques and collectibles. On his death, he donated the home to the Egyptian government and it has since been preserved as an example of life of that period. Inside the four storey museum it is stifling hot and a bit worse for wear, but still well worth the effort.

We also visited the huge Mosque of Ibn Tulun, which shares a wall with the museum, and climbed to the top of its tall minaret for impressive views of Old Cairo and the city's hilltop Citadel.

Egypt can be a bit weird at times, lots of people here are friendly and helpful, but lots of other people see you simply as a mark. On our way back from the museum we stopped at a group of fruit stands to buy a couple of apples. One vendor with a nice display waved us over so we drifted that way. The moment we walked up he began talking to us in rapid-fire Arabic. Thanks to our two weeks of classes in Morocco, we were able to understand and respond to "Where are you from?" Beyond that we were limited to "I don't understand," and "How much?" When the vendor responded; we still didn't know how much. After a couple of tries, we gave up and handed him a five pound note. We expected change, but none was forth coming. Instead the vendor began to cackle gleefully and wave the five pound note at other vendors. Loosely translated, he was clearly spouting something on the order of, "Look at this! These stupid tourists gave me five pounds for two apples and a pear! What morons!" To put this "rip-off" in perspective, the poor guy was gloating extravagantly over cheating us out of the difference between what we should have paid and $0.88; pretty sad. Just down the street, we purchased several pita breads from a woman for $0.44 and she thanked us profusely and kissed the coins; go figure.

Walking in Cairo is an extreme adventure sport not for the faint of heart. The sidewalks are broken and uneven, mined with holes of various sizes, cluttered with trash and impromptu sheesha cafes, and punctuated at intervals with odd bits of metal set into the concrete (pedestrian tank traps). It's simpler to just walk in the street, but traffic makes that even scarier. We thought crossing the streets in Marrakech was tough. Getting around in Cairo is like starring in a live action version of Frogger. Even when lights are red, traffic rarely stops; eventually you just have to step off the curb, pucker your sphincter, and make like a running back. Be it fragile old ladies, pregnant women with toddlers in tow, suited businessmen, or terrified tourists; cars do not stop, they just lay on the horn to let you know that if you don't dodge fast enough you're dead meat. On really busy streets people congregate at the corners until combined weight gives them a false sense of security. When that critical mass is reached, everyone moves quickly into the traffic braving the blaring klaxons and angry protests of harried drivers. Thank God for rare Metro underpasses and the occasional traffic cop (also largely ignored).

Back at the hotel, we spent the rest of the day on the Internet once again trying to find tickets for an exit flight from India. We purchased our inbound tickets without too much agony because we knew more or less what we want to see in Egypt and how long it will take. But India; sheesh, we have no idea! We just haven't thought that far ahead. Finally, at about 11 PM we tired of banging our heads against the walls and grabbed a flight that puts us in Phuket, Thailand just before Christmas.

Day 260 - September 21 - Tuesday

Today's first order of business was to ferret out an Internet place where we printed copies of our airline tickets. At about 9AM, paperwork in hand, we trotted back to the India Embassy.

"Yes, everything looks good. Just come back on Thursday and your visas will be ready." *Arrrgggh!*

"But, we've already purchased train tickets, by Thursday morning we'll be in Aswan!"

"I'm sorry, (paraphrased) but there are still I's to be dotted and T's to be crossed. Perhaps if you take a seat for a while I can pawn you off on someone else who won't be able to help you either but will make nice conciliatory noises." After a while we were ushered into the office of a pleasant consular officer whose main interest was the U.S. economy and where all the U.S. money went.

"Hey, hows about that recession?" The upshot is that we have to change our plans and make a second visit to Cairo. "Your visas will be ready no problem, by uh Thursday. Anytime after that you can just walk in and pick them up." *Great!*

Day 261 - September 22 - Wednesday

Several trains a day run between Cairo and Aswan, but because of security concerns, most are off limits to foreign tourists. Our sleeper train for Aswan doesn't board until about 10 PM, so we spent most of today more or less waiting. We checked out of the Hotel Osiris at noon, put our bags in their storage room, and hopped the Metro down to Coptic Cairo. Coptic Cairo is the old Christian section of the city and it boasts atmospheric cobbled alleyways that twist and turn amid high stone walls. Scattered along the alleys are Coptic and Greek Orthodox churches and monasteries some dating from the 3rd and 4th century. Underlying the entrance to the Coptic compound stand the remains of two Roman gate towers built in AD 98 by the Emperor Trajan to guard a riverfront fortification then called, "Babylon in Egypt." The highlight of the area is a beautiful museum that houses an impressive collection of Coptic, Islamic, and Greco-Roman art. Exhibits range from sculpture and woodcarving to textiles and frescos. We managed to kill a couple of sweltering hours wandering its halls.

Having exhausted Coptic Cairo's attractions, we rode the Metro back downtown. We ate a late lunch at a good restaurant called FelFella, and then headed back to the "lobby" of the Osiris to watch the clock and wait for our taxi to the train station.

Day 262 - September 23 - Thursday - Aswan, Egypt

Today was a good day. We woke up around 6:30 AM to the rhythmic clickty-clack of the train wheels. Outside, the Nile's greenbelt paraded past our window: date palms, plantings of corn and bananas, turbaned farmers already at work in their fields, donkey's, water wheels, camels, brown mud-brick villages, an occasional glimpse of felucca sails, and the river itself; not a bad way to wake up. Open our cabin door and look to the East and the scene is completely different: barren rock, sand, desert, here and there the occasional work of man huddled at the edge of a wasteland. The Nile is without a doubt the lifeblood of this country.

On arrival in Aswan we caught an overpriced taxi to our hotel. Unless you have inside information, it takes a couple of taxi rides in each new place before you get a handle on what you should really pay; in the meantime you get burned. This ride cost us twice the going rate. The only saving grace is that taxis are so cheap that even paying double we only spent an extra two dollars.

Nabil, at the Osiris recommended, and booked, the Hotel Keylany and it was a good steer. Set on a side street a half a block from a pedestrian souk and just one block from the Nile, it is situated in a great location right in the center of town. Our room is plain but includes a fridge, always a big plus, and AC, pretty much essential. On its fifth floor rooftop, breakfast is served in a Bedouin-tent-style shaded enclosure which shares the space with a small but refreshing plunge pool ($30/night).

Once we settled in, we headed off to explore. Our first stops were several Nile-side travel agencies where we shopped for a cruise from Aswan back to Luxor. After hitting three places, we decided that we'd done our due diligence and handed our credit card to a Thomas Cook agent. They did the best job of describing (selling) their package, but since they weren't the cheapest we managed to squeeze them for a small discount. In Egypt fixed prices are always more of a suggestion than a reality.

Next up on our agenda was a long hot (aren't they all) walk to Aswan's Nubia Museum. You'd think that by this point we'd be starting to get jaded by museums, but it just isn't happening. The Nubia Museum is excellent. It was established in 1997 with the help of UNESCO to preserve the Nubian culture, much of which was lost when the waters of the High Aswan Dam flooded their homeland. Arranged in chronological order (we didn't know and walked backwards) the exhibits carry you through 6,000 years of history. Everything is beautifully displayed, and before we knew it several hours slipped by.

Since it was now way too hot to walk, we took another taxi back to the Keylany. This ride cost us twenty-five percent less. Overcharging was still the order of the day, but with the sun cooking on broil we weren't in the mood to haggle.

Day 263 - September 24 - Friday

This morning we took the public ferry to Elephantine Island in the middle of the Nile. Locals pay one pound for the out-and-back ride. We were nicked five pounds each. Oh well, we're getting used to it; sort of.

Elephantine Island is a terrific spot to while away part of a day. At its north end are scattered the ruins of Ancient Abu which date from around 3,000 BC. At their entrance you also encounter the Aswan Museum. Walking south, you pass through a living Nubian village, an agricultural area, and then another village.

Our first stop was the museum. Its dusty collection of Aswan and Nubian artifacts are housed in a rundown nineteenth century villa that once belonged to the architect of the Old Aswan Dam. A newer wing was added in 1998. Nothing on display was standout and we breezed through in about thirty minutes.

Walking around behind the museum, we passed through the remains of the villa's garden, and entered the ruins of Abu. As soon as we stepped inside a pair of caretaker's latched onto us and began to show us around. We knew that this was going to lead to an obligatory outlay of baksheeh, but since they seemed to know their stuff, we didn't quibble. The best trick they pulled out of their turbans was a live brightly colored scarab beetle which went nicely with the impressive wall art. Abu is really interesting. It's not as well preserved or as highly decorated as some other sites, but it's highly evocative of a once living city. We really got a kick out of the "Nilometer of the Satet Temple." This is a long series of steps that lead down to the river dropping through what was originally an enclosed passage. As you descend, you see niches in the walls that once held oil lamps and etched into the stone is a scale for measuring the river's rise and fall. More than a nicety, this was essential stuff. The height of the spring flood determined the abundance of the year's harvest, and in turn told the pharaoh's bureaucrats how heavily they could tax the local farmers.

After about five minutes with our "guides," one of them left us for greener pastures in the form of a German tour group. The other "guide" stuck with us for another twenty minutes or so, poking into the various temples, and showing us the highlights. When the "official" tour ended, we slipped him twenty pounds ($3.55) and he went merrily on his way. We wandered on our own for another half-hour and then headed back toward the garden. As we were stepping through the fence, the other "guide" reappeared with another scarab beetle in hand and suggested that we keep it as a souvenir.

"Uh, no thanks, no way to carry it."

"Okay, (paraphrased) where's my baksheesh?"

"We already gave to the other guy."

"But, what about me?"

"Talk to your friend." *Sorry dude, it ain't going to happen!*

Back in front of the museum, we strolled in the direction of the first Nubian village. As we approached, a man in a traditional outfit came toward us.

"Hello, where you from? Welcome to my village. I'm the chief. This is my village. Would you like a tour? Cheap price, only fifty pounds! I'm the chief."

If you're the chief of anything, I'm friggin Lawrence of Arabia! "No thank you. We're just out walking."

"Cheap price, I'm the chief!" Blocked in that direction we turned back toward the ferry dock. When the "chief" was sufficiently far behind, we turned and walked back into the village by a different route.

The village was colorful, tranquil, and easy to navigate on our own. After a few minutes stroll we passed into cool irrigated gardens that make up the center of the island. Here a man works his field, there a woman hurries with bundles on her head, here another man washes his goat; walking along the sometimes shady sometimes sun splashed path was a joy.

As we worked our way into a second village, we saw small hand painted arrows reading, “Nubian House.” They pointed in as good a direction as any and we let them lead us along narrow streets, between mud walls where goats sheltered from the sun and old men sat smoking. The “Nubian House” turned out to be traditionally painted, bright and colorful; a home that was a sort of café/crafts store/guesthouse perched on the island’s east shore. Stepping through the home’s blue picket goat gate into its entrance hall we were greeted by Mustapha, its owner. Mustapha brought us a couple of cold Sprites and then sat down with us in a cool breezeway. The three of us spent the next half hour in easy conversation; Denise and I asking questions and Mustapha telling us about his life and culture. Although into his thirties, our host wasn’t married. It turns out that traditional Nubians believe that when a couple marries they must move into their own home and everything in that home must be new; new bed, new sofa, new chairs, new TV, etc. Mustapha is still saving.

After this enjoyable experience, we ferried back to the mainland and spoiled the warm fuzzy feeling with another rip-off. Although we’re perfectly comfortable at the Keylany, we decided to go check out another fancier hotel called the Sara that is located on a bluff with stunning views of the Nile; the grass is always greener. The Sara was a couple of kilometers away so we grabbed a taxi. We know what you’re thinking, but no, this one charged us a fair price. When we arrived at the hotel, we spoke to a receptionist and asked to see a room. The room was a little better appointed than the one we were in and the views were great but not worth the $75 a night rate. We asked for a discount, everything in Egypt is negotiable, and they agreed to knock off another $5. That still didn't get our motors running, but as long as we were there and it was lunch time we figured we might as well grab a bite.

The receptionist escorted us up to their restaurant (nice, sort of upscale), introduced us to our waiter, and explained that we weren't staying in the hotel but that we were going to eat lunch.

"What you like to drink?"

"Uh, I don't know, may we see a menu?"

"We have beer, cola, wine, everything what you like?"

"How much is a Stella (beer)?"

"Twenty Bob." *Hmm, that's a little high.*

"Okay, I'll take a Stella."

"What you want to eat?"

"We're not sure, may we see a menu?"

"No menu, we got everything; chicken, fish, kabab, kofta, what you want?"

"May we see a menu?"

"We got everything, what you want?"

"Uh, how much is the kofta?"

"Sixty Bob." *Hmm, that's a little high.*

"Okay, we'll take a chicken and a kofta."

"One chicken, one kofta, one Stella, okay!"

The beer arrived first, then tiny bowls of lentil soup. This was followed by small green salads, some bread, and then the chicken and kofta dishes. Everything was edible but nothing to suggest the place was worth a second visit. The meal finished with a bit of fruit while the waiter hovered nearby chatting us up.

"Here is picture of my daughter, etc, etc, blah, blah, blah." Then he presents us the bill and yikes it's like 200 pounds!

"Hey, we thought you said the kofta and chicken were sixty pounds."

"Yes, but soup, salad, bread, fruit, taxes, blah, and blah, blah." Even though the only things we actually ordered were the beer and the two mains, we paid the bill and even reluctantly tipped him; little daughter and all.

As we were walking back through the lobby, the hotel's manager approached us.

"Are you going to stay with us? Did you enjoy your meal?"

Denise gave him an icy stare, "Frankly, we're upset!"

"What; why?" We explained about the meal and he asked to see our receipt.

"We don't have one."

"Wait here, I'll be right back." A few minutes later the manager returned with the sheepish waiter in tow. Parking the guy in front of us, he spoke harshly to him and made him dig in his pocket and hand us fifty pounds. Turns out, the guy kept the menu from us so that he could overcharge us, and then trashed the receipt so that he could pocket all the cash instead of putting it in the till. After the waiter left, the manager sat down and explained that many people in Egypt don't make much money and because of this they try to take advantage of tourists.

"You need to always be on your guard." *No kidding, what a pleasant custom!* He then he offered us the hotel room for $50 per night by way of apology. *Uh, thanks but no thanks.*

Day 264 - September 25 - Saturday - Abu Simbel, Egypt

There are undoubtedly certain light sleepers who like to leap out of bed at 2:45 AM. Denise and I don't fall into that demographic. First the telephone rang; our wake up call. While I fumbled for it, the alarm went off; our backup. Then, someone knocked on our hotel room door; their backup. The goal of all this wee hour commotion was to get us up and moving for our 3:10 AM day tour to Abu Simbel.

2:45, 3:10; you gotta be kidding, why that early? The answer lies with a 1990's Islamic Insurgency and with the 1997 massacre of tourists at Luxor. Watching the spigot of tourist dollars twist closed (twenty percent of its total revenue), the Egyptian government cast about frantically for a way to protect tourists (and their dollars). Voila, the convoy system whereby foreigners can only travel to certain areas in guarded police convoys. Over intervening years, tensions and incidents have decreased and much of the convoy system was dismantled in 2009. So where is the convoy system still firmly in place you ask? Why between Aswan and Abu Simbel of course and evidently some gung ho type decided that the best time to depart is long before the crack of dawn.

We might be naïve but the whole thing seems like a farce. At 4 AM we waited at the convoy assembly point drinking over priced tea, purchased from a noisy vendor who cackled with delight as he gouged one tourist after another, while assorted flavors of tour buses, mini-vans, and taxis gathered waiting to reach some unfathomable level of critical mass. When the moment finally came, drivers started their engines, tourists scrambled for their seats, and the whole caboodle roared off down the road. Like Dale Unger wanta-bes on an off day the drivers jockeyed for position; passing and being passed as if a first-place prize waited at the end of the trip and we wouldn't all arrive at the same time. If there were police with the convoy, we didn't see them. There were uniforms and guns in evidence at the assembly point, but once we hit the highway it seemed to be every man for himself. We passed a decrepit checkpoint just outside of Aswan and another just before Abu Simbel but that was it. All the drivers hauled ass at their own speed and you were lucky to see the tail lights of another bus much less an escort. The system may no longer offer anything in the way of security, but it does guarantee that every tourist who visits Abu Simbel pays top dollar to get there. The only sanctioned methods are: airplane, cruise ship, or tour bus /private taxi in convoy. "Oh, we got a great big convoy... Come on; sing along, you know the words."

Despite the overpriced tea, the trip was a blurry, head-nodding, jerk-awake three hours with little to recommend it. On the good side we arrived at Abu Simbel just after sunrise when the light was beautiful. The Great Temple of Ramses and the Temple of Hathor sited at the edge of Lake Nasser are amazing. Even though you know they were moved, it's still hard to look at the four colossal statues of Ramses II and not imagine them sitting sentinel; unchanged for thousands of years. The temple was supposedly built to watch over Egypt's southern border and warn potential miscreants of pharaoh's power. It works. Walking under his gigantic statues makes you feel like a piss-ant. Inside The Great Temple, are more statues and mind blowing carved reliefs; Ramses in his chariot shooting arrows at his fleeing foes, Ramses and Nefertiti in front of the gods, one scene after another; many still bright with color.

Hathor's temple is smaller in scale; its six statues of Ramses and Nefertiti only reaching to a measly thirty feet tall. In this temple Nefertiti dresses up as the goddess Hathor and gets equal billing with Ramses. Usually pharaohs had their consorts carved about knee high but Ramses thought so much of his squeeze (she looks hot) that he ordered her carved as tall as himself (well almost). The artwork in this temple is concerned more with feminine themes, respect for the gods and daily life, and less with Ramses' prowess as a warrior. Somehow it feels more accessible.

There were lots of people at the site, remember we all arrived at the same time, but it was definitely worth the hassle to get there. There aren't too many places in the world that have the overawing presence of Abu Simbel. Mount Rushmore might reach that point in about three thousand years, but right now Abu Simbel has the inside track.

An hour and a half after we arrived, we dutifully tramped back to our mini-bus to catch the return convoy. What a great system! The three hour drive back was, if anything, worse than the drive out; at least on the way out it was dark. With the sun fully up, we got to see the unlivable side of Egypt in all its glory, or lack thereof. Talk about wasteland, nothing but stony desert in all directions as far as the eye can see. To be fair, the land has a harsh grandeur about it, but that only manages to hold your attention for ten to fifteen minutes. After that, it's read, nod off, or squint at the far off horizon. Maybe that early wake up was a good call after all.

Are we glad we went to Abu Simbel? You betcha! Was it worth it? Sure! Would we do it a second time? No way, unless we fly, sail down the Nile, or Egypt cans the convoy.

When we signed up for our tour we booked the "Long" option which threw in three more sights, each of which also carried an additional entrance fee. The first of these was the mighty High Aswan Dam. It wasn't on our "must see" list but we figured, *Why not?*

Since the dam was on our way back to Aswan, we rolled up to its entrance gate with eighteen passengers on board, about half of whom had gone for the "Short Tour" option. The driver opened the door and with the help of an English/Arabic speaking passenger told all of these people that they each needed to pay the dam's twenty pound entrance fee or get off the bus and wait twenty minutes or so until the rest of us, and the bus, returned. Outside the bus' door it was maybe 120 degrees and there was nothing out there but a concrete sidewalk baking in the scorching midday sun. Some of the "Shorties" got off; others wanted to stay on board but didn't want to pay. Still others, got off, experienced the heat, and immediately climbed back in. One Japanese girl shrilly snapped, "Alright! Alright! I give you money!" Eventually things were sorted out and most of us rolled off to see the dam while a few diehards stayed behind for a close encounter of the solar kind. The diehards got the better deal. The admission fee was about $3.50 per person, but all that bought you was a ticket to stand at an equally sweltering view point and gaze at a totally uninteresting rock slope. "What about the power plant and the flood gates?" you ask; far out of sight and completely off limits.

As we climbed off the bus the driver dutifully handed each of us our official entrance ticket. We then had to present the ticket at a security booth, pass through a metal detector (everyone beeped), and have our hand bags and knapsacks run through a scanner (no one watching the screen). As we exited the booth we looked back and realized that it wasn't an actual entrance to anything. The checkpoint just stands there by itself with people milling around on all sides. We suspect it's there to give tourists the feel that they get something for their money. We could have walked right on past and we seriously doubt anyone would have cared.

Back on the bus, with the Shorties still in tow, we next drove to Shellal the jumping off point for Philae and the Temple of Isis. This time the driver dumped us "Longies" off with a stern admonition to be back at such and such a time and continued back to Aswan with our short trip companions.

Lakeside Shellal, where we were dropped, features a semi-obligatory row of tat stands, a ticket booth, a dock, and its own bit of craziness. You buy a $10 ticket to visit the archaeological site, but that doesn't get you there. Philae is an island and like the sign says "Boot not included." Before you can hand your ticket to anyone, you have to negotiate with boatmen on the dock to ferry you out to the island (and back). After a bit of confusion, our group split into two boats and headed out. Our hotel had warned us about the boat thing so for us it was no big deal, just another $2 per person; like part of the entrance fee. Some of our companions didn't take it as well. About a hundred yards from the dock, the other boat made a U-turn and headed back. As it passed us the Arab speaking guy, Israeli by way of Australia, cupped his hands and yelled, "I'm refusing to pay!" After complaining at the ticket booth and getting police involved to enforce an "official" price, he did manage to pay less, but the upshot was that his boat blew half their sightseeing time haggling over a dollar. Their time would have been much better spent at the Temple of Isis which turned out to be a really cool place.

On reaching the island you walk uphill from the dock and, as you climb, the temple's structures rise into view. First your eyes are caught by the imposing Kiosk of Trajan a square of monumental columns topped with huge artistic capitals. To the left stands the equally impressive temple of Isis itself; with monumental fifty-foot high towers and a sprawling colonnaded forecourt. Everywhere you turn the ancient walls and columns jump to life with fascinating relief carvings depicting offerings to the gods and aspects of ancient life. If it hadn't been so hot, we'd probably have wished for more time.

After motoring back from the island on our launch the "Missy," we hooked up again with our driver and bus. Next on our planned itinerary, was a visit to the "Unfinished Obelisk," a 42 meter long, 1168 ton, chunk of unadorned granite. About two kilometers outside of Aswan, it lies in a quarry where ancient Egyptian stonemasons left it in disgust after it developed a flaw.

By this point in the day, the idea of another 30 EGP per person entrance fee just to see a bare rock sitting under the unrelenting sun didn't fire anyone's imagination. We all took a vote and decided that the Unfinished Obelisk could wait for another visit. The Israeli/Australian guy told our driver, but he didn't buy it and asked for another show of hands. With all of us voting to bag the obelisk, the confused driver said that we still had to go. We didn't have to go in, but he still HAD to take us there. After a ten minute drive we pulled up in front of the quarry ticket booth. "Does anyone want to go in?" Blank looks of disbelief; flummoxed, the driver took us back to our hotel. Nobody tipped him.

Day 265 - September 26 - Sunday

The Keylany is a nice budget hotel. We had a little visitor this morning. *Eeek, a prospecting mouse!* We shooed it out of our room and stuffed a towel under the door.

Day 267 - September 28 - Tuesday - On the Nile, Egypt

We spent the past two nights on a Nile cruise. It's a semi-obligatory thing to do in Egypt and we'd probably do it over again but the reality is less romantic than the idea. At 11 AM a Thomas Cook town car with two suited representatives (we were impressed) picked us up at our hotel, took us to our ship, and helped us to register. At first they were going to put us into a water level cabin where you can't see over the Nile's banks, "Nope, no way!" We bitched that the Thomas Cook office had promised us an upper deck.

"Sorry, but the ship is full, blah, blah, blah..." At that point we both dug in our heels and pitched a minor hissy.

When I let loose with, "I guess we'll never travel with Thomas Cook again," suddenly an upper cabin became available.

Although nicer than most of the other ships that we saw working the river, ours was still only on a par with a midrange hotel; okay room, mediocre food, overpriced drinks, cheesy entertainment, and so-so amenities. Also, you don't cruise that much. We boarded at noon and then sat at the dock in Aswan until around 2:30. By 5:00 PM we were tied up amid thick reeking clouds of diesel exhaust, along with about twenty other boats, for a one hour stop at the excellent temple at Kom Ombo.

When we returned early from our shore excursion, our boat was pulling away! *Oh Crap! Where's it going?*

Ships raft up to the dock three and four deep, and if you're on an outer one you need to walk across gangways and through other vessels to reach the shore. If one of the inner ships gets ready to leave, all the outer ones have to cast off and find a new position. We stood on the dock for roughly twenty minutes while our boat sailed back and forth playing musical chairs. Once it finally managed to dock, it was moored at a completely different location from where it let us off! *Well, that's interesting.* Before re-boarding, we waited another twenty minutes while the ship that was closest to the shore figured out how to lower its jammed gangplank.

Once we all stampeded back on board, a short cruise in the dark left us and the rest of the flotilla rafted together at Edfu for the night. After breakfast we motored through the Nile's locks and tied up at Luxor by early afternoon. We spent the rest of that day and night sitting on the docked ship next to thirty other docked ships. The following morning, we took an overpriced taxi into town. The "new" cruise dock is located seven kilometers from downtown so, unless you are part of a group tour, taxi drivers have you by the short hairs.

Despite its drawbacks (and there were a lot) the cruise was fun. The time we spent topside simply soaking it all in as the shores of the Nile slipped by was a not to be missed experience.

Day 272 - October 3 - Sunday - Luxor, Egypt

It's the evening of our fourth full day in Luxor and according to locals it's unusually hot (120° F). When Denise can't spend more than an hour by the pool, you know it's sweltering. We're holed up in the Hotel St. Joseph which, at $30 per night, might be our best deal so far. Our 5th floor room is large, clean, and comfortable. We have: AC, a fridge, cable TV (mostly Arabic), and a private balcony with killer views overlooking the Nile and the West Bank Necropolis. In the interest of full disclosure, the view also includes a defunct sewage treatment plant (next door to the Club Med), but it's not something that grabs your attention. A great buffet breakfast is included in the room price, and there's a rooftop bar/restaurant and swimming pool. A second restaurant is located on the ground floor, and there's a second bar in the basement (haven't tried it but we know it's there). The hotel is located on Luxor's main drag, the "Corniche" a street that parallels the east bank of the Nile. It's only about a fifteen minute walk from the hotel to Luxor Temple and ten minutes by taxi to Karnak. As an added bonus, the street that runs along the hotel's north side is lined with good restaurants and cafes.

The afternoons here cook, so we do most of our out-and-about stuff in the morning. The mornings are still warm but the temperature doesn't start to reach insufferable until around noon.

On our first day after we transferred from the cruise dock, we didn't do much; just settled into our hotel, tested out the pool, watched dozens of white-sailed feluccas flit back and forth across the river, and investigated the local restaurant scene.

On day two, we walked to the train station and purchased sleeper car tickets for our return trip to Cairo (safer to reserve in advance). The ticketing isn't computerized and we waited in the stifling station for twenty minutes shooing flies and feeling sweat drip down the back of our knees (about 9 AM). Meanwhile the ticket agent with a phone in each hand made repeated calls trying to confirm our booking. Finally, as we reached a stage of doneness just short of broasted, the tickets appeared. We beat a measured retreat and headed for the marginally cooler locales next to the river.

We walked up the sidewalk by the Nile, ogled Luxor Temple from outside the fence, and then went on to the Luxor Museum, where we spent a couple of hours inside. The Luxor Museum has a much (much) smaller collection than the museum in Cairo, but it wins the esthetics competition hands down. It is air conditioned and everything from statues to mummies is tastefully displayed and clearly labeled. We really enjoyed the visit. After that it was back to our hotel for pool time followed by a quality AC fueled nap.

On day three we set our clock and hopped out of bed dark-and-early, 5:00 AM, so that we could catch The Temple of Karnak right when it opened. By the time we sleep-walked down to the restaurant a half hour later, bleary-eyed waiters were laying out the buffet. Fortified with food and more importantly coffee, we stepped out of the restaurant and Denise spied the lobby clock. It read 5:05.

"Hi, is your clock slow?"

"Time change! No see notice in elevator?" *Okay, so exercise is good but there's a downside to using the stairs.*

The unexpected change threw us for a loop, but after we piddled around for a bit, it turned out that our timing was just about right. A taxi drove us past the remains of a three kilometer sphinx lined avenue (few remain) and we arrived at Karnak right at the crack of dawn. We sat on stone steps and watched a glorious sun rise while we waited fifteen minutes for the ticket booth to open. The entrance fee for two is about $25 USD; Egypt nicks you pretty hard for its sights, but you can't really blame them.

Because we beat the ticket seller to his post, we also beat the daily hordes of other tourists. For almost an hour and a half we shared the temple with only four other people; a most excellent way to see it.

"Monumental" immediately leaps to the tip of your tongue, but it doesn't do the temple justice. Karnak transcends, and its tumbledown grandeur overwhelms. The path from the ticket booth took us between a row of ram-headed stone sphinxes and then on through an enormous unfinished gateway known as the First Pylon. Our footsteps were the only sounds amid the ancient stone; everything bathed in the soft glow of morning light. To our left and right stood temples dedicated to Theban gods and pharaohs of old, before us towered huge statues and a single sixty foot column.

Karnak is vast, a massive complex that sprawls over more than two square kilometers. According to historians, construction began around 1950 BC and the temple was continuously built, enlarged, torn down, added to, and restored for an astonishing 1,500 to 2,000 years! Called Ipet-Isut, "Most Esteemed of Places," by the Egyptians of the Middle Kingdom, Karnak was revered as the place of creation, the spot where Amun-Ra made the first mound of earth rise from the dark waters of chaos.

At its height, the temple was staffed by more than 80,000 people! Its scale is enormous.

Stepping through a second great stone gateway, we entered the Temple of Amun, reputed to be the largest religious building ever built. We can buy it. The space beyond the Second Pylon is called the Great Hypostyle Hall, and great it is! Huge rounded columns tower above your head; the shadowy interior of the hall, a symbolic papyrus swamp. Standing among those pillars is like standing amid the hushed primordial giants of an old growth forest; their air of age and mystery conspicuous, their presence tangible. Each of the columns is exuberantly incised with hieroglyphics, symbols that are at once both familiar and inscrutable. When we looked closely, we could see faded colors hinting at a brighter past.

The Great Hypostyle Hall is Karnak's heart but it's only one of the temple's amazing sights. Everywhere we looked our eyes played across colossal wonders: titan sized statues, pharaohs ankh in hand, soaring obelisks, a shimmering sacred lake, gargantuan stone blocks, a giant stone scarab, a grinning life-size baboon, and hieroglyphics far and wide.

As we wandered through another of Karnak's main structures, the Temple of Khonsu god of the moon, a man dressed in a traditional galabiya and turban stepped out of the shadows.

"Hello, where you from? You want to see pictures?"

"Uh, sure." Leading us forward, he waves us past a rickety barricade and a sternly worded "Keep Out" sign. *Hmmm!* Next, he pulls out a key and opens a padlock securing a wire cage-like door. Pointing at a "No Admittance" sign tacked to the door, he puts a finger to his lips, "Shsssss!" *Okay, we get it; this is another no-no baksheesh experience.*

Past the wire door, we entered a small sweltering room. White plaster covered its walls and painted upon them; dramatic hieroglyphics and a handsome linen-skirted pharaoh making an offering to his god. The room was stuffy, but the colors were as bright and wonderful as the day the artist first dipped his brush. We don't know the age of the paintings, but Ramses III built most of Khonsu's temple sometime between 1186 and 1155 BCE; awesome!

Later, slowly poking our way here and there, we walked over to the Temple of Ptah, a structure that nestles against the Amun Temple's north enclosure wall. As we neared the cult temple, an armed and uniformed security guard approached. "Hello, where you from..." *Okay-dokey, here we go again.* Chatting us up, the guard tagged along. When we reached the temple he smiled. "You want to see statue?" At that point, he called over another man. After a moment of slightly heated discussion (in Arabic), the second man pulled out a set of keys and opened yet another locked door.

Entering a darkened chamber we found ourselves staring at an otherworldly statue of the lioness-headed goddess, Sekhmet. Standing perhaps eight feet tall, the dark granite figure is as beautiful as she is strange. Lissome and regal, with a staff in one hand and an ankh in the other; a sun-disk behind her head, she stares out across the ages with feline intensity. Denise and I were both excited when she agreed to pose for a couple of pictures.

As we again stepped out into the sun, the guard held out his hand, "Baksheesh." I dug into my pocket and handed him what seemed an appropriate amount.

The second man held out his hand. "Baksheesh."

I turned to the guard. "We already paid you."

"You pay him too!" We weren't happy, but he had the uniform and the gun so I went back into my pocket. We gave five Egyptian pounds to the guy who showed us the pictures and he went away happy. These two bandits held out for twenty. Egypt's constant demands for baksheesh are a real buzz-kill, but they're also a way of life. You go with the flow.

At the end of our Karnak visit, we strolled over to a waiting calèche. Calèches are horse-drawn carriages that ply the Luxor tourist trade offering a leisurely alternative to the town's hurtling taxis. The upside is open air sightseeing at a clip-clop pace; the downside is uber-haggle before you climb aboard.

"How much do you want to take us to the Hotel St. Joseph?"

"Hotel St. Joseph? That will be ..."

"No, that's way too much, how about ..."

"I can't accept that, you must pay at least ..."

"No, that's still too much, we'll give you ..."

"No, that's not enough I can't take less than ..."

"Okay never mind, we'll walk." We turn and head off down the street. By the time we get twenty yards the guy realizes that we really mean to walk.

"Okay, okay, I take you."

The ride back to the hotel was pleasant, but then we looked more closely at our coach's horse. The unfortunate beastie was skinny and wheezy and there were bald patches on his back and flanks from a poorly padded harness. We're talking a horse with one hoof in the glue factory. Since we'd pushed a hard bargain, our driver wanted to be shed of us quickly, and forced his sad animal along at a trot. When the horse stumbled, that was enough. We told the driver to stop, thanked him for his service, and hopped out. We hear that Egypt has some sort of organization for the protection of working horses; somehow we don't think this guy belonged.

As we already wrote, today is day four of our stay in Luxor. Since no visit here is complete without a pilgrimage to the Valley of the Kings, that's how we spent our morning. Luxor sits on the east bank of the Nile. For millennia the west bank, the direction of the setting sun, was considered a hopping off spot for the afterlife, a land of the dead and the perfect place any upscale royal tomb. The easiest way to get there today is on a private guided excursion so we booked a half day through our hotel. The cost was a reasonable $44 US not including tips or entrance fees (another $61) for both of us.

After breakfast, our driver and our guide, Kamal, picked us up in their sedan and we headed across the Nile. The west bank is home to a number of interesting sights, but our first stop was the Valley of the Kings itself. Barren and isolated there's little about the valley to make you suspect the treasures buried beneath its rocky soil. Of course, we suppose that was the whole point.

When you arrive, you park in a lot, and then you take a tram to the entrance where you begin walking. Although the entire area is riddled with tombs, almost nothing is visible on the surface, just gravel paths leading to yawning entrances. To prevent overuse, access to individual tombs is limited on a rotating basis.

At each open tomb, Kamal gave us some background about its owner and its construction, and then turned us loose to plunge inside while he smoked a cigarette. Between looting and removal for preservation, furnishings are long gone, but the crypts still fascinate.

Some consist of a single chamber others are multi-roomed and elaborate. To enter, we walked down steep shafts where the air was close and hot. Several sweltering tombs were enough to wear us out, but the payoff was stellar. Chambers are bare, but elaborately decorated walls remain, some monochromatic, others brilliant in their color. Along one wall Isis and Nephthys worship the solar disc, along another sweep scenes of Nut the sky goddess, pharaohs at prayer, the Book of the Gates, the Book of Caverns, the Book of Day and Night, and the Book of the Dead; room after room filled with strictures for an eternal life. Standing in those stuffy vaults it was easy to imagine, flickering lamplight and scribes hard at work. It's a wonderful thing when art holds the power to transcend the passage of time.

That's the upside. Unfortunately, The Valley of the Kings also has an unpleasant other side. We arrived well before the day's motor coach hordes, but as we left they were wandering in, aggressively pursued by an army of persistent vendors. It's difficult to overstate Egypt's hard sell. We watched appalled as a French woman, literally in tears, tried to escape from an in-your-face merchant. He sensed her weakness, knew that he had her on the ropes, and waving his trinkets flatly refused to take "no" for an answer. Talk about killing the goose that lays the golden egg; simply unbelievable!

Leaving behind The Valley of the Kings with its wonders and its ugly sales tableau, we headed over to the temple of Egypt's female pharaoh, Hatshepsut. This beautiful limestone building is even more impressive because of the spectacular cliffs that soar upward behind it. Larger than life statues of the god queen, resplendent with her fake beard, stand before square pillars of the temple's colonnaded façade and dark recesses hide ancient traces of color. By the time we finished exploring the sun was out in full force and we were both dripping in sweat.

A cold overpriced soda at the snack bar and we were off to The Valley of the Queens. Like its male counterpart The Valley of the Queens is another necropolis, but this time the maze of underground tombs was built to house the mortal remains of: queens, princesses, and other royal relatives. For the casual visitor (us) the sightseeing experience is enjoyable, but much the same. *Hmmm, maybe we're experiencing tomb overload?*

The last stop on our half day tour was the Colossi of Memnon. The Colossi are two giant enthroned statues, each cut from a single block of stone and each weighing as much as 1,000 tons. Once upon a time, they were center pieces of a huge memorial temple; a great mud brick structure that has weathered away until all that remains are two enigmatic faceless giants and their lonely vigil; way cool!

Day 275 - October 6 - Wednesday - Cairo, Egypt

We haven't kept up our journal so now we're playing catch-up again. From Luxor, we caught another sleeper train back to Cairo. Compared to the train we took in Turkey, the sleepers here in Egypt are adequate, but a little shabby. The cars look like they're maybe thirty years old and indifferently maintained. Our sleeping compartments on both trains were clean, but in Egypt you don't want to look too closely. Included meals are served airplane style in your room and are unbelievably mediocre. It's as though someone worked at it to make them uninteresting and bland. And the toilets; well... let's not go there.

We arrived in Cairo, and haggled a cab from the train station back to the Hotel Osiris where we'd booked one more night. Our idea was that we'd scamper over to the India Embassy, pick up our visas, then the next morning an outfit called Samo Tours would pick us up and drive us to the Sinai. Fitting action to plan, we dropped our bags at the hotel, grabbed our passports, and headed for the embassy. As we approached, we noticed that the grubby flag was missing from their balcony. *Hmmm, that's weird.* The building was unusually quiet and our foreboding grew as we climbed the dirty stairwell toward the third floor. Suddenly, there it was, a white computer printout taped to the door; "Closed for Egypt Victory Day, will resume regular business Thursday 10/07 at 8:30 AM." "Aaarrrgggh!" in harmony. The rest of the day was a waking nightmare as we tried to reschedule our Sinai transfer and subsequent accommodations. Thank God for beer and hazelnuts on our balcony. Finally, about 9 PM, our emails got responses, our phone calls were returned, and everything appeared to fall back into place.

Day 276 - October 7 - Thursday - Sinai Peninsula, Egypt

Today started with our visa hassles belching out one last rattling gasp. We woke up early, showered, grabbed breakfast at the hotel, and yet again hiked over to the India embassy. Early birds that we are, we stepped through their door right after they opened.

"Hi, we'd like to pick up our visas."

"Yes, your passports please and 375 Egyptian pounds each." I pushed over the passports and 800 EGP.

"You don't have 50 Bob?"

Evidently no one in Egypt carries change except for tourists! It doesn't matter what you're paying for or to whom, you're expected to cough up the exact amount. It's not that they can't make change; they can. They just don't want to give it to you. Everyone wants to hoard what they have. Now that we've caught on, we've taken to shaking our head sadly and saying that we're so sorry, but that's all we have; regardless of what's actually in our pockets. If you don't follow this strategy, pretty soon you end up with a wallet full of 200 pound Egyptian notes that no one wants.

Anyway, the receptionist behind the counter takes the fifty I give her and hands me back one of the hundreds. Sometimes it's politic to be flexible.

"Ok, thank you. Your visas will be ready when you come back on Saturday"

Aaargggghh! "No I'm sorry, that won't work, were leaving Cairo."

"When is your flight?"

"We don't have a flight; we leave on a tour to Sinai at 10:00 this morning!"

"That's too soon the visas must be signed."

"Look, we've been waiting for three weeks. The man we spoke to said that when we came back everything would be ready."

"He's not in."

"When does he get here?"

"Umm," she looks at her watch, "maybe 9:00. Take a seat." With locomotive-like steam whistling out of our ears we perched ourselves on the "Group W bench," gnashed our teeth, and counted the minutes as they ticked by.

The last thing our tour operator told us the night before was, "Be standing in front of your hotel at 10:00.

There's no parking outside, so we can't wait." As we slowly approached meltdown, the counselor officer wandered through the door. "Umm, let me see what I can do." It's all about knowing the right person; about 15 minutes later we hurried out with our visa stamped passports.

We hear that India learned the art of bureaucracy from the British. We didn't have the heart to tell the Canadian at the counter, who'd just been bumped from his flight to India, no visa, and needed one today, that he was shit out of luck. *Sorry dude; better just scratch that ten day visit off your itinerary and move on to your next country.*

A quick stop at an ATM to re-stuff the kitty and we still managed to hoof it back to the Osiris, grab our bags, and walk out onto the sidewalk just as the "Samo Tours" mini-van rounded the corner. We were on time. They were on time, so far so good. We stowed our gear in the back and settled into our seats while our driver, Mohamadi, and our guide, Hassan, introduced themselves. Then, Hassan asked that we pay in full and the haggling began.

We'd agreed on a price by email for a "private" transfer and tour that was supposed to take us from Cairo to St Katherine on the Sinai Peninsula, provide overnight lodging, a guide to assist with climbing Mt. Sinai, and then transfer us to Dahab. The problem was that the company wanted to drive from St Katherine to Sharm el-Sheikh to pick up four more people before continuing on to Dahab. This was fine with us, but we argued that since it added two hours to the trip and was no longer a private transfer that we should get a discount. Hassan called his boss who grudgingly authorized a $10 reduction. Did we mention that most of Egypt demands payment in U.S. dollars like they don't have a currency of their own! We were angry, but hey, we were already in their van whizzing out of Cairo; at some point you just have to grin and bear it.

Our route took us past a million dusty half constructed apartment buildings sitting in the desert east of the city. Evidently, someone thinks they're going to need a lot of burbs and elbow room. Right now the empty shells look like insanity.

Leaving behind the suburbs of tomorrow, we continued through empty barren lands that lead to the Suez Canal. Not much to see; this was all war zone forty years ago and today it still doesn't hold much except small isolated, *I'd kill myself if stationed here*, military camps. As the road approached the canal, we passed a series of round concrete guard posts. The sun is beating down. It's above 100 degrees outside and probably 212 inside the tiny oven shaped huts. Each phone-booth-sized hut casts a narrow sliver of shade and inside each sliver leans a bored looking young guard seeking elusive relief from the unremitting heat. *Holy Promised Land, glad we're not out there!*

We pass under the canal via a tunnel without ever seeing it. "Welcome to Asia!" Now were driving with the Gulf of Suez on our right and the dessert on our left. Hussan is feeling a bit sheepish about squeezing us on our bill so he throws us a bone by stopping for a quick peek at Ain Musa. Ain Musa or "Moses Springs" are the remains of a couple of brackish wells where Moses, with God's help, may or may not have performed a miracle that turned the water sweet and slaked the thirst of the Israelites. Whatever Moses did, it didn't last. Today, he'd need to change trash into water because that's all the wells contain. Add a few dusty date palms, a row of rickety tables selling trinkets, and a Korean tour group singing hymns, and you've got a darn good five minute rest stop.

Do you remember that scene in the movie "Lawrence of Arabia;" the one where he stumbles through the desert and suddenly sees the superstructure of a ship on the Suez Canal that moves mirage-like through the sand? We didn't see the ship or the Canal but we saw plenty of sand. On our right we slide past one large rundown or partially built beach development after another, a few cars parked here and there, but otherwise apparently empty. Hassan says that they're weekend places for Cairo's elite, and that right now it's midweek and kids are in school. We don't think we buy it; the places have an air of disuse.

To our left, the landscape is harsh and empty. A Bedouin woman wearing a black head-to-toe burqa walks out of a dry wash carrying a large bundle on her head. An existence hard to imagine; there's nothing out there.

As we turn inland to head toward St. Katherine the landforms become wild, eroded, and interesting; shades of tan, soft shapes, ragged shapes, eons of relentless wind, occasionally a town or structure that looks precarious and out of place. Isolated mud-brick houses sprout incongruous solar panels and satellite dishes. It's a magical hill country laced with the Zen of a Japanese rock garden.

Day 276 - October 7 - Thursday - Saint Katherine, Egypt

Last night, we again slept under mosquito nets; this time at the Hotel Daniela in St. Katherine. Mosquitoes seem weird in the middle of the desert, but there was also a can of bug spray on the dresser so evidently they're a problem. At 1:00 AM a waiter knocked on our door; another wake-up call, even earlier than the one for Abu Simbel. This one got us up and moving for our 2:00 AM hike up "Gebel Musa," Mt. Sinai. We threw on our clothes, I guzzled a cup of coffee, and then we crawled into our van for a five min drive to the trailhead and security checkpoint. After registering the two of us with the authorities, Hassan introduced us to our Bedouin guide, Salah.

Salah set a quick pace, and for the next two hours, 4.2miles, we wound ever upward through pitch blackness. Our world was steep and rocky, its limits defined by the soft glow of Denise's headlamp. The night was moonless, but overhead, stars whorled in frantic profusion, rare meteorites adding to the gaudy splendor.

Mt. Sinai is a popular place and our trail was far from empty. One minute we'd be walking in absolute silence and the next we'd find ourselves surrounded by a chattering group of Korean pilgrims practicing broken Arabic at the top of their lungs or a gaggle of Romanian peasant women softly singing hymns with their priest. Unlit lines of towering camels move past, specters from some dream of the Arabian Nights, saddles quietly creaking, tourists hanging on for dear life.

About a quarter mile below the summit the going gets steeper and the path switches from a trail to a series of 750 ragged stone steps. At this point everyone who made the climb by camel has to continue under their own power. It's a strange procession as many of the people shouldn't be there at all. Old, out of shape, way worse than us, and ill shod, they shuffle forward, driven huffing and puffing by their faith.

With forty-five minutes to spare before sunrise, we reached the top of the mountain and stood at the spot where Jehovah is said to have delivered his commandments to the Israelites. Perhaps 200 people waited for the dawn running the range from bearded chanting robed priests to board-short clad twenty-something day hikers. There was a palpable sense of anticipation and we listened carefully as the flaming red sun crested the horizon. Despite a crush of the faithful, and the obvious majesty of the moment, no one received any new commandments. Oh well, Salah said it was an off day!

On a busy day as many as a thousand people attempt the climb. One enterprising Bedouin built an outhouse at the summit; "Toilet! Toilet!" He probably does a land office business.

Once the sun was fully up, we beat a hasty retreat to avoid the returning crowd. The journey down was even more amazing than the climb up. With the morning sun setting the surrounding mountains ablaze, shadows of every possible hue crept across the crags and valleys. The views were so fantastic that it was difficult to decide where to look next. By 7:30 we were back at the trailhead gazing up at the 3rd century AD monastery of St. Katherine; "Closed on Fridays." *Doh!* We'd hiked for 8.4miles and were Jonesing for breakfast.

After we ate, Hassan informed us, without explanation, that instead of dragging us to Sharm el-Sheikh, our previous bone of contention, he and Mohamadi would drive us straight to Dahab as previously agreed. *Go figure?* He then introduced us to our armed guard Ali. *Say what!* It seems that the direct route from St. Katherine to Dahab is a little sketchy and that American and Japanese (*Huh?*) tourists are only allowed along it with an armed escort. Ali adjusted the machine gun slung under his sport coat and took "shotgun" in the passenger seat.

The drive was uneventful, just more awesome desert scenery, colorful gorges, fanciful eroded shapes, and sand spilling glacier-like over craggy ridges. Two beautiful hours and a couple of police checkpoints later we were staring at the blue waters of the Gulf of Aqaba.

Day 278 - October 9 - Saturday - Dahab, Egypt

Today is our second full day in Dahab. We're lying on a couple of padded lounge chairs, sipping beer, listening to Reggae, and watching waves lap the shore. Just across the Gulf of Aqaba rises the mountainous coast of Saudi Arabia. Cool breezes off the water break the desert heat; nice place!

If Dahab isn't Egypt's number one chill spot, it's still close enough that it works for us. It's a bit like slipping back to the Playa del Carmen, Mexico of maybe fifteen years ago. Dahab's vibe is post hippie beach camp in the early stages of transition to upscale resort. A long concrete boardwalk lines the coast backed by small hotels, backpacker places, and dive shops. At the heart of the action, the seaward side of the walk is lined with open air restaurants, all touting their fresh seafood and drinks. Across the way, there sits a row of colorful shops that sell everything from carefully displayed Bedouin scarves to tourist t-shirts and sheesha pipes.

Our accommodation is at the Blue Beach Club and at $60 a night it's a good deal. Our balcony room overlooks the garden. It's large, attractive, and comfortable with private bath and AC. The beach front club, which is across the street from our room, features two nice bars, a good sized pool, lots of lounge opportunities, a restaurant, and excellent included buffet breakfasts. We are going to stay for eight nights and recharge our batteries. The sunset is magnificent.

Day 283 - October 14 - Thursday

Went snorkeling today and we should have gone sooner. There's an amazing reef wall just off shore and it's easy to float for hours watching the fanciful coral and sea life. Most of the fish are small but they make up for it by being brightly colored. We did see a couple of poisonous spiny rock fish; way cool!

Chapter 12

JORDAN

Day 285 - October 16 - Saturday - Aqaba, Jordan

Dahab is more rambling dive shop than beach paradise, but "low key" is clearly its niche. Compared with the rest of Egypt, Dahab's easy breezy vibe whispers, "kick back;" think budget tourist Shangri-La. Get up, take a walk, wear shorts, lay by the pool, have a beer, choose a restaurant for dinner. Feeling really energetic; snorkel a bit. Our eight days passed is a flash. When the time came for us to move on, this morning to be exact, it required Herculean resolve to stow our sandals and hit the road. Shangri-La or not, airplane reservations to India now drive our schedule.

Our plan was to take the "fast" ferry to Aqaba. One final tasty breakfast buffet, a goodbye to the Blue Beach Club, and we were travelers again; well sort of. Our first step was easy. Small pickup-truck taxis cruise Dahab nonstop trawling for fares. We just plopped our bags into the street and flagged the first one that rolled by. Our turbaned driver's command of English was nearly as sorry as our own command of Arabic; "Where you from? Oh, very nice." He was a friendly garrulous old guy, so the language barrier didn't hold him back. While we nodded and smiled politely, he kept up a lively banter in Arabic all the way to the bus station. By 9:50 AM, our tickets for the 10:30 bus to Nuweiba were in hand and we were set to hit the highway. As it turned out however 10:30 was more of a suggestion than an actual schedule. Our bus didn't chug into the station until about 11:15. Oh well, who's in a hurry.

We paid a small additional fee to stow our bags in the luggage compartment under the bus and climbed aboard. The hour plus ride was mostly uneventful. One short middle-of-nowhere stop so a cigarette smoking armed security officer could walk through the bus and scrutinize IDs (can't be too careful); otherwise we watched a drama of craggy weathered rock play out against the proscenia of our dirty windows.

When we hit Nuweiba, our air-conditioned bus disgorged us on a dusty street simmering in the noonday sun. Denise popped open her umbrella, we retrieved our bags, and then we trundled off toward the nearby ferry port.

For some illogical reason, the Nuweiba office where you must buy ferry tickets isn't located at the port. Instead, it's housed in another official building a couple of blocks away. Rather than drag our bags any further and both of us risk heat stroke, Denise waited with them in the shade, only 90 plus instead of 100 plus, while I trotted off for the tickets.

I thought the day was setting a standard for hot until I heard the sizzling "foreigners' price" for two tickets. $140, only payable in US dollars, for a one hour ferry ride, now that's scorching! *Oh well, scrimp when you can and spend with abandon when ya gotta.*

At the port, all the signs are in Arabic. Slightly confused, we stumbled our way along a path of oddly arranged bureaucracy that wound around a couple of buildings and eventually squirted us through passport control. The Unnamed Guide book strongly suggests that you arrive two hours early to make your way through the "Shambolic" boarding procedures. Procedures were a little hazy but far from "Shambolic," whatever that means. We breezed through and began to worry that we'd arrived too early. The prospect of an hour or two parked on the port's hard wooden benches looked pretty grim.

Our main concern was we didn't know how much of a wait we really faced. No times were printed on our tickets. Nothing appeared to be posted, and when we tried to determine the ferry's schedule, things moved quickly from slightly vague to downright muddled. No one spoke much English and answers ranged from 2:00 PM to 5:00 PM. We'd just been assured by one uniformed port official that 4:00 PM was the correct time and that we should take seats at a snack bar, when another official hurried up and told us that we needed to come immediately to catch the "last" shuttle to the ship; what great organization!

Bags in tow, we scrambled onto a beat-up bus where we joined an Argentinean tour group and other sundry passengers headed for Jordan. Denise, always the Good Samaritan, convinced the driver to hold the shuttle for a couple of clueless (*there but for the grace of God go I*) young Scots who were still dawdling in the terminal. Once they were on board, the bus zipped us right to the boat. *So far so good, it looks like a 2:00 PM departure is on the mark.* Well, maybe not so much. At 5:30 or so in the middle of the tourist class lounge's second movie, The Expendables, the engines finally kicked to life. The "fast" crossing normally takes one hour; two hours if conditions are bad. There was a beautiful sunset and the water was like glass, but for the second time on our trip we found ourselves on a "fast" ferry that resembled a snail with water wings. Aqaba by night; we were so looking forward to it.

During the passage, Denise struck up a conversation the young Scottish couple that turned into a suggestion that we all share a cab. Aqaba's ferry port is seven kilometers out of town so you're pretty much stuck with a taxi; especially if you unexpectedly dock way after dark. Once we cleared immigration and walked outside we were immediately met with taxi offers.

"How much to the Al-Amer Hotel?" asked Adam, the aforementioned young Scot.

"Ten JOD," replied the taxi driver. The Unnamed Guidebook (Have we mentioned that everyone carries the damn thing) claims that five JOD ($7.13) is the going fare.

Adam astutely balked, "Gee that seems kind of high; how about five?"

"No. Ten is fair price."

Back to Adam, "Okay we'll take it."

This sudden collapse elicited a grunt of mild disgust from Jemma, the other aforementioned young Scot; "So much for Adam's bargaining skills."

As we've said before, Taxi drivers aren't dumb. When they've got the upper hand they know it and seven kilometers from town in the dark looks as good as a royal flush.

The driver carefully slid our bags into his trunk, tossed Adam's and Jemma's backpacks in afterwards (age before beauty), and motioned us to pile in. Since his obvious intent was to drive off with his trunk hanging open and Adam's and Jemma's packs hanging precariously over its lip, Adam again astutely balked. While the driver stood by making repeated assurances that there was "no problem" with this configuration, Adam rearranged luggage until the trunk reluctantly closed.

Once we reached downtown, our driver pulled over, pointed down an alley and said, "There is hotel." The four of us looked skeptically down the street and again astutely balked. Nobody was getting paid until we actually saw the hotel. "Is just there. Yes, Yes, Hotel Al-Amir (notice spelling difference)." Denise and Jemma scooted down the alley and determined that the Al-Amir was definitely not the place we wanted. This was followed by further discussion.

"Yes, Yes, Hotel Al-Amir is there!"

"No we want the Al-Amer."

"Is Al-Amir!" A couple of locals sitting on the sidewalk were added into the mix.

"Al-Amir."

"No, Al-Amer."

"Al-Amir, Al-Amer. Oh (a light goes on) you want Hotel Amer!" Once again The Unnamed Guidebook leaves something to be desired, the hotel's correct name is "Amer," not "Al-Amer" and that makes all the difference.

Taxi driver again points down the alley, "Yes, Yes, Hotel Amer is just there around corner." Denise and Jemma again take off for a validity check and I slip the fidgeting driver two JOD ($3) to keep him calm until they report back.

"Yep, it's there!" It's after 11:00 PM when we finally tugged our bags into the lobby of the Hotel Al-Shula. The Amer a couple of doors down was less expensive, but was dealing with quality issues; not a stellar day for public transport.

Day 286 - October 17 - Sunday - Wadi Musa, Jordan

Our first full day in Jordan started out a little shaky, but turned itself around quite nicely. We planned, silly us to make plans, to spend two nights in Aqaba and squeeze in an organized day tour to the Wadi Rum Nature Reserve in between. Our thought was that the "fast" ferry would get us into Aqaba around 4:00 PM, we'd hot foot it over to an Unnamed Guidebook recommended tour company, and at the crack of dawn we'd be rolling for Wadi Rum.

By the time we crawled groggily out of bed, dawn was well beyond cracked, and a short pre-breakfast exploration informed us that the nearby Unnamed Guidebook recommended "branch" tour office was now a t-shirt shop. *Doh!* Since our house of cards had crumbled, we decided to bag the second night in Aqaba, pick up our rental car a day early, and head straight to Wadi Rum on our own; flexibility, the hallmark of the seasoned independent traveler.

Leaving Denise in our room to make herself even more beautiful, I hiked a few blocks over to a Europcar office to see what I could arrange. "Open seven days a week from 7 AM until 10 PM;" at 8:50 AM, they were firmly locked and shuttered. *Great, just great!* Fortunately, the aforementioned Scotts were also renting from Europcar and we knew they were scheduled to snag their car at 9:30. A half hour later, we tagged along when they walked over. Low and behold, a guy was sitting in the office smoking a cigarette while his young son played with office supplies.

After a yummy sidewalk breakfast of baked cheese pastries and thick sweet Arabic coffee, we threw our stuff into the spacious truck of our free-upgrade rental car (we later discovered they charged our credit card three times; maybe or maybe not an error), and hit the road. After months at the mercy of: buses, taxis, trains, and tour vans; it felt liberating to once again be masters of our own transport. Yeah! Stop when you want to, go when you want to; visit this spot or visit that spot. What can be better? Driving in Jordan is easy. Everything is well signed. The roads are well maintained, gas stations are plentiful, and distances are short.

An hour and a half out of Aqaba and we rolled into the Bait-ali desert camp. We figured we might spend a night at Wadi Rum and Bait-ali just outside the entrance is the area's only option besides Bedouin tent camps. The tented camps sound romantic, but their reality runs to basic digs, sweltering heat, dust, and pit toilets. On first impression Bait-ali looked good. It's a walled desert compound (to keep out blowing sand), with bungalows, common areas, and a pool.

"Do you have a room available for tonight?"

"Oui (French woman), but only a basic bungalow or a tent, both with shared bath."

"May we see one?"

"Oui, they are being cleaned right now. Perhaps you can wait a bit?" She then led us to an attractive plein aire dinning pavilion where we were served sweet tea and asked to relax. Minutes ticked by and the "bit" stretched to forty minutes before the rooms were "ready."

Second impression, not so good; the basic bungalow was a square concrete room with three beds, one of which looked slept in, and no aesthetic appeal whatsoever. The tent was even worse and made our budget Masai Mara safari tent look positively luxurious. Even with the drawbacks, we might have stayed until we heard the price, $114 per night with an extra $7 per person facilities fee if you want to use the pool. *Oh well, the tea was good.*

Back in the car, we continued the short distance to the Wadi Rum Visitor's Center. The center is an attractive modern sandstone complex with raised lookout platforms that afford expansive breathtaking views of the "Seven Pillars of Wisdom," and other craggy promontories. From a U.S. perspective, it's also a tad strange. Signage is minimal and confusing. Walk to the window labeled "tickets" and you're told that tickets are sold in another building without a sign. Walk to the interpretive exhibit hall and you find it locked. Backtrack to the theatre for the ten minute introductory film and you discover that it is also locked.

Moments after we arrived, a "guide" glommed onto us and began trying to sell us jeep and camel rides. He wasn't overtly high pressure, but he was annoyingly persistent and simply wouldn't take "no" for an answer. He just kept trailing us around helpfully pointing out things and repeating his offers. On the plus side, he scrounged up a guard with a key who let us into the theatre. After the film, we thanked the guide and ducked into the WC to shake him.

When we came out of the toilets, there he was waiting, "My jeep very nice, you like to see?"

"No thanks, we're not interested." The guy just did not get it and was ruining our whole experience. To shake the little tick, we were finally forced to tell him that he was pissing us off and that he needed to go away!

So why didn't we want a camel or a jeep ride? You ask. The truth is; for us they were just too expensive. Wadi Rum is beautiful, heck it's gorgeous, but it's not all that different from sights we've seen in the American

West. The going, official/posted, price for a two hour jeep ride is $52. Unfortunately, that's not the end of the story. The ride doesn't include your admission to the reserve which runs another $21 per person. Throw in a tip and suddenly you're talking $100 for a bumpy two hour excursion.

When we ate lunch at the visitor center restaurant and it set us back $28 we finally got the hint that maybe Jordan isn't such a cheap place. We could have paid the $42 entrance fee and continued on our own into Rum Village fifteen minutes up the road, but it didn't sound like there was much there too see.

In the end, we decided to self-cater the experience. We enjoyed the free views from the visitor center, and then we drove back up the road and explored the nearby village of Diseh, another spot where the scenery is spectacular, and also free.

Since Bait-Ali was out of our price range, we decided to overnight in Wadi Musa, the gateway to Petra. Leaving Wadi Rum behind, we put pedal to the metal and cruised up the amazing King's Highway. *Ah, the flexibility of the independent traveler!*

When we arrived, we located the Petra Gate Hostel, a popular backpacker place where we'd reserved a room for the following night. We were a day early but there was space available so we went ahead and checked in. The room was as shabby and basic as any that we've tried, but at $26 per night, we really couldn't complain. Still..., for a place that Hostel World rates as the "Best Hostel in Jordan," we don't think your knees should be pressed against the wall when you sit on the toilet. Throw in unrelenting street noise, crumbs on the floor, and plump dust bunnies cavorting under the bed, and we decided that our next two nights in Wadi Musa were probably better spent in other digs.

Day 287 - October 18 - Petra, Jordan

Following our included basic-but-not-bad breakfast, today's first order of business was to change hotels. We rolled down the street to the "El Rashid" and for $7 more per night made a serious upgrade to an air-conditioned room with a large bathroom and a couple of comfortable chairs.

After dumping our stuff, we were off for Petra. The entrance was only a kilometer or two away so as we left the hotel, we asked the lobby guy if we could just walk down. "No," he told us, "take your car. It's easy going down, but the way back is all uphill and you'll be tired." It was one of several good tips today.

At the Petra Visitor Center we bought two two-day passes and two tickets to the Petra After-Dark program. Together they came to a whopping $140 USD. The entrance fees seemed stiff while paying, but as our visit unfolded, we decided they were a bargain.

Petra is easily one of the coolest places on Earth! From the visitor center a dirt road winds through a sandstone landscape, past three "Djinn Blocks," large squat stone funerary monuments, and a couple of medium-sized tombs carved from the living rock; tantalizing tastes of things to come. After an interesting twenty minutes we reached the "Siq" where twin niches mark the remains of a monumental arch and the start of the true entrance to Petra.

The Siq is a deep canyon or more correctly a dramatic 1.2 kilometer crack in the rock that leads to the hidden city. As we entered, the space between the canyon walls drew together; shadows replaced the harsh desert sunlight. Carved channels that once flowed with water trace the sides of the gorge and ancient cobbles pave its floor. Enigmatic stairways climb broken and crumbling into the heights. At one point the floor widens to reveal a bit of greenery and a small tomb. At another we gazed at a weathered life-size relief; a camel caravan forever plodding through the ancient stone.

Yes, there are lots of tourists, and yes, an occasional horse-drawn cart rattles by, but they don't detract from the experience. The drama of the Siq is hard to overstate. Even if the gorge was unadorned by man it would still be a place of wonder. The coolness of the air, the play of light and shadow, the remarkable shapes and colors of the stone; all of it enthralls. Just when we thought it couldn't get any better, the walls drew closer together, dampening sound, and further shutting out the sun. Our anticipation grew and suddenly we rounded a bend and there glowing in the sunlight soared the iconic Hellenistic façade of the Treasury.

At that point, you just stand there with your jaw hanging open. Hidden and protected from the elements the perfectly preserved Treasury is beautiful and unique. Its monumental scale, 43 meters high by 30 meters wide, its superb craftsmanship, and its incredible location, all worked to plaster our faces with goofy awestruck expressions; simply remarkable!

The Siq and the Treasury are hard acts to follow, but they're just the beginning. The ancient Nabataen city of Petra was vast and what's left today, 800 registered sites and 500 tombs, sprawls over a wide area of mountains and wadis.

Finally tearing ourselves away from the Treasury, we continued into the "Street of Façades." Here the walls of the Siq fall back and the passage widens to become a broad avenue. More than forty tombs rose around us towering on all sides. Dark doorways beckoned us to stop and peer into their shadowy recesses. A short distance further we came to Petra's weathered amphitheater, a half circle with over 8,000 seats that dates back more than 2,000 years.

As we continued, the wadi widened still further, and to the right tall west-facing cliffs loomed above us. Carved into their vertical faces gigantic burial chambers, known as the Royal Tombs, leap out of the stone. Almost everywhere your eyes alight, something amazing awaits.

We haven't mentioned it, but up to this point our visit was guided. All entry tickets include a free group tour and we figured; *Free, why not?* There were only a couple of other people in our "group" so it was really like having a private guide. Making the situation even better, our guy was sensitive to the majesty of our surroundings and he gave us plenty of space to enjoy them without a constant stream of chatter. After we saw the Royal Tombs, the tour wrapped up with free mint teas and what proved to be the best part of the freebie deal; good advice on what to see next. We told our guide that we liked to hike and he gave us a couple of easy-to-follow yet off the beaten track paths that would take us to less visited parts of Petra.

After an al fresco sack lunch of bananas and peanut butter sandwiches, Denise and I took our bearings from the "Pharaun" a lone surviving column of a Nabatean temple and set out east along a dry desert ridge toward a place called Wadi Farasa, Butterfly Valley. As we moved out of Petra's core, we left the crowds behind and began our own Indiana Jones experience.

Dropping down from the ridge we continued through a beautiful desert and sandstone landscape into the wadi. Walls of colored stone rose on each side and the canyon floor held bits of greenery that hinted of water. Once again we began to encounter the bones of ancient Petra.

First came the Garden Triclinium a great hall used for feasts, decorative carving still visible on its inner walls. A few paces further on our right rose the impressive Roman Soldier's Tomb, so called because of a martial statue carved over its door. Continuing up the canyon we came to the Garden Tomb, a building whose huge dry cistern suggests the once elaborate Nabatean water system. From this point our path followed ancient cliff hugging steps that rose precipitously from the valley floor.

After about twenty minutes of climbing we reached the Lion Monument another impressive example of Nabatean hydraulics. Carved into the cliff face, towers the badly weathered form of a five meter long lion and behind the lion a stone channel that once brought water gushing from his mouth. A small stone altar opposite the fountain hints at long forgotten rites.

Today, the dry fountain is a place of business for a wizened little Bedouin woman who makes the difficult daily climb to sell postcards or trinkets to the occasional tourist like ourselves. We're suckers for the soft sell so we paid $1.43 for a stack of postcards we don't intend to use.

Past the lion we followed in the footsteps of ancient priests and climbed the ceremonial path that leads to Al-Madbah, the Altar, also known as the High Place of Sacrifice. Here the Nabateans leveled the top of a mountain to create a platform where animals were offered to their gods. Little remains of the site except for two tall stone obelisks that stand as mute testimony to the altar's past grandeur. The amazing thing about the eighteen foot pillars is that they weren't set in place; instead they were carved from the living rock. It's mind boggling to look at them here on the top of a mountain and imagine the amount of stone that must have been removed to create them.

Walking past these sentinels, we climbed a last set of steps and were rewarded with sweeping views that take in all of central Petra. With only the sky above and the ancient city spread out below it's easy to understand why the spot was chosen as a place to commune with the gods.

We sat for a while and chatted with another Bedouin woman whose tiny place of business seemed to perch on the edge of the world. Although difficult to reach, it would be hard to beat its location.

After resting, we returned to the obelisks and started down another set of well maintained steps. For the next half hour we continued down one unrelenting step after another, twisting and turning through gaps and fissures in the rock, until abruptly we stood on the last step and were back at the theater and the Siq.

This was without a doubt one of the most amazing hikes either of us has ever taken. No question we're going to remember it as one of the true high points of our trip.

By the time we worked our way through the Siq and back to the visitor center, we were both worn out, and really, really, really glad our car was sitting nearby. *Thank you hotel guy!* We drove back up the hill to Wadi Musa, freshened up at the El Rashid and grabbed some dinner on the square. As we pushed back from our outside table, the sun was setting and it was time to head back to Petra for the night program.

We felt tired as we trudged the access road for the third time, but the moment we reached the Siq we caught our second wind. Full night had fallen and before us stretched the sinuous stone corridor; both its sides now lined with flickering luminaria (paper bags with candles inside). By day the Siq is powerful and awe inspiring. Candle lit, by night, it's mysterious and magical.

Along with a throng of other tourists, we walked quietly through the soaring, softly glowing, halls. Shuffling feet, silence, and dancing shadows; it felt as though we were participants in some ancient rite, a procession to honor long forgotten gods. When we reached the Treasury, hundreds more luminaria bathed the space in a soft and welcoming glow; shifting patterns of yellow, orange, and shadow. We sat down on carpets that were spread on the ground and our Bedouin hosts moved quietly among us serving small cups of sweet tea from large silver trays.

We've seen many "sound and light" spectaculars where ancient monuments are lit in dramatic fashion and polished narration plays out to orchestral crescendos. The night program at Petra is none of that and it strikes just the right note. A lone Bedouin story teller, the plaintive melody of a single-string violin, and haunting chant-like singing; it was the humble entertainment of a desert camel camp, a fitting counterpoint to Petra's stony majesty.

Day 288 - October 19 - Tuesday

After a good night's sleep, we felt ready to tackle a second full day of exploring. We ate a nice included breakfast at the hotel, and soon we were again negotiating the Siq's amazing twists and turns. We paused to again admire the artistry of the Treasury, it demands it, and then we continued to where the towering face of massif Jebel Al-Khubtha looms over the valley. Under a blazing sun, we turned east and climbed a steep path to reach burial sites known as "The Royal Tombs."

Built on an enormous scale, these multi-storey tombs are some of Petra's most spectacular. The "Urn Tomb," so called because of a gigantic urn perched at the top of its pediment; the "Silk Tomb" where brightly colored veins of white, yellow, and pink stone swirl across its façade; the "Palace Tomb" with the ancient city's largest façade; each one is different and each one a wonder. Constructed around AD 70 as burial places for Nabataean kings the structures were later altered by Greeks, Romans, and Byzantines. As late as AD 447 the Urn Tomb was in use as a Greek cathedral.

We edged around the base of the tombs, nosed into open doorways, and skipped from shadow to shadow to escape the desert heat. After we finished our tomb "exploration," we followed a set of winding stone stairs that took us back to the valley floor.

Rubber-necking as we went, we continued down the wadi past the stump-like remains of marble-clad sandstone pillars. Built around AD 100, these broken columns were part of a mighty colonnaded carriageway that ran through the heart of Roman Petra. Today, baking under the bright sun they resemble nothing so much as the bleaching bones of some long dead leviathan.

Near a service area with a restaurant, a few trees, and a bit of green, we left the wadi and began a slow climb up the hill of Al-Habis, the prison. A couple of flights of stone stairs brought us to a small museum set in caves carved into the rock. We spent a few minutes with its statues, stucco paintings, and figurines, and then found a bench on the museum's entrance terrace. The narrow ledge was deep in shade, so we parked ourselves for a sack lunch, guzzled water, and enjoyed the sweeping views.

At the edge of the museum's terrace, a little-used trail snakes toward the backside of Al-Habis. This offers another chance for outback adventure, so after lunch, we ducked under a bush and headed up the path. The trail hugs the cliff, works around the side of the hill, and affords great views of the watery pools and dense greenery of Wadi Siyagh and also of its junction with Wadi Numeir. Here and there we saw the scattered cave homes of some of Petra's last residents. Further up the path we reached the "Covenant Group;" tombs where bands of multi-hued sandstone swirl like colorful rippled ice cream.

Leaving the tombs, the trail continues up steep steps that eventually reach the top of Al-Habis. It was the hottest part of the afternoon and with the sun cooking us inside and out, we decided to eschew the pleasures of the climb, turned around, and headed down.

We planned to finish our second Petra day with a visit to "Al-Deir." According to our reading Al-Deir, called "The Monastery," is a spectacular monument, similar in design to the Treasury, only larger. Unfortunately, we didn't make it. Mid-afternoon is the best for the climb (shade), but by the time we reached the Al-Deir trailhead, the idea of another hour of uphill walking, an hour that includes 800 rock-cut steps, was a non-starter. There were donkeys, but we're on a budget and the people riding them looked a little too much like baggage. Oh well, it's always good to save something for next time, and if ever a place deserved a next-time, it's Petra.

A sweltering trudge back toward the entrance highlighted the wisdom of our decision. By the time we reached the Colonnaded Street, Denise was drained and ready for transport. Luckily, since she wasn't Petra's first overly ambitious visitor, a steady stream of camel and horse jockeys troll the wadi looking for weary tourists; the fancier the animal's livery, the higher the fare.

We flagged down a Bedouin leading an ordinary looking camel and began a lively negotiation. The dickering started at $28 for a fifteen minute ride to the Treasury; for one person! After a lot of back and forth and feigned disgust, Denise climbed aboard for twelve Jordanian dollars ($17.12). As we said, Jordan isn't cheap.

Since we drove a hard bargain, her camel jockey tried to recoup his loss with a quick turn around. No sooner was Denise mounted on her ship of the desert than the Bedouin plunged off at a ground eating pace. As I shouldered my bag, I watched her disappear up the wadi, bouncing, pounding, and swaying atop her dromedary.

When I reached the Treasury, not that much worse for wear, Denise had been waiting fifteen minutes; just long enough to make a personal vow to avoid further camels. After listening to her recap, it's my impression that their uncomfortable ride falls somewhere between plowing with a roto-tiller and that mechanical bull from "Urban Cowboy."

Denise walked through the Siq, but she was really dragging at the other end, so we entered another negotiation. This time the dickering was for her "included" horseback ride up the entrance road. Since the ride is "free" we managed to get the price down to an acceptable five dollars Jordanian ($7.12). Denise mounted from a low wall and her handler led her horse up the access road at a slow but steady gait. Thanks to the walking pace, I managed to keep up.

After we cooled down and cleaned up at the El Rashid, I quaffed my most expensive beer of the trip (so far); more than a horse, less than a camel. Muslim country that it is, local stores sell several non-alcoholic brews, but if you want the real deal, you have to look. We ended up in the small lounge at a nearby "licensed" hotel. Denise watched patiently while I rewarded myself for my overheated walk with a Lilliputian $8.56 shot of lager. The beer wasn't what you'd call cold, but on the upside, the glass wasn't hot.

We finished our day at the Midtown Restaurant, a second-floor place with good views and better food. The highlight of the experience came when we ordered dessert. We finished our meal, were invited to move to comfortable lounge chairs, and then our waiter brought out an enormous tray of assorted Arabic sweets. The dessert price was low, so we expected only one or two bites. Instead, we ate flakey pastries, chewy nut and fruit morsels, and honey drizzled confections until our stomachs were full and our fingers sticky. Despite our gluttony, we still walked out of the Midtown with a carefully wrapped box of "leftovers."

Day 289 - October 20 - Wednesday - Karak, Jordan

Today, we climbed back in our car and again hit the road. Our first stop, just a few kilometers up the tarmac, was Siq al-Barid, better known as "Little Petra." Unlike its big brother, admission to Little Petra is free.

Except for a lone tour bus and a large Bedouin tent the dirt parking area lay deserted. Although it was only 10 AM the sun was already working overtime. With thoughts of our rental's dark interior slowly morphing into a sweltering inferno, we snuggled the car in as close to the bus as we could get and hid in the behemoth's shade.

From the car park, an obvious path leads to an unlocked iron gate. We stepped through and entered the world of Little Petra. Siq al-Barid means "Cold Canyon" and as we walked into the 400-meter-long cleft the name sort of made sense. Outside it was hot, but inside large sections of the Siq lay in cooling shadow. The canyon alternates between well lit open spaces and narrow towering walls where the angry sun struggles to penetrate.

The ancient community of Little Petra was contemporary to its larger neighbor and may have served as an agricultural suburb that catered to the resupply needs of passing camel caravans. Just past the entrance we climbed a short flight of steps and peeked into the dark interior of an imposing Nabataean mausoleum. The tomb's door is flanked by square columns and topped by an elegant arched pediment which features four raised disks. At its outer edges the façade is bordered by two even larger horned columns which "support" an even larger triangular pediment; capped at its peak by a finial urn. We stood there in the silence and marveled at tool marks left by long-forgotten sculptors when they liberated the tomb from its surrounding rock. Archeologists date the tomb to between 100 BC and 100 AD.

As we moved further into the Siq we were struck by a sense that we were in a place that once pulsed with activity. Everywhere there was evidence of the hand of man; houses carved into the rock, tombs, and stairways that led away to unknown destinations. Four large rooms flank the second open area. The rooms contain what appear to be tables and benches carved from the rock so (surprise, surprise) they've been tentatively identified as dining areas. Standing there quietly, it's easy to imagine ancient camel traders and merchants chatting and laughing over wine and dates.

A little deeper into the Siq we climbed other stairs to reach the "Painted House." The Painted House is another small dining-room-like structure that features a "biclinium;" that's a sort of ancient Roman dining couch for two persons (we didn't know either). The stone biclinium was sort of interesting, but the room's big claim to our attention was its frescoes. When we looked closely we could just make out the faded shapes of vines, flowers, and birds. Unfortunately, most of the walls are blackened with the soot of countless Bedouin campfires. Supposedly there's also a winged cupid and a Pan-like guy playing a flute, but we couldn't see them. Still, what remains is one of the very few examples of Nabatean painting to have survived the ravages of time; and there we were staring at the frescoes all by our lonesome.

Just beyond a final wide area, the Siq narrows to a width of maybe eight feet and worn rock-cut stairs lead upward into the narrow gap. Of course we started to climb. At the top of the stairs the way flattened. A few more paces between soaring walls and we entered a small alcove where an enterprising local had set up shop. Two rugs were spread on the ground and arranged around them were four or five plastic patio chairs with plastic footstools pressed into service as small tables. Opposite sat two benches draped with sheepskins and two more plastic footstools. Behind these a rope stretched along the rock wall and served as a display rack for scarves, necklaces, and other trinkets. Cups waited on the tables, but leery of the water, we passed on tea.

A short way further the narrow rift opens onto a flat ledge and we were treated to picturesque views across a wonderful landscape of time weathered rock. A diminutive Bedouin woman was seated in the Siq's last shadow. Despite the day's warmth she wore a handsome embroidered black woolen robe and her head was wrapped in a black woolen scarf. Piles of dark fluffy wool were spread before her on a blanket and she was patiently twisting the tufts into coarse thread which she then wound onto a simple wooden spindle. Smiling, she beckoned us over and launched into what we could only assume was an explanation of her process. When the unintelligible but brief introduction, and possibly sales-pitch, ended she indicated by sign that we should take her picture; cottage industry meets eco-tourism. Standing at full height she didn't reach to Denise's shoulder.

Upon leaving Little Petra, our road curved and meandered through scenic highlands of olive groves, rolling hills, and rural communities until eventually it took us back to the King's Highway. On an ancient route that witnessed the passage of: Christian Crusaders, Moses on his way to the Promised Land, and countless Muslim pilgrims on their way to Mecca; we headed toward our next goal, Al-Shobak Castle.

We're both partial to medieval castles and the crusades left Jordan with some doozeys. Baldwin I (you remember, that crusader guy from the movie "City of Heaven) built Shobak around AD 1115 so that he could control the surrounding area, and of course, extort payment from merchants and pilgrims unfortunate enough to travel past. Baldwin's Castle remained a force to be reckoned with off-and-on through the 14th century, but its crusader era ended in May of 1189. That's when the Muslim hero Saladin, who'd grown fed up with the castle's predations, finally starved out its defenders after a protracted siege. Shobak today is largely unexcavated and un-restored, but it's still an imposing place to visit. Baldwin picked his building site to be defensible and as a result what's left of the castle crowns a steep rocky butte; a scenic spot with sweeping panoramic views across the neighboring plateau.

If you have even a smidgen of imagination, Al-Shobak (also spelled Ash-Shawbak) is an adventure. It has plenty of everything you expect from a proper medieval castle: cisterns, two churches, a market area, secret passages, a keep with arrow slits, watchtowers, catacombs, and a subterranean spring reached via 350 scary stone steps. What the castle lacks is any helpful signage. We thought about muddling through on our own but decided that we'd get more out of our visit if we engaged Shobak's caretaker to show us around.

For a negotiated price of $8.56 our "guide" led the way pointing out salient features. His moustache and his commentary were both marginal and we quickly realized that his primary talent lay in touching and brushing up against Denise as frequently as was humanly possible while at the same time trying to appear innocent enough to avoid a direct rebuke. It was sweltering at the castle, but in hindsight a thin peach tank-top might not have been Denise's best Islamic sartorial option.

After bidding "ma'a as-salaama (goodbye)" to our slightly lecherous guide, we continued our drive up The King's Highway. A route favored for 3,000 years; the highway is flanked by an unmarked, or barely marked, chain of historical and natural attractions: tombs of the Prophet's martyred companions, neglected Nabataean temples, impressive canyons, more decrepit Crusader castles, and even an improved, men and women in separate pools, hot spring or two. We looked, but we didn't tarry. With our flight to Delhi only four days away, it's going to be difficult just to squeeze in the sights that are already on our radar. Pushed by a need to keep moving, we skirted the beckoning Dana Nature Reserve, enjoyed the varied arid landscape outside our windows, and rolled through the unremarkable towns of Tafila and Mutah. Late in the afternoon we arrived in Karak.

Karak, our planned stop for the night, is home to another Baldwin-built Crusader castle; this one in a much better state of repair. Following sporadic signs we drove into a maze of narrow one-way streets that dominate the town's center. We didn't know where we were going, but dumb-luck held, and eventually we arrived at our goal; well almost. When the castle finally hove into sight, our obstructed view was from the back of a traffic jam. While I scratched my head, Denise spotted an open parking space at the curb. Both of us quickly declared it an unambiguous omen that we were within walking distance. The traffic snarl was caused by three gargantuan tour buses as they jockeyed for position in the castle's small parking area. *Hmmm, isn't there a better way to do that?*

According to The Unnamed Guidebook the Karak Rest House (their pick) is the most "convenient" bed in town. The hotel sits within spitting distance of the castle and since it was also close to where we parked, we headed over. Inside a slightly garish lobby, we found the front desk deserted. We rang the bell and waited. Nobody came. Two European tourists joined us. They rang the bell. Nobody came. We hailed a passing employee, but front desk wasn't part of his job description. After we fidgeted for fifteen minutes a man finally appeared and took an interest in our presence. "Would you like a room?" Always cautious, we asked if we could look before we leapt. The cost for a double was $67 and the room we were shown was probably last cleaned just before Baldwin checked-in. We were shuffling back and forth trying to make a decision when one of the Europeans turned on the bathroom faucet. Nothing came out. "Don't worry, the water come back soon." *Uh oh, we've heard that one before.* We turned and beat a hasty retreat. The Europeans bought the story and the smile, and took the room.

Happily, a few doors down there's a budget place called the Tower Hotel. Its reception area cum lounge is shabby and not very promising, but the staff is friendly so once again we figured, *what the heck.* "May we see a room?" The reception guy escorted us outside into a dingy alcove that leads off the street. One wall features a roll-up steel door and the other features chipped plaster and peeling paint. A Sixties style plastic light fixture dangles from the twenty-foot ceiling and giant black drapes of cobweb hang in the corners. On one side of the rear wall a short set of concrete steps lead down to a closed door. On the other side, a dim stairwell reaches upward. It looked like a great place to get mugged.

Misgivings aside, the stairs led to an extremely modest, but clean room. The water in the bathroom worked, there was a fan, a TV, and the unglazed window offered up terrific far-reaching views across Wadi Karak. We plunked down our $25 JOD ($35.66 US, breakfast included) and considered ourselves lucky. Later, we ran into the two Europeans. The water never came back on and they'd moved.

Karak Castle was already closed for the afternoon, so after we settled into our room we headed out to explore the town and grab an early dinner. The dinner was a no-brainer. The tables at Kir Heres, located almost next door, are set with cloth. Their menu is varied. Their prices are reasonable. And, last but not least, we were able to wash down our meals with a cold beer and a glass of wine (only on-sale place in town).

Traveling with a plan keeps you focused and sometimes it can smooth out the bumps, but truth be told it's usually the unplanned stuff that makes your journey. After dinner we strolled into the old center of town simply enjoying the ebb and flow of daily life. Karak is a city of about 23,000 that dates from biblical times; a strategic stop on the road to Jerusalem with a long history that includes: caravans, Greeks, Romans, and of course Crusaders. Today, it's a typical Jordanian town. At the small main plaza we mugged in front of the dashing equestrian statue of Saladin. We peered into stores, bought pastries, and mingled with evening shoppers. As dusk approached, we ducked into a tiny corner market to buy water before heading back to the hotel.

We greeted the shopkeeper and quickly depleted our minuscule repertoire of Arabic pleasantries. Like most people the world over, he had a functional knowledge of English which put us to shame. He was interested in where we came from, what we were doing, and our impressions of his country. We tried our best to answer his questions and in turn he told us about his life, his family, and his long hours running his shop. After a bit, he motioned us back behind his tiny counter and invited us to sit on a pair of low stools. Once we were seated, he went to his shelves. He opened a small package of sweets, and politely offered them to us as his guests. While we were nibbling and discussing food, a call to prayer echoed through the streets. Our host encouraged us to remain seated, but explained that we must excuse him while he prayed. That said, he unrolled a small rug onto the floor and kneeling between sacks of grain and boxes of dry goods, he went through his devotions. I think he hoped to share the experience and shed light on his religion. We both felt slightly awkward, but also felt like we'd stumbled onto something special.

After our host finished his prayers, our conversation returned to food and this eventually led to a suggestion that we take a meal at the shopkeeper's home. Burn me for a cynic, but something about the offer suddenly gave me the uncomfortable feeling that we were slowly backing into a money transaction. I reluctantly apologized that we couldn't accept his generous offer, made a self-conscious goodbye, and steered Denise into the street. Her "scam-dar" wasn't pinging like mine and she was pretty damn sure that I'd just blown an awesome cultural experience. I couldn't help it. I kept having visions of the holistic healer guy in Marrakech whining, "You hurt me. This is not about money," just before he tried to gouge us for $100; once burnt, twice shy. Denise barely spoke to me for the rest of the night.

Day 290 - October 21 - Thursday - Jerash, Jordan

When tickets for the castle went on sale at 8 AM we were outside waiting. We marched across a bridge, over a dry moat, and passing through the "Ottoman's Gate" entered our second Crusader castle. Karak sits on a promontory where it overlooks Wadi Karak and farther in the distance Numeira, the supposed location of doomed Sodom and Gomorrah. We caught nary a whiff of fire or brimstone, but the castle was still a treat. Its dry moat separates it from the town and on its other three sides rocky slopes fall steeply away from its massive stone walls.

According to historians, one of Karak's Crusader owners, Reynald de Chatillon, took a particular delight in flinging unfortunate prisoners from its parapets. This practice didn't go over well with the locals and when Saladin captured Chatillon in 1187 he took up his own sword, and citing the Crusader's evil acts, promptly chopped off his head.

Like Al-Shobak, Karak Castle features plenty of crumbling medieval architecture to fire the imagination. Unlike its neighbor to the south, it's much better restored. Best of all, extensive signage meant that we didn't need the services of a touchy-feely guide.

The Kings Highway continues from Karak toward Amman, but with our castle spelunking finished, we laid out a saltier plan. We tossed our bags in the trunk, wove our way through old town, this is where our on-foot exploring paid off, and in due course rambled down a road toward the town of Safi and "Al Mazraa," the Dead Sea.

A huge expanse of water in the middle of a desert; a body of water that's 1,237 ft deep, nine times saltier than the oceans, and whose waves lap at the lowest elevation on the surface of the earth; how awesome is that? We drove down a steep-sided valley and about fifty minutes later the water came into view; a startling field of blue, forty-two miles long and eleven miles wide. You stare in wonder at its rising and falling surface and suddenly it hits you; not a single fin or a single bit of kelp flutters in those salty depths, Dead Sea.

We mapped out a full day of sightseeing for ourselves: first, some canyon hiking, next, a dip, or at least a bob, in the sea, a rinse-off and then a short drive to an amazing viewpoint. We planned to conclude our day by delving into the heart of the New Testament. Ah, the best laid plans of mice and independent travelers ...

Following the Dead Sea Highway with the water on our left and the Moab mountains rising on our right, we crossed the Wadi Mujib Bridge and pulled into yet another dirt parking lot. Wadi Mujib is a narrow rocky water-cut gorge that empties into the Dead Sea at a point 400 meters below sea level (the other sea). It's also home to the Mujib Reserve, the lowest nature reserve in the world. The reserve's simple visitor center was our first stop.

Wadi Mujib is home to a wide variety of wildlife and reportedly some of the best canyon trails in Jordan. To truly experience the wildlife and most of the trails you need a full day and a mandatory guide. We didn't have the day and we didn't want the guide, so we set our sights on the lone exception, the "Siq Trail," an easy do-on-your-own, two-kilometer-long, "wading" excursion that leads to a nearby waterfall.

What we didn't set our sights on was a wall-o-flies and a $17 per person entrance fee. The moment we opened the car doors, a whirling buzzing invading host swarmed inside. In an instant it made itself completely at home. We shooed and swatted, but the energetic flies had the upper hand. Faced with certain defeat, we left the fly crusade in possession of the car and walked over to the visitor center. Inside, we enjoyed photo displays about the reserve's ecology and then succumbed to sticker shock. Faced with a $34 entrance fee for an hour-long nature walk, we balked. Wadi Mujib looks really inviting, but living in Oregon we've experienced more than our share of waterfalls, wet gorges, and natural wonders. We just couldn't bring ourselves to cough up the money. We used the restroom; climbed back in the car and with all windows down did our best to encourage our "guests" to leave.

Our second balk came just up the road at the Amman Beach Tourism Resort. The Dead Sea has a reputation for therapeutic and rejuvenating properties and its upper end is dotted with upscale resorts and fancy spas. Amman Beach is a less swanky municipal option that provides "affordable access" to the general public. Peering past the security gate and the ticket counter, we could see: sun umbrellas, showers, swimming pools, a restaurant, and a bare unappealing stretch of beach. "Affordable access" translated into $21 per person.

There you are, halfway around the world and you know that you might never come back. Should you, or shouldn't you? Purchasing decisions like this are tough. Sometimes we flop one way. Sometimes we flop the other way. We don't always make the right call. The easy answer is; "Sure, it's only money." The more difficult answer is; "No." Just because you're in a foreign country that doesn't mean that every activity is worth doing or that every transaction is a bargain. Of course, sometimes you're just in a penny-pinching mood.

The amenities at Amman Beach Tourism Resort were too rich for our blood so we did what a certain guidebook claims many locals do. We went looking for an isolated spot for a discrete free dip. Showers were the main reason that we sought out the beach and they were also the biggest drawback of our decision not to fork over $42. The Dead Sea's salt content hovers near thirty-one percent. That concentration pretty much guarantees that if you go for a swim you'll come out encrusted with an itchy eye-burning film. Figuring that we could use drinking water to at least rinse our tootsies, we opted for a wade. A few miles back down the highway toward the Wadi Mujib Bridge we found likely looking spot, parked near an army checkpoint, and worked our way down to a rugged shore.

The Dead Sea is a "terminal lake," a low spot where water flows in but can't find its way out. For centuries mineral-carrying water from the Jordan River together with the runoff from assorted springs and wadis has settled into the valley of the Jordan Rift. With nowhere to go but up, evaporation steps in and minerals and salts get left behind. We were still yards above the waterline when we gradually realized that we were walking on a dirty crust of salt; not just a sprinkling, mind you, but a deep hard layer, a shell many inches thick. Near the shore, the salt resembles the damp sparkling floor of a limestone cavern; a frozen morass of strange undulations and half-formed shapes. The water itself is clear, but even when wading its salinity and buoyancy are immediately obvious. We bounced with each step, and the deeper we got; the more we felt a ridiculous urge to moon-walk.

Denise standing in the surf, the desert in the background; after all these years she still takes my breath away!

By the time we got back to the car and reached for our jugs of water, our legs were simmering and we were glad that we'd gone for the wade instead of a full immersion. Okay, maybe showers are worth $42.

A side trip to "The Dead Sea Panorama Complex" provided the opportunity for our third balk. We'd read about the panorama and deemed it worth a visit. The complex is run by Jordan's "Royal Society for the Conservation of Nature" and includes a museum where you can learn about Dead Sea: geology, ecology, archaeology, history and industry, and of course observation areas where, we're told, you can revel in killer "banoramic" views (remember, no "P" in Arabic). We don't know. We never got there. It was just one of those "bite off more than you can chew" sort of things. The turn off is well marked, but the road up to the complex was more concrete than our waning interest. After twenty minutes of uphill turns we'd had our fill of panoramic views and whipped a one-eighty. Our destination was probably just around the next bend, but on the bright side; most of the flies were gone.

Four is a nice round number so we finished out our day with one more balk. At the top of the Dead Sea we left the highway and took a scenic secondary road through fertile agricultural land which borders the badly polluted Jordan River. We enjoyed the change of scenery and if we'd kept going, we'd have reached "Bethany Beyond The Jordan;" a riverside location that some scholars claim is where Jesus said, "Let it be so now," and John the Baptist did his thing. As an added bonus many of the faithful also believe that it's the exact spot where the 9th century Samarian prophet Elijah hopped into his fiery chariot and whirled off to heaven; signs and wonders! It was the signs that did it, and by signs we don't mean the wondrous "horses of flame" kind; "admission $7JD." "$10 per person, Uh... I'm just not that interested. Are you that interested?" "Nah, I'm good."

Late afternoon found us tooling through the outskirts of Jerash. Known as the "Hills of Gilead" in biblical times, it's an appealing region of olive-covered rolling hills. The Unnamed Guidebook claims that if you squint and use your imagination, the hills will remind you of "Tuscany." We've never been to Tuscany so we have to take their word on the resemblance, but any way you squint at it, Jerash is a nice locale.

Tired and ready to wrap-up our day, we searched for a hotel called, The Olive Branch Resort. According to our directions the resort, a modern spacious place with a pool, is reached via a turnoff five kilometers before town. Our problem was; we couldn't seem to find it. We peeled our eyes, and we hunted diligently, but suddenly with no Olive Branch in sight we found ourselves rolling into Jerash. *Drat!* We turned around, set our trip odometer, and crept slowly back up the highway. Around the aforementioned five kilometer mark, a small unpromising road rolled off to the left. *Okay so there's a road, but still no hotel sign.* Short on options, we shrugged our shoulders and turned. A kilometer down the pavement, we spotted a notebook-paper-sized, hand-lettered board that pointed us to an even smaller dirt road. Another kilometer down that track and we pulled into the wide circular drive of a spiffy three-story winged hotel with a pool, a picnic-and-play area, a restaurant, and its name emblazoned in meter-high red letters across the roof. Go figure! We guess you just have to know that it's here!

What the "Olive Branch" lacks in highway signage, it makes up for in other amenities. Our room is spacious and is reasonably priced. The "Tuscan" views out our window are suitably pastoral and there are even better views to be enjoyed from the restaurant and pool area.

First stop, the pool; hot from a long day in the car, we dove right in and just as quickly sproinged back out. The water wasn't salty, but it was bracing or more accurately unheated and mind-numbingly cold. While we toweled off on the patio, wine, beer, and the appealing landscape eased our shock and rounded over the day's rough edges.

We might have rated the Olive Branch a top-notch layover if it hadn't been for dinner. We were prepped for a yummy meal by reviews that talked about hardy "country fare." Ah, there go those unfettered expectations. Tonight was flat-out the worst meal that we've eaten since we started our trip!

The hotel's restaurant is on the second floor and, to throw it a bone, its views are great. Inside the windows everything is pretty nondescript. There's a wood-burning fireplace for winter use, but the overall impression is stackable chairs and empty cafeteria. The menu features ethnic Jordanian and Western food and touts their kitchen's use of local olive oil in the preparations. We decided that a comfort meal was in order. Denise chose "pasta with cheese sauce" and I opted for, "chunks" grilled in vinegar. We rounded out our selections with baba ganoush, olives, and local wine.

Yeah, I know what you're thinking; who orders something called, "chunks?" In my defense, I figured the description was another case of content lost in translation. Where the menu fell short, my mind helpfully substituted its own vision; succulent nuggets of roast meat gently simmered in olive oil and vinegar. What I got was, you guessed it, "chunks;" little bits of tasteless unchewable gristle that were probably chipped off a well-worn radial tire or scooped from a back-kitchen slop bucket. Denise's pasta was equally disgusting; pulpy over-done macaroni slopped on a plate and topped with lukewarm yellowish goo; something from a can, obviously exported by a country where no one has ever seen real cheese. The baba ganoush was terrible. The olives were mushy. The wine; along with our meal, we left most of it on the table. Our bill came to $20.85.

Would we stay at the Olive Branch again? Sure, no question. Would we eat there again? Not so much!

Day 293 - October 24 - Sunday - Amman, Jordan

It's the end of another day and we're seated in the Queen Alia International Airport outside Amman waiting for our overnight flight to India. With our sojourn through Jordan winding down, time has swung back and forth between hectic sprints and snail-paced crawls. Right now, it's crawling. Over the last two days it mostly ran flat out.

Back around 64 BC Gnaeus Pompeius Magnus better known as Pompe the Great was busy winning the Third Mithridatic War and tramping through what was soon to become the Roman province of Syria (and much later Jordan). On the heels of his victorious campaign, the area around Jerash tumbled into the Roman Empire as another of its far flung provinces. Jerash was originally settled by Greeks in the time of Alexander and then prospered under Roman and later Byzantine rule for the next seven centuries. The Roman emperors Trajan and Hadrian lavished attention on Jerash and when in due course the fortunes of the ancient city declined it left behind an architectural skeleton that makes it onto our not-to-be-missed list.

The archeological site nestles against present-day Jerash. After breakfast (included and not horrible), we left the Olive Branch and drove straight over. We like early starts because they usually put you ahead of the tour groups and give you time to explore without jostling shoulders. When we arrived the gate had just opened and the commercial area around the entrance was slowly shaking itself awake. We left our car in an adjacent parking lot, walked through the semi-obligatory gauntlet of sleepy vendors, and bought our tickets.

You enter ancient Jerash through the massive two-story gate known as "Hadrian's Arch." A monumental work of stone; the main arch is flanked by towering columns and a pair of lower one-story arches. Somewhat diminished from its original glory, the gate still soars to over forty feet. Elaborate niches sit above the smaller arches, the huge structure is capped by an elegant pediment, and everywhere you look you spy the remnants of the master stone carver's art. In the late morning light the tan and earthy shades of the façade seemed to glow against the backdrop of blue-grey skies and rolling green hills. Erected in 129 A.D. the arch was built to impress and after nearly two millennia it still does a good job.

With an unrealized expansion in mind, Hadrian's Arch was built well outside of Jerash's existing walls. Since the anticipated growth spurt never arrived, it's a walk of about three football fields to the remains of another gate where the old city actually begins.

Along the way, we stopped at the Hippodrome a sprawling athletic field also built outside the walls. Once the home to authentic gladiatorial contests, tests of prowess, and careening chariots the arena has been extensively restored and now hosts a twice daily tourist spectacular, "The Roman Army and Chariot Experience," with faux examples of similar activity. We considered taking in a show, but were turned away by the twelve JOD entrance fee. We'd just plunked down about $23 U.S. to get through the main entrance and another $34 for theatrical chariots felt like a budget buster. Since the show didn't start until 11 AM, we asked the guy with the rickety wooden table, cash box, and rubber stamp, if we could just step inside and peek at the arena. With a nod of the head, he shooed us in and we walked through a stone tunnel, that although hoary with age, still screams, "sports arena." Even without gladiators the huge oval tweaks your imagination. Today its stone bleachers only seat about 500, but it's easy to imagine it in its heyday when it was packed with 15,000 cheering, toga-clad, fans.

By the time we began to explore Jerash proper, the clouds were gone, the sun was out, and Denise had deployed her umbrella for shade. The bones of the old city are amazing. The Forum, a huge oval plaza paved in limestone, was the nexus of ancient activity. With the remains of a fountain at its center and Ionic columns fifteen to twenty feet high, some capped with massive stone lintels, ringing its perimeter, the plaza anchors the "cardo maximus," or old main drag.

The cardo is also lined with columns and its ancient flagstones still bear the ruts of countless carts and chariots. *Way cool!* A couple of other main thoroughfares branch off to the east and west and along the way you encounter broken temples, monumental staircases, the remains of fountains and baths, whimsical relief carvings, theatres and public gathering places. Don't get us wrong, Roman Jerash is a jumbled ruin. Good imagination is definitely required to fill in its blanks, but like Pamukale, Ephesus, or Rome itself, it's a place where the spectral ghosts of empire still roam.

We spent several hot hours climbing hills and temples, gazing across fabulous views, and poking into nooks and crannies. At one point, we even caught a slightly bizarre (free) performance in one of the amphitheaters; four Jordanian soldiers in antiquated desert uniforms performing martial bagpipe (*Huh?*) and drum tunes. At another point we watched self-assured young schoolboys march along the cardo proudly chanting "Allahu Akbar!"

We also tried to sneak a free peek at the chariot races. From a viewpoint in the city, we noticed locals picking out freebee seats among the weeds and unimproved ruins at a far end of the arena. This seemed like a good idea so we wandered down and picked out a couple for ourselves. The seating was lumpy, but it looked like we were on track for some no-cost gladiator action. At least it looked that way until the first flourish of trumpets, then a security guard came over and shooed us all away; oh well, something saved for next time.

After we left the archeological site we took a recommendation from the Unnamed Guidebook and ate a light lunch at a patio restaurant called the "Lebanese House." It was a good steer. The open-air place was bustling with local families, the service was friendly, and the food was tasty.

Next, it was back in the car and on to Madaba. With only two nights left in Jordan, we made a decision to skip Amman. The capital is a major tourist destination, but it's also thoroughly modern and boasts a population of nearly three million. We wanted to rest up before our plunge into India and the intensity of another big city experience didn't seem the way to go about it.

Madaba, 32 kilometers southwest of Amman, is a more manageable option. With a population of about 70,000; it's easy to get around, offers a variety of accommodation and services, and is only 28 kilometers from the airport.

Our cell phones didn't work at the Olive Branch and the hotel didn't have Internet so before we left we asked their front desk to call ahead and make us a Madaba reservation. We don't always feel a need for reservations, but since we were arriving on Friday, the Muslim holy day, we figured it was a good precaution. As it turned out, it wasn't just a good precaution it was an over-the-top great precaution. We picked out a couple of places we thought sounded promising, but the Olive Branch was on phone call number three before it found one with a vacancy; their last room. Later, as we stood in the lobby of the Mariam Hotel in Madaba, we watched the receptionist turn away one anxious hopeful looking group of tourists after another. *Whew, glad that's not us!*

Most of the drive from Jerash followed well-signed highway and despite the traffic encountered while skirting Amman, we arrived in Madaba in plenty of time to partake of cold poolside beers and late afternoon sun; our preferred wrap-up for a busy day.

Like Karak, Madaba is a typical Jordanian market town with a long history. Its streets are easy to navigate and there are plenty of distinctive shops, points of interest, and restaurants within easy walking distance of our hotel. Unfortunately by the time dinner rolled around, Denise felt headachy and out of sorts. Our plan was to wander the town and sample its offerings. Instead, with the blahs hard at work, we took all of our Madaba meals in the hotel. On our last full day in Jordan, Denise hung out in bed while I made occasional forays in search of aspirin, Panadol, and snacks. Luckily, she climbed back into the pink by this morning and, although pressed for time, we managed to squeeze in a brief walking tour before we headed out to the Airport.

Madaba is a good layover, but it's more than a wide spot on the way to the airport. About a third of the town's population is Christian (unusual), descended from a population that fled Karak in the late 1800's amid conflict with their Muslim neighbors. When they arrived in Madaba they quickly began to build new homes and churches and in the course of digging their foundations stumbled onto something unique. In a number of locations, the excavations brought to light amazing Byzantine-era Christian mosaics. Delicate pieces of art, that defying both time and intentional destruction had lain buried for a thousand years.

Today, the mosaics are carefully preserved, and of course on public display. Since we were short on time, we didn't visit as many as we would have liked, but we did take in the granddaddy of them all. Embedded in the floor of Saint George's Church is a sprawling 6th century map of the "Holy Land" assembled from countless bits of earthy colored tile. The captions are all in Greek, but we were still able to pick out: the Jordan River, Jericho, the Dead Sea, and a bunch of other biblical sites. The map isn't just places. It's embellished with palm trees, swimming fish, boats, lions, antelope, and other touches of whimsy. A tangible link with history, the mosaic is credited as the oldest map of Palestine in existence; two thumbs up!

Chapter 13

INDIA

Day 300 - November 1 - Monday - Rishikesh, India

O*m...My God; Holy Cow!* Today is our eighth full day in India and our seventh full day at the Phool Chatti Ashram.

Our Royal Jordanian flight from Amman left on time, arrived on time, and served free drinks with dinner; no complaints. Its only shortcoming was an 8:30 PM departure time that dumped us into the Indira Gandhi International Airport at 4:30 in the morning. Befuddled by lack of sleep and a two-and-a-half hour time change (who knew there was such a thing), we wheeled our bags away from the luggage carrousel; our brains screaming; "It's only 2 AM! Go back to bed!"

Although we were functioning with the motor skills of a pair of George Romero zombies, a cab to our chosen hotel still went smoothly. To prevent rip-offs (a favorite taxi pastime the world over) and increase overall security, Dehli police require that all taxis leaving the airport be pre-paid. You go to a police counter, tell them where you want to go, pay them the price, hopefully fair, and they give you an official voucher. With our voucher clutched tightly in hand we walked outside and flagged a cab; a cute little black and yellow Morris Minor type job. The driver shoved our bags into the front seat (propane tank in the trunk), we showed him our voucher, and away we went.

We only planned to stay one night in Dehli, so we encamped at a hotel called the EuroStar, a modest place about ten minutes from the airport. When we arrived at 6 AM they were expecting us. They told us apologetically that our room with AC wouldn't be ready until 9 AM so in the meantime we would have to use a room with only a fan. *At the half day rate of sixteen dollars, who cares? Just get us into bed.*

We handed over our passports; they always make copies, and then waded through the other registration rigmarole. In most of the countries that we've visited the governments are sticklers for bureaucracy around foreigners and hotels. In India, each place that you stay requires you to fill out forms (in triplicate of course) listing your permanent address, how long you intend to stay, where you plan to go next, your passport number, where it was issued, ditto for your visa, etc. etc. God only knows what these governments do with the oceans of paperwork this generates. We can only hope it provides a good living for people who file it away into dank forgotten archives.

While we registered, we noticed a man asleep on a thin pad that was shoved against one of the lobby walls. When the forms were complete, the desk clerk walked over, shook the poor guy awake, and told him to carry our bags up to our room; heavy bags, three flights. We tried to decline, but you can't buck the system. We felt really bad. The sleepy bellhop opened the door and turned on the fan, we tipped him, flicked the fan back off, and dove into bed. The only way that bellhop beat us to sleep was if he ran back to the lobby.

Our room was quiet and windowless so we slept like logs until 11 AM when the desk called to say that our "real" room was now ready. The room we were in was fine, but when we booked online we paid $28 for a room with AC and the hotel wanted to make sure we got our full value.

Our half day in Dehli zoomed by as we wandered nearby streets. Despite the presence of several hotels, our location near the airport wasn't a tourist area and we felt lucky to have our first taste of India be the real deal. All sorts of shops lined the streets: hole-in-the-wall markets, eateries cooking almost on the sidewalk, clothing stores, fruit stands, tailor shops, fabric stores dyeing brightly colored cloth, tiny stationary supplies, motorcycle repair shops, cellular phone stores, banks, and more; everything small, squeezed together, bustling and exotic. The traffic makes Cairo look tame, and the number of people on the street has to be experienced to be believed. Our sudden immersion into the crazy world that is India felt like a recipe for culture shock, but seasoned travelers that we now are, we soaked up the chaos and enjoyed every minute.

Offerings of the food stalls and sidewalk cafes looked great and smelled terrific, but discretion is the better part of valor. With another day of travel ahead, we played it safe and opted for a slightly upscale restaurant in another nearby hotel (popular with Chinese businessmen). Our vegetarian lunch: paneer kofta, garlic nan, and rice for $16 was so good that we went back again for dinner.

The next morning, our hotel arranged another 200 rupee ($4.55 US) taxi and we rode back to the airport to catch our 9:30 AM "Kingfisher" flight to Dehra Dun. Our goal for the day was Rishikesh, but Dehra Dun's "Jolly Grant" airport, eighteen kilometers away, is as close as you can get by air.

In Dehra Dun the taxi stand was outside the airport and the offered fare was 610 rupees ($13.86 US). Since this was twice what we expected, we quibbled a bit until we were shown an "official" price list. Oh well, to get dollars you divide by forty-four. Like a shrewd vendor told us in Egypt, "That much won't make you broke and it won't make me rich."

The next taxi queued at the stand was piloted by "Mr. Toad;" he of the wild ride. There was an elaborate little Hindu shrine on his dashboard and we were glad it was there. This guy clearly needed all the divine protection he could muster. He raced his car down the highway (they drive on the left) at breakneck speed, careening around corners, passing anything that was moving slower or fixed in place, and swerving around random troops of monkeys!

Supposedly, if an Indian Taxi driver has to choose between mowing down a pedestrian and plowing into a group of monkeys, the pedestrian is in serious trouble.

Denise and I both wore white faces and rictus grins when we finally slowed into the congestion of Rishikesh. After a few minutes of bumper to bumper, Mr. Toad reached a "no cars beyond this point" sign and we gratefully peeled ourselves out of his backseat. With our bags in tow, we followed a narrow shop lined street that after some uphill, some downhill, and a twist or two brought us to the Lakshman Jhula cable bridge that stretches across the "Ganga," Ganges River.

Only two bridges cross the river at Rishikesh. Both are limited to foot traffic and a steady flow of motorcycles. If you want to take your car or truck to Lakshman Jhula, you need to drive another eighteen kilometers downriver.

The street to the bridgehead opens suddenly and the sight revealed is exotic and impressive. Rishikesh sits at the edge of the Himalayas where the mighty Ganga flows strong and heavy with silt, rushing down out of the foothills. Monkeys line the suspension bridge cables and a thirteen story wedding-cake Hindu temple dominates the far shore.

We joined the stream of people and scooters and strolled slowly across, stopping from time to time to snap pictures or just to stare. Everything here is lush and green and after so much time in deserts it's a welcome sight.

Turning left, we walked past the front of the temple and up a colorful noisy music filled street; past more small shops and fruit stands, busy with people, wandering cows, and sadhus (wandering holy men) dressed in orange robes. Another taxi stand, a bumpy six kilometer jeep ride, and we arrived at the gates of our ashram.

Day 307 - November 8 - Monday

When today is over, we'll have been here at Phool Chatti for two weeks. I was tired this morning so when our alarm went off I ignored it, pulled my blanket tighter around my shoulders and drifted back to sleep. Denise, who was probably equally tired, refused to be infected by my defection and headed off for our morning activities. It's now several hours later. I'm still lazing, and Denise is probably performing the asnas of Hatha Yoga.

Our first impression as we entered through the ashram's corroded metal gate was something on the order of; *Uh Oh, this looks a little rundown.* Closer inspection revealed this wasn't really the case. It rains a lot here and pretty much anything that wasn't painted or whitewashed yesterday needs attention. Yes, there's some peeling paint at Phool Chatti and some of its walls and roofs look mossy and or moldy, but the ashram is no different in that respect than everything else in this part of India (and some parts of Eugene, Oregon for that matter.) By way of comparison Phool Chatti looks positively immaculate when measured against the Lakshman Jhula Government Hospital, a building whose outside creeps you out so badly that you hope fervently that you'll never see its interior.

The ashram's front gate opens onto a central courtyard. On the right, the space is bordered by a three sided room with an open hearth at its center. This is the oldest part of Phool Chatti dating back two hundred years. Next to this sits the dining hall. The courtyard's other two sides are enclosed by white, two and three story, buildings that contain living quarters. The far corner of the courtyard is filled by a small Hindu temple dedicated to the god Shiva, its roof domes adorned with orange and red lotus blossoms and garish hooded cobras. Behind the temple is a large chanting room, the yoga hall, the private residence of Swami Dev Swaroop Nanda Ji (Ayurvedic Doctor, Vedic Astrologer, and director of the ashram), and also the grave of a Hindu saint; buried sitting in the lotus position, or so we're told.

Life in the ashram moves at a slow predictable pace. To be here and be a part of this life is a hard experience to match. It's a small peek into what it must be like to be a novitiate in a monastic order. A copper gong is stuck four times at 5:30 AM to wake us from slumber. We have thirty minutes to splash water on our faces, brush our teeth, use the shared toilet, and get dressed. By 6:00 we're expected to assemble in the darkened yoga hall for silent meditation. For a half hour or so we try to still our "monkey minds" and find the space between our thoughts. "Thoughts come and thoughts go." It's in the space between one thought and the next that something interesting happens and conscious awareness awaits.

Following is a meditation we chant for fifteen minutes:

"Om trayambakam yajamahe
Sugandhim pustivardhanam
Urvarukamiva bandhanan
Mityormukchi amamritat."

Translation: "I worship the three eyed lord Shiva who is full of fragrance," and so on.

By this time, the sun is up and we file outside and down to the garden for yogic cleansing. To prepare for breathing exercises we clear out our nasal passages by pouring a pot of warm salty water in one nostril and letting it run out the other (no bullshit)!

Back in the yoga hall our teacher, Sadhvi Lalitambay Ji, "Lalita Ji" for short, leads us in fifteen minutes of Pranayama practices that link mind and breath through respiration control. Once all the bad air is out, our lungs are full, and all sickness has left the body, we move on to an hour and a half of Hatha Yoga.

Of the two yogic asana forms we're being taught, Hatha is the less strenuous. It's more about stretching and getting your body into positions that nature never intended, or maybe into positions that nature intended but that us couch potatoes have forgotten, than it is about jumping around. Lalita Ji demonstrates and then it's our turn.

"Just you watch me, then, you do. Place left foot on right hip. Reach left arm around behind your back and hold big toe. Stretch right arm into air and now slowly, slowly bend waist until right palm is on the floor and head is touching the knee."

At this point she is standing on one leg, folded in half at the waist, and our mouths are hanging open. "Not everybody can. If you can't, just you do this..." Guess which group we're in? It's amazing, at least to us; that an exercise which really boils down to stretching can be so physically demanding. From the second day on; we've been running on Alleve and aspirin; forced to bum them off fellow travelers. The good part is that aside from some semi-continuous joint aches and muscle pain we both feel great.

A little before 9 AM, we chant a few Oms, a mantra or two, and a Namaste and shuffle out of the yoga hall for breakfast. If we're lucky, we have about five minutes to change out of sweaty clothes and pee before the gong calls us to eat. Breakfast is served "buffet style" and al fresco in the courtyard and it's the only meal of the day that we get to eat sitting in a chair (yeah!) instead of on the floor. The fare which never varies consists of porridge, fresh fruit, and chai. Weird though it sounds, we think breakfast gets a little yummier each day. Denise and I both feel it's the best breakfast of our trip so far.

After we finish eating, we go to an outside set of sinks and wash our utensils with anti-bacterial soap. Each participant in the program is issued a segmented stainless steel plate, a matching drinking cup, and a spoon. You keep these in your room, bring them to each meal, and wash them when you're done. Any leftovers get fed to the Ashram cows.

If you don't dawdle over breakfast, you have about half an hour of free time before the next activity. We use it to wash up, do hand laundry, straighten our beds, and take care of other personal stuff. Of course, some days we just sit in the sun and sip our hot chai.

At 10 AM the gong sounds again and its time for "karmic yoga." Basically, this is a half hour of communal house cleaning to keep the ashram neat and tidy: clean the bathrooms, empty the trash, sweep the common areas (short brooms), straighten the yoga hall, etc.

The next gong rings out at 10:30 and we all assemble for a contemplative walk. The destinations for the walks vary from day to day. One morning we walked along a narrow aqueduct, winding past rice paddies where farmers labored using methods already outmoded a hundred and fifty years ago. Men led oxen which pulled a wooden plow with a straight metal blade. Behind them worked women, again and again swinging large wooden mallets to break up the clods. At the end of the aqueduct we reached a clear fast-running tributary of the Ganga where we paused to meditate and swim. Another day, we walked up a steep forest trail to a beautiful waterfall. Another walk took us to a beach along the Ganga where we chanted, "Om Ganga mai Ganga mai Ganga mai mai," meditated, and performed ritual bathing, offering flowers to the goddess river. We might add that it's a rather interesting experience to be standing waist deep in a rushing milky river and see a bloated human corpse float past. A different walk that again took us along the Ganga led us past a cremation ceremony. A crowd of men sat quietly on the bank and chatted as a large pyre burned on the shore with a hot blue flame.

The thing that all our walks have in common is silence. We haven't mentioned it yet but silence or

"Mauna" is a profound aspect of ashram life. Participants in the program are expected to be in silence from the start of evening meditation (we'll get to that) until the finish of lunch each day. Dinner is also taken in silence. Silence is more than just not talking. It means maintaining a calm inner directed focus and allowing others to maintain theirs. It's a unique and rewarding experience that we rarely encounter in our hurried day to day lives.

After the contemplative walk, the gong again sounds at 12:30 PM to signal the start of lunch. Lunch is taken in the main dining hall. This is a large bare space with mat runners along three walls and two more in the room's center. With plate, cup, and spoon in hand, you kick off your sandals; no footwear is worn in any ashram building, and take a seat on one of the mats. Sitting cross-legged or lotus (if you can) you put your plate and cup on the concrete floor in front of you and wait quietly. Two young men, Muna and Mitu, a priest in training, move quickly around the hall with large stainless steel buckets and ladles dishing out food. First comes dahl, a soupy bean or lentil based dish. This is usually followed by a vegetable, homemade yogurt or raita, sliced tomatoes, radishes, and cucumbers, rice, and chapatti, a tortilla like bread. Once everyone has been served a couple of items and chapatti, Swami Ji or Lalita Ji says a quick prayer and everyone tucks in. Muna and Mitu continue to circulate with their buckets and as long as you stay seated they continue to offer you food. Mitu's repeated mantra of: "Chapatti, chapatti? Chapatti Sir? Chapatti Mam? Chapatti?" immediately endears him to everyone.

For a couple of "aged" people, Lalita Ji's comment not ours; eating two meals a day seated cross-legged on a concrete floor is one of the ashram's biggest challenges. Thankfully, the scales are balanced by food that's consistently delicious.

After lunch, a large pot of chai is available in the courtyard, silence ends, and we all have free time until 3:00 PM. Some socializing goes on, but the reality is that everyone is fairly tired at that point. Most days things quiet down pretty quickly as people wander off to read or catch a quick nap.

Our next activity is a lecture and discussion session. The gong assembles us in the yoga hall and Randy Ji (a volunteer from the U.S.) and Lalita Ji lead discourse and discussion about how to apply ancient yoga philosophies to modern life. Questions are encouraged and it's an opportunity to learn from the two teachers and from each other. Topics range from; the eight limbs of yoga to, why do Swamis wear orange? Some sessions are deeper than others but most are equally engaging and interesting. Lalita Ji and especially Randy Ji both do a great job of making alien concepts accessible to Western thinkers.

About the time we reach saturation, we're told to break for ten minutes, use the bathroom, and then reassemble for Astanga Yoga. Like the morning session, the afternoon is devoted to movement, balance, stretching, and postures that enhance physical vitality and mental clarity. Unlike the morning session, Astanga calls for more power moves, jumping, and tough stuff like arching yourself backward and standing on your head. "If you can't do, just..." I finish the sessions drenched in sweat (Denise perspires), but except for aching joints, we feel better than when we arrived.

The Asana practice finishes with some more breathing exercises, some relax position, "savasna," inner focused meditation, and again a mantra and three or four repetitions of "Om, shanti, shanti, shanti (a prayer for peace). After that we've got another five minute break and then we gather at the Shiva temple for the evening pooja; worship ritual. This is religion pure and simple. No one is required to attend, but most everyone does. Hindus are very open about their faith and are happy to have you participate or just snap a few pictures and observe. The brief ceremony begins with the blowing of a conch shell horn and the loud ringing of bells. Adding to the cacophony of sound, the ashram's two dogs get into the act and howl in chorus with the bells. Swami Ji or Mitu then makes a ritual offering within the temple, and a ritual purification with a lighted lamp that chases away the darkness. The bells and dogs cease, a couple of prayers are said by the faithful, and the lamp is then offered to everyone so we can take in the light and release the darkness from our hearts.

Next, it's on to bhajan singing. During our first weeklong session the singing was held in the old meditation hall which involved more cold cross-legged concrete sitting. For the second session, because the weather was getting colder, we sung next to the ashram's ancient fire pit; a much better if still slightly uncomfortable proposition. Sandals are again left outside, you pick up a cymbal-like noise maker (you know, like the Hare Krishnas used to use at the airport), grab a song sheet, and for the next half-hour or more everyone sings sacred Hindu songs.

The quality of the bhajan singing depended heavily on the energy of the group. Sometimes the devotional songs were lively and fun; other times they bogged down. The songs are sacred and have a traditional way they are to be sung. Unfortunately some of the program participants in our second group missed the point. They were into music or gospel singing, or whatever, and wanted to improvise or sing something different. Not a great way to endear yourself to your Hindu hosts.

On good nights the singing didn't last too long and we had a few minutes to rest before the 7:30 dinner gong. Dinner is essentially a repeat of lunch, except that it's dark outside and the concrete floor is a little colder.

At 8:30 the gong rings a final time for evening meditation. Unlike the morning meditation, this one is directed. During the sessions Lalita Ji and Randy Ji introduce a variety of techniques that encourage present moment awareness. One evening was "Yoga Nidra," guided relaxation that induces a state of conscious sleep through body awareness and imagery. On another night we chanted a powerful mantra for fifteen minutes that when stopped led immediately to a meditative state. Other practices involved music, breathing, or focus on opening the heart to develop unconditional kindness toward all expressions of life; no kidding, heavy stuff. The meditation ends with another prayer for peace, we exit in silence, go to our beds, and the cycle begins again.

When we lay it out this way, ashram life sounds strict and regimented, but Phool Chatti is both fascinating and liberating. Bianca, a really sweet woman from Brazil (met her in Turkey) put the ashram on our radar. What a great gift! We're really glad we stumbled in and both of us feel refreshed and reenergized by our experience. We'd be going over the top to say that we're on the road to enlightenment, but if we're interested, it's just possible that after another week or two here we'd know where to look for the trailhead.

The daily routine was a big part of our experience at Phool Chatti but there was lots of other stuff that made our stay enjoyable. We have to say it again, the location is phenomenal. Several times between sessions we made the seven kilometer trek into Lakshman Jhula and each time it was a world class walk. The narrow road winds up and down, bordered by lush semi-jungle on one side and the noisy rushing Ganga on the other. Steep hills rise on all sides and everything is vibrant and alive. Birds chatter in the trees, a huge monitor lizard moves sedately through the underbrush, and troops of monkeys sit on the road shoulder grooming. With each stroll you see something a little different and entirely new.

Other highlights at the ashram included a Diwali celebration; sort of a Hindu New Years festival where we prepared and lit hundreds of tiny oil lamps (to help lead Lord Rama home from the forest) and set off fireworks.

Each session at the ashram also wrapped up with a huge bonfire on the beach with chai, sweets, and singing. Participants were asked to get together by country of origin and sing something in front of the whole group. It didn't matter what you sang; commercial jingles, rock and roll, lullabies; everything fit the occasion. With apologies to the Beach Boys, Denise and I croaked out a chorus of Good Vibrations with slightly changed lyrics, "Om's giving us good vibrations..." The best performance was delivered by a German guy named Andre who held tiny iPod speakers to his ears, rocked to the music, and belted out what sounded to the rest of us like a Ramstein-type heavy metal number. When he finished, he thanked everyone for their applause and said, "That is German nursery rhyme."

Another end-of-session event is the fire ceremony. Everyone gathers together in a rounded open balcony overlooking the Ganga and sits cross-legged on the floor (natch) around a special brazier in which is built a sacred fire using seven kinds of wood. The ceremony begins with us passing around a tray on which sits a tiny statue of Ganesha, the elephant-headed god of good luck. You make an offering by placing flower petals on the tray and then pass it to the next person. Meanwhile the fire is lit and Lalita Ji feeds it with ghee (clarified butter). After Ganesha has made his rounds we begin to chant a sacred mantra. At the end of each repetition, each person tosses a small offering of fragrant wood chips into brazier, an offering to the fire god, Agra. The chanting goes on for 108 repetitions, a propitious number that takes about half an hour to complete. At the end, we each toss a small scrap of paper into the fire on which is written something that we would like to drop from our lives: fear, hate, envy, obsession, etc. The smoke then carries our petitions to the gods.

Last among the ashrams highlights, but not by any stretch least, were the other participants in the program. There were around thirty people in each session and they came from all over: the US, Mexico, Germany, Israel, Russia, Holland, Sweden, Finland, South Africa, Slovakia, England, Switzerland, Canada, and India. Ages ranged from eighteen to maybe sixty. There was one woman slightly older than us in the first group, one man close to our age in the second, and a smattering of forty-somethings in both. Other than that, younger people were a heavy majority with the first group hovering around thirty years old and the second group mostly in their teens and early twenties (two gap-year tours). Most everybody was lively, interesting, and engaging. Add to the mix the fact that many participants were on spiritual journeys and you have a recipe for fascinating interaction and stimulating conversation.

Just so you won't think we made too much progress towards enlightenment, there was one thing at Phool Chatti that pushed my weird button. That was the whole business with the honorific, "Ji" that they use after names as in "Swami Dev Swaroop Nanda Ji." Okay, it works in that case and if you take our yoga instructor's name, "Sadhvi Lalitambay Ji" that's not so bad either. When you shorten it to: "Lalita Ji," hmmm, not so much. Use it to address Randy, the friendly and helpful American guy who facilitates stuff, and it grabs me firmly by the funny bone. My problem is that "Ji" is pronounced "gee" as in "Gee whiz!" So what we've got is Randy "G." Every time I hear it, or worse yet say it, my chattering monkey mind leaps off the yogic path and goes totally Hip-hop. "Yo, yo, you gotta meet my homies: Chedda Cheese, White Boy Bob, and yo, yo, Randy G!"

In all seriousness, Phool Chatti is a wonderful experience. Denise and I thought long and hard about staying for a third session. If my knees were in better shape or we had more ibuprofen, it might have happened. As it stands, the ashram is on our short list of places we want to revisit.

Day 311 - November 12 - Friday

Today, we say goodbye to Phool Chatti and move on. After lunch around 2 PM a taxi is going to scoop us up for the hour plus ride to Haridwar. We'll hang out there until about midnight and then, with luck, we'll catch a sleeper train to Varanasi; on to the crazy beating heart of India.

Day 312 - November 13 - Saturday - Varanasi, India

Holy Hanuman! Everything went off like we planned but what a stretched out wringer of a trip. Our taxi showed-up on time and we set out down a rough narrow road that twists and turns its way along the Ganga. The driver kept it smooth as possible, but it was still the kind of ride where we swayed from side to side and grabbed for handholds. If you've ever driven on an old mountain-hugging logging road you know the feeling. The scenery was great and the views of the Ganga spectacular. Monkeys were in the trees and although we didn't see any, there were signs telling us to watch out for elephants!

Following forty-five minutes of wonderful bumpy scenery, we crossed the Ganga, turned onto a main road, and rolled towards Haridwar. It was somewhere along this stretch that we decided that Mr. Toad hadn't been such a bad driver after all. It wasn't that the current guy was worse; in fact he seemed a little more cautious. Our sudden change of heart toward Mr. Toad was due to an equally sudden epiphany. All of the drivers in India are partially crazy, and a small but important percentage are lock-me-away, bat-shit, bonkers! Over the years, we've seen some pretty knarly traffic. Heck, we've driven in Mexico City at rush hour, but we've never experienced traffic that compares with India.

They have some secret formula for determining right-of-way. We can tell that it has something to do with the size of your vehicle. Trucks and buses trump cars; cars take auto-rickshaws and motor scooters, pedal rickshaws trump bicycles and pushcarts, and of course everything on wheels beats a pedestrian. This would be straight forward except that a bunch of other stuff apparently alters the game. Are you driving on the side of the road appropriate to your direction of travel or are you rushing headlong into oncoming traffic? Is your vehicle new and shiny, or is it an old and dented beater? Is your three passenger auto-rickshaw carrying twelve or more people? Is your truck loaded with straw or bricks? Do you value your life?

Horn honking is also extremely important. You must do it constantly and vigorously. Honking adds bonus points to your vehicle and if performed stridently enough it allows you to compete outside your weight class. If a sudden brain aneurysm should make you inadvertently forget to apply your horn. All trucks are conveniently labeled with large eye-catching signs that read either "BLOW HORN" or the less demanding "HORN PLEASE."

Farm tractors and two-wheeled medieval wooden oxcarts are moving obstacles that everyone is required to pass. Cows have right-of-way over everything. Goats and pigs also receive limited invulnerability points. Dogs are roadkill.

We're only guessing you understand. We suspect things work like this, but as foreigners we're deep in the dark. We're pretty sure that driving skill in India is inherited genetically; some kind of stockcar race memory that simply emerges full-blown when they pump the gas pedal.

Driving from the backseat takes it out of you. When we reached Haridwar we'd only been traveling for an hour-and-a-half, but it felt oh so much longer.

"Hotel Sachin International" is the fancy name for a nondescript slightly dated establishment that's conveniently situated directly across from the Haridwar train station. Making good use of their location (it's everything in business) they offer a partial day rate of $14 to people waiting for trains. That's us! We registered (triplicate) and checked in. On most days we'd have given the room a pass, but it did have a bed and a bathroom, and it was located, literally, across the street from the station. With our sleeper scheduled to pull out at 11:55 PM, it fit our needs to a T. We tossed our bags inside, steel-cabled them to various immoveable objects, and set out to find the status of our tickets. This proved an interesting exercise in patience.

Indian trains have this wonderful efficient online ticketing system that when push comes to shove is nearly as confusing as the country's driving rules. It's easy to get to the website. It's easy to locate the trains you may want. As you go to book, things start to get murky. What ticket should you buy: AC1, Second Class, AC2, AC3, Third Class, Sleeper, AC chair, First Class? It turns out that for long distances and overnight, AC1 and AC2 are considered the way to go. Second, Third, and Sleeper class passengers get packed into cars that to the uninitiated resemble deportation scenes from the Holocaust.

Once you make your class selection, you're shown what's available. Invariably, this is a "waitlisted" ticket. At this point you go down the rabbit hole. What the heck is a waitlisted ticket? Well, it goes something like this. Tickets can be purchased months in advance and cancellation fees are ridiculously low. As a result, the limited numbers of confirmed AC2 seats (AC1 cars are pulled by unicorns) sell out immediately. Once all the confirmed seats are gone, the train company begins selling "Reservation Against Cancellation" or RAC tickets. Snag one of these and it means that you can board the train. It doesn't however mean that you have the sleeping berth that you paid for. If the train is full and if no one cancels, you may be stuck in a stiff hard backed seat and told to count yourself lucky. RAC tickets also sell out quickly, which brings us to waitlist tickets. Buy one of these tickets (usually all that's available) and you've purchased a place in a queue. You pay your money and you're assigned a "WL" number. As people cancel and special reserved quotas (elderly, disabled, foreign dignitaries, etc.) are released your number drops. When it reaches zero, congratulations you now have an RAC ticket and are in another queue waiting for that elusive confirmed seat.

Our WL numbers started at 3 and 4 which are darn good and most people assured us that anything under 15 or 20 was a sure thing. When we checked online before setting out for Haridwar, we were at 1 and 2; better, but not good enough to get us on the train. Most of the action in the queue takes place in the last twenty-four hours so we figured no problem and walked over to the station to find out where we stood. Where we stood was in a non-moving line in front of ticket windows where all the signage was in Devanagari script; that's Hindi, and you thought Arabic was tough! Except for a few signs in English listing the platforms and the location of public toilets the station suffered from a severe lack of useable information. After shuffling around a bit, we decided to bag it and go check on the Internet.

Back across the street at a hole-in-the-wall Internet/Travel Agency with old bags of rice and dusty cans of cooking oil stacked against the wall its helpful young proprietor logged onto the ticket system and displayed our status. Only five and a half hours to go and we were still at 1 and 2! The young guy explained that any further waitlist action would wrap up by 8 PM. We'd then either be canceled or issued a boarding pass. *Hmmm, okay dokey; still a little vague.* We thanked him and left saying that we'd return in a couple of hours.

We were getting tired at this point and the uncertainty with the tickets didn't help; *Om...* Anyway, we did what we usually do when the going gets confused; we went looking for something to eat. When in doubt, either get prone or gobble something. Actually, we first went in search of the city's ghats, waterfront steps that lead into the Ganga and are used for ritual bathing and ceremony.

Haridwar is a holy city and its nightly riverfront aarti (ritual prayers) are supposedly among India's most interesting; sort of a Varanasi "light." The upshot was that we walked for an hour dodging wheeled traffic; swimming along in the colorful bubbling stream of people, bicycles, carts, and cows while an exciting mix of sights, noises, and smells buffeted us from all sides. We thought we knew where we were going, but eventually the sun set and the time for the aarti came and went. We never found our way to the ghats, but we still had a good time. We especially enjoyed our $0.91 splurge for a pedal rickshaw back to a restaurant near the hotel.

Once we fueled up, we walked back to the Internet/travel agency to recheck our status. Now it was only five minutes before 8 PM and there we were; still number 1 and 2 on the no fly list! At that point the agency guy's older brother showed up. "No problem, for 200 rupees each, I can go over to the train station and be back in fifteen minutes with your confirmed tickets." This ability appeared to stem from an intimate knowledge of the arcane inner-workings of the waitlist and priority quota systems. The fifteen minutes turned into forty-five, but at last big brother called back and told little brother to recheck our status. Sure enough, our status had moved from WL right past RAC into confirmed.

"Now you give me 400 rupees."

"Uh, sure." *Okay, we're confirmed, but we still don't have paper tickets.* "Don't we need paper tickets?"

"No, no, this number all you need."

"You're sure?"

"Yes, yes no problem." More or less satisfied that we now had confirmed seats we retired to our "luxurious" digs to await the witching hour. At about 11:30 we gathered our stuff and hustled over to the station. As we approached the main building, where at least a hundred locals were asleep on its concrete steps under blankets ostensibly awaiting trains, a garbled loud speaker was already announcing boarding for ours. With minimal help from the station signage, finding our platform and then our "AC Tier 2 Sleeper Car" was more a matter of blind luck than actual directions.

Hauling our bags on board, we stumbled down the aisle, only to discover that our berths were already occupied and that all available luggage space was crammed with other people's stuff.

The car is divided into open curtained compartments with four upper/lower seats/berths on one side of the train and two upper/lower seat/berths on the other, across the aisle. We were supposed to have the two upper berths in the four seat compartment (two side by side seats by day). An old woman and two fifty-something men, however, had already folded down the beds and encamped.

"Excuse me, but we have seats 8 and 10. Those are our beds."

"Yes, yes, no problem. You here and here." "Here and here" referred to one of the upper berths and a lower berth on the two seat side of the car that was piled with bags and boxes.

"I don't know, we're supposed to be in 8 and 10."

"No, here is good. No problem." Tired and not at our most persuasive, we acquiesced.

After a bunch of rearranging, Denise climbed into the upper bunk in the four-bunk compartment. I made up the coffin sized lower one across the aisle. Our luggage, with nowhere else to go, ended up smack in the middle of the aisle, where everyone had to step over it.

"Are these your bags? You should move them."

About this time, the conductor came around and asked for our tickets. "We don't have paper tickets, but here are our PNR (reservation) numbers and our Ids."

"Where is ticket?"

"We don't have paper tickets. We were told we didn't need them; just these numbers."

"Where you buy your ticket?"

"We bought them online, they're e-tickets."

"Online?"

"Yes, Internet, they're e-tickets." The guy is holding a clipboard. We peek and can plainly see that it lists our names, our seat numbers, and our magic PNR numbers.

"Where is ticket?" Despite earlier assurances to the contrary, it appears that boarding with a PNR number written on a piece of paper and not one that's been printed on a hardcopy of a random Internet page is somehow a major bureaucratic faux pas. The conductor fined us fifty rupees for being rule breakers and scofflaws. He then wrote us out a paper ticket that no one ever looked at again.

The conductor went away and I searched for sleep in the narrow bouncing bunk; lost cause. It was too cramped to use my CPAP. It was too hot. It was too stuffy. It was too uncomfortable. Worst of all, the train's engineer was a virtuoso on the whistle and he played a never ending solo. Morning found me alive but feeling like I'd slept in an old ashtray (something I haven't actually done for many a year). Denise got a little more sleep, but didn't fare much better.

Making the coffin bunk into a chair for day travel was only a marginal improvement. I don't like to whine, but this was a really crummy ride; cramped, uncomfortable, almost no food, and disgusting bathrooms. Adding to our discomfort, the train ran five hours behind schedule. What was supposed to be a pleasant thirteen hour overnight jaunt turned into a grueling eighteen hour saga. Instead of rolling into Varanasi in the middle of the afternoon, we rolled in with the setting sun. At that point we were like; *We don't care! Just get us off!*

Exiting the huge Varanasi station, we threw caution to the wind and hooked up with the first autorickshaw guy that stepped into our path.

"How much to take us to the Misrha Guesthouse?"

"200 rupees."

"Yes, okay." *Anything, just get us to the hotel.* "You do know the Mishra Guesthouse?"

"Yes, yes, I know; drive then walk."

A few minutes later we were in his tuk-tuk threading our way through hair-raising Varanasi traffic. Based on our progress, we can only assume there was carnage and mayhem in our wake. After about fifteen minutes, we neared the Ganga and moved into narrower and narrower streets. First the trucks couldn't fit, then it was the cars, finally our driver had to pull over and park his three-wheeler.

Transitioning from driver to guide, he hopped out and set off at a fast pace with us dragging our bags in his wake. The alleys twisted and turned and got darker and darker. Just about the time we were starting to think of muggings and trails of breadcrumbs we stumbled, tired and grateful, into the lobby of the Mishra. Train travel had just moved from the top of our India transportation list into the "over my dead body" category.

Day 314 - November 15 - Monday

Getting here was an ordeal, but two days in Varanasi made up for the effort. What an amazing, twisted place!

The Mishra, where we're staying, is a backpacker type hotel; recommended to us by a fellow traveler at the ashram. Like most backpackers it's a mixed bag. Cleanliness is only average. The building is two hundred years old and the rooms have seen better days. On the other side of the scale the people who run the place are friendly and helpful, rates are less than $12 per night, the rooftop restaurant has excellent food with even better views, and when the power fails, as it does on a daily basis in India, the guesthouse has battery backups.

When the owner showed us to our room he proudly unlatched a door that opens onto a small balcony; one of the features which justify the "extravagant" cost. After showing us the balcony, he looked at us and with a straight face and told us, "If you go out, do not to leave balcony door open, or monkeys will come in and take your things." *Monkeys, swell, no doubt a euphemism for cat burglars!*

After a leisurely (their service is so slow that there's no other kind) meal on the rooftop. We crawled into bed and were out in a wink. The next day I got up and stepped out onto the balcony to enjoy the morning. I stretched and looked up the alley to my left; then I stretched again and turned to my right. *Holy Crap! Big scary monkeys! Don't look 'em in the eye. Hey, the male is grinning. Oh God, he's not grinning, he's showing teeth. Back through the door. Slowly, don't make eye contact. Lock it!* "Hey Denise, I don't think we'll get much use out of the balcony."

On a couple of other occasions we watched a woman next door hang out her laundry. Each time she came out onto her roof she was accompanied by a girl with a long pole whose job was the keep the monkeys at bay. Okay, so no euphemisms, honest to god monkeys!

Despite its furry neighbors, the Mishra Guesthouse has a stellar location. It hunkers on a tiny alley in what was once medieval Varanasi. Behind it stretches the labyrinthine maze of the old city and fifty yards from its front door wind the banks of the Ganga. The views from the rooftop are awesome taking in everything from river action to ancient Hindu temples.

Varanasi is one of the holiest spots in India and also one of the world's oldest continuously inhabited cities. Where the old city meets the Ganga the entire riverfront is lined with ghats. Each long section of steps leads to the river and carries its own special name. Most of the ghats are used for ritual bathing and pilgrims from all corners of India flock here to wash away their sins in the Ganga's holy, albeit polluted, waters.

The ghat closest to the Mishra is called Manikarnika and it's a special case. Manikarnika is Varanasi's main "burning ghat" and it's considered the most auspicious place possible for a Hindu to be cremated. As we exited the alley from the guesthouse, we immediately encountered the smell of smoke and moments later we were walking between huge mountains of firewood. Giant scales sit next to the wood so that each log can be precisely weighed to determine the exact cost of each cremation. Threading our way through the stacks of wood we emerged onto the burning ghat itself.

Before us were perhaps a dozen funeral pyres; some nearly spent, others not yet burning. Outcasts called doms were at work tending the cremations, raking coals, adjusting the logs. A body waited near the shore while workers removed its wrappings of gold foil and flowers and tossed them into the river. Another body was laid on its pyre and wood was carefully stacked over it. Still another was already engulfed in flames; burning head and shoulders jutting from its bed of logs. Public cremations aren't for the queasy and they're definitely not a sight we'll soon forget.

Varanasi's other ghats are less spectacular, but just as interesting. Moving on, we worked our way from one to another soaking in the city's heady mélange of life. Boats ply the river. Sadhus, priests, flower sellers, bathing pilgrims, people washing clothes, wandering cattle, beggars, touts, hawkers, entertainers, ascetics, and tourists swirl together in a colorful chaotic mix that makes for first class people watching.

Our prize probably goes to a hunched-over, wizened, little guy wearing diaper-like pants and a t-shirt. As far as we could tell, his job was to collect cow shit with his bare hands! Watching him carefully and diligently scoop it up and pat it into little piles was about as weird as it gets.

As the sun set, we wandered back to Dasaswamedh Ghat, the city's liveliest, to catch the nightly "Ganga aarti." Each evening around 7 PM the ghat fills with people and five priests standing on raised platforms perform an elaborate worship ritual involving copious clouds of incense, flaming braziers, and lots of noise; conch horns, bells, and gongs. The ceremony was essentially the same that we participated in at Phool Chatti except writ large; more drawn out, more theatrical.

When the aarti finished, we purchased a ten rupee pooja offering, a lighted candle with flowers in a small cup, and Denise set it adrift to join the hundreds of other twinkling prayers swirling away on the river.

On our second day here in Varanasi we went on a "free" tour facilitated by the guesthouse. The "free" is in quotes because there's no free lunch, everything has a cost. In this case, nothing was asked up front, but if we enjoyed ourselves our consciences would surely dictate a heartfelt tip; that and the fact that we were going to get a close up look at an outlet store for silk.

The tour was a blast. Jaffe, our guide, was an interesting old guy and our companions were three affable women from Spain. For nearly three hours we explored mazelike pedestrian streets; picking up tidbits of history and culture, and slipping out of our sandals to visit temples and a mosque.

Since Jaffe is Hindu he was permitted to escort us inside the temples and that was pretty cool. As we said, Hindus are very open about their religion, but normally as a non-Hindu you have to have an invite or stay outside. The various temples were dedicated to different deities or incarnations; this one to Krishna, that one to Hanuman, another to Vishnu, and so on. At one stop, we saw a priest performing smoky rituals in a "smallpox temple." At another a priest gave us small pieces of offering sugar to eat.

To western eyes, ours at least, many of the temple decorations look garish. One or more statues usually take center stage. Painted in loud bright colors, they invariably have a cartoonish or "sideshow" appearance that's an exact opposite to the somber iconography of European Christian churches.

Varanasi is a hard city to describe because it comes at you on so many levels. On one level it's filthy. A layer of grunge covers everything. The alleyways are cracked and uneven. The air smells of urine and incense.

Cow poop is literally everywhere. As you walk your eyes are constantly drawn upwards to interesting architecture and soaring temple spires, but you have to just as consistently watch your feet. It's either that or embrace the pleasure of wet cow dung between your toes. From watching Jaffe who wasn't sufficiently vigilant, we'd say it's an experience best avoided.

Arm-span wide streets are lined chock-a-block with dark dingy literally hole-in-the-wall businesses. Many are just big enough for the owner to sit cross-legged behind his small display of wares, cooking brazier, or sewing machine. Food looks and smells enticing, but we wouldn't touch it with a ten-foot pole. A rat lies dead in the gutter. Any unused wall space is a urinal.

On another level, there's a magic about Varanasi. It vibrates with a religious fervor and these same alleys are packed with life, color, and spectacle. Hidden temples lie just around every corner and a peek through most any doorway reveals something fascinating.

Our tour with Jaffe finished up with the close-up look at the silk shop which to be honest, wasn't such a bad deal. The salesmen at the store made a valiant effort to sell us something. They chatted us up, plied us with tea, and laid out samples of nearly all their wares. We both nodded politely and Denise tried on a sari, but, when push came to shove, all we bought was an inexpensive scarf. The salesmen did better with the Spanish gals who undoubtedly had bigger suitcases. Denise had fun helping them pick things. While I waited, I had fun watching tiny mice scamper in and out of the store.

We can't leave the subject of Varanasi without mention of a further "feature" of the Mishra Guesthouse, "The Cult of the Really Annoying Speaker." When we arrived at the Mishra it was already dark. Since we were dog tired, we just went up to the roof, ate dinner, and immediately went to bed. Because of our late arrival we failed to notice the proximity of a large ominous looking speaker mounted on the wall opposite our monkey laden balcony. The next morning, it called itself to our attention in a manner that even quality earplugs couldn't lessen. Evidently, the building across the alley housed a cult of cat stranglers that were religiously compelled to amplify their caterwauling at both 4 AM and 6 PM. We're not sure about the Cult of the Really Annoying Speaker's actual affiliation, but obviously all its members were enthusiastic if untalented Yoko Ono imitators. By our last morning, we were praying for destructive monkeys and torn wires.

Day 321 - November 22 - Monday - Jaipur, India

As so many seem to, our last week went by in a rush, and once again we're playing catch-up with our journal. On our third morning in Varanasi, a tout met us at the guesthouse and lead us through the maze to a point where we could climb into an auto-rickshaw. An hour of put-putting later our driver turned into the local airport only to discover it closed and mothballed. A new airport had just opened the day before and the guy didn't know it! Fortunately, the new field was only fifteen minutes away and we'd allowed ourselves plenty of time before our flight. When we arrived at the new airport, the auto-rickshaw guy asked us to pay extra since he'd been forced to backtrack. *Dude! It ain't gonna happen.*

Before we could board our Kingfisher flight to Khajuraho, we had to queue up to pay a special airport development tax. This was absolutely priceless. They'd built Varanasi a brand spanking new modern airport, but every single passenger was required to wait in the same long, snaking, single-file, line to pay the tax. At the front of the queue sat a makeshift plywood kiosk that looked, more than a little, like a Charles Schulz Peanuts psychiatry stand. Seated behind it, a single harried civil servant struggled to keep up with a ballpoint pen and his grandfather's triplicate receipt book. To make matters worse, he accepted payments in both Indian rupees and foreign currency. Each time someone presented Dollars, Euros, or whatever, he laboriously figured the exchange rate on a hand calculator. Our flight wasn't due to depart anytime soon so it was no big deal. For other tourists with higher blood pressure and tighter schedules it was meltdown and lose-it time.

The new airport was fairly spiffy but it also looked slightly grubby and unfinished. Unfortunately, we think we probably saw it on the best day of its existence.

Our flight to Khajuraho was a pleasant forty-five minute puddle-jumper and when we exited the airport a taxi guy was holding up a sign with our name; definitely the upside of reservations.

Like everyone else who comes to Khajuraho, we went there to see its famous carvings. The small town, a World Heritage Site, is home to three sets of temples, twenty-five in total, that boast some of the finest artistic stonework in the world. The superb quality of the life-like sculptures is eye-catching but it's their blatant eroticism that makes them unique. The carvings depict the lives of gods and goddesses, warriors and musicians, real animals and mythical beasts, but the overarching theme is sex and lots of it. Acrobatic sex, group sex, oral sex, bestiality; if it's popular on the Internet today, it was also popular in stone in the year 950!

After we checked in at our hotel, we walked over to the main temple group and spent a couple of hours oohing and aahing until we were shooed out at sunset.

The next day, I woke up sick and a sudden fondness for a proximity to toilets put a swift end to my Khajuraho sojourns. Denise felt sympathy for me, but not enough to hang out in our room and watch me sleep. While I took pills and recuperated, she visited a local folk craft museum, sampled a couple of restaurants, and walked past the other temple groups.

By day two I was on the mend, so Denise suggested that we partake of ayurvedic massages. Ayurvedic comes from "Ayurveda" a Sanskrit word meaning "the knowledge for long life." Today it refers to an ancient system of Indian traditional medicine. The Unnamed Guidebook says that a local massage place called Ayur Arogyam is "the real deal" so we strolled on over. Denise was excited. For my part, I felt crappy but figured it couldn't hurt.

The center is modest and clean. Each of us was introduced to our practitioner, male for me, female for Denise, and then we were shown to small private rooms. We were asked to remove all our clothing. Towels were draped strategically over our genitalia, and for the next hour we were pummeled, kneaded, and drenched in aromatic essential oils as our therapists worked to purge unwanted toxins from our bodies. It must have worked, because when the massage ended I felt like a wet oily noodle, but much better than when we first walked in; total cost for two, 2,800 rupees ($63.64).

The friendly couple who own the center are from Kerala in southern India and while we relaxed with post-massage cups of tea, the man engaged us in conversation. Waxing spiritual, he shared his devotion to Sathya Sai Baba. Baba (deceased since our visit) was an 84-year-old guru who rocked orange robes and a halo of dark frizzy hair; a slightly bizarre religious figure revered by millions as a living Hindu god. After explaining about Baba's healing powers, his miracles, and his love, our host shifted gears to talk about American involvement in the Middle East. "America is making big big mistake! Is not Iraq you should be bombing, is Pakistan!" *Oh well, so much for the love.*

After the massage, I recovered enough so that we could book a four-and-a-half hour taxi ride and move on to our next destination, Orchha. Orchha is a quiet village of about 8,500 that sits on the banks of the Betwa River. Unlike Khajuraho which crawls with persistent touts, Orchha is pleasant and hassle free. Our room at the "Fortview Hotel" smelled slightly moldy (incense works wonders), but lived up to its name with large windows and impressive views of the fortified seventeenth century palaces just across the river.

Now it was Denise's turn to get sick. It was probably something she ate, either that, or a wave of massage released toxins leaving her body. She didn't go off the deep end like I did, but she vomited and felt sickly enough that we cranked our plans down a notch and took things nice and slow.

While we're on the subject of Denise's health, you may have wondered what became of her Zanzibar beach,

Doxycycline induced, photo-onycholysis. Well, her nails didn't come tumbling out, but lifting from the nail bed wasn't the end of the tale. While we were staying at Phool Chatti her nails started to take on a greenish cast. We're not talking sci-fi glow-in-the-dark radioactive, but there was definitely a green tint taking hold under the surface. Concerned that it was a fungus, we made a fruitless trek to local hole-in-the-wall pharmacies and medicinal shops in search of an appropriate remedy. Empty handed, we turned back to the Internet; Medhelp to the rescue. Pseudomonas Bacteria (the yucky green stuff) is the result of trauma, not fungus! Prescription; "leave it alone," hide it under polish for six months and supposedly it goes away on its own. We're waiting to see.

After two nights in Orchha, a little sightseeing, and a couple of good meals, we were both back in the pink and it was time to leave.

Following our successful taxi ride from Khajuraho to Orchha, we both decided that car hire is the way to go in India. Sure, it costs more than a couple of train tickets. And true, you don't rub shoulders with the locals like you do on the bus, but other than that, there's no downside. Taxis pick you up when and where you want. They take you to exactly where you want to go and they stop anywhere you want to along the way. Best of all, car hire is ridiculously cheap. So far, the most we've shelled out is $53 per day for exclusive use of a car with driver, and that's with them paying for gas and picking up any toll charges.

Anyway, in Orchha we bipped into a closet size travel agency and arranged for the interesting but slow six-hour trip to Agra (Taj Mahal). With the exception of a couple of forgettable transport towns the drive took us through rural areas and small villages.

India is a nation of wild extremes. In the heart of its big cities it's an Internet powerhouse with a veneer of hip western culture and a bright Bollywood outlook. In the countryside it's a third world country where wooden camel carts and communal village water pumps are more common than private cars. Tiny farms and makeshift businesses line the roads. Women in flamboyantly bright saris walk the dusty shoulders with bundles of wood, baskets, and bright metal pots balanced securely on their heads. People shepherd small herds of goats and cattle. Partially dressed men and boys bathe in streams or at the village pumps. Every vehicle imaginable rattles and clatters down the bumpy road.

Our driver was a strange little bloke named, Panchi. Compared to our previous drivers he wasn't very aggressive; bit of a pokey-Joe. On the other hand our road was tough and congested with detours and poor pavement which required lots of attention and constant maneuvering. Overall, Panchi did a good job, and despite being speed challenged we agreed to meet with his boss and see if we could hire him for another five days.

When we reached Agra, he drove us to his office, which was a bathroom-sized travel agency a couple of blocks from the Taj Mahal. Panchi's boss, "Bobby," leaned toward the slick-Willy persuasion, but after some mild sparing we reached an agreement that seemed mutually satisfactory. To sweeten the deal, Bobby threw in a complimentary drive to a riverfront viewpoint where, along with Paulo a traveler from Portugal, we watched the sun set over the Taj.

We spent that night in a hotel just down the street from the monument. It wasn't our first choice, but at least it featured a convenient location. The next morning at 5:30 AM Paulo knocked on our door to say that Bobby had our Taj Mahal tickets and that he'd be here in a few minutes with our guide. During our negotiations, Bobby, as another deal sweetener, had offered to pick up our tickets. At the time, we shrugged and said, "Sure, why not?" The plan was that he'd save us from waiting in line and that we'd get to the Taj right when it opened, see the sunrise, and avoid the crowds. The guide was an unexpected and annoying twist. Bobby had asked us if we wanted one and we'd told him, "No, not interested." We figured that since a guide was coming anyway; Paulo must have requested her. It later turned out that he'd also declined a guide, and assumed that we'd asked for one. *Bad tout! Bad guide! No tip!*

By 6:30 we were queued up in front of the Taj Mahal's East gate waiting to pass through security; separate lines for men and women. You shuffle through some stiles, step through a metal detector, let them poke around in your bag, and then you're in.

"What's this, a computer?" The guy is holding my Kindle book reader.

"Yeah, it's sort of a computer." The guy looks at the thumb keyboard and the blank screen.

"Computers aren't allowed!"

"Uh, it's not a computer it's a book;" *actually much more dangerous.*

"Okay, you can go in."

Once you're past security, you pass through a huge ornate gate and there framed in the entrance is your first view of the Taj Mahal. This is where a scrum of stressed tourists jostles, shoves, and yells at you for getting in their picture. Beyond this funnel, you find yourself facing Taj's gardens and its empty reflecting pool (it's only filled for visiting dignitaries). Despite obnoxious tourists and an ultra annoying guide who kept demanding our attention, the Taj was pretty spectacular. Like the pyramids, we'd seen a million pictures, but the reality is still impressive. There's a peaceful symmetry about the famous building that makes you simply want to sit and stare.

Outside, the Taj Mahal is a marvel; inside, not so much. Its walls are elaborately inlaid with coral and semi-precious stones, but we found it all a little cold and ho-hum. It is after all a mausoleum for the dead, not a place intended for the living. In keeping with its somber nature, the drafty marble interior is so dimly lit that it's difficult to appreciate its details. We did a quick in and out and then spent the majority of our visit admiring the building's wondrous exterior.

Agra is home to other popular sights besides the Taj Mahal, but we decided to give them a pass. We met Panchi at 10 AM and rolled for another World Heritage Site, Fatehpur Sikri. Located about forty kilometers west of Agra, Fatehpur Sikri boasts the well preserved remains of a Mughal empire capital which dates from the late 1500's.

Since cars aren't allowed in the historical area, Panchi stopped at a free dirt parking area a short distance away. Not realizing how close we were, we took Panchi's advice and climbed into an overpriced auto-rickshaw. Before we got moving however, I lost it on a persistent wanta-be guide.

"Namaste, would you like a guide?"

"No thank you, were fine."

"You really should have a guide, blah blah blah."

"No thank you, we just want to be on our own."

"I can blah blah blah."

"I'm sorry, we're not interested."

"But blah blah blah."

"No, we don't want a guide!"

And, so on, "Blah blah blah."

With no end in sight I snapped at the guy, "Look, why don't you just go away!"

"I can't go away, I live here."

Denise said he looked ready to cry, and I've felt like a shit-heel ever since. Faced with near constant sales pitches, it's easy to forget that many of the touts, vendors, and guides that you encounter in hard-scrabble countries aren't just aggressive and persistent, they're truly desperate. That you're rich and they're poor is an inescapable reality of independent travel; one that calls for continuing patience and sensitivity.

Fatehpur Sikri's two main points of interest are a large impressive mosque and a set of palaces. Of the two, the palace complex is the more interesting. Most of the buildings are only one or two stories tall and the predominant building material is red sandstone. Carving and decorative work is ubiquitous but understated. Wandering about, we both enjoyed the site's openness and austerity. There was an Eastern aesthetic about the architecture that put both of us in mind of China's Forbidden City, a last emperor sort of vibe.

Much to the disappointment of our auto-rickshaw driver, we walked back to the parking lot.

Our day ended at the Pearl Palace Hotel in Jaipur which at $18 per night is a steal. Our room is spacious, bright, and well decorated. The bed is comfortable. There's free in-room Wi-Fi and the rooftop Peacock Restaurant is the bomb. If they weren't fully booked we'd stay an extra day.

Day 322 - November 23 - Tuesday - Pushkar, India

Today started off normal, but ended up a little weird. We got up, ate a leisurely breakfast, and then Panchi picked us up at our hotel.

Our first stop of the day was on a busy downtown Jaipur street where we snapped quick photos of the "Hawa Mahal" or The Palace of the Winds. The palace is an impressive five-storey pink sandstone building that was constructed in 1799. The thing that makes the palace remarkable is its front façade; honey-combed with delicate lattice windows, places where ladies of the royal household used to stand behind small shutters and watch the life of the city without being seen.

From there we drove into the rugged hills north of town and visited the enormous sprawling palace-fort of Amber; pronounced "Amer." This is the ancient capital of Jaipur another 1500's era relic. Although ancient ramparts snake Great-Wall-like into the distance the feel is totally Maharaja. Buildings soar with domes and turrets. Tile and marble work is detailed and ostentatious. Mirrored audience halls and creature comforts like an elaborate hammam (bath) take center stage. With its honey-colored courtyards, pavilions, and defensive walls Amber Fort is probably as impressive a castle as we've ever visited.

It would have been nice if at least one or two rooms had featured some furnishings, but even bare it was possible to imagine the glory of the former Raj. Painted elephants slowly hauling tourists up the hill helped with our visualization.

Next, it was on to Pushkar. This was only a hundred mile drive from the fort, still it took us nearly four hours. Much of the road was six-lane highway, the best we've seen in India, but even there traffic only rolled along at about 45 mph. In the cities and on rural sections it literally crawled.

All of that was normal. Here comes the weird. We arrived in Pushkar around 4:30 PM checked into our hotel and surrendered our passports to their front desk. With bureaucracy out of the way we headed to our room to settle in and unpack. A few minutes later we heard a light knock on our door and the reception guy was standing outside. "Excuse me, but you gave me your daughter's passport." *Say what? What daughter?* "Yes, this is your passport, but this is not your wife's." *Oh God, no!* But, oh God, yes! At our last hotel, they'd swapped Denise's passport with someone else's. We had Leah somebody-or-other's and presumably she had Denise's!

This nightmare in the making could easily have gone from bad to worse, but fortunately we were handed the relatively clean end of the stick. A quick call discovered that the Pearl Palace was still holding Denise's passport at their front desk. *Whew!* Luckily, Leah hadn't picked it up and blithely moved on. The Pearl Palace promised that they would get it to us before we left Pushkar (DHL or something) and told us to just hang on to the other passport until they decided what to do.

A short while later we heard another knock on our door and the reception guy told us that the Pearl Palace had called back; they were going to send a car with Denise's passport and pick up the other. We assume that this sudden change was initiated by a freaked out Leah who'd just been apprised that a couple of strangers in Pushkar were thumbing through her passport.

That night we were called out of our room by the sound of trumpets and raucous drumming. On the street below a wedding procession was repeatedly marching a loop between a pair of nearby temples. We never saw the bride, but the groom, dressed as a Raja, rode by several times on horseback accompanied by musicians, male friends, and guys carrying large electric candelabra-like table lamps. Cords from the lamps snaked back to an auto-rickshaw that we assume carried the generator. After a couple of circuits, the procession stopped at a corner just up from the hotel and the guys began to dance and shimmy to the beat of tribal sounding drums. This appeared to be a men only affair (bachelor party?) and we watched as several local women were shooed away. Female tourists on the other hand were encouraged to get down and join in the dancing. Loose foreign women to liven things up; who knows?

Day 323 - November 24 - Wednesday

We woke up this morning to the sound of water running, splashing, dripping, and pounding from the eaves. Outside our shutters a heavy rain was soaking the town and had turned the street in front of our hotel into a small lake. After so many dry months it feels odd to see everything wet and soggy.

We hadn't planned to do much today, but now it looks like we might do even less. The hotel's rooftop restaurant is closed because it's too wet so food is being served in the shelter of the portico around its ground-floor patio. The street in front is maybe a foot and a half deep in water and there's an inch of it standing just inside the hotel's front door. A raised ledge runs along the wall of the hotel. If the rain lets up and the water subsides a little we may be able to wade along it and reach higher ground. Only parts of the town are flooded, so a walk isn't out of the question. If the rain doesn't let up we'll just hole up in our room and take it easy.

Our current hotel is called "Seventh Heaven." It's located in a restored havali, which is a traditional Indian house set around a courtyard; sort of the Indian version of a Moroccan riad. We're staying three nights so we decided to splurge for "Silk Sari" the fanciest room in the place at $35 per night. The main reason we picked the second floor room was that two of its walls are set with large windows that overlook the street. What we didn't expect when we pre-booked was that the windows would be screened, but unglazed. "If we put glass in the windows the monkeys break it." *Damn those monkeys!* Unfortunately, with the rain and unseasonable cold unless we keep the windows tightly shuttered the room is a refrigerator. Given a choice between light and heat, we chose heat. Even with things buttoned up we still had to request a space heater and an extra blanket. Oh well, only a few more days in Rajastan then we fly to southern India and a return to warmer climates.

Still waiting for the passport; hope the roads are clear.

Day 324 - November 25 - Thursday

The rain stopped, the water receded, and the passport arrived. About 6 PM we realized it was Thanksgiving so we celebrated with mashed potatoes, steamed vegetables, and apple crisp ala mode. Pushkar is a holy city (veggie only!) so no wine, no turkey!

Day 327 - November 28 - Sunday - Udaipur, India

Our deal with "Bobby" was for chauffeured transport from Agra to Udaipur; not necessarily all of it in the same car. When we arrived in Pushkar, Panchi decided that he didn't want to hang around (father sick, looked healthy to us, blah blah blah) so he arranged for another driver named, Kanea, to take us the rest of the way. That was three days ago. We scraped the mud of Pushkar from our feet and rolled for Udaipur, a city billed as the "most romantic" in Rajasthan.

Kanea proved himself a more aggressive driver than Panchi, better and faster, but once again roads were congested and despite his valiant efforts Pushkar to Udaipur stretched into a six hour journey. Denise read a book, I watched the rural scenery; time passed.

High points of the drive, literally, were a pair of fortified mountain passes where medieval castle-like gates once controlled access from one valley to the next. Just looking at them conjures up images of soldiers on the battlements and the gates barred against the marauding elephants of some rival Raj.

Another roadside attraction was marble production. For miles the roadside was lined with heaps of quarried marble; everything from small piles to Herculean chunks dumped like some giant's forgotten Legos. Amid this jumble of marble stood small businesses; one after another, crowded shoulder to shoulder with competitors. Each of them offered acres of the stuff, all the same, for sale by the slab and by the block. We've never seen so much marble in one place, Taj Mahal included.

India is a smorgasbord of incredible sights; stuff to warm the cockles of any travel agent's heart, but not everything makes it into the travel brochures. Take public urination for instance. No seriously; India has got to be the pissingest country in the whole world; or at least the parts of it we've seen. Driving down the road it's hard to go even a few miles before you're treated to the sight of some guy relieving himself on a bush or against a wall. Men wearing turbans and traditional garb, men dressed in sport coats and ties; it's as if hordes of Indian males from all walks of life are in training for some secret outdoor pissing Olympics. On one drive, I started counting, sort of like the spotting white horses thing. When my count reached fifty, I figured my attention was better served elsewhere. Still, full busloads of people whizzing by the roadside are hard to ignore.

Okay, in for a pee, in for a poo; public urination is only half the picture. One day while out walking, we came upon a small boy. Apparently glad to see us, he looked up with a beatific smile and greeted us with a warm, "Hello!" He was also squatted in the middle of the sidewalk happily taking a big dump. Public defecation is usually a little more discrete than this, but like the pissing it's part of the genuine India experience. Different and unexpected, sure, but we don't think these are selling points you'll ever see touted on a travel poster.

Tonight's our third night in a lake-view room at the Krishna Newas Havali, and pissing aside, it's true; Udaipur is a fairly romantic city. The old town stretches along the shores of a pretty, but don't look too closely, lake with still waters, fairy-tale-white island castles, and colorful sunsets. Almost every building is an old havali hotel and all of them sport rooftop restaurants with decent food and splendid views.

We've been lazy since we arrived, but we still managed enough motivation to take in a few of the sights. Our first evening, we visited the nearby Jagdish Hindu Temple. This is an elaborately carved tower that closely resembles the temples at Khajuraho but without their in your face eroticism. We kicked off our shoes and spent a few minutes inside listening to the nightly bhajan singing. The chants weren't the ones that we'd learned at our ashram so we stifled the urge to sit down and join in.

The next day our big outing took us to the "City Palace Museum" a large rambling slightly rundown structure built and expanded by a series of Maharajas in the 1600's. It was something of a strange visit because Indian bureaucracy at the museum was running at full throttle.

Admission was only 60 rupees per person, but if you wanted to use a camera, and we can't imagine why you would, that cost another 200 rupees. On entering the building your tickets are checked by a uniformed guard in red beret and polished jack boots. All bags are searched, and if you're carrying a camera without a camera ticket you're sternly told that you must check it at a special booth before you can proceed. We turned in our camera and then moved to a set of stairs where another guard checked our tickets a second time and also clipped them with a hole-punch. At the top of the flight of stairs, with no entry or exit possible along the way, yet another guard was waiting and our tickets were checked a third time. To ensure we didn't attempt any ticket hanky panky, this guard carefully made short tears opposite the punched holes.

Totally weird; the "museum" consists mostly of dusty second rate paintings of boring historical scenes; nothing that seems of value. Besides the paintings there are a few sparsely furnished rooms that try to give you a feel for the palace's former grandeur. Doesn't work; most of what's there is shabby and reminded us of rundown second hand stores.

The best parts of the City Palace weren't the things on exhibit but instead its passageways and other visitors. Painted signs directed us through the building via strange narrow windowless halls that twisted and turned and did odd things like leading you down a flight of stairs only to hit a flat spot and then lead you back up two more. Sometimes ahead of us through this maze, sometimes trailing there was a tour group from a rural area; men with turbans and wild moustaches, women in brightly colored saris. It was a real kick to watch them look at the historical exhibits. Since they were speaking Hindi we couldn't understand a word they said, but it was obvious that they were admiring various tools and furnishings and discussing their relative merits. "Hey Kumar, check out this hayfork, its just like the one you gave your son last Diwali." "Sita, look at this cracked butter churn! Isn't it the one your cow stepped on last fall?"

Later that night, we went to a cultural program that featured traditional music and dance from various parts of Rajasthan. It was outdoors under the stars and we both thought that the energetic performance was good fun. The show opened with a stylized reenactment of a confrontation between a demon and a god that involved the "demon" picking up real burning coals with his teeth. That was a hard act to follow but the rest of the program was equally entertaining ranging from dancing marionettes to three women who swung tiny corded cymbals like a group of dangerous ninjas working their nunchucks. For the finale a woman danced barefoot on a bed of broken glass with nine feet of pots stacked above her head. Yeah! That's what we're talking about!

Today we took a long walk through the honking chaotic crush of the city to a popular lakeshore spot called Sunset Point. Along the way we poked our heads into the "Tibetan Market," sort of a flea market where locals came in droves to buy contemporary clothing from stalls run by (naturally) Tibetans. Clothing is already so cheap in India we couldn't understand the attraction. Judging from the enthusiastic crowd, we figure the ordinary looking clothes must be bootlegged items from China carried over secret mountain passes by clandestine yak trains.

Back at the hotel we watched fireworks explode over the lake.

Day 329 - November 30 - Tuesday - Fort Cochin, India

Sometimes when you travel everything is an excellent adventure, other times, with a nod to Bill and Ted, it's most heinous. Like our train from Haridwar, yesterday was most heinous!

Our first cautionary hint came at the airport in Udaipur when we checked in for our 3:45 PM flight to Kochi (Southern India) via Mumbai (old school, Bombay).

"Is our luggage going to be checked all the way through to Kochi?"

"No, I'm sorry sir. You must pick up your bags in Mumbai." *Okay, that's a drag but no big deal.* Our first leg was an hour and ten minutes on Air India; then, we had an hour and forty-five minute layover before our Air India Express flight to Kochi. *Plenty of time.*

The second warning sign came when an omnipresent loudspeaker announced that our Air India flight was delayed and wouldn't depart until 4:15 PM. *Okay, that's going to be a little tight, but an hour and fifteen minutes to collect our luggage and re-board, we should be fine.*

We didn't board the plane until 4:20 and by the time it sailed over Mumbai's cardboard slums and taxied to our gate it was 6:00 PM. *Oh crap! We only have forty minutes to grab our bags and get checked-in.* "I'll wait for the bags. You run to the Air India counter and let them know we're on our way." Our bags we're first off the conveyor. *Yes!* I grabbed them and scuttled after Denise.

Her experience went something like this.

"Hi, we just arrived on your delayed flight from Udaipur. We're supposed to be on the 6:40 Air India Express flight to Kochi. Could you please let them know that we're on our way."

"No I'm sorry; Air India Express is a different company."

"What, but you're Air India."

"Yes, is same name but different company." *Say what? We booked the tickets at the same time!*

"Okay, where's their counter?"

"No counter here; is at International Terminal, but is too late counter closed." *Huh?!!*

So here are two pertinent bits of information. One, if you're on a domestic Indian flight and you haven't cleared security forty-five minutes before departure, you're screwed. Two, Air India Express is a subsidiary of Air India and both are owned by the Indian government.

I caught up with Denise about the time she was telling the Air India counter agent it was their fault that we'd missed our connection. "Well, what are you going to do about it?"

"You need to go the second floor and talk to the Duty Manager."

On the second floor, we walked up to the first Air India counter we saw and re-explained the situation. "You need to go to the customer service counter on the first floor."

Back at the same first floor counter that we'd just left, we re-explained the situation to a different customer service representative. Fortuitously, we were now joined by two Indian passengers who were also in the same fix; strength in numbers.

"Well, what are you going to do about it?" This representative tried to paint a brighter picture.

"Maybe we can honor your tickets on a later flight, we need to go to the second floor and talk to the Duty Manager." This time the counter guy, "It's my pleasure. You are our guests," led the four of us upstairs to the Duty Manager's office.

The Duty Manager had a different perspective on our predicament. "No, I am sorry, but we cannot help you. We are not the same airline. Air India Express is much cheaper. You must get a refund for your ticket from them and purchase a new one from us." *Say what?!!!*

"And just how do you propose we get a refund?"

"No problem, I'll make a note in my log. You just talk to your travel agent."

"We bought our tickets online, it'll take months."

"No problem, I'll make a note in my log." *Right, that's gonna work!*

"So you're saying that if we don't have the money to buy your tickets that we're stuck here in Mumbai?"

"You must buy new ticket."

"And, how much is that going to cost?"

"I don't know; you have to talk to the Duty Manager in the International Terminal." *But, it's a domestic flight! Arrrgh!*

This went round and round. The four of us passengers kept repeating that it was Air India's fault that we missed our connection and the Duty Manager kept repeating that we would have missed the connection anyway and that we had to buy new tickets.

At length we wore on her nerves and she asked us to take a seat while she did some checking. About fifteen minutes later she reappeared and again announced that we must to talk to the Duty Manager at the International Terminal. *Is this a brush off?*

The counter rep lead us back downstairs to the free, because no one would have the gall to charge for it, inter-terminal shuttle bus. Before you can board the bus you have to present your valid ticket and pass through military security.

The reason we needed to speak to the Duty Manager inside the International Terminal was because we'd missed our flight. Catch 22! We missed our flight; therefore our tickets were no longer valid. "I'm sorry. You can't be admitted to the International Terminal without a valid ticket." *You're kidding?!!!!!*

Since we were his "guests," the Air India counter rep took our side and worked his way through the chain of command. On his third try, he convinced someone in authority that we weren't dangerous terrorists and they reluctantly agreed that we could board the shuttle. Of course by that time the shuttle had left the Domestic Terminal and we were told that we would have to wait thirty minutes for the next one.

We sat in a special holding area (Group W Bench?) and watched a monitor that perpetually read, "Next shuttle will arrive in 20 minutes." After about forty minutes a bus finally pulled in and the four of us climbed aboard. We sat for another fifteen minutes waiting for the bus to fill. When it began to roll, it crept around the airport as if pulled by a team of scrawny octogenarians who'd lost their walkers. Traveling at the speed of stale catsup, it took nearly an hour to cover maybe three kilometers. The Domestic Duty Manager was right! We'd never have made our connection!

At last, inside the terminal, we made a beeline for the International Duty Manager. Once again we repeated our tale of woe in four part harmony. She made note of our details, scrutinized our e-tickets, scowled at us, and told us that we needed to walk across the terminal and talk to the "mini-booking office."

At the mini-booking office, we talked to another representative who again made note of our details, scrutinized our e-tickets, and then went to the "dark place" (DOS style text screen) on his computer terminal. At the end of this process we were holding dot matrix printouts that listed our details and said that we'd missed our connection because our Air India flight was delayed.

"You need to go just over there and talk to the lady."

"The Duty Manager?"

"Yes." *Déjà vu!*

Back at the Duty Manager's counter, she scowled at us again and said, "You wait." Another twenty minutes ticked by before she again acknowledged our existence. At that point she collected our e-tickets and the printouts we'd been given. She handed everything to a guy in blue coveralls who looked like a janitor and told him to take them somewhere. Once again, she told us to wait. We watched the guy stroll off and then pause in conversation with another janitor. *Patience is a virtue! Patience is a virtue!*

Eventually, he wandered back and returned the papers to the Duty Manager. She handed them back to us and then looked at a guy at another counter. "Hey Suresh, (paraphrased) check these losers into the 1 AM flight to Kochi."

Yes! Somewhere along the line, someone decided that they were sick of dealing with us and that it was easier to just put us on a plane and get rid of us.

True, three hours passed since we landed and we faced another four hours before we got back in the air, but at least no one was talking about refunds and re-buying tickets. We ate crummy overpriced airport food, passed through a ridiculously confusing international immigration queue to reach a domestic flight, boarded an almost empty plane, stayed up all night, and arrived at our destination at 5 AM; most heinous! *Repeat after me, "Only book non-stop! Only book non-stop!"*

Day 330 - December 1 - Wednesday

I've been fighting a cold for the past two days. I'd like to blame it on our horrible flight, but I think I have to lay it at the feet of a Pneumococcal Mary that sat next to me in a crowded Udaipur Internet cafe and hacked and wheezed contagion into my airspace.

If you need to recuperate, Fort Cochin in the state of Kerala where our travel challenge ended isn't a bad place to do it. The Unnamed Guide Book describes the town as the result of "an unlikely blend of medieval Portugal, Holland, and an English village grafted onto the tropical Malabar Coast." That's stretching things to the breaking point, but it's true that those three nations along with the Chinese did trade and settle here and bits and pieces of all four cultures do still add tiny dashes of flavor to the current local mix.

As usual on our first day in a new place, we didn't do much except wander around and get our bearings. We're lodged at the Daffodil Homestay which is sort of a cross between a bed and breakfast and a boutique hotel.

We'd picked it from the Web sight unseen, which is always a crapshoot, so we were pleased when the room turned out to be nice, the included breakfast good, and the location even better. All the local sights are only a short walk away and a number of good restaurant choices are also nearby.

Just up the street is Santa Cruz Basilica a large ho-hum Catholic structure, originally built by the Portuguese in 1506.

A little beyond the basilica, lies what locals call "the beach." There's nothing even vaguely beachy about the spot except that it's a shore and it faces the Arabian Sea. It's more of an estuary cum oily shipping channel, but it does have its appeal.

Trinket stalls and fishmongers line the shore and you can't help but notice the gigantic spindly Chinese fishing nets. When traders from the court of Kubla Khan introduced the nets around 1400, these huge contraptions were the height of modern fishing technology. Today, not so much; they can only be operated at high tide and require at least four men to lift their clunky counterweights. Luckily for us camera-toting tourists, they remain just profitable enough to not to be sold for firewood.

Circle a few more streets and you pass St. Francis Church where erstwhile Portuguese explorer Vasco de Gama was buried in 1524. They dug him up a few years later, but the headstone's still there. If you are a history buff wanta-be like I am, Fort Cochin can hold your attention.

The town itself is low key and tropical. We're not sure exactly why, but it reminds us of a shabby rundown Key West with less wood, and more concrete, trash, and mold. Maybe it's the palm trees or the smell of sea air.

Maybe it's because Fort Cochin sits on an island that's connected to the mainland by long bridges.

We finished our first day in Southern India with dinner at Linda's Café. The décor was nondescript and at $15.68 it was our most expensive Indian meal to date, luckily the food was excellent. Denise snarfed prawns cooked with dry spices and I ravaged a fish steak (no idea what kind) cooked with coconut milk and herbs. These were our first non-vegetarian meals since we hit India and if we're going to fall off the wagon they were a great way to do it.

We spent most of our second Fort Cochin day exploring other "must see" attractions. To guide our wandering we picked up a crummy walking map that I couldn't seem to align with the streets. I blame it on my cold. Luckily, Denise had a better sense of direction and, despite my disorientation; we still managed to find our way to Mattancherry Palace. The palace is a large moderately well preserved building that was built by the Portuguese in 1555. After completion, they presented it to the Raja of Kochi; Kochi, Cochi, Cochin there are several spellings for everything, as some sort of a bribe. The Dutch got into the act in 1663 and performed some major renovations that left the building with the popular nickname, "The Dutch Palace."

Portuguese, Dutch, whatever, the best thing about the palace is its well preserved Hindu murals. Paintings cover several interior walls and illustrate religious scenes from the Ramayana, Mahabharata, and Puranic legends. The colorful details are faded, but the murals still fan the flames of imagination; really cool stuff.

After touring the palace, we made our way around behind it and entered "Jew Town," an area of antique stores and curio shops. In the past this was a port area and a Jewish enclave, the heart of Fort Cochin's once bustling spice trade. We ate lunch at an upstairs joint called, "The Crafters' Café" and then visited the 1664 synagogue that anchors the area.

No purses or cameras were permitted inside so you had to check them with an old guy in a little annex room. You toss all your stuff on a bed (his?) and then he gives you a numbered plastic token. When you pick up your belongings, returning his plastic token takes precedence over whether you walk out with your possessions or someone else's.

With our bags and camera "safely" secured, we paid our $0.11 per person entry fee. First stop is a small room where several slightly funky, mildly interesting, paintings depict Jewish history in Fort Cochin. From there, we walked into a forecourt, removed our shoes, and entered the synagogue itself. An ornate gilded pulpit sits front and center in the hall but the rest of the furnishing were a little understated; in other words, kind of dull. The painted floor tiles are from China and the chandeliers from Belgium, but the synagogue left us yawning. Once again, we're confused why someone felt photography needed to be prohibited.

When we left the synagogue a light rain was falling. We headed down Bazaar Road which loops around the tip of the island and strolled into an interesting industrial area filled with small import and export businesses selling: rice, bulk spices, and the like. At one point, the narrow road was blocked. A large truck was parked next to the buildings on one side. The driver of another truck had tried to inch by but instead had almost wedged his vehicle against the building across the way. Neither truck was touching the other. Neither was pressed against the buildings, but they were both stuck. There wasn't enough room for pedestrians, much less cars, to squeeze by, so we waited while a growing crowd of spectators honked horns and threw increasingly angry suggestions at the harried drivers. It was good entertainment.

By the time one truck maneuvered enough that we could slip past, it was raining steadily. After waiting under an awning, we decided that it wasn't going to let up and hailed an auto-rickshaw. A $0.45 fare took us to the Tea Pot Café where coffee, tea, and "Death by Chocolate" helped me forget my sniffles and both of us forget the weather.

Day 332 - December 3 - Friday - Munnar, India

I'm on the mend and we're back on the move. We negotiated another car and driver deal ($32/day) and for the last two days we've been traversing Kerala's Western Ghats, mountain regions, with Jose, pronounced Joe's, behind the wheel. Jose is far and away our best driver so far. His driving is good. He's got a sweet personality and he likes to point out stuff.

To get out of Fort Cochin we drove across the long toll bridges that link it to Ernakulam, its uninteresting mainland counterpart. From there, we headed straight for the hills.

The first thing you notice about the state of Kerala is that you're back in the tropics. The air is warm and heavy. Palm trees wave overhead and groves of pineapple, rubber trees, and cardamom line the road.

The second thing you notice is that you're out of the "cow belt." You still see cows grazing along the shoulder, but they're cut a lot less slack than their northern counterparts. In fact, a fair number of cows sport decidedly beefy tags stuck in their ears. We think it must be the Christian thing.

Only 2.3 percent of India's population is Christian but thanks to the Portuguese and the Dutch something like eighty-five percent of those are found in Kerala. Suddenly, shrines to Jesus and various Christian saints outnumber those to Vishnu and Ganesh. The weird part is that most of the Christian shrines have a decidedly Hindu appearance. If you don't look closely the garish statues are hard to tell apart. Pink, three and four storey pagodas with large glass windows and a statue on each level are popular. There was a particularly creepy life size Mother Theresa near our home-stay.

You also notice a related shift in business names. Instead of "Krishna's Family Restaurant," you now see names like "Holy Mother Mary Fruit Stand," "Saint Joseph's Lumber," and even better, the "Instant Jesus Tire Service."

Strangely for an area that's staunchly Christian, Kerala is also staunchly Communist. The state has a freely elected Communist government and the highest level of literacy in the country. It's weird to see the old Soviet hammer and sickle prominently displayed on sign bills and fluttering red flags.

We made an early start out of Fort Cochin and so beat Ernakulam's supposedly hellish rush hour. We could have waited for the traffic to thin, but we wanted to be at the Kudanadu Elephant Training Camp by 8 AM to catch the morning bath. No, for real; elephant bathing is cool.

Jose parked the car and we walked down a cobbled road until we came out onto a landing at the edge of a wide foliage lined river. Just to our right were the elephants. Four of them we're lying in the water getting the whole beauty spa treatment. Each elephant had two or more handlers who were hard at work scrubbing the pachyderms with pieces of dried coconut husk. The husks made loud sandpaper-like scritching sounds. Over the eye, scritch scritch, scritch; behind the ears scritch scritch, scritch; along the trunk scritch scritch, scritch; between the toes scritch scritch, scritch; and the elephants obviously loved every minute of it. What's not to like? From time to time one of them would get so relaxed that their bowels would cut loose and the handler at the rear, probably the trainee position, would toss cannon ball sized turds into the river; not something you see every day.

When the bath was over we drove to a nearby wildlife "preserve" that was the elephants' home. Billed as a forest eco-park, it featured a huge antique wooden elephant kraal or cage, interesting but no longer used, a child's play area with suspiciously dangerous looking equipment, an overgrown garden with a skeetery pond topped by a cheesy big breasted mermaid, and perhaps the saddest little zoo that we've ever seen; small bare wet cages, lots of mud and mold and neurotic looking animals. We used the toilets, enjoyed the scenery, and moved on.

Our next stop was at one of the highway's many "spice gardens." These are sort of botanical roadside attractions that, judging from their popularity, are must-sees for Indian tourists from the north. You pay a 100 rupee ($2.25) per person entrance fee and then a guide takes you on a half hour stroll along a path through the grounds. "This is a pepper plant. This is ginger. You just are using the root. This medicine plant. Called power plant, makes man very, very strong, Indian Viagra," and so on. At the end of the tour you (surprise, surprise) have the opportunity to visit their store where all of these wondrous botanicals are sold.

From Ernakulam our road climbed and with each bend the scenery became more mountainous; beguiling us with sweeping panoramas, plunging cliffs, and tall cascading waterfalls. Just when we thought the views couldn't get any better we passed into the misty mountains and tea plantations that surround Munnar. The beauty of the tea plantations stuns the senses. They cling to steep undulating hillsides, monocultures of startlingly verdant green, broken only by large magnificent rocks, and skyscraper tall eucalyptus trees. The whole area reminds us of nothing so much as an epic bonsai garden laid out by the hand of some gigantic Zen master. It's a landscape that made us want to stare for hours.

Of course tea is the reason for all this beauty, so our next stop was the Munnar Tea Museum. Here we rubbed shoulders with Indian tourists, sampled cups of spiced tea, heard a brief unintelligible description of tea production, walked through a demonstration factory floor where clattering machinery converted dried leaves into sorted graded bags of tea, and watched an overly long video about the settlement of Munnar.

After that, it was off to our home stay. This time our digs were more home and less hotel. The house, owned by an apparently prosperous advocate (civil and criminal law), is located about seven kilometers out of town. A small creek runs under the driveway and steps from the backyard climb into a tea plantation. Since we were the home's only guests, we were given their best accommodation. For $34 a night, the second floor room is a good deal. Just inside, there's a sitting area with a couple chairs and also a small dining table with chairs.

These were a big plus. In about ninety percent of the hotel rooms in India, at least the ones we stay in, the only place to sit is on the bed. That gets old really fast. The bedroom is huge. There's also a separate dressing area, and the bathroom is good sized too. The floors are tile and most of the walls are paneled with dark wood which gives the room a sort of hunting-lodge feel. A good breakfast was included.

The only drawback to our two night stay was cool rainy weather that emphasized the fact that our room lacked heat. Add shower water that never gets above tepid and, when we let ourselves get chilled, warming back up was a challenge.

For our second day in and around Munnar, we let Jose take us wherever he chose. It was a good day. Our first stop was at a junction with a small paved road signed, "Manager's Bungalow." Jose suggested that we get out and walk for a while. This set the tone for the day, good sightseeing from the car interspersed with interesting walks. The bungalow road wound down into a tea plantation and treated us to great views and the opportunity to watch pickers at work.

All the tea picking, actually trimming, is done by women who stand on the steep slopes and move among the chest-high plants. Male supervisors stand on the level road and watch. The women use hand hedge-shears that have been modified for the job. On one blade a container has been attached that resembles a deep tin shoebox. On the other, there's an upright tin flap that runs the length of the blade. When the women use the shears, the flat flap pushes the cut leaves into the box. When their boxes get full, the women dump them into large plastic mesh bags. Eventually, a woman is lugging around her shears and two big bags, each crammed with maybe forty pounds of leaves. She drags them down to the road for pickup, grabs a couple of empty bags, and starts over.

This is really tough work and making it even nastier; the tea plantations are full of leeches! The women wrap themselves in thick sheets of plastic that cover them from their calves to their armpits, but most of them work barefoot and so they get munched anyway. One woman showed us her feet with blood oozing from her heel and between her toes; yuck!

Despite what has to be tough lives, these people are unfailingly friendly. They smile, they say "Hello," they strike up conversations, and in contrast to so many other places, they're not looking for a way to reach into your pocket. Sure, they might ask you if you have any chocolate to share, and kids may ask you to give them a pen, but refreshingly, most of the time it's just interaction for the shear fun of it.

We saw lots of spellbinding natural beauty around Munnar and got in some good walking, but two of our stops are worth special mention; not because they fit into the spellbinding category, but because they also fell into the "*that's weird*" category.

Take the Munnar "Floriculture Center," it's a botanical attraction just out of town. Cars were double parked along the side of the road and Indian tourists were queued up to get in. The countryside was so fantastic that we were a little nonplused by the idea of a flower garden, but the price was only $0.22 each and the place seem wildly popular. Inside people were snapping close-ups of flowers, taking pictures of sweethearts posed by flowers, and generally "ooing and ahing." We looked at each other and went, *Huh?* The place was a nursery and a fairly ordinary one at that. It was like we'd just paid

$0.44 to visit an end-of-the-season garden center at a Home Depot.

Our other odd stop was, "Top Station." The name sounds like some type of terminus, but today its claim to fame is as a view point. The road up there is in poor condition and because of recent rains there were a number of mudslides that made it even worse. Muddy going, one-lane blind corners, steep drop offs, and aggressive traffic were only the half of it. As we neared the "station," we hit dense fog. Visibility dropped, and suddenly Jose was hunched over the wheel and we were creeping along. Then, just like that, we reached a gate at the end of the road. He stopped the car, and we stepped out into a drizzle to go searching for the viewpoint.

After a hundred yards, we looked at each other. "This is ridiculous. It's all socked in. Even if we find the view point, we're not going to see anything. Do you want to go on?"

"I don't want to go on. Do you want to go on?" Back up the road we found Jose waiting by a roadside shack where he'd just ordered a bread omelet. Since it was either head back for the view or order omelets of our own, we turned around.

This time, questing a little farther, we reached the overlook or more correctly the entrance to the overlook. Some enterprising locals had installed a gate, a few "Top Station" signs, a snack shack, and were charging admission.

"I don't know; 15 rupees each seems a little high. It's all fogged in. If we pay you, are we going to see anything?"

"Oh yes, no problem." Like a couple of dunces, we paid our $0.68, shuffled through the metal gate, and started down a series of steep muddy steps. Of course when we reached the viewpoint everything more than fifty feet away was lost in the mist. Indian tourists were also squinting into the fog so at least we weren't the only rubes. By the time we got back to Jose, his omelet was long gone.

On the drive back to the homestay Jose must have decided that since Top Station was a bust we needed an attitude adjustment. "You want beer before go hotel?"

We looked at each other, "Uh sure, why not?" We thought he'd probably take us to a licensed restaurant, but instead we ended up at Munnar's state liquor store. Who knew such a thing even existed? Once again, we think it must be the Christian thing. You know; more guilt, more original sin; more reason to drink. Anyway, Kerala has the highest rate of alcohol consumption, and alcoholism, in the country.

The liquor store was a gruddy hole-in-the-wall place with a grimy counter across the front and racks and stacks of dusty bottles behind. A green plastic tarp was stretched as a screen between the counter and the street so that customers and their transactions were hidden from the sensitive view of the public at large. Behind the counter two taciturn men handled the sales, one retrieving the selected liquor and the other taking the money. The emphasis was clearly on potency over flavor and frequently involved the pouring of some generic brew from a large container into an unlabeled plastic bottle.

I queued up with the other red faced twitching customers and bought two tiny, twice airplane size, bottles of rum. When they turned out to be good, we went back to stock up. No luck, that brand was gone. "Here, take this rot-gut instead." People who don't drink socially don't get it. All liquor, and beer for that matter, does not taste the same. Young Muslim Turks aside, these same people don't make exemplary bartenders or sympathetic liquor store clerks.

Day 334 - December 5 - Sunday - Kumily, India

We spent the best part of today at the Periyar Tiger Reserve. The name sounds exciting and the reserve draws big Indian crowds, but your chance of seeing a tiger are on a par with catching the Tooth Fairy red handed. In addition to its elusive population of forty-six tigers the reserve is home to 1,000 elephants and herds of bison. We didn't see those either, but the pictures looked swell. That doesn't mean that the reserve isn't worth a visit. The sanctuary covers hundreds of square kilometers of mountainous forest and jungle and includes a twenty-six square kilometer manmade lake courtesy of the British (1895). Its two big drawing cards are boat trips and nature walks; we did both.

Arranging these activities was another enlightening exercise in bureaucracy. To go into the details would be tedious, but here's a taste of the madness. You purchase entrance tickets at the park gate where you have to provide them with address information and show your passport. A kilometer inside the park there's an "information center," but they can't tell you about the nature walk. The place to ask about that is in another signed building. You can ask there, but if you actually want to go on the walk, you must purchase your tickets at a forest service office one kilometer back outside the front gate! Oh by the way, if you want to use a camera in the park, you have to purchase a ticket for that at the information center.

The boat tours were nearly as confusing. Tickets for one category of boat sold at the information center for 40 rupees. A hundred yards away, another window sold tickets for different boats for 150 rupees. The boats looked virtually identical. They all left from the same dock at the same time. Their crews were all dressed in identical blue camouflage outfits and all the boats followed exactly the same itinerary around the lake. The only obvious difference was the price. Naturally, the cheaper boats were full so we ended up with the 150 rupee tickets.

On board, we were ushered to our assigned seats; plastic patio chairs bolted to the deck. We ended up in the "nose-bleed" row at the very back of the boat, seats number 30 and 31, while a Belgium couple who bought tickets at the same time ended up with the first two "court-side" seats at the bow, numbers 32 and 33. *Huh?*

Before we could leave the shore the crew helped everyone into their annoying, compulsory, life jackets. The way the story goes, a few years back someone on one of the tours sighted something interesting, all the excited passengers rushed to that side of the boat, and over it went, taking two decks of sightseers to a watery grave. Today, the rule is orange lifejackets one and all and there's a metal railing down the center of each boat; just in case.

Considering that our one hour tour was sort of like a Disneyland Jungle Cruise minus the commentary and the audio-animatronics it was still moderately entertaining. We putt-putted quietly up the lake and from time to time we did see animals; nothing that made us all rush to one side of the boat, but animals just the same. First there were cormorants, then a herd of wild boar. After that came some deer, a monitor lizard, some turtles, more cormorants, and a couple of wild dogs. Except for the lizard and the turtles, everything was cavorting at an uninspiring binocular distance from the boat; black dots on the shore. Just the same, the scenery was green and lush and it was a fun way to spend an hour.

Now, our afternoon jungle walk; that was different! We signed up for it with the aforementioned Belgium couple and for two hours it was just the four of us, a ranger, and the leeches. Holy blood sucking fiends! Did they just say leeches again? You bet we did! If you ever want to add spice to a quiet jungle walk, just make it muddy and mushy and sprinkle around a few zillion mini-leeches. The scary little things resemble tiny inch worms and give you the creeps without even trying. Stop for a moment and they scent your blood. Look down at your feet and there they are moving toward you through the grass or climbing up your shoes. Yuck! We can't imagine how the tea workers even get up in the morning.

We began our excursion at the "Jungle Patrol" hut where we paid $0.57 each to rent leech gaiters; money well spent! The gaiters were essentially canvas booties with attached leggings. You take off your shoes, tuck your pant legs into your socks, and then slip the gaiters over the top and tie them off at your knees. Your shoes, or in Denise's case sandals (creepy), go on last. Next, since the little suckers like to climb, we tucked our shirts into our belted pants. The ranger, Raj, sprinkled tobacco dust over our shoes and gaiters as a further deterrent and off we went.

Except for a tendency for our skin to crawl any-time we stood still, it was a fun walk. We hiked away from the patrol hut and followed small paths and game trails that wound through a variety of muddy terrain: hilly woodland, semi-jungle, and grassy meadows with streams and ponds. Along the way we saw teak and rosewood trees, coffee and sandalwood, and a mix of other interesting plants. The animals were also pretty good. There were wild pigs, this time close enough to see, lots of deer, wild chickens, and our personal favorite, a teak-nut munching Malabar Giant Squirrel.

It was neat just walking quietly through nature, and the reserve was wild enough that it hinted of unseen possibilities which fed our sense of anticipation. What's going to appear over the next rise or peak out from behind the next tree? At one point we saw elephant tracks by a stream and Raj glided off to try to trail it for us. At another spot, frightened monkeys began a raucous "Oo Oo Ahh Ahh Ahh" in the trees. Raj whispered, "It might be a tiger." A little encouragement and an active imagination can make for a great time!

Our home for the two nights while we're visiting the tiger reserve is Claus Garden, a bed and breakfast located in the neighboring town of Kumily. Its name tells it all. The bright and well appointed B&B nestles in a profusion of greenery and is owned by a German ex-pat named Claus. His per-night price of 1,470 rupees ($33.41) is about what we've been paying but when Claus trots out crusty homemade bread at breakfast it feels like a bargain.

This morning as we stood on our balcony enjoying the sun, we noticed that our car was parked in the garden. Next, we saw Jose peal himself out of the backseat and stretch. While we'd slept comfortably in our room, the poor guy had sacked out in the car! If you travel with a driver, most places that you stay have a space where your driver is allowed to sleep. Jose didn't mention that Claus Garden couldn't put him up, and we didn't think to inquire. Embarrassed by our oversight, we apologized and asked Jose how much he needed to get a room for our second night. He replied that he'd slept okay in the car and not to worry. We persisted and he hmmed and hawed. After a bit of back and forth, he agreed to accept 300 rupees ($6.82) which he said would get him a bed. Tonight, our car isn't in the garden, but we have a sneaking suspicion that Jose stuffed the money in his pocket and made up the backseat anyway.

Day 336 - Dec 7 - Tues - Backwaters of Kerala, India

The day after our Periyar visit, Jose drove us back down to sea level and dropped us at the Tharavad Resort Hotel, another nice homestay, in the costal town of Alleppey. Alleppey is a moderately appealing place with several wide leafy streets which parallel water lily clogged Venice-like canals. Okay, "Venice-like" is a reach, but it's a pleasant enough place to do a little wandering.

Alleppey's streets however aren't what put it on the tourist route; that honor goes to Kerala's "backwaters." The backwaters are a 900 kilometer spider web of coconut palm lined lakes, rivers, and canals and Alleppey is a main jumping off point for exploring them. Walk down the street and you can't help but notice that everyone and their brother are in the business of selling: canoe excursions, Gilliganesque three hour tours, or the gold ring itself, twenty-two hour overnight houseboat trips. We thought we might do all three, but first on our agenda was the houseboat trip.

Prices range from a low of about 4,500 rupees ($102 US) for a scow, to well over 20,000 ($455 US) for a travel agent arranged luxury boat; preferred by cardiologists and Saudi princes. We decided to shoot for something in between. Anybody in town can set you up with a trip, but the best way to go at it is to walk down to the docks, talk to the boatmen, and check out the houseboats in person.

By the time we hit town, my cold had jumped hosts and Denise was down with the sniffles. After a light lunch at a beachside, sand but no people, restaurant, she headed back to the room for a nap and I walked the docks. It was about 5 PM and a lot of houseboats were out for the evening. 9 AM would have been better, but there were still enough boats tied up that I was able to sniff around and walk onboard a couple that looked promising. Nothing I saw made me shout, "Sign me up!" but after about forty-five minutes I had a good idea of what was on offer for 6,000 rupees or less. At that point I hopped an auto-rickshaw back to the homestay, and asked them about their boats.

To cut to the chase, the next morning they showed us a boat and we dickered about price. They wanted 6,500 rupees. We offered them, 6,000. They countered with 6,250. Denise suggested that we'd meet the 6,250 ($142 US) if they'd throw in a couple of cold beers, and we had a deal.

We went back to our room, packed our gear, and by 11:30 our captain was sliding his houseboat away from the dock. We waved to the Saudis that were pulling out at the same time but they didn't feel the love. Oh well, their loss.

Compared to what we've been spending, houseboats are a splurge so we almost passed them up. Just a few minutes away from the dock, we knew that we'd made a really good decision. The backwaters are totally relaxing. You sit on the boat's foredeck sipping your included beer, and a wonderful quiet world slips by around you. Canals link lakes and rivers, and raised causeways separate the canals from miles and miles of egret dotted rice fields. Isolated homes and small bucolic villages sit on the causeways and lives, little changed in generations, play out by the water. Men with umbrella hats move by silently in their canoes or cast fishing nets from the shore. Women pound laundry on rocks and hang it to dry on convenient shrubs. Children with schoolbooks walk shoreline paths laughing and talking. The backwaters are road, bathtub, food larder, drinking fountain, and kitchen sink; what a fascinating place. Adding icing to the cake, our cook on the boat is the bomb! Everything he puts on the table is mouthwatering and it all comes in embarrassingly large portions.

Day 337 - December 8 - Wednesday - Kollam, India

We tied up for the night with the river on one side and rice paddies on the other. When we crawled out of bed it was about 7:30. We made our way out to the deck and sipped Masala tea while we watched the backwaters wake up. An overcast sky turned the still river into a mirror reflecting clouds and foliage with equal perfection. Birds squabbled in the palms. Egrets zipped overhead. Fish jumped in the river and frogs hopped on the shore. Long shaft canoes putted by, their sound drowned by the deeper throb of heavily loaded rice boats. Wakes set us gently rocking. After a time, our own engine rumbled to life, the crew cast off, and the cook called us to breakfast; not a bad way to start the day.

Our houseboat docked at 9 AM and we caught an auto-rickshaw to Alleppey's main bus terminal. We were going to Kollam about eighty-four kilometers away and figured that short a distance would be a safe test of India's bus system. At the station, buses pull up out front and you simply climb onto the one that's yours. We'd discussed our plans with the people at the home-stay and they'd told us, "No problem (you hear that a lot) just look for the bus that says "SuperFast." Right off the bat we noticed that "SuperFast" was painted on a bunch of buses. Unfortunately, that was pretty much the extent of English signage. All the destinations were in Hindi.

I scuttled over to a couple of arriving buses and asked the drivers if they were headed to Kollam. Evidently my pronunciation of "Kollam" is way off because my question tended to elicit blank stares until I repeated it several times. Trying a different tack, we struck up a conversation with an Indian man who was also waiting. This worked better, and he pointed out our bus when it pulled up. He also told us to board at the front (bus has two doors) because we could stow our bags next to the driver, and because the front door is often less crowded.

Good advice; Indian people are almost unfailingly polite but when it comes to boarding public transport all bets are off! Something switches on in a deep primal recess of their brains and an animalistic herd mentality takes over. One minute, they're all "Hello sir. Hello, mam. Where from?" and the next they're wide-eyed cattle trying frantically to squeeze down the knackers shoot. Queue, shmoo! Men shove ahead of you, old women turn into linebackers, young women wriggle forcefully past, and everyone jostles and pushes. If you don't push back, you end up standing on the curb. I managed to wrestle our bags inside and Denise made it onto the stairwell by the door.

The "SuperFast" bus isn't a "Chicken" bus; i.e. no livestock and no ceiling-high piles of bags and bundles. That's not to say that it isn't crowded. For the first forty-five minutes of our trip Denise remained perched precariously in the stairwell. I stood in the aisle squeezed in like an all-meat weenie in a vacuum-sealed Wal-Mart value-pak. Because she was able to look out the window Denise had the better "seat." Our bus was designed for passengers half a head shorter so I resigned myself to a view of its walls and a four-inch wide blur of the road's shoulder.

After a couple of stops things improved. A woman at the front got off and waved Denise into her single seat. At about the same time, the bus driver took pity on me and suggested that I sit on the engine cowl. As long as the bus was moving the cowl was okay. When the bus slowed or came to a stop in traffic, the cowl heated up and my butt felt like overdone chapatti. I wasn't complaining; at least I was sitting and I could see out.

Almost at the moment we climbed into the bus, it started to rain. This was a good hard monsoon kind of rain. It came down in big wet drops, made everything drip, and turned the roadside into muddy lake-sized puddles. Since the "SuperFast" didn't have any glass in its side windows, it also made for an interesting ride. At first passengers ignored the weather, but as more and more water flew in, one by one they began to pull down metal accordion shutters. The shutters stopped the water, but they also shut out the air and light. The temperature inside soared and the steamy interior soon resembled a darkened hot house set from *Attack of the Mushroom People.* By the time we reached Kollam and climbed off; we were both medium parboiled and really glad to be there. The "SuperFast" covered the fifty miles in two hours and thirty minutes. *Okay, not bad, but maybe we'll try the train again.*

Day 338 - December 9 - Thursday

We spent our first night in Kollam at a homestay called the Valiyavila Family Estate. The place was actually a bit out of town, but it was recommended to us by the local tourist office and at 1,200 rupees the price seemed right. We later learned that a German couple had paid 2,000 rupees for the same room the night before. We really hate that in a hotel, as it makes you question their honesty at every turn.

To get to the estate we took a fifteen minute, six rupee, ride on a government backwater ferry and then we walked a couple of hundred yards in the rain. As a spot to hovel and wait out the weather, the estate made a good layover. Our room was large and Spartan: bed, small table, and cold water bathroom, but lots of windows. A good included breakfast, and a covered semi-private veranda with a table and two plastic chairs made up for any short comings.

The estate sits on the tip of a small peninsula, so you're surrounded on three sides by water. We spent most of our time sitting in the chairs, enjoying the quiet ebb and flow of backwater life. Boats and canoes come and go and rain or shine people go about their lives.

As we sat, we watched one fellow shinny up a nearby palm tree with a clay jug strapped to his back. When he got to the swaying top, there was another jug hanging among the fronds and he poured its contents into the one he carried. We later learned that he was collecting "toddy," alcoholic palm liquor. When the palm flowers; someone scrambles up, slits the bud, and covers it with a clay pot. Sap flows into the pot and when enough has collected someone climbs back up to retrieve it. Toddy is a popular budget drink found in roadside "toddy bars." Sadly, the locals like their toddy strong so unscrupulous bartenders sometimes make unsavory additions to increase its potency. "There've been deaths," a guide whispered ominously.

The estate's most prominent feature is also hard to ignore. Located right at the tip of the peninsula, filling twenty percent of our view, towers the grandiosely titled (or is that tittied?), "Goddess of Light." The Goddess, a Titanic tribute to lawn "art," is this huge tacky concrete statue of a woman climbing a tree stump while holding up a Statue of Liberty style torch. Unlike Lady Liberty, this gal is voluptuous and brazenly nude. Think attack of the fifty foot naked woman. Oddly, other prominent decorations at the estate feature life size depictions of Jesus and other conservative Christian imagery.

Dawn brought better weather and we decided that despite the local attractions a move into town was in order. The estate was pleasant, but it was also isolated. The only place to get food was from their kitchen and the government ferry service was intermittent so it was going to be tricky to coordinate our activities.

Our next stop was a downtown Kollam hotel located in a dusty business area mostly lacking in charm, but charm wasn't why we picked it. The Hotel Nani was well situated between the ferry dock and the train station and according to The Unnamed Guidebook, "Even the cheaper rooms have mod cons you'd expect at double these prices, including flat panel TV's, feathery pillows, and sumptuous bathrooms." When we also read on their website that they had in-room safes and Wi-Fi, we were hooked.

Of course, their prices are now double (*thank you Unnamed Guidebook*) and the Wi-Fi doesn't work. "I'm sorry sir, the Wi-Fi not working. There is temporary problem." This phrase is a stock answer at Indian hotels, sort of a fill-in-the-blank sentence where you can substitute any advertised amenity for the word, Wi-Fi. "I'm sorry sir, the Wi-Fi, pool, restaurant, hot water, elevator, fan, etc, etc..." The "temporary" part is wishful thinking. Yes, the feature worked at some time in the past, but you can safely bet your last dollar that it's not going to work again during your stay.

As for the in-room safe, that also suffered from a temporary problem that no amount of bellhop fiddling could rectify. Considering that the safe was small, portable, and not mounted to anything, we really didn't care. The rest of our room was up to snuff and although a little over priced, there was plenty of hot water in the shower.

Around 2 PM we went back to the boat dock and signed up for a "DTPC," government tourist office, canoe trip through the backwater canals of a place called Munroe Island. This was the other backwater experience on our Kerala must-do list and it was another good one.

At the DTPC office we were joined by two young couples, one from France and another from Denmark. The first leg of the tour was a forty-five minute taxi ride that took us out of town and then wound along smaller and smaller roads. When we arrived at the rural community of Munroe Island, the six of us climbed out and were met by our local guide. Five minutes later we were seated in a large canoe and he was punting slowly down a backwater canal. The next two hours moved by at a comfortable snail's pace as we wound through twisting green waterways, past small rural homes, a Technicolor Hindu temple, and shrimp farms. We ducked to slip under low-slung bridges, stopped to watch coconut oil being extracted, and laughed as a young woman jumped up and down trying to harvest us a papaya. Women washed clothes, men fished, small naked children blew us kisses, fish sellers conducted business from their canoes, and behind it all, singsong chanting echoed through the palms.

Day 340 - December 11 - Saturday - Varkala, India

Our painful Haridwar to Varanasi trip has faded in memory so yesterday we opted to take a train from Kollam to Varkala. Lots of trains make the trip so you don't need to buy tickets in advance, and it's only a twenty-five minute run. We figured it was a safe bet. Besides at $0.59 each it's a bargain of the first order.

We arrived at the station an hour early so that we'd have plenty of time to buy our tickets and find our platform. As it turns out, Kollam's station is small and navigable; five minutes would have been plenty. With tickets tucked safely into Denise's bag, we settled into uncomfortable metal seats to wait. We watched as a train in the opposite direction pulled in, loaded, and then pulled out. *It's right on time; could this be a favorable omen?* And, we waited, and we waited... Our train rolled in more than an hour behind schedule; evidently it was of a different species.

Boarding was another hands-on lesson in herd mentality. The moment the train stopped, Indians rushed the door and began to push and shove like the golden gates to paradise had just opened and only three general admission seats were left. I was fed up and pushed back. Denise entertained visions of being crushed under train wheels and plaintively asked, "Please don't push." With perseverance and a bit of elbow, we squeezed through the sphincter and reached the interior of our cattle-class car. The seating arrangements made our vacuum-pak-weenie SuperFast bus look luxurious. We both stood the whole way, Denise next to the open door and me swaying over our bags in the aisle. Fortunately, twenty-five minutes goes by pretty quickly.

Varkala is the payoff for our train time. Like Dahab, it's another kick back beach resort that's just starting to outgrow its backpacker roots. There's an oceanfront cliff-side walk that's lined with open air restaurants; perfect for setting sun worship, small stores, clothing shops, and trinket stands. We're in a second floor room at the Sea Breeze Resort with a balcony, a hammock, and a view of the ocean just past a grove of waving palms. There's a black sand beach a hundred yards away and the room service is good.

Day 346 - December 17 - Friday

For the past week, we've lived "La Vida Beach." We get up in the morning and eat breakfast on our balcony. By 11:00 or 12:00 we manage to overcome inertia and leave the hotel for a healthy, or unhealthy according to your dermatologist, dose of sun and surf. A couple of days stayed overcast, but most of the time it cooks; plenty of sunscreen and the occasional rented umbrella. Waves are big enough for body surfing, but also calm enough for just bobbing around. The bottom sand is soft and the drop-off gradual; pretty much your ideal beach. The only real drawbacks are a serious lack of beach chairs (non-existent) and a tendency for Indian men to stand around and gawk at delectable bikini clad tourists.

Afternoons, when it's too hot for sunbathing, we go for walks or hang out at the room and practice yoga. The walks are really pleasant. From our hotel, easy-to-follow stone paths run along the top of ocean hugging cliffs for about an hour in each direction. One way takes us through the heart of Varkala's tourist scene with its multitude of restaurants and colorful shops. The other direction passes: palm groves, streams, and small fishing villages.

For tourists, Varkala is mainly about kicking back and working on your tan, but it does have its sights. As with nearly everywhere else in Kerala, there's a local "Kathakali" troop that puts on nightly performances. Kathakali is a traditional play in which elaborately made-up and costumed actors present archetypal stories from Hindu mythology. What sets Kathakali apart from an ordinary play is that aside from some drum and cymbal music, a little singsong narration, and a grunt or two the story is presented through elaborate hand movements and exaggerated facial gestures.

Three tourists at a restaurant in Fort Cochi described a performance they attended as "painful." They'd been seated in the first row, but suggested that if we go, we take seats at the rear where unseen escape is still a possibility. This "recommendation" placed Kathakali exhibitions on a low rung of our to-do list and so far we avoided the concerted and persistent attempts of drivers, homestay owners, and touts to get us into one. Things probably would have remained that way if a pair of German tourists, Wolfgang and Annunciata, hadn't invited us to join them at the Varkala show. They're both professional musicians, he's a composer and she specializes in esoteric Italian folk music, and they convinced us that Kathakali was worth a try.

Happily, they were right. Although a bit shabby: tattered curtains, plastic chairs, three actors, bare light bulb over the stage; the performance was colorful and mostly entertaining. What we experienced (from the back row) was a one-and-a-half hour tourist version of Kathakali; the real deal goes all night. The show left us yawning; still it was a far cry from painful.

We paid 400 rupees ($9.09) for the Kathakali show, but Varkala's best sight is free. Every morning except Friday (mostly Muslims here) fishermen work on the beach. They row out past the surf in large canoes and lay out football-field-sized horseshoes of netting. The two ends of each net are returned to shore and a hundred or so men begin a daily tug-o-war with the sea. Slowly, ever so slowly, they draw in the nets while other men, paddling prehistoric three-log boats, patrol the outer edges to watch that the nets hold their shape. As the giant U's near the shore, beaters take to the water and pound its surface to drive fish deeper into the nets. At last the catch is landed and everyone crowds around to see what the ocean has provided. Some days the catch is good, merchants on motorcycles stacked with double-milk-crate sized boxes dicker with the fishermen over purchases, and everyone goes away with smiles on their faces. On other days the catch is bad, and tempers flare as arguments erupt over who should get what. It's an amazing cycle that has certainly played out unchanged for hundreds of years.

India is an incredible, frustrating place. It's an exquisite exotic flower that you bring to your nose only to find that it smells of urine and cow dung. Two days later you're still thinking about its beauty, but you discover it's left a rash on your hand.

This is supposed to be Varkala's high season, a time when all accommodations are booked and walking-wallets fill every shop. Unfortunately, this is a slow year. Things are tough all over the world and fewer tourists are on the prowl. As a result, the locals are worried and testy.

The other day Denise stopped in a clothing stall and looked at a blouse. “How much is this?”

“950 rupees madam,” replied the saleswoman. *Holy Cow! That’s $22!*

“Whoa that’s expensive.”

“That’s my high season price. For you madam I make better deal, 650.”

“No that’s still too high.”

“What you pay? What you pay?”

“I’ll give you 150.” Based on our other India shopping experiences 200 rupees was about right and 150 should have been a good counter offer. Instead of coming back with another price, the saleswoman rolled her eyes in disgust. At that point, Denise figured the blouse was a no-go so she turned her attention to a bedspread. “How much is this?” In a repeat of the previous negotiation, the saleswoman refused to bargain.

Since things are tight, many of the small shops have decided that they need to make up for the shortfall by double or triple charging. The result is that even the tourists who are here aren’t buying much of anything.

“Okay, thank you. I’ll think about it.”

At this juncture the saleswoman turned nasty. “Why you come into my store and no buy? You just look! Don’t come back!” We talked to other tourists who encountered this same experience in other shops.

In another stall the owner guilted Denise into a bedspread purchase. “Things very hard. No business. I have three children. You rich. Me poor. Etc. etc. blah, blah, blah.” If ordinary sales techniques don’t work try to shame the customer into buying with anger, guilt, or intimidation. Somehow, we don't think those were chapters in "How to Win Customers and Keep Them for Life."

Lying on the beach today, I glanced up and couldn't believe my eyes. "Hey Denise, look at this!"

"What?"

"Those two women."

"Wow, they're actually cleaning the beach." In this land of knee-deep perpetual trash, the two women in question were clearly a cleanup detail. They were both dressed in tan fatigue caps, brown wrap-around skirts, and tan khaki shirts labeled, "Sanitation Department." One woman carried a bag and the other carried a rake. Every couple of steps the woman with the rake made several anemic unenthusiastic passes with her tool and pulled together a few pieces of trash. The other woman collected the stuff with a gloved hand and shoved it into her bag.

It quickly became apparent that not only was their method haphazard; their rake was worthless. The rake's handle was tied with bits of string from a multitude of previous repairs and writhed like an angry cobra with every stroke. On about the third small pile after we spotted them, their rake gave it up and fell in two. Its owner tried a few half-hearted scritches at the sand with the now handle-less head and then gave up. The two women looked at each other. Their unspoken communication was obvious. "Well, that's it for today Lakshmi. Guess the beach'll just have to wait. Let's go get some tea."

The woman with the rake pieces trudged away through the sand while the other woman walked over to some rocks and dumped the contents of her bag back onto the beach. *Out of sight, out of mind; India we love you, well sort of.*

Near Chiang Mai, Thailand

Chapter 14

THAILAND

Day 350 - December 21 - Tuesday - Phuket, Thailand

India gets into your head. After fifty-seven days of bureaucracy, grime, dysfunction, and chaos, Thailand caught us by surprise. We walked into the international airport in Bangkok and teetered on the edge of culture shock. Neither of us slept on our overnight flight from Chennai. It was 5 AM and everything was: clean, bright, and efficient; moving walkways and escalators that work, walls and floors that gleam, fresh cut flowers in the bathrooms! When we checked in for our 8:30 flight to Phuket, the counter person smiled at us. "There's an earlier flight at 7:40. If you'd like, we can put you on that one." *Hold on Toto; I don't think we're in Kansas anymore!*

Immigration was a breeze (no visa needed) and our checked bags sailed through all the way to Phuket. If we'd stayed away from the currency exchange counters our introduction to Thailand would've been perfect. We considered exchanging our remaining rupees for dollars at the airport in Chennai but couldn't stomach the fifteen percent loss. Idiots that we are, we left India with rupees in our pockets. At the airport in Bangkok everyone cheerfully offered us sixty cents on the dollar; ouch!

Phuket's airport was also a snap. We retrieved our bags, whisked past customs, bought a bottle of rum in the duty-free, and followed the clearly labeled "Exit" signs. Outside, standing behind barriers, waited the usual scrum of chattering humanity: taxi drivers with signs reading "Mr. Conrad" or "Lundquist Party," similarly equipped limo drivers, hotel touts, taxi touts, people waiting for relatives, and more touts. The air felt humid and smelled of the tropics.

We were a few beats ahead of our originally scheduled arrival, but we only stood around for a minute or two before we spotted a taxi guy holding aloft our misspelled name. Good spelling, bad spelling; when you're exhausted, pre-arranged transfers are hard to beat.

We both detest reservations, but Christmas and New Years are nipping at our heels. With everyone beating their "high season" drums, we figured that Phuket wasn't a place to show up unannounced for a fourteen night stay. We read guidebook recommendations, checked out Trip Advisor, looked at pictures, and surfed dedicated websites. Working through a process that we've both grown to abhor, we tried to get a feel for Phuket's hotels and what each one offers. Without being there and in the absence of personal recommendations (people you actually know), pre-booking is a lot like spinning the roulette wheel and yelling, "Let her ride!" You might think you have a system, but it's mostly a matter of blind luck.

The first couple of places we tried were fully reserved, so we ended up at "The Golddigger's Resort." The "resort" is a ten minute walk from the beach (and yes, we know it has a cheesy name) but once again our blindfolded dart hit a bull's-eye. The Golddigger's is owned by a Swiss expat, Hans, and his Thai wife, Aie (like Canadian, "eh"). Hans made his fortune prospecting in the wilds of Australia hence the resort name, and a slightly weird accent. He may be many years from his Switzerland roots, but Hans' small hotel still runs with that country's famous efficiency. The grounds are landscaped and immaculate. The pool is clean and inviting. Our room is spotless. The staff is friendly. The onsite restaurant serves good food, and prices are reasonable.

Day 360 - December 31 - Friday

The last ten days disappeared faster than a magician's pretty blonde assistant. It's mind boggling how fast time can fly while you do nothing. Breakfast at the hotel or on the beach, lying by the pool, swimming in the pool, strolling along the sand, lunch at the hotel or on the beach, reading, napping, a little yoga, happy hour, dinner at the hotel or on the beach, a movie on TV, $10 dollar hour-long massages; these are the building blocks of our days. We don't do everything everyday and we constantly tinker with the order, but the overall result is the same. Could we get any lazier? Probably not; we're close to perfecting an art.

Now that we've taken off our rose colored glasses, our first impression of Thailand still holds. Admittedly, there's some litter along Phuket's roads but nothing like the sea of trash to which we've grown accustomed. Buildings look well kept and people are friendly.

Local women dress for the tropics. Many wear shorts, sleeveless tops, and flip-flops. On the beach, they wear bathing suits. They all smile, laugh, and look you in the eye. They say, "Hi," as they walk past. After months of travel through countries where such behavior is generally regarded as shameless or tantamount to prostitution, Phuket's easy freedom comes as both a shock and a refreshing revelation. One night at a restaurant, the hostess who was showing us to our table put one hand on my arm and her other on Denise's back. It was all the two of us could do not to flinch! Our unsolicited reactions were immediately followed by relief at again being in a country where a friendly smile and an innocent touch don't equate to grease on the hot rails to perdition.

Our hotel is located in an area called Hat Nai Yang, a quiet beach in the northern part of the island about ten minutes from the airport. Since Nai Yang isn't touted as one of Phuket's hot spots, we made a couple of excursions to see what we were missing.

For our first exploration we traveled by bus. There's a main road about two hundred yards away and that's where we caught the "Airport Bus." Like a shark constantly on the move, the Airport Bus trawls the pavement between the airport (duh) and Phuket Town. Armed with a printed timetable, we only waited five minutes before we climbed aboard. The first half of our air-conditioned ride ran along scenic rural road, the second half through the less-appealing outskirts of town. The fare for the fifty-minute run was 85 baht ($2.89) each which took us to the end-of-the-line at Phuket's main bus terminal.

Using a decent map, we frittered away the afternoon wandering Phuket Town's busy but navigable streets. We stopped at a bakery for tuna sandwiches and yummy cookies. We strolled up and back along the length of the local ho-hum market street, and last but not least we paid a visit to the town's branch immigration office.

When we landed in Bangkok, our passports were stamped with on-arrival visas valid for only thirty days. Sitting out the holidays on our bums in Phuket was going to burn half that time so we figured an extension was in order. At the immigration office we learned that what was in order was a change of plans. For about $40 each we could add another seven days. *Wow, that seems like a low value option.* If we made a day trip to a nearby land border we could cross over and back, paying fees on both sides, and add another fifteen days on our return. *Hmmm sounds tempting, but no.* Our third option, explained by a friendly immigration officer, was to fly out of Thailand and then fly back. That would entitle us to another thirty days. *Okay, looks like we're going to visit Thailand twice!*

This is supposed to be Phuket's dry season but monsoon-like weather is bucking tradition. On our ride back to Nai Yang, it poured rain; buckets of the stuff. Traffic snarled because of an accident, the air-conditioner on the bus was set to "mind-numbing-cold," and the quick trip stretched into several hours. We watched our driver dial up the temperature but apparently the AC had other ideas. Eventually the bus grew so cold that its windows fogged on the outside! By the time we climbed down and stepped out into the warm tropical rain, hypothermia didn't seem all that far fetched.

To give ourselves maximum flexibility, and ensure control of the air-conditioner, we chose a rental car for our second exploration. We loaded our swim suits and towels into the trunk and set out for adventure. Our plan was to do a slow circuit of the island, stopping along the way to see the sights and visit the "must-see" beach spots like Patong and Kata Karon. We have to say, we've spent better days. Thais drive on the left. Phuket's roads are narrow and most of the time they're either congested, winding, or both. Patong and the other "hot spots" are over-touristed, crowded, and unappealing. We made a couple of short view-point stops, but none of the beaches we rolled past enticed us out of the car. Mostly we just drove; white-knuckled, five hours behind the wheel, with both of us watching the road instead of the scenery. Sadly, at the end of the day we agreed that our high-point was a visit to the "Big C," Wal-Mart-like department store.

If you you're in the mood to drink yourself blind, buy Hard Rock Café t-shirts, indulge in a little sex tourism, and rub shoulders with mobs of the like-minded; low-key Nai Yang Beach probably isn't your oyster. Maybe we're just getting old, but we think it's the bomb. Our room at The Golddigger's is quite possibly the cleanest and best appointed of our entire trip. Its pool and lounge chairs are seductive. The nearby beach is lined with good restaurants and is bookended by national parks. The sand is powder fine and the sea is calm. If there's any drawback to Hat Nai Yang, it may be that it's a little too quiet. Lots of people hang at the beach sunning and scarfing seafood but all of it is done in a sedate laid-back manner. A bit of rowdiness and the occasional pumping beat of music might have jazzed our stay. Oh well, better too little than too much.

In keeping with the Hat Nai Yang vibe, our Christmas and New Years eves were low key. Christmas Eve, we ate dinner on the beach with the sand between our toes. Later, as we walked back to The Golddigger's fireworks exploded overhead. We stood inside a tree covered corridor with our heads tilted back and, "Ooohed" and "Aaahed," as pyrotechnics lit the sky. When we emerged from under the trees, it was into a warm hard tropical rain. By the time we reached our room, we were both soaked but happy.

On New Years Eve Hat Nai Yang cranked up the excitement a tiny notch; fun but still family oriented. This time the fireworks started early and ran late. While we lingered over our dinner, again on the beach, sporadic skyrocket concussions shook the sand and fiery cascades of color illuminated the heavens. Adding a quiet counterpoint, people lit dozens of tissue paper lanterns the size of large trash cans. When the air in the glowing lanterns heated, they floated off like miniature hot air balloons, lifting slowly at first then shooting high into the sky to ride the wind out to sea.

About the time we finished our meal the aerial display wound down and nothing new took its place. Instead of heading for a beach bar and cocktails on the sand, we wandered back to our room and settled for a bit of TV. After a year on the road, most of it without TV, a decent movie was kind of fun. Oh crap, we are getting old! Around 11:30 PM we ushered in the New Year with some meditation. We lit incense and Denise set our clock to buzz us back from the "Now" when 2011 arrived.

No need to set the alarm; at midnight the pyrotechnics restarted with a whoosh and a bang! Perfectly framed in the picture window above our headboard, it was like the fireworks were planned for us alone. Flipping around, we lay naked on our backs; our heads propped on our pillows, and watched the extravaganza unfold. There were dozens of floating lanterns; a shifting constellation of soft golden stars that drifted silently amid the roar and splash of fireworks. The display continued for more than half an hour. One gigantic flash of color overlapped another, each explosive flash of brilliance trying to outdo the last. What a great way to bring in a New Year, thunderous and thrilling, beautiful and peaceful.

Day 365 - January 5 - Wed - Koh Phi Phi Don, Thailand

We'll see your one beach, and raise you two. A couple of days ago, we stashed most of our luggage in The Golddigger's storage room, shouldered our day-packs, and traveling light, headed out to spend four nights on the fabled island paradise of Koh Phi Phi.

Travel has its ups and downs and this little excursion featured both. Things started smoothly. We hopped the morning's first Airport shuttle to the downtown bus station and then easily found a shared 100 Bhat ($3.43 US) taxi to take us to the Koh Phi Phi ferry dock.

When we reached the dock, things turned decidedly murky. A raft of assorted ferries was tied up at the pier and the port was crammed with surging tourists and their luggage. The object of the tourists' attention was a line of small tables. Each table was selling tickets for a different ferry, and each ticket came at a different price, with different options; beach stops, snorkel stops, included lunch, etc. etc. With minimal extras the bottom price seemed to be about 600 baht ($20.60 US) one-way or 1,000 baht ($34.34 US) round trip. None of this was what we wanted. We'd been led to believe that a basic one-way no-frills ferry ticket cost 300 baht ($10.30 US). There go those expectations again; could we find it? No sir, we could not; and surprise, surprise, no one at any of the tables wanted to help us with our quest.

We worked up and down the port, but quickly ran out of time. We'd arrived with only fifteen minutes to spare before departure and, strangely, all of the island ferries were scheduled to depart at the same time! Finally, we gave up, gritted our teeth and bought a pair of 1,000 baht round trip tickets.

All the boats cast off at once (weird) and made for Koh Phi Phi. The crossing was advertised as a one-and-a-half-hour trip but actually took closer to two-and-a-half. Helping to make up for the scheduling discrepancy, our tickets included free coffee and donuts; *donuts la-la-la.* On the downside, again, when we neared our destination, instead of steaming to the pier at Koh Phi Phi Don, our "excursion" tickets got us a leisurely sightseeing jaunt around the uninhabited sister island of Koh Phi Phi Ley. On the upside, the scenery was great and Denise spotted a sea turtle. Returning to the downside (or is that dark side?), after Koh Phi Phi Ley, our ferry went over to Phi Phi Don's "Long Beach" and made a tender stop so that motor launches could take sunbathers ashore; great for day trippers, but the delay left us with our undies in a bunch.

When we finally landed, paid our port tax, and carried our daypacks down the pier we were greeted with an abundance of in-your-face signs advertising 300 baht one-way direct ferry service to Phuket. *Arrrggghh! Okay, that's over, here we are in paradise. Dump the bags, grab a beer, get some sand between the toes; it'll be smooth sailing from here;* dream on oh walking wallet!

A short walk carried us to the reception desk at the Chaokoh Phi Phi Lodge, the site of our envisioned beer and sand. Indifferent receptionists looked at their records and informed us that the lodge was full and that they had no record of our confirmed pre-paid reservation. We showed them our booking voucher and they again repeated that they were full and couldn't accommodate us. They made no offer to help, and as far as they were concerned, that was the end of the matter. *Arrrggghh!*

Grinding our teeth (going to need dental work), we called the online booking service, Agoda, at our own expense ($1.39 US/min). After a couple of calls, some time on hold, and some checking; an Agoda customer service rep called back to happily ask if everything was now, okay. “Huh? Uh no!” The Chaokoh Phi Phi Lodge had told Agoda that they’d walked us down to another “more expensive” hotel and given us a room there. *Say what?!!* We were still standing in their lobby, as we had been for over an hour. No one had spoken to us, much less taken us anywhere.

Once again, Agoda customer service did some checking and after a bit called back. Okay; now they were sure that things were straightened out. We were told that shortly someone would take us to another hotel, but that we would still take our included breakfasts at the Chaokoh Phi Phi Lodge. Agoda also told us that to make up for our inconvenience the lodge had offered to give us free dinners during our stay. *Say; now that’s sounding better!*

After we got off the phone, the Chaokoh’s receptionist rolled her eyes at us and told us that we would eat breakfast at the other hotel and that the most she would do for us was give us was a voucher for 500 baht at Chaokoh’s restaurant; less than one meal and less than what we spent on phone calls.

At that point their bellhop led us to the other hotel called the Phi Phi Don Chukit Resort. When we arrived it was obvious that they weren’t expecting us and that they had no idea why we were there. After some phone consultation between the two hotels, we were shown a room and asked if we wanted it. We were also told that it was their last room and that if we didn't take it we were on our own! *Wait a minute, we're on Phi Phi Don where The Unnamed Guidebook warns; "you MUST book a room in advance!" We've already learned that several other places are full, and we've already missed the afternoon ferry back to Phuket. Swell, just swell!!!* Rather than look for something else and face the hassle of trying to get a refund, we accepted what was obviously a substandard room.

We've put up with intermittent electricity, cold water, mice, and scary monkeys, so what doesn't meet our standards? You know, it's that room that never gets rented; the one that's twice as rundown as everything else. It's musty. The front door doesn't seal. The air-conditioner clatters. It's sandwiched next to a storage room and a public toilet. The furnishings are shabby. Cleanliness is superficial. Bathroom fixtures are rusted out. Random light bulbs don't light, and of course there are cockroaches.

If we'd been charged say $30 per night we would have considered it a reasonable deal. After all, cockroaches or not, Koh Phi Phi is a popular island paradise. If we'd been charged $60 we wouldn't have liked it, but we wouldn't be writing about it. Unfortunately, $90 per night deserves a damn good whine. Oh well, rip-off or not, you don't stay at the beach to hang out in your room. We locked our bags to a desk, threw on our swimsuits, and left our troubles behind.

The Phi Phi Don Chukit Resort doesn't have much of a beach, but it does have a small ocean front swimming pool with lounge chairs and bar service. *Okay, not perfect, but we can make this work.*

Next morning's buffet breakfast was reasonably good so we decided to ignore our room's occasional foraging cockroach and stick it out for our full pre-paid four nights. We'd thought to spend the day on the beach, but the weather had its own plans. Under an overcast sky and amid an intermittent drizzle, we explored Koh Phi Phi Don's back streets. Just your basic time passing stroll; we checked out restaurants, peered into bakery cases, tried on souvenir t-shirts, all too small, and scoped possible venues for an evening's night-life.

Around noon the weather improved. It still drizzled occasionally but in between the drizzles the clouds broke apart and sun blazed through. On a mission to make the most of our island experience, we grabbed our beach accoutrements and made for Koh Phi Phi's best sand. A fun twenty-minute walk along the island's luxuriant shore brought us to Long Beach; a quiet stretch of grainy stuff flanked by upscale resorts and great across-the-sea views of nearby Kon Phi Phi Ley.

After test driving several blanket locations, we were reluctantly forced to admit that it was indeed still raining. Rather than give up, we ducked into one of the many restaurants to wait. Lunch worked its magic and by the time we finished our stir-fry vegetables and beer, the sun reemerged. We settled on a dry spot, near where a couple of Italians were putting the finishing touches on their new dive shop; watched them struggle with the work, offered suggestions, and did as little as possible while the rest of the afternoon slid away.

That evening we overcame inertia and dragged ourselves out in search of nightlife. We might be getting picky, but we couldn't find anything that met our taste. That's not to say that there isn't a lot of nightlife on Koh Phi Phi; there is. We were itching for a little island music so the first place we tried was a Reggae bar. We're not sure what live Muay Thai boxing has to do with Reggae, but that's what they had on offer. We weren't in the mood for gladiatorial combat so we moved on. The next place we tried advertised live Rock and Roll. The band was alive, but that was about all you could say for them. Songs; old, moldy, and butchered were their specialty, so on to the next place, and the next, and so on.

The common theme for most bars on the island is loud Techno or Hip Hop that precludes both conversation and dancing (for everyone, not just the aged) and lots of flashing lights. This timeless party mix is of course fueled by lots of alcohol.

Koh Phi Phi's drink of choice is the "bucket," a sort of do it yourself alcoholism kit for people who can't get shit-faced drunk fast enough using ordinary methods. Buckets are sold in bars, markets, souvenir shops, and impromptu stands that sprout at night. There are whiskey buckets, vodka buckets, and rum buckets. You name it, either there's a bucket to suit your taste or someone will fix you one.

The "bucket" was no doubt invented at a frat party that ended badly. So what does this wonderful island culture kit include? First off, there's the bucket. This is usually a run of the mill plastic or tin bucket that began life as a child's beach toy. Inside is a can of mixer, Coke, Sprite, whatever. Nestled beside the mixer is a bottle labeled, "Shark Bite," "Tiger Piss," or something of that ilk; a concoction of caffeine and assorted potency enhancers strong enough to tear off the Red Bull's wings and stuff 'em down his throat. Last but of course not least, there's a pint of your poison of choice. Pop the lids and pour everything into the bucket. Drink it through a straw or guzzle it straight and you're ready for an evening of serious inebriation.

Tempting, but at our age we have far too much common sense to indulge in something that blatantly foolish, besides. . . the hangover would probably kill us.

Day 366 - January 6 - Thursday

Today, we devoted our morning to a four hour snorkel tour to Koh Phi Phi Ley and Maya Beach. Maya Beach is that "perfect beach" which served as the namesake location for Leonardo DiCaprio's "The Beach." With the movie's release, a visit to Maya Beach became a sort of semi-obligatory pilgrimage for anyone staying on Koh Phi Phi. Not ones to buck tradition, we shopped around and signed up for a discount tour that featured some picture stops, a couple of snorkel opportunities, and of course a visit to Maya Beach.

At about 9AM, we collected our masks and fins from a tour office and followed a guide through a small souvenir market to a quay where several other tourists were already waiting. Once more people arrived and we reached the auspicious number of thirteen, we were ready to depart. We picked our way off the end of the concrete quay, waded through knee-deep water, and climbed, somewhat ungracefully, up a three-rung metal ladder into our appointed "long-tail" boat.

Long-tails are the ubiquitous watercraft of Thailand. They are large wooden vaguely canoe shaped boats; swept up at the prow and flat on the stern. Mounted at the rear is an uncowled car engine set on an angled pivot that allows it to swivel from side to side. Stretching back from the engine is a ten foot shaft that ends in an unguarded propeller, the "tail." When maneuvering in tight quarters, the boat's helmsman stands in front of the engine and, leaning on a short countershaft, swings the tail up out of the water to attain his new heading.

A bit of shuffling, a little rearranging, and everyone found a seat. Our skipper whipped the tail around and with a throaty growl from the engine we were bouncing across the bay. Instead of making for Phi Phi Ley we spent the first fifteen minutes of our tour motoring over to Long Beach. *Huh?* It seems that if you book from an upscale resort you get curbside service while the cheap seats get to wait. Oh well, the detour added two more people and everyone knows that when facing the vagaries of ocean travel the number fifteen is far superior to the number thirteen.

Viking Cave was our first advertised picture stop, and it was, well yes, a cave. We bobbed around in rough water, nice shade of green (the water not us), under an overcast sky. Everyone snapped a picture or two of the cave's gaping maw, the skipper gunned the engine and we bounced off again.

A short time later our long-tail chugged into a shady inlet. "Okay, this is your first swimming stop. Who wants to swim?" Nobody's hand went up. We bobbed up and down on the swell and everyone eyed the dark water. With a cool breeze blowing and rain threatening a quick dip wasn't high on anyone's agenda. "Uh, maybe we can skip the swim and have more time to snorkel at the next spot."

"So nobody wants to swim? Who doesn't want to swim?" Everybody's hand shot up and we were back at sea.

Phi Phi Ley's coast is spectacular. Yes we saw it on the way ovcr, but up close it's more impressive. Sheer limestone cliffs tower over your head. Water shifts from deep ocean green to light emerald as it surges against their base; crashing, pounding; eroding. Caves large and small pock the waterline. Look up; lush greenery clings precariously to vertical walls and more greenery crowns craggy summits. In places, limestone flows like melting ice cream. No wonder someone chose this island as a backdrop for their movie.

Our second lagoon was larger and the water calmer. Overcast still hid the sun but the old guy was making a good effort to peek through. The skipper tied up to a buoy and this time most of us went over the side. Visibility was only so-so, but the water was more or less warm and our loaner snorkels only leaked at a manageable pace. Mounds of coral decorated the bottom and enough finny scaly stuff called it home to hold our interest. Schools of small yellow and black striped fish nosed about. Colorful parrot fish nibbled at rocks. An angelfish or two played hard to get and a slightly scary, sea-snake showed us how fast it can swim (*yuck*). Denise and I love to snorkel and everyone else was back on the boat long before we climbed the ladder.

Next stop, legendary Maya Beach; we motored around the tip of the island and entered the mouth of a protected bay. Just as advertised, there it was: quiet turquoise water, a romantic pocket of white sand, and gently waving palms. Except for a scrum of tour boats tightly beached side by side, a little roped off area so that you can swim without getting run over, and a gazillion tourists exploring Maya's "hidden" charms, it's just like the movie! Well, to be honest you also need to ignore the ticket booth, concession stand, and the busy public toilets. What can we say, we spread a blanket.

We were allotted an hour to soak up the "mystery," then it was back on the long-tail. The water was choppy and as we entered the channel between Phi Phi Ley and Phi Phi Don we slammed into a running swell. Our skipper kept the engine revved, the boat plowed ahead, and a continuous waterfall of spray cascaded over the bow. With each new swell a great splash swept across us from stem to stern. There wasn't enough water to cause problems, but in seconds everyone was drenched and dripping. A steady stream of cool salty water played into our faces. Like drinking from a showerhead, it was difficult to see and even to breathe. First one person and then another donned their snorkel gear. In a minute all fifteen of us were wearing goggles, sucking on tubes, and laughing like ninnies. The unplanned wild ride, something missed by larger more expensive boats, was a high point of the day.

In the lee of Phi Phi Don, we wrung out our clothes as the skipper maneuvered us up to our last stop, a tiny patch of sand and overhanging trees unapologetically dubbed, "Monkey Beach." The attraction here was of course, monkeys, a well established troop of which lives full-time at the spot shamelessly working the tourist trade. Most of our companions were excited and scrambled off the boat in search of close encounters. India gave us our fill of smelly monkeys with questionable manners so Denise and I opted to stay on the boat. Unexpectedly, this choice provided us with the best seat for beastie viewing. As soon as everyone else was on shore, opportunistic primates hopped aboard to rummage through their stuff. "Hey! Bad monkey! Put that down!" Shooing them away was definitely touch and go as the big one with the pointy teeth, an obvious seasoned professional, clearly knew who was in charge. We stood there waving our arms and yelling. He glared at us and pretended that he cared. We think the only reason he didn't steal anything was because it was less work to just be handed bananas on the beach. With an annoyed hiss he turned and made an indifferent arboreal exit.

Day 370 - January 10 - Monday - Chiang Mai, Thailand

If it isn't obvious by now, let me make it perfectly clear. Denise and I are beach people. We love all sorts of activities, but a sunny day on a warm beach is right up near the top of our shortlist. Thailand is blessed with an embarrassment of island paradises and we barely scratched their surface. Hat Nai Yang and Koh Phi Phi drifted past in a sandy sea breeze haze. If we hadn't been short-timing our visas, we probably would have continued to drift. As things stood, the holidays were over, and the clock was ticking on our time in Thailand. Reluctantly we wiped the sand from our feet and moved on.

The ferry ride back from Koh Phi Phi to Phuket was smooth and only about half-again as long as advertised. It was also a cultural experience. We arrived at the pier at our appointed time, 8:30 AM, and after turning down various Phuket-pier-to-hotel transfer offers we were pointed toward our boat. By the time we walked on board, a good-sized stack of oversized luggage had taken root inside the main cabin door and most of the choice seats were already taken. We found a couple of empties, tossed down our day packs, and retreated back on deck to enjoy the sun until departure.

For the next fifty minutes (the ferry was supposed to leave at 9:00) we sat and watched an unbroken line of passengers stream aboard. This was the cultural part, i.e. the part you'd never experience in the U.S. The day we arrived on the Koh Phi Phi Don a number of ferries were tied at the pier disgorging tourists. Now on the way back, it seemed as if each and every one of those tourists was climbing aboard our boat. The luggage mountain in the cabin began to reach prodigious proportions and precarious heights. With each new bag the aisle to the cabin grew narrower and narrower. As more and more people clambered across the gangway, the crew started a second luggage pile on deck. If there was a "Maximum Capacity" sign; we didn't see it. By the time we cast off, the second pile had also grown precarious and passengers filled the cabin and overflowed across all the outside spaces. Denise looked over at me. "Where was it that overloaded ferry sank?" I didn't have an answer, but I thought it a pertinent question.

Ten minutes out from the dock, we rendezvoused with another ferry boat and our crew asked everyone on deck to move inside. "You need to make room; fifty more people coming aboard." *Yikes!* At least it was a calm day and our luggage wasn't being slowly crushed.

As we neared Phuket, Denise suggested that we go out on deck. "Naw, let's just stay in our seats. Things will go quickly once we dock." Bad call! There was absolutely no organization and it was every passenger for themselves at the luggage piles. Instead of letting others off and waiting for their luggage to be delivered ashore, tourists crowded the aisle and struggled frantically to retrieve suitcases and backpacks that were buried under five feet of other people's excess baggage. Denise and I shuffled our feet for thirty minutes before we finally contrived to wiggle past the chaos and gain the gangplank.

On shore the situation wasn't much better. There weren't any regular taxis available at the port, which may or may not be *an insidious plot.* After a bit of fruitless searching, we queued up at a special kiosk where you must pre-pay for a shared mini-bus into town. The kiosk was a madhouse with several lines going at once and the counter people helping more than one person at a time. "I'd like two tickets to the downtown bus station."

"Yes, yes! (strident) 100 baht!" ($3.43 US) The gal at the counter wrote me a receipt and then left me holding out my money while she moved on to the next person. When she finished with that customer, she turned and began a conversation with a co-worker.

Still waving a 100 baht bill, "Hey, do you want my money or not?" The counter people were too busy gossiping to respond so I just pocketed the hundred and went looking for our "pre-paid" mini-bus. Sometimes chaos works in your favor.

A short ride to the downtown bus station and we were once again seated on the airport shuttle rolling toward Nai Yang. Golddigger's put us up for a final night, we ate one last dinner on the beach, and the next morning we headed up country.

An easy two hour Air Asia flight spirited us away from sea-surrounded Phuket and on to mountain-surrounded Chiang Mai. Just a few minutes off the plane and our post-beach regrets were gone. We knew that we'd made a good move. The Chiang Mai airport was clean and smooth to navigate. The weather was clear and warm. Our hotel called "3Sis" is located right in the heart of the old city and a pre-paid taxi made it a snap to reach.

According to one of our guide books, Chiang Mai is a city of around 175,000 inhabitants with: a university, a bunch of Buddhist temples, and a long history. The old city area where we're staying is a square surrounded by a moat (now a decorative canal) and the remnants of ancient city walls.

By dint of dumb luck, always better than talent, we flew in on a Sunday which serendipitously happens to be the day of the city's weekly "walking market." Starting around four in the afternoon several major streets in the old section are closed off and vendors set up stalls. By about 5 PM commerce is in full swing. Catering to both locals and tourists the market sells: clothing, crafts, sculpture, perfumes, paintings, house wares, and oddities of all description. Food offerings also vie for your attention, ranging from the common, like Phad Thai, to the exotic like: fried worms, beetles, and grasshoppers. Bands of blind street performers work the crowd. The market is a swirling blend of sights, sounds, and smells.

We spent several happy hours strolling among the booths. At the food courts we sampled one unfamilar dish after another; no bugs, but plenty of exotic fare: coconut cakes, fried fish bits, fried basil, battered quail eggs, fried "green vegetable," taro, bamboo, sweet sticky rice on a stick, and more quail eggs, this time fried and presented in a basket. Food displays strive for maximum appeal; colorful and enticing. Cooking aromas tugged at our brain stems, making our mouths water and our stomachs growl. Everything looked and smelled so impossibly good it was hard to decide what to eat next. We're lucky that our stomachs have shrunk.

We finished the evening at one of the market's impromptu massage concessions. These sprout among the stalls and do a land office business. The one we chose had nearly forty chairs and mats set up, all of them occupied. I went for a half hour foot and calf massage. Denise started out the same, but added a half hour of shoulder, back, and neck. Clean, professional, and top quality, by the time our massages were finished we were both relaxed and ready for bed; total cost, $6.87 USD.

At 11 PM sharp, vendors began to close their stalls, cart off their cooking utensils, load massage chairs on to trucks, and quickly slip away. By the time we got back to our hotel, the streets were open again and it looked as if the huge walking market had never been.

Day 375 - January 15 - Saturday

Yet again, the days have scurried by and we've been too busy living life to write about it. When we hit Chiang Mai, we planned that we would spend five nights and then move on. After just a day and a half we knew that five nights weren't enough. The city has so much to offer and its vibe is so relaxed that we decided to linger the full nine days until our visas run out.

We devoted our first full day to aimless wandering; a local market here, some Mexican food (*huh?*) there, but on the second day we jumped into the tourist scene with both feet. Chiang Mai is a city that gears up for tourism in a big way. The old section of town is jammed chock-a-block with hotels, hostels, restaurants, cafes, tat stores, and tour companies; and all of them offer activities to fill your visit and fulfill your fantasies. Canopy tours, zip lines, elephant farms, tiger encounters, rock climbing, abseiling, mountain biking, trekking, whitewater rafting, and Buddhist meditation; if you want it, they offer it. Since our hotel lobby is equipped with an expansive array of brochures and binders, we figured that was as good a place as any to start. Some perusal and a little discussion helped us decide that Thai cooking would be a good thing to know; best to start slow.

So... on the second morning of our stay we were picked up at 9 AM by "Boom," the instructor and co-owner of "Basil Healthy Thai Cookery School." Boom led us out to a waiting "sorng-taa-ou," a pickup truck with a canopy and bench seats; a kind of shared taxi that can be chartered or that follows a route at the driver's discretion. She lowered the tail-gate and we climbed in to join Yohana and Dinu from Romania, our fellow students. After introductions all round, the sorng-taa-ou took us to a local fresh food market; a warren of open stalls gathered under a corrugated roof. Boom handed us each a woven straw basket and we set off to shop for ingredients.

Denise and I already visited the same market the day before, but it was still a neat experience. Boom led us from stall to stall explaining the vegetables, spices, pastes, fruits, and other foodstuffs on offer. We purchased: lemon grass, fresh shredded coconut, eggplants the size of grapes, turmeric rubbed tofu, eggs, "mouse shit" peppers: small, stinky, and potent, cabbage, and more.

Next, with our baskets full, the sorng-taa-ou took us on to the cooking school. The school is located in Boom's house, but features a spacious purpose built kitchen. Basil Healthy Thai Cookery School is a hands-on experience. Each of us had our own counter space, cutting board with utensils, and hooded gas stove with wok. We also got to choose six dishes that we wanted to prepare, one soup, four main dishes, and a dessert. We set to work almost immediately, chopping, dicing, and stir frying.

The order of the day was, prepare a dish, sit down and enjoy it at a dining table, then prepare your next dish. Since each of us chose different dishes, we had a chance to sample twenty-four Thai specialties. We prepared: green curry, pa-nang curry, stir fried prawns with tamarind sauce, papaya salad, spring rolls, coconut milk soup, and sticky rice with mango to name just a few. Everything was easy to cook and mouth watering delicious. This was better than a gourmet restaurant experience and we can't wait to try the recipes at home.

After class, Boom gave us each cookbooks and certificates of completion and then shuttled us back to our hotel; what a fun day!

We spent day three in Chiang Mai on a self-guided temple walk. As a Buddhist holy city Chiang Mai is second in importance only to Bangkok. Something on the order of 300 temple compounds, "Wats," lie within the area, and as many as 130 of these are packed inside the walls of the old city. Denise didn't think we should visit all 130 so we compromised on three. I was skeptical, but with quick flyby visits to one or two others, three was plenty.

Our first stop was at Wat Phra Singh. This large compound prominently features the two essentials of wat architecture: "chedi," solid, mountain-shaped monuments that portray Buddhism's lasting stability, and "wi-hahn," buildings that shelter revered Buddha images. Inside one of these rests the city's most important Buddha, the Phra Singh or Lion Buddha from circa 1300. The Lion Buddha, suitably serene and enigmatic, is cool but so were all the others. There is a two-storey standing Buddha, an equally gigantic reclining Buddha, a pair of fat happy one-storey seated Buddha, big Buddha, little Buddha, Buddha of all sizes and poses, gilt Buddha, wooden Buddha, jade Buddha, stone Buddha; anyway you slice it that's a lot of Buddha!

Sprinkled among the Buddha were shrines to the memory of particularly revered monks. The drawing cards to these are life-size wax sculptures. The detail is remarkable; wrinkles, wispy hair, nails, age spots. Encased in glass, it looks as if the old monks sat down to meditate, achieved Nirvana, and at that moment decided to remain immobile for eternity.

Our other two stops were Wat Chedi Luang and Wat Phan Tao, a pair of venerable temple complexes conveniently located right across the street from our hotel. Both are similar in their appeal to Wat Phra Singh; beautiful temple buildings, impressive Buddha, and pleasant grounds. Wat Chedi Luang centers on a massive partially restored thirteenth century chedi that's decorated with giant mythical serpents, "naga," and life-size stone elephants.

The high point of our day was the time we devoted to Wat Chedi Luang's "Monk Chat." Most of the wats in the city are live-in monastic communities where monks of all ages work, study, and pray. For many young men born to poor hill families the free education offered by these monasteries is their only path out of poverty. As part of this education, monks learn English and what better way to practice than to sit down for an hour and shoot the breeze with a couple of American tourists.

Supat, who talked with us, was a soft-spoken young man of thirty. The youngest of five children from a Karen hill tribe on the outskirts of Chiang Mai, he came to Wat Chedi Luang as a novice at the age of sixteen. At the age of twenty he became a monk. He explained that as a novice you must follow ten rules of behavior, but as a monk you must follow 200. Of these, the four most important are: you must not kill another human being; you must not steal; you must not lie to make yourself seem more important; and, you must not engage in sexual relations. Supat also told us that he was free to leave the monastic life at any time, but could return later as long as he didn't violate those four rules.

In broken English, he described his day: up at 5:30, wash, chant for a half hour, meditate for ten minutes, go on an "alms walk;" monks walk around with baskets and people donate freshly prepared food and other items to their support, eat breakfast/lunch, only one meal per day, attend classes, chant for an hour, meditate for ten minutes, and then retire. Except for their late morning meal the monks at Wat Chedi Luang are supposed to fast. Supat follows this rule, but admits that some monks are less strict and sneak the occasional snack. The rigor of each monk's observance is a matter of personal choice.

We got a particular kick out of talking with Supat about his clothes and other possessions. Monks aren't allowed dark colored clothes; no reds, blues, greens, or other ostentatious hues. That pretty much leaves shades of yellow and orange. Supat was rocking mustard colored robes that leave his right arm and shoulder bare, but covered his left arm to the wrist. He explained that the off-the-shoulder style was reserved for inside the wat and then demonstrated how his robes could be re-wrapped to cover both arms. He also unwrapped for a moment to reveal that he was also wearing a mustard colored skirt and a mustard colored off-the-shoulder polar fleece vest. Who'da thought?

We commented on Supat's cell phone and his Costco-type shopping card (a friend returned it while we were talking); he responded that he also has a computer in his room and that the Internet is great for games! *Okay, monks roll high-tech; good to know.*

At some point, Supat hopes to leave the monastic life and experience the rest of the world. He was a sweet guy and we have our doubts.

On day three, we gulped hot coffee, munched cold cereal, and trooped out the door of our hotel at 7:30AM. The reason for our bright and early start (okay, bright and early for us) was that we'd signed up for a half-day bicycle tour pedaling through the outskirts of Chiang Mai. A car was waiting, and along with a young couple from Boston, we were whisked to the home office of "Recreational Bangkok Biking." At their "headquarters," really more home than office, we met Foek, the owner, a Dutch expat, ex-chef, who was going to be our guide. Foek and his wife handed out water bottles and helmets, fitted us for our bicycles, and away we rolled.

Everything about the excursion was well done. The bicycles were good quality and like new. Our route was flat, scenic, and mostly traffic free. Foek, by the way, that's pronounced like "folk," was a personable guy and a knowledgeable guide. Icing on the cake; all of our stops were interesting.

We visited an over-the-top-garish Chinese temple complete with giant Technicolor dragon; sampled fresh donuts and coconut buns at a local bakery; pedaled through a former leper colony; talked to excited children at an elementary school; poked around an outdoor crematorium; ate a yummy lunch at an orphanage; watched potters turn twenty-pound rounds of clay into thrown pots at a rate of one every three minutes; tasted sticky sweets at a commercial candy factory; walked around ancient temples; and sampled more food at a bustling local market. It's hard to believe, but we also managed to squeeze in twenty-five kilometers of biking!

At the last temple we visited, Denise joined locals who were making small donations in exchange for fortunes printed on thin sheets of paper; kind of like fortune cookies without the cookie.

"You're like a mute being basted and couldn't express what you think. The patronage you get is just an illusion like a dream that vapors when you wake. Don't think of coupling, otherwise you'll be in such trouble!"

Hmmm, not sure if I like that last part. Foek assured Denise that it was okay to try again until she got a "good" one.

The "Colors of Chiang Mai" tour crammed a lot of doing into four hours, but we loved every minute. In fact, we liked the excursion so much that if it works out we want to do another with the same company in Bangkok.

To maintain our momentum and roll with our "do the tourist thing" theme, we allocated day four to a full-day "Simple Trek" to Doi Inthanon National Park. This time, we were part of a small guided excursion that included a married couple from Australia, their two sons, aged seven and nine, and a young Swedish couple.

As we walked out of the 3Sis lobby the hotel receptionist cautioned us not to tell the other tourists what we paid for our tour. A moment later "Bang," the excursion's guide, put his finger to his lips and whispered the same warning. The implication of such a "wink-wink" warning is that you've paid much less than your fellow travelers and that blurting it out in public would be the social equivalent of a fart in church. We've heard it all before and we're not sure we buy it. Our sneaky suspicion is always that we're the ones who paid way too much and that the whispered warnings are a time tested ploy to insure that we don't find out and throw a hissy fit. It works! Good team players that we are; we keep our mouths shut. If you're satisfied with the price, why ask? If we paid more, we get grumpy. If we paid less, someone else gets grumpy. Either way, you're going to have a better, happy, happy experience if you don't know.

An hour-long ride in a mini-van transported us from the hotel out into rural farmland and then into foothills. Our first stop was an "elephant camp." Bang led us from the van to a roof-high platform which serves as a sort of an elephant loading dock. Climb up its rickety steps and you're on the same level as a pachyderm's seat-equipped back. Elephants sidled up to the platform in a good imitation of 1940's town cars at valet parking, and two by two, like animals shuffling onto the Ark, our fellow tour-ons climbed aboard.

When our turn came, an elephant docked against the platform and we stepped gingerly onto his back; ladies first. "Yes, right there. Just step on him. He doesn't care." Our mahout tapped the elephant's ear and off it strolled gently rocking from side to side.

Right from the get-go it was obvious that our elephant was about to go rogue. The last thing that he, or maybe she, it's hard to tell from up top, wanted to do was carry another pair of tourists on another hour-long jaunt. Our elephant was obviously more interested in eating than walking. A few paces from the loading platform it grabbed a stump sized chunk of banana tree and began a loud and vigorous munch. When that snack was gone, it paused at every convenient bit of greenery and foraged for more. The elephant would stop, the mahout would shout at it, poke its ear with the pointy end of his stick or bop it on the head, the elephant would snort or growl (no really! sort of a "Grrrrrr" sound), the driver would poke it or bop it again, and reluctantly the behemoth would resume its plod. Every couple of minutes the scene replayed. The elephant sounded pissed! It was really big and the guy with the stick was really small. Each time Jumbo snorted, we expected him to reach back, dash the mahout to the ground, and stomp him into Thai jelly. Of course no such thing came to pass, but uncertainty is sauce for the goose.

We rocked along in fits and starts and wound our way down a narrow well worn jungle trail. It was fascinating to watch the elephants ahead of us slowly and carefully place their ponderous feet one in front of the other. It was also a thrill and a bit scary when, to avoid a "traffic jam," our mahout urged Jumbo (who knows its real name) to step off the trail and head up a steep incline. There we were far above the ground, rocking from side to side, and leaning back at what had to be a ninety degree angle while our mount performed its mutant elephant-Spiderman thing. *Do elephants ever roll over backwards?* Heading down hill; just flip everything around 180 degrees.

About half way into our ride, we came upon an enterprising woman sitting on an elephant-high platform amid stacks of bananas. "Hello madam. Bananas for your elephant? Only 20 baht." Twenty baht is about $0.68. Jumbo was obviously hungry. This seemed like a no-brainer. The moment our transaction was complete; a large muscular trunk with a grasping snout snaked back to our seat and began to grope about. Clearly, Jumbo was familiar with the routine. Denise tore a banana off the stalk and passed it to the snout. The trunk went away and our driver urged Jumbo forward. Two steps and the trunk came back. Denise passed it another banana. One more step and the trunk whipped back again. After that, it was no more steps. The trunk just whipped back and forth snatching bananas until the stalk was bare and our mahout had to bop it with his stick. We're not sure who was training who.

Near the end of our ride, we paused in a field for a photo opportunity. While Jumbo foraged, another elephant's driver swung to the ground and urged the young Swedish woman to climb into the driver's seat. Seeing us watch her sit on her elephant's head, our mahout turned to Denise and warily signed that he could also hop down if she wanted to give it a try. Our elephant reaches for a bush and makes the growling sound. *Are you certifiably crazy! This elephant wants to stampede! It's been waiting for it all day!* "Uh, no, that's okay. We're fine right here."

After dropping us back at the loading platform, Jumbo made a beeline for another banana trunk. As we walked to the van he could be seen (and heard) munching contentedly.

Our next stop was a small hill tribe village. Other than well behaved chickens and a few sleeping pigs Animal Planet was behind us. We wandered among the scattering of huts and watched Karen women weave cloth on their hand looms. The visuals were nice since each woman sat surrounded by colorful displays of her finished cloth and other assorted tourist tat. The cluster of huts and stalls was probably more of a tourist set up than a working village, but it still made for an interesting visit. We bought a pair of seed bracelets from two little girls for 5 Bhat each ($.017).

When we finished with the village, Bang led us on an easy thirty minute walk through farmland and jungle to a mountain waterfall. "Okay, thirty minutes here. You swim Mr. Don?" Along with the two Australian boys and the Swedish couple, I slipped into my trunks and went swimming. Everyone else sat on the rocks and admired the crashing water. Okay, to be honest the two boys swam, the Swedish couple and I dipped into the water a couple of times, shivered, and scrambled out. How do you ask, "As cold as at home," in Swedish?

After the falls, we walked another hour through more jungle and more farmland until we reached a second small village. This community was Hmong instead of Karen. Denise tried on clothes, the Australians tried their hand at a crossbow, and we all toured a typical hut.

By now, everyone's appetite was awake and paying attention so we loaded back into our van and rolled for a roadside café. Lunch consisted of rice, stir fried veggies, and fruit; not exceptional, but fresh and filling.

Our final "Simple Trek" activity was a river trip on a bamboo raft. At the put-in point, we changed into our swim suits and split up onto two rafts. The four Australians took one and the rest of us the other. Each raft was constructed of nine goal-post-sized bamboo poles held together with loops of old bicycle tire. We all sat down and our "captains," standing at the front, poled their crafts into the shallow river. For the next hour they skillfully navigated currents, bends, and gurgling riffles. We glided past overhanging jungle, bounced through tiny rapids, got splashed, saw snakes, and enjoyed a major Huck Finn experience.

When we reached our take-out point, workers popped the bike tires off the poles and that was the end of our rafts. The dissembled pieces were quickly tossed into a pickup truck and hauled back up stream for their next trip; ingenious, reusable, and low-tech.

On the ride back to Chiang Mai, everyone (driver excluded) fell asleep; good day, good time.

Chapter 15

VIETNAM

Day 379 - January 19 - Wednesday - Hanoi, Vietnam

With our visas about to expire, we left Chiang Mai and caught an easy flight to Bangkok. Since we plan to hit Thailand again, we've saved the big 'B' for next time around. We stayed over night in an airport hotel called the Orchid Resort; convenient and comfortable and the next morning at 6:50 AM, that's a 3:30 AM wake-up for anyone who's interested, we winged off to Vietnam. An hour and fifty minutes later, under overcast skies, we alighted at Hanoi's international airport.

Immigration was efficient if a little bureaucratic. We stood in a line in front of a thick plate window, a procedure common to every immigration counter world-wide, and then handed our passports to a uniformed officer. Vietnam requires U.S. citizens to obtain visas before they leave home. We cavalierly overlooked this requirement, but fortunately we had the foresight to pay an online facilitator $50 USD to issue us a "pre-approval" letter. If you haven't done your homework, this "official" document somehow obviates your past sins.

Add another $50 at the counter for an official stamp and voila, visa on arrival for two.

We walked to the other side of a glass enclosure. Inside, other uniformed types were diligently at work scrutinizing and reviewing. We stood patiently with other waiting travelers (actually the Russian guy was antsy) and after a short time our patience was rewarded with our visa-stamped passports; easy as pie.

Luggage retrieval didn't go quite so smoothly. When we reached the baggage area our flight and another were listed on the sign board and a carousel was looping round and round. There weren't any bags but eventually a few began to circulate. We waited. At first there were a few people from our flight standing there expectantly, but after a time the crowd began to thin. We waited; still no bags. Half-an-hour slipped by and still nothing. As the crowd dispersed, Denise looked away from the carousel. "Hey, isn't that my bag?" I walked over to where she pointed and sure enough, there was her bag sitting next to a Vietnamese family and their luggage. I grabbed it and rolled it back to Denise. "What the heck! How did it get there?"

At that point I look up and there's a skycap-looking guy scuttling away with my bag in tow! "Whoa, hold it right there! That's my bag!"

"Yes, yes, it there long time. Go round and round." *I don't think so!* The only thing we can figure is that our luggage double-timed it from the plane and that some "helpful" soul pulled it off the carousel while we waited for official stamps.

As usual, we'd arranged an airport pickup, but by the time we pushed our luggage cart through the exit, it was long gone; no one holding up a sign. Left to fend for ourselves, we walked over to an information counter and managed to convince a helpful attendant to call our hotel. This led to assurances that our driver was still in the area and that he would reappear momentarily. Sure enough, we'd barely said "Thank You" to the helpful attendant when a man walked up.

"You Mister Donald, go Hidden Charm Hotel?"

"Yep, that's us." This looked like a positive development, but I have to own up to a moment of skepticism. Everything you read warns you about the infinite variety of taxi scams found in Vietnam. There are quoted rates which on arrival turn out to be per person rather than per trip, meters that run too fast, hotels that purportedly burned down, hotels that clone the name of other better known establishments, and so on. *I gave the helpful attendant our name and the name of our hotel. How do I know this guy is on the up and up?* A little paranoia is healthy, but too much is a pain in the rear. Thank you, Unnamed Guide Book!

When we walked out of the exit to our car, we suddenly came face to face with the first really cool weather of out trip. We're talking, overcast, cold, see-your-breath weather! After a full year of mostly sweltering tropical heat, this was a decidedly unwelcome development. My first thought was of Charlie Sheen's character (Chris Taylor) in the movie "Platoon." "Grandma, I think I made a big mistake coming here." This weather might be fine for January in Eugene, Oregon, but darn it, we're in Southeast Asia!

The well appointed lobby of the Hidden Charm Hotel was as cold as the proverbial well digger's ass. It seems that central heat is virtually non-existent in North Vietnam. Whether this is a political commentary on decadent Western Civilization, a lack of infrastructure, or merely a function of our own budget restrictions, the result is the same. The reception and bell staff at the hotel were bundled in scarves, sweaters, and wool hats that made us shiver just to look at them.

When we arrived we were offered a lobby seat and hot tea while our room was readied. It was only about 10 AM which admittedly is early for check-in, but the real motive was to give the receptionist a chance to pitch local tours. “So what tour you like? Best if you book now.”

Tough as it was; we resisted, “Hmmm, we’ll think about it.” As it turned out, a low grade sales-pitch was an ongoing theme at the Hidden Charm; not enough high pressure to make us cranky, but a consistent background buzz to all our staff interactions.

Our room was sixty-three degrees Fahrenheit; warm enough that frost didn’t form on our luggage, but cold enough that we layered on our clothing. Thankfully, our air-conditioner was equipped with a “heat” setting. It wasn’t what either of us called a real heater, but it did eventually warm the room.

While we waited, we decided that it was probably no colder outside so we might as well be sightseeing. The Hidden Charm is unquestionably a touch chilly, but its address is unbeatable. It’s located right in the heart of Old Hanoi on a quaint street behind the cathedral and only a short walk from Hoan Kiem Lake. Clad in clothes that we almost mailed home, we walked the small streets near our hotel. We soaked in the atmosphere, ate to-die-for brioche, scoped out the local scene, bought some wine at a supermarket, and ate a reasonably authentic Italian dinner.

Day 380 - January 20 - Thursday

Hanoi is a smorgasbord of sights, sounds, and smells! Fueled by exotic hustle and bustle, Asian mystery, and French Colonial charm, it's a multi-level assault on your imagination. The city exudes a palpable air of history. For the two of us, and we assume for many others of our generation, Hanoi is iconic. This is the place that B52's pounded on our nightly news. It's the place where downed American pilots were paraded for newsreels; where Jane Fonda irked the conservatives of our nation, and where Ho Chi Minh preached defiance and resistance. Hanoi is one of the world's great cities and as Americans of a certain age, simply being here is an experience.

On our first full day, we continued our plan from the day before, which is to say we wandered without plan. Our first stop was a nearby bakery for a redo of the mouthwatering brioche. Munching happily, we ambled along the shores of Hoan Kiem Lake. We watched a photographer snap photos of two newlyweds on the Rising Sun Bridge and then strolled across ourselves. The graceful wooden span arches, red and flag-lined, to a small island and the "Ngoc Son," Jade Mountain, Temple.

As an introduction to Vietnamese multipurpose temples Ngoc Son is a good one. Dedicated to a general named Tran Hung Dao, who defeated Mongol hordes in the 1200's, it also serves as a shrine to La To, patron saint of physicians, and a random Confucian scholar named, Van Xuong. Resplendent in colors of red, black, and gold, the temple features altars with statues of the deified general and his scholarly buddies. Locals kneel reverently. Incense wafts through the air, piles of colorful offerings adorn the altars, and giant brass cranes stand an eternal watch. We didn't exactly get it, but we liked the mummified 500 pound lake-turtle on display in a glass case. According to signage, giant turtles still ply the lake's waters, appearing now and then to the chosen few. We didn't see one.

Back over the bridge and across a busy street sits the Martyrs' Monument. Think uber-sized 1930's WPA concrete and you have a general idea. Continuing into Hanoi's Old Quarter, we wandered traditional market streets, avenues where most shops specialize in a single ware. On one street it's all mirrors and tin. On another it's hardware. Another thoroughfare features merit-making offerings and brightly colored temple supplies, yet another fruits of all shapes and sizes; all of it lively, crowded, and congested. We visited a "Culture House" where traditional furnishings were displayed and ate a lunch of rice and cabbage at the Ladybird café. Exotic scents fill the air and everywhere around us buzzes with activity.

Crossing streets in Hanoi isn't the live-action Frogger we experienced in Cairo, but it's nearly as harrowing. It's an art form, and a completely new experience. The population of Vietnam is around 84 million. A wealthy 4 million of these own private cars. The other 80 million whiz around on 40 million motorcycles. According to our own unscientific estimate, on any given day, most of these jostle through the streets of Hanoi. Signals or not, you don't ever have the right of way in Vietnam. Nothings stops for pedestrians. So how do you cross a busy boulevard? Fortune favors the bold. You pucker up and step off the curb. Immediately you're engulfed in a noxious stream of honking scooters. You try not to flinch, move unpredictably; or, worse yet, run. Meanwhile, the heavily laden motor bikes flow around you like giant mechanical salmon rushing upstream to spawn. You want to close your eyes, but you're afraid not to look. As you timidly place one foot in front of the other the scooters race straight at you. Just as your life passes before your eyes, they swerve. If your nerve holds, you make the far curb. We usually attempt such crossings in designated crosswalks, but we're not sure exactly why.

Walking through an area of meat and seafood stalls we stumbled across the day's cultural highlight; a frog butcher. We've seen chickens get their throats slit and cuddly bunnies waiting for their turn on the block, but this was a first. A woman sat on a small stool. In front of her was a big square tin pan. In the pan was a flat chunk of wood. In her hand was a large serious looking cleaver. Beside her was a squirming bag of the biggest, greenest, bug-eyed toads you ever saw. In a steady rhythm, she'd grab a frog, hack its head off, gut it, peel its skin off, toss it in a basket and reach for another. She was a regular one woman amphibian apocalypse.

Day 381 - January 21 - Friday

We know it's cliché to say that the world is small, but it is. This morning, we met up with Chris and Bob, the couple who shared our dinner table crossing the Atlantic. They emailed us a couple of weeks ago to ask how we were doing and in passing mentioned that they were about to visit Vietnam. As chance would have it, they arrived in Hanoi the day after we did and ended up in a hotel only a half block from ours. Chris and Bob are fun people and after so long on the road it was a pleasure to see familiar faces. We shot the breeze for a while and then, since we all plan to visit Angkor Wat, we walked over to the Cambodian embassy to arrange our visas.

The Cambodian Consular Immigration Section was one guy sitting in a dark office. “Yes, yes, visas are no problem. You pay twenty dollars US and come back Tuesday.” *Okay, we went down that road in Cairo.*

“Uh, is there any way to get them faster?”

“Yes, you come Monday; pay twenty-five dollars.”

“So you’re saying that if we pay $25 on Monday we can get visas the same day?”

“Yes, same day.” At that point the guy gave us forms to fill out and told us that he had to close in a couple of minutes to run an errand. Evidently, he then thought better of his decision. “You *all* want same day?”

“Yes, same day.”

“Okay, you come back at 4 o’clock and I get.”

“You mean we can all come back at 4 PM today and get our visas today?”

“Yes, same day.” The upshot was that the four of us came back, paid our $25 each, and received our visas. The whole process took fifteen minutes, which is a heck of a lot better than fifteen days! Check that India! Still, bureaucracy isn’t supposed to work that smoothly. It’s an unwritten rule! We figure the embassy guy pocketed the $5 same-day fees and made big plans for the weekend, but hey; who looks a gift horse in the mouth?

We finished the day with dinner at another Italian place that we’d discovered. Sure, it’s sort of weird to be in Southeast Asia and eat Italian twice in one week, but Denise and I have cabbage and rice dripping out of our ears. A nice pasta dish and some red wine really hit the spot. Thank you, expats!

Day 382 - January 22 - Saturday

Day three and we set out early for some serious sightseeing. Bob and Chris joined us right after breakfast and the four of us shared a cab over to the Ho Chi Minh Mausoleum Complex. In a communist country where ancestor worship is deeply ingrained in the national psyche, this is the Big Poobah. Before Uncle Ho died, he stated his wish for a simple cremation. Instead, in the best communist tradition; Lenin, Stalin, and Mao got the same treatment; he lies perpetually in state in a sort of creepy father-of-our-country immortality.

The mausoleum complex is a huge pedestrian open space with sweeping parade grounds, stirring memorials, manicured lawns, shady parks, serene lakes, and ancient pagodas. The center piece of the complex is the monumental edifice that houses Ho's glass sarcophagus. Set on a tiered platform the enormous square building is surrounded on all sides by towering square columns, and capped by an angled tiered roof said to evoke a lotus flower or a traditional communal house. It was definitely impressive, but probably evokes more Third Reich than flowering lotus.

On most days the complex is crowded with Vietnamese come to pay their respects or just catch a glimpse of an almost mythical figure. Sixty-five percent of the country's citizens are under the age of 30, so Ho is the stuff of legends. Often the queue to view his body winds back for hundreds of yards from the mausoleum itself. We got lucky. After a brief wait in a covered breezeway, the line moved quickly. We walked past the honor guard: snow white uniforms, white gloves, and chrome bayonets, and entered the silent marble halls of Vietnam's holy of holies.

The scene is slightly bizarre and knowing that Ho's embalmed corpse travels to Russia once a year for "maintenance" only adds to the weirdness. We would dearly have loved a picture or two, but such crass activity is strictly forbidden. To ensure that no one succumbs to temptation; surrender of all cameras, cell phones, and other electronics is a precondition of entry.

Every five steps we passed another white-garbed guard. As we entered the viewing chamber, the marble hall split to enter two galleries separated by a metal rail. I entered the inner gallery nearest to Ho's case, while Denise accidently took a step into the other. When she tried to turn and join me, a scowling guard sternly gestured for her to stay where she was. Another cultural faux pas; I swear, I can't take her anywhere.

Uncle Ho was smaller than we expected, but for someone who died more than forty years ago, the old guy's in pretty good shape. With his wispy white hair and beard, he lies pale and serene in his glass case; looking for all the world like someone's recently deceased grandfather. Locals and tourists alike shuffle reverently past. You're not allowed to stop or slow down; and just like that, your brush with history is over.

Back outside, Bob and Chris took off to explore the markets of the Old Quarter and we headed deeper into the mausoleum complex. 30,000 dong, about $1.57, gained us admission to Ho Chi Minh's Stilt House and the presidential palace. This is essentially an opportunity to wander in a park-like setting past gardens and carp ponds and view the outside of several historical buildings.

The stilt house is a simple open structure modeled on traditional rural dwellings. According to signage, Ho occupied it from 1958 to 1969 and it's been kept "just as he left it." If this latter is true the guy must have been something of an ascetic. The house is pleasing, but still pretty sparse.

The presidential palace is a restored colonial mansion constructed in 1906 for the Governor General of Indochina. You're able to peek into a few windows but that's about it. We thought the garage was the best part. Carefully preserved behind glass are several cars that at one time or another ferried Ho Chi Minh on his appointed rounds. The cars are sort of a yawn, but the signage is great, "Garage of Ho Chi Minh's Used Cars." Hey, my dad was a used car guy too! "Coupes! Sedans! Town cars! You want 'em, we got 'em. Come on down! Free rice hats and pork-on-a-stick for the kiddies."

We wrapped up our visit to the mausoleum complex with a stop at Hanoi's landmark "One Pillar Pagoda." A hefty concrete pillar rises from the center of a small pond and supports a wooden one-room pagoda. Like the roof of Ho's mausoleum, the small wooden structure is supposed to evoke a blooming lotus. Uncultured person that I am, it reminded me of an upscale version of a tree-house I once built. The One Pillar Pagoda was constructed by an eleventh century Emperor to honor the Goddess of Mercy for giving him an heir. Of course we're talking about the original. The one we saw is a copy. Sadly, Vietnam has lost much of its cultural heritage to the ravages of weather and war. The original One Pillar Pagoda lasted nine hundred years before embittered French troops destroyed it in 1954.

Our next planned stop was a visit to the Hanoi Museum of Fine Art, but just walking in Hanoi turns up the unexpected. Leaving the mausoleum complex we passed through a lively market and then along a busy street. As we stepped up on a corner curb, we spotted a large concrete WPA-style plaque mounted on a wall. Dated, May 19, 1967, the plaque features a rough stylized relief of brave citizen soldiers and an American war plane spiraling down in flames; weird and a little eerie.

The Hanoi Museum of Fine Art is located in an impressive pair of buildings that once upon a time housed the French Ministry of Information. The art collection inside is even better: ancient stone and wood carvings, oodles of contemporary art, ceramics, and more. We especially liked the paintings executed over lacquer and the ethereal watercolors done on silk.

By the time we finished poking into the museum's assortment of galleries and returned to the street, our stomachs were growling. Serendipitously, just around the corner, we stumbled onto a neat little restaurant called Café Smile. From chefs to waiters and waitresses, the staff is made up of disadvantaged youth training to work in food service. Eating at Smile helps young people in need, but it's not a totally altruistic experience. Their food is delicious; it's also dirt cheap, and presented with gourmet flair. It took significant will power for us not to order lunch twice.

Just across from the restaurant hunkered our next destination, a square block of traditional Vietnamese architecture dubbed, The Temple of Literature. A wall surrounds the complex and provides market space for small-time entrepreneurs ranging from barbers clipping away al-fresco to crowd-drawing calligraphers who carpet the sidewalk with their papers and ink.

The temple was dedicated to Confucius in 1070 and consists of five serene courtyards. Arranged around these are buildings and pavilions honoring assorted Vietnamese scholars. Wandering the grounds is a pleasant break from the hustle and bustle outside. Among the temple's artifacts are 82 huge stone tablets standing on the backs of equally huge stone turtles. These stelae date from around 1500 and record the accomplishments of renowned men of letters, historians, mathematicians, and poets. The inscriptions are worn, but the turtles are excellent. Gold and red statues of Confucius, a giant gong, a giant drum, sweeping dragon topped roofs; a Well of Heavenly Clarity, low-slung pagodas, and fanciful landscaping were well worth the temple's $0.50 admission fee.

Sight seeing is usually a passive activity. You drift by something, make a few comments, "Oooh, that's pretty!" Snap a few photos and then move on to the next thing. Every once in a while it's something else. Some sights demand more of you; they excite your imagination or stir your emotions. That was our last stop of the day, Hoa Lo Prison. Hoa Lo, which commonly translates to "Fiery Furnace," was a sprawling complex built by the French in 1896. Designed to house 400 prisoners and later expanded to 600; by 1954 they were using it to house nearly 2,000 in unspeakable conditions. In 1993 two thirds of the complex was razed to build a skyscraper. What remains is maintained as a thought provoking museum.

Most of the museum exhibits depict the heroic tribulations of Vietnamese freedom fighters; captured by the French, shackled to their bunks, tortured, abused, and marched to the guillotine. This is interesting and more than a little gruesome, but it's Hoa Lo's recent history that brought us here. Walk through an arch labeled, "Maison Centrale," and you step into a prison better known to aging Americans as the "Hanoi Hilton."

Over the years, we've traveled to a lot of museums that preserve the memory and perhaps the glory of

American military actions. It's a very different experience to visit a museum that denounces American aggression and praises American defeat. Most of the exhibition is propaganda. Photos of happy-go-lucky American prisoners enjoying parties, recreation, and attentive medical care are images that stand in sharp contrast to the returning aviators' tales of torture and deprivation. No matter what your opinion of U.S. involvement in Vietnam, it's a sobering experience to stand before a glass trophy case and gaze at the flight suit of a captured American pilot (John McCain's). The Hanoi Hilton once loomed so large in the American psyche that walking its halls is a real taste of history.

Day 384 - January 24 - Monday - Halong Bay, Vietnam

We just spent the past two days, and one night, as joiners on a packaged excursion to Halong Bay. Designated a World Heritage site, Halong Bay is home to what has become Vietnam's signature scenery; a "must do" if you visit Hanoi. More than two thousand iconic limestone islands are the draw. Majestic outcrops of all shapes and sizes jut from placid green waters creating a spectacular almost magical landscape. According to legend, with a lash of his powerful tail, a giant dragon gouged the bay as he plunged into the sea. A warm day floating among the fairyland isles is probably sublime. We say "probably" because despite repeated assurances, "Oh yes, much warmer in Halong," the bay was goose bump cold!

Our tour group was ad hoc, and numbered about twenty. A small bus scooped us up from our hotel and, with luggage in the overhead and behind the seats; we set out on the three hour drive to Halong City. We made the usual semi-obligatory ceramics factory and pearl store restroom stops. Several Mentos later, "Tony" (liked to refer to himself in the third person) our guide, shepherded us on to a bobbing tender, and we chugged off toward a Chinese-Junk-style cruise boat.

Everybody and their Hanoi cousin try to sell you Halong Bay tours. They range from you-get-what-you-pay-for $23 per person trips to excursions of atmospheric luxury; and price. We dickered around with our hotel and settled on $119 each which scored us an upgrade "sea-view" cabin on a newer boat and a couple of thrown-in "free" airport transfers.

Our designated boat, the "Golden Lotus," met our expectations. When the hotel sold us our tickets, they claimed that the "junk" was only a couple of years old. It probably was. Everything looked well kept and, as far as we could tell, in reasonable working order. Painted wooden decks, furled sails, and classic lines even gave the "Lotus" a hint of romance. Our cabin was smallish, but it was equipped with an air-conditioner which included (thank you God!) the coveted "heat" setting.

Leave our cabin and everywhere else on the boat was bundle-up and blow on your fingers cold! Rows of padded lounge chairs lined the roof. On warm days passengers probably while the hours in solar fueled comfort praising the ethereal scenery. "Oh my God! That's beautiful! Honey, would you rub some sunscreen on my back." With coats, scarves, and gloves, Denise and I lasted ten minutes. "Okay, (sound of chattering teeth) that was good. Let's go back inside." A quick retreat into the main lounge took us out of the wind, but that was as far as it went. Several key doors remained permanently open on the Golden Lotus rendering the boat's out-to-in distinction, shall we say; subtle. Meals (mediocre) were perforce al fresco and required nearly as much clothing as off boat excursions.

Cold or not, Halong Bay lives up to its hype. The weather compensated for the temperature with a minimum of surface fog, and what little mist swirled about rendered the limestone archipelago mysterious and exotic rather than invisible. After we scrambled off the tender and stowed luggage, we enjoyed a welcome drink of fruit juice, and the Golden Lotus motored away into the maze of limestone outcrops.

The breathtaking kaleidoscope of sparsely forested towers was the focus of our trip, but a couple of extras were tossed in that kept things lively. Wind and waves eat away at the islands and grottos pock their shores. Our first stop was "Hang Dau Go," Cave of the Wooden Stakes. We have to admit, we sort of like monumental caves and Hang Dau Go is a good one. The Golden Lotus threaded its way among other boats (you're not alone at Halong) and into a storybook bay where we were tendered ashore. We ascended ninety (we counted) stone steps which rose steeply from the quay. At their top, we paused, caught our breath, and then stepped into the cave's first chamber. Technicolor lighting effects illuminate the cavern and Mother Nature does the rest. Stalagmites, stalactites, curtains of flowstone, pools of still water; nearby a group of gnomes appear to hunker in conference. A ways farther, a proud male phallus juts from the wall. "Men only, come here. Tony show you something." Amazing geology and titillating commentary, who wants more?

In the "small world" category, we ran into Chris in the depths of the grotto. She and Bob booked their own semi-obligatory Halong tour with a different outfit, but as they say, "all roads lead to Rome."

After the cave, we motored to a small floating fishing village where kayaking among the karsts was offered as an included optional experience. Denise and I looked at the deep icy green water, readjusted our gloves and scarves, and decided that kayaking Halong was an experience we'd live without. We did however wave encouragement to Chris, an adventurous soul, as she paddled past. You go gal!

Scenery isn't the only thing in Halong Bay that's surreal. Whenever the Golden Lotus paused in her journey, small rowboats magically appeared alongside. One minute we were in the middle of nowhere; the next impromptu convenience stores bobbed beside the rail. Bundled in wool hats and heavy coats oarswomen maneuver oversize baskets (no kidding, the boats are oval and woven from bamboo) while touting their wares. "Hey Mister, you want Snickers?" Cases of beer, bottles of wine and hard liquor, boxes of Custas and Choco Pies (Vietnam equivalent of Moon Pies), stacks of Oreos, softdrinks galore, cup-o-noodles by the gross, and Pringles of every conceivable flavor; each rowable basket is a veritable 7/11 of the seas. "Mister..., (with a nasal whine) Pringles!"

"Uh, no thank you. We're good."

That night, we anchored in the lee of Cat Ba Island. You can't say you've truly lived until you've experienced Karaoke performed in an icebox. Imagine a pair of Esquimaux, actually Australian art school grads, bundled from head to toe, belting out Celine Dion. "Every night in my dreams I see you. I feel you. That is how I know you go on..." You get the idea. The Vietnamese are crazy for Karaoke. Parties, hotels, bars, any locale, any excuse; it's a cultural staple. Long after that one annoying guy quit butchering Stairway to Heaven and the rest of us tourists tucked into our beds, ear plugs firmly in place, our crew still crooned away with undiminished gusto.

Day 385 - January 25 - Tuesday - Hoi An, Vietnam

We purchased killer-price, $35 economy tickets to fly from Hanoi to Danang. Even better, we snagged a flight that left at 10:40 AM, an infinitely reasonable hour! Calculations for our departure went some thing like this, "Let's see, Jetstar ticket counters close thirty minutes before domestic flights. Okay, that means that we need to get to the airport by 10:00 AM to be safe. From downtown Hanoi to the airport by taxi; give-or-take, forty minutes; we should probably leave the hotel by 9:00." We're slow to crawl out of bed and we enjoy a leisurely breakfast, so we set our alarm for 7:00 AM.

We know what you're thinking, but no, the alarm went off on time. While Denise hopped into the shower, I decided to check my email, and low and behold, there it was! "Dear <Sir/Madam>, We, at Jetstar Pacific, would like to thank you for choosing our services! Unfortunately, due to our schedule change, your reserved flight will have earlier departure time. Please note that the new departure time of your flight will be 09:10." *Huh? Let's see, 9:10 minus 30 minutes equals 8:40. Take away another 40 minutes and ...Holy Crap!* "Denise, get out of the shower!"

Denise toweled off. I went stinky. We shoved stuff into our bags and ran for the lobby. Panting, we explained our predicament and then waited fifteen agonizing minutes for a taxi to arrive. When one finally showed, we settled into its back seat with sighs of relief. Then, as we wound our way through town our sphincters began to clench. Despite his best efforts heavy traffic limited our driver's top speed to a hair pulling, nail-biting, twenty miles per hour. With the clock ticking and our sanity teetering, we at last rolled into the airport and sprinted for the check-in counter. Minutes to spare; piece of cake! Breakfasts are overrated and who likes to wait around in airports anyway?

Danang is a large commercial city, without much to recommend it as a tourist destination. Its small neighbor, Hoi An is different story. Nestled on the banks of the Thu Bon River a short distance from the sea; Hoi An enjoyed nearly four centuries as one of Southeast Asia's preeminent international ports. Influential traders from China and Japan came and stayed, stamping their indelible mark on the region's art and culture. Treasures of the orient: silk, tea, exotic spices, porcelain, and more, once filled town warehouses, and merchant ships from a dozen nations tied up at its wharves. Fortunately for the tourist, that's ancient history. The river silted up, commerce moved on to Danang, and Hoi An went peacefully to sleep. Amazingly, despite neglect, war, and repeated flooding, a large architecturally significant section of Hoi An's riverfront survives. In 1999 the narrow streets and ancient buildings were given UNESCO World Heritage status.

When we landed in Danang, earlier than expected, we caught a prepaid, $18, taxi and asked that it run us straight to Hoi An. We mention this detail only because the ride brushed us up against yet another taxi scam. After we settled in, our driver asked us if we'd already booked a room. This question is a given because every taxi driver who spots you with luggage salivates for the chance to take you to a commission paying hotel. Our assurances that we had a room seemed to satisfy him and we rolled merrily along. As we approached Hoi An, however, he suddenly expressed uncertainty about his ability to locate our hotel. Then, "serendipitously," he spotted someone standing on a corner and pulled over. "This is my friend. He live Hoi An, can show us hotel." "No way! We do not want him in the car! He does NOT get in!" Letting a stranger climb into your taxi is always a very bad idea.

In this case the situation was more about avoiding potential nuisance than actual danger. Several days earlier we'd spoken with another couple and their Hoi An experience had put us on our guard. While not an actual robber, the "friend" was still a highwayman of sorts; a commission paying tout for a tailor shop. Let him into your cab, and a few pleasantries later you're suddenly the focus of a mind-melting high pressure sales pitch.

Hoi An is nuts for tailors! Large and small shops line street after street, literally hundreds of them, and they all sell, remarkably similar, custom made, clothing. Suits, gowns, bathing suits, you name it, twenty-four hours after your fitting it's ready to wear. It's nearly impossible to walk down the street without someone suggesting you need a new jacket or a dress. Of course competition is fierce; hence the taxi-tout. If he can drag you into his shop before you even hit town, well hey hey, hey, hey, he's got a leg up on his competitors. Let the tout into the cab and he'll stick to you like a limpet mine. If you're not confrontational you'll probably end up with custom clothes as a precondition of reaching your hotel.

Forewarned is forearmed, so we kept the doors firmly closed. Strangely, our driver was then able to find our hotel without a hitch.

Day 389 - January 29 - Saturday

The place we landed in Hoi An is called the Thien Thanh Hotel and for $42 a night it's a good find. Our first two nights, we stayed in a "family" room on the top floor. That was a little odd, but also sort of fun. It featured a dark beam ceiling, a tile roof, lots of dark wood, and several beds. On the upside it had a good bathroom, space-to-spare, and felt like an upscale loft in some yuppie's converted farmhouse. The downside was a lack of window glass and screens which meant that to keep out cold and skeeters you had to leave the windows shuttered and the room dark. Forget light bulbs. We haven't seen anything over 40 Watts since we left the U.S.

Our second room was smaller and located on the ground floor, but thanks to large glassed windows that looked out onto the hotel's back deck, it was much brighter.

Their rooms are comfortable, and Thien Thanh's staff is friendly and helpful, but flat-out the hotel's best feature is its included breakfast. They lay on a morning spread that warmed our hearts: breads, fruits, juices, coffee, yogurt, and more. Making their offering even better, they supplement the buffet with a station where you can order several styles of eggs. The breakfast is served on a wooden deck overlooking rice paddies and a small nearby farm; what a great way to start your day.

Hoi An is all about wandering its atmospheric Old Town and until today, Denise did most of the foot work. Somewhere out on Halong Bay, I contracted my third cold of the trip and by the time we dropped our bags in Hoi An, the only sights I wanted to see were a pillow and a comforter. Not one to hovel in someone else's sickroom,

Denise left me to my recovery, and went exploring. From time to time, she'd come back, drag me out to a restaurant or something of particular interest, then, with a wheeze, I'd crawl back into bed. This system actually works fairly well. By the time I was feeling better, I'd hit a few of the high points and Denise knew exactly how to lead me to the rest.

It's too bad that I felt puny, because there's a lot to see and do in Hoi An. More than 800 buildings have historical preservation status. There are various temples and pagodas to visit. The town architecture fascinates and a number of well preserved homes are open (for a fee) as living museums; sometimes more gift shop than museum, but still interesting. There's a small graceful "Japanese" bridge that dates from the 1590's; a great spot for photo ops and people watching. Women in rice hats walk down the street with baskets of chickens and ducks slung from poles across their shoulders. Elders squat on the sidewalk and gamble. Toothless old women pose to have their picture taken. The town's open market is lively. The riverfront is festooned with bobbing boats. Colorful silk lanterns hang from the eaves and the choice of good inexpensive restaurants is outstanding. And bakeries... don't get us started.

In one of the living museums a smiling docent (owner, employee, who knows?) urged us to toss I-Ching-like coins in a heads-or-tails manner and determine our fortune. Another couple who were in the house at the same time went first. "Ah, so sorry, bad luck. You try again." The woman tossed her coin three times, evidently the max that fate allows, but failed to improve her result. "Oh, so sorry!" The man took his three turns and again fate frowned. This time the docent was ominously silent. While the couple grumbled that it didn't mean anything, the universe selected us for good fortune on our first toss. When push comes to shove, give us luck every time.

Since I'm on the mend, Denise decided to test my stamina with a bike ride out to Cua Dai Beach. It's still cool and drizzly so this was strictly a coat and gloves affair. We rented two bicycles for a dollar a day each and pedaled off to check out the sand and surf. The round trip was only about ten miles. Despite the weather, if I'd felt well it would have been a pleasant ride. As it was, it was tolerable. The short distance pushed my limit, but the scenery proved excellent: swaying palms, quiet rivers, heroic political billboards, and verdant rice paddies dotted with egrets. As for the beach itself, glowering grey skies presided over towering windswept waves; a scene that to our minds better suits the Oregon coast than the Asian tropics.

Day 390 - January 30 - Sunday - Hue, Vietnam

Hoi An gets lots of tourists and some of what you see feels staged, but it's still a neat place. If we weren't under pressure from another flight reservation we'd surely have lingered. As things stood, Jetstar made us another offer that we couldn't refuse; Hue to Ho Chi Minh City for the mind blowing price of only $22 per ticket! With our departure clock once again ticking, we said "goodbye" to Hoi An and headed for Hue.

Some goodbyes are short and sweet, others are long and drawn-out; protracted affairs that end awkwardly. We'd decided that the least hassle way to travel from Hoi An to Hue was on a daily "tourist" bus. The $6 a seat "luxury" coach picks you up at your hotel and three-and-a-half hours later, you're in Hue. Hope springs eternal, but as we've learned over and again on this trip, times and distances are often quite subjective. The bus was a half hour late picking us up, but no complaints. It looked like it was in pretty good shape and most of the seats were empty; *Ah, room to spread out.*

When the door closed and the coach pulled away from the curb, we figured, *Hue here we come!* Not! We spent the best part of the next hour driving around Hoi An in circles, "Didn't we just pass that?" while the driver picked up other passengers. When our bus did finally hit the road, it only crawled as far as Danang, before it stopped to fill more seats. By the time we made any real distance-eating progress, the coach was crammed to capacity and any chance of stretching out was long gone.

The road between Danang and Hue climbs a mountain pass and a certain Unnamed Guidebook waxes poetic about the journey's beauty; if you're from downtown Cleveland, maybe; if you're from the Pacific Northwest, not so much.

We were two hours behind schedule and a light rain was falling when we finally rolled into Hue. Luckily, the tourist bus pulled up on a side street that was only two blocks from our reserved hotel. A couple of minutes dragging our bags along uneven pavement and we reached the door to the Hong Thien.

Day 391 - January 31 - Monday

We booked and paid (Internet) for four nights at the Hong Thien, but we only lasted one. At $17 per night there was nothing wrong with the hotel. It was one of those tall, thin, multi-story, one-room-wide places that are common all over Vietnam; steep staircase and no lift. Our fourth floor room featured great views, a comfortable bed, and decent furnishings considering the price. The thing that drove us away was a total soul-sucking lack of heat. Not to put too fine an edge on it, the Hong Thien was a way station on the road to hypothermia! Even in our room, coats and gloves were required attire. In bed, blankets, down bag liners, and silk sleep sacks barely kept out the chill. When we ate breakfast in the lobby, we bundled for the outdoors, and our breath hung before us in icy clouds.

After breakfast, which didn't stay warm from the kitchen to the table, we went looking for another hotel. Okay, we'll admit that it was a wussy thing to do, but darn it, this journey is supposed to be a chance for growth and soft adventure; not an exercise in Arctic survival! A block up the street we stepped into the Orchid Hotel and slipped firmly back into the comfort zone. Mercifully, everything in the hotel was warm and cozy. We gave them a deposit for three nights, and before actually changing hotels, walked off to explore.

Hue, another UNESCO World Heritage site, brings fragments of pre-communist imperial Vietnam to life. While old buildings, wide streets, and picturesque riverside locations beg to be experienced, it's Hue's Citadel and Forbidden Purple City which are the jewels. On the north bank of the Perfume River on a site carefully chosen by geomancers sits Hue's nineteenth century citadel; ten kilometers of two meter thick walls that encircled the ancient city. Narrow, one car at a time, fortified gates are the only means of access. Inside the walls stands another enclosure; the six meter high walls of the imperial residence, and at its center the Forbidden Purple City.

From the early 1800's until the mid 1940's, this was home to Vietnam's ruling Nguyen dynasty. As emperors are wont to do; they built lavish palaces and surrounded themselves with beauty and luxury. At one point the imperial enclosure contained pools, gardens, and more than 140 exquisite buildings. The French sacked the palace in 1885, burning much of what they couldn't carry off. In 1968 the Viet Cong held the Citadel and American warplanes pounded the enclosure. Toss in a couple of typhoons and today only about twenty buildings remain.

So is it worth a visit? You betcha it is! The imperial enclosure is awesome. Some buildings are restored to gilt and lacquered perfection. Others sit in atmospheric ruin. The whole compound exudes an aura of mystery and tarnished majesty. Slightly overgrown paths lead you into forgotten corners and if you squint carefully, you glimpse weathered remnants of a past glory. It was cold and sprinkled rain during our visit, but that didn't dampen our enthusiasm. Poke in here and peek in there, and just like that three fascinating hours slip by.

Back at the Orchid Hotel, we officially checked-in and were handed our welcome fruit drinks. The Orchid cost $23 more per night than the Hong Thien, but the added expense raised the comfort bar to a whole new level. Our room oozed boutique ambience. The bedding was stylish, artistic touches enlivened the walls; there was heat, sitting space, free Internet, in-room computer, and a DVD player with a free movie library. They had us at, "heat," but throw in a good bathroom, a fridge, a daily fresh fruit basket, slippers, silk bathrobes, excellent breakfasts, and bend-over-backwards service, and we quickly knew we made a good decision.

Day 393 - February 2 - Wednesday

This morning at breakfast we pilfered a baguette, two yogurts, and a pair of Laughing Cow cheese wedges. Add bananas from our room's complimentary fruit tray, a plastic bag, and our "free" picnic lunch was ready to travel. A planned all-day boat tour to pagodas and imperial tombs triggered our petty larceny. The deal included lunch on the boat, but our hotel warned us that it was pretty meager. "You should bring snacks." At a tour cost of only $6 per person, meager was fine with us.

At 8 AM a tiny gal, bundled in a thick wool coat and hat, led us, along with a few other tourists, through a light drizzle to where our "dragon boat" awaited at a dock on the Perfume River. The boat was a houseboat-party-barge affair with a glass enclosed seating area and a pair of large gaudy tin dragons jutting above its twin prow.

The captain cast off, an engine somewhere under the deck rumbled to life, water churned, blue smoke swirled, and away we chugged. Racing other dragon boats for prime mooring space, our first stop was an octagonal gothic wedding cake called, Thien Mu Pagoda. Originally founded in 1601; the pagoda's current structure dates from 1844. Each of the tower's seven levels is dedicated to a different incarnation of the Buddha and in the 1960's the temple complex was a focus for political demonstrations. Today, the temple compound plays quiet host to a steady stream of tourists.

Next to the tower hangs a ginormous two ton bell. According to the sign, you can hear it six miles away. Who knows? One of us wanted to give it a good whack, but cooler heads prevailed and we agreed that a really big "bong" probably didn't justify an international incident.

To our monkey minds, the best attraction at the Thien Mu temple is Thich Quang Duc's Austin motorcar. Doesn't ring a bell? Set the "Wayback Machine" to 1963. There's Thich Quang Duc on the front page of nearly every newspaper in the world, sitting serenely in the lotus position while the gasoline he's doused on himself lights him up like a campfire marshmallow gone bad. This act of self immolation (and questionable judgment), a protest against the policies of the South Vietnam government, earned the monk lasting veneration. It's claimed that Thich Quang Duc's heart wasn't consumed and despite later attempts at cremation, refused to burn. The rusty Austin on display at the temple was the car the monk used to reach the site of his fiery protest. Whew, we don't know! We're thinking maybe a terse text message or a stern email.

Following the pagoda, we spent the rest of our day wandering tombs and mausoleums of the Nguyen emperors. We visited four enclaves and each one was unique. There were beautiful temples, magnificent sculptures, expansive stone courtyards, and tranquil lotus ponds; all arranged in harmony with their natural surroundings; everything an emperor might want to ensure his eternal rest and continued veneration. As our hotel warned, lunch was a little sparse, but the tour was definitely not about the eats. A bus took us to the last couple of tombs and then back to Hue.

At the stroke of midnight we watched the first fireworks of Tet burst in the sky outside our window. You know, it's an amazing world! Some days you can't swing a cat without hitting something wonderful.

Day 397 - February 6 - Sun - Ho Chi Minh City, Vietnam

The first thing we noticed as we stepped out of the airport in Ho Chi Minh City, Saigon for those of us with long memory, was blessed warmth. Our flight from Hue lasted only an hour and forty-five minutes, but suddenly we were back in the tropics. *Oh, yes!*

That was four days ago and our time in the big city has roared past in a cloud of swirling blue motorcycle exhaust. We found a reasonable hotel in a backpacker district and immediately headed out to pound the pavement, take in the city's sights, and measure its pulse.

Ho Chi Minh City buzzes. Compared to Hanoi, it's frenetic and brash. Both cities exude a reach-for-the-moon vitality and energy, but in Hanoi it's tempered by Old World charm. Ho Chi Minh City is on the go. People rush hither and thither, motorcycles surge, and neon charged commerce sprouts everywhere.

We hit town on the first day of Tet carrying high hopes that we'd catch a banging New Year's party. Unfortunately, that's not how Tet works. Instead of boisterous festivity, everyone closes up shop and heads home for quiet-time with the family. Who knew? Our search for rowdy celebration led us to elaborate park-side flower and bonsai displays. The flower shows were interesting and well attended, but banging? Well, not so much.

Ho Chi Minh City offers an abundance of sights and we situated ourselves within reasonable walking distance of more than a few. Each day, we set out with one or two goals in mind and walked until fatigue reeled us back in. We hit art museums, history museums, historic buildings, busy malls, and quiet parks.

If you discount people squatting on the sidewalk picking lice from each others hair and squeezing nits between their fingers, Ho Chi Minh City's standout attraction is the War Remnants Museum. Originally dubbed the "Museum of Chinese and American War Crimes," this collection documents horrors of war that were inflicted on the Vietnamese people. Like the Holocaust museum in Washington, D.C. the War Remnants Museum is disturbing and thought provoking. As Americans, it's not often that we look in the mirror and see ourselves reflected as the bad guys.

The museum's most powerful exhibits are: a collection of moving photos taken by a multitude of war correspondents, all of whom lost their lives in combat; and an extensive and horrific documentation of the effects and after-effects of the defoliant Agent Orange. Lower on the impact scale, but still decidedly weird; the plaza in front of the museum is littered with captured and abandoned American: aircraft, tanks, and artillery.

On the walk back to our hotel we saw a pair of motorcycles slam into each other, one of them spewing its three female passengers onto the pavement (no serious injuries). We were all, "Oh my!" but everyone else treated the mash up like the common occurrence it probably is. Ho Chi Minh City is the home to something on the order of five million motorcycles. Given that statistic, the riding habits of the Vietnamese, and their propensity for squeezing whole families on the seat (four is common); it's a wonder there's not carnage on every corner. Motos clog the streets at all hours, continually jockey for position, anticipate signals, and generally invite disaster. It's the norm to see people ride against traffic, i.e. you need to look both ways even when crossing a one-way street. If traffic gets congested, aggressive riders simply guide their mounts onto the sidewalk. This is also a popular way to cut a corner and avoid a stop. Caveat pedestrian!

Day 398 - February 7 - Monday

Today we opted for a taste of the Mekong Delta. After breakfast, a twelve passenger van picked us up at the hotel. Eight or so tourists were already on board, but as the "old guy," I got the deference and sat shotgun. Denise made do with a slightly cramped seat behind the driver. Our first destination, two hours away, was the riverside port of My Tho.

Since Vietnam's population is predominately young you don't interact with many older people. Hotel staff, store clerks, restaurant employees, tour guides, touts, and taxi drivers all tend to be young. Somewhere near our own age, our day trip guide was an exception. He was also a bit of a character with a wry sense of humor. When we asked him his name, he said, "You can call me 'Charlie.' That's what the American army used to call me." That was the only name he gave us. "Charlie" later mentioned that he'd worked with the Americans. We never figured out which leg he was pulling.

The Mekong is a world class river that snakes 5,000 kilometers through China, Laos, and Cambodia before it crosses southern Vietnam and spills into the sea. My Tho, an important jumping-off point for tourism and commerce, sits thirty-nine miles inland.

Charlie herded us from our bright red van onto a bright blue water taxi and we ferried across. The first stop on our itinerary was an open-air "factory" where women busily stirred, rolled, patted, chopped, and wrapped hand-made coconut candy. We tasted a sample or two, sort of addictive, and of course made a semi-obligatory purchase.

Next, we piled into horse-drawn carts and trotted off through the rural countryside. Four to a cart, the fifteen minute clop was contrived and touristy, but we still had fun; the scenery was lush and green. The horsey-ride ended at a café-cum-gift-shop. We sat at outdoor tables and sampled sweet tea, peanuts, candied coconut, and slices of exotic fruit while musicians serenaded us with traditional song. Afterwards, the least squeamish of our group shouldered pythons for a photo op (no snakes in our photos).

Once the constrictors were back in their cages we walked through a village to a backwater dock and transferred onto small sampans. This was the best part of the day. For the next fifteen to twenty minutes we sat quietly while a small rice-hatted woman rowed us through a twisting backwater channel. Standing at the stern working a single vertical side-mounted paddle she sent us gliding along. The water was still and green; the banks muddy. Exuberant tropical vegetation stretched away on both sides. We floated past small streams and fish traps. Boats passed us in both directions; some rowed, others chugging along. It was a thoroughly enjoyable, albeit brief, experience.

Next up was our included lunch; rice, cabbage, the usual vegetables, and a shaving of pork (which we skipped). For an additional fee, we could have purchased a fried "elephant fish." The rather large fish is presented whole in a wooden stand that makes it look ready to mount on someone's wall. At your table, a waitress flakes off the meat and makes it into spring rolls; easily enough food for two or three people and not a bad presentation for $7.50. Despite the appeal, we passed. Later, we spied a slimy fish farm operation and we were glad that elephant fish hadn't squirmed its way onto our plates.

At lunch, Denise sat next to three young men from China who were on vacation from their Vietnamese language studies in Hanoi. One of them struck up a conversation.

"Where you from?"

"America."

"I like America. You have good sitcoms. 'Friends' is my favorite. I like music, Rock-n-Roll, Kurt Cobain. Since I've been in Vietnam, you the first Americans I meet. You are vegetarian?"

"Yes."

"Are many Americans vegetarian?"

"Some are; why do you ask?"

With stars in his eyes, "Phoebe is a vegetarian!"

A "free time" bike ride came next, but mostly fell short of expectations. There weren't enough bicycles for the tour groups that wanted to ride, so we stood around twiddling our thumbs. One after another other tourists returned their bicycles shaking their heads with disgust. If the bikes had been horses, a glue factory would have been their next stop. Tires that were underinflated, brakes that didn't; collapsed pedals, and broken seats; frames that were too small, chains that fell off; these were old bicycles that wanted to crawl off and die. We found two that more or less worked and pedaled off with our knees up to our chins. "Be sure to check out the garbage heap," groused one returning rider, "that's particularly appealing."

After a minute or two of squeaky clattering progress we discovered that we were right back to where we'd been on the horse carts. With the whole of the Mekong Delta to explore, we're given free time in a place where we'd already been! Denise, good at ordering off the menu, salvaged our ride when she spotted a dirt track snaking away from the road. The bumpy path was just what we wanted. It led us under palm and banana trees, past simple homes, and across small canals. Our road less traveled was fun while it lasted, but ended abruptly in a yard full of barking dogs. "Nice doggies. Good doggies. See, we're leaving." Oh well, you do what you can.

The rest of the tour involved lots of standing around, and our return to Ho Chi Minh City. At $9 per ticket we got our money's worth, but on the other hand neither of us would've felt slighted if the excursion had wrapped early.

Day 404 - February 13 - Sunday - Phu Quoc, Vietnam

Five days ago, we left Ho Chi Minh City and flew to Phu Quoc. At first, we thought we'd travel overland by bus and then catch a ferry to the island. Instead we opted for speed, comfort, and Vietnam Airlines. We froze our ninnies off up north and then spent three weeks walking smoggy uneven urban streets. We figured we deserved another beach and that we were better off sitting in the sand than on a bus. Good call; Phu Quoc is a swell place to lose yourself and an even better place to work on your tan.

A van picked us up at the island's small airport and shuttled us straight to our beachfront digs at the Hiep Thanh Resort. "Resort" is a bit pretentious, but the place more than meets our needs. $69 per night snagged us a one-room bungalow with AC, a porch, a sea view, and a slightly boring but completely adequate included breakfast. The good stuff is down on the beach: fine sand, a swimmable ocean, plenty of padded recliners, and large well anchored umbrellas. Gentle surf crashes along the shore. Palm trees wave overhead. The sun shines and soft breezes keep you from cooking. Top that with a concession selling ice cold $1 beers and a talented woman selling muscle-relaxing, melt-into-the-lounge, $2.10, forty-five minute massages and you have a recipe for world class idle indulgence.

We're not total slugs! We walked far enough up the beach to qualify as exercise. Both directions; no, we swear! We also walked into town where we checked out the port's comings and goings, people fishing from woven basket boats, and the local lighthouse cum Buddhist temple. We used an ATM, ate a couple of meals, and bought ice cream. It was all good, but truth be told, Phu Quoc is about sun and sand and little else. We love it!

Okay, the love only goes so far, today's lunch was the last straw! We're compelled to write about restaurant menus that lack any measurable synchronization with reality. We were walking along Phu Quoc's main road and what do we spy? "Hey look, a German Bakery." After months of rice, we're both Jonesing for crusty whole grain bread. "Okay, this is lunch!" We sit down and peruse the menu. "Oooh! Look at all the sandwiches available on 'German brown bread'." We each order a tuna sandwich. "And, we'd like that on the German brown bread please." The waiter writes "2 tuna" on his pad and gives us an odd look. Fifteen minutes later while Denise is sipping her strawberry smoothie and I'm working on my beer, the waiter comes back. "I'm sorry Madame, brown bread finish today." The implication is that there was brown bread several minutes ago and that there will again be brown bread tomorrow. The reality is that the "bakery" quit baking brown bread two days after they put up the sign and the only thing German about the place is the grizzled expat drinking beer at the bar.

A chronic disconnect exists between menus and reality and it's an ongoing cultural aspect of our trip. Just so you won't think that we're laying this problem at Vietnam's feet; it happens everywhere.

"Hi, I'd like the Thai veggie pie."

"I'm sorry Madame, veggie pie finish today."

We come back the next day. "I'm sorry Madame, veggie pie only Friday."

We come back on Friday. "I'm sorry Madame, veggie pie tomorrow."

When restaurants open, excited entrepreneurs create menus listing the foods they plan to offer. Somewhere between the printer and the kitchen something goes terribly awry. Mango pancakes without mangos, banana smoothies without bananas, mixed vegetables with nothing but cabbage, buttered toast without butter, feta salad without feta, stir fried cashew nuts without cashews; the list goes on and on. There is no veggie pie! Please! Just scratch it off the menu!

Chapter 16

CAMBODIA

Day 405 - Feb 14 - Monday - Phnom Penh, Cambodia

The rough edge of traveling is the travel itself. When we get ready to change locations we want to know what's around the corner. We check our guide books. We surf the web. We talk to the locals. Once we understand the available options, or think we do, we make our arrangements. Our deluded thinking is that by doing homework we'll somehow secure an optimal and enjoyable experience. The reality is that it's often a huge waste of time. Today was another case in point.

Lazy from our sunny days on the beach, we delegated and let "Toto," the go-to guy at the hotel, handle our booking. We'd done our due diligence. It was the path of least resistance, and gushing on-line reviews seemed to bear out our choice. We probably could have done better if we'd pinned options to a board, blindfolded ourselves, and thrown darts.

Toto told us that a shuttle would pick us up at 7AM. "Uh, how about breakfast? Will we be able to eat before we leave?"

"Yes, no problem breakfast start at 6AM."

The reason the shuttle picks you up at 7:00 is so that it can speed across the island and arrive in plenty of time to connect with a small morning ferry that runs to the mainland. No worries; we're getting used to early starts. We packed the night before and then got up at 5:30 AM so that we'd have plenty of time. When we walked into the restaurant at 6:05 for our leisurely meal, only one light was lit and no one was in sight! Five minutes before the shuttle arrived we were wolfing down a semblance of breakfast that had reached our table in fits and starts. *Well, that wasn't what we had in mind, but c'est la vie. The experienced traveler is flexible!*

"Plenty of time" translated into a sleepy hour-and-a-half wait at the port. Eventually, we were told to drag our luggage out to the pier and queue up for the boat. When the guy checking tickets looks at ours, a stamped piece of paper, he pulls us out of line. "You wait here." *Huh?* We watch as other people board. After a time, the ticket guy confers with the boat's captain and, following much nodding of heads, he waves us on. *Hmmm, that was weird.*

We entered the cabin, found a couple of empty seats, and settled in. A few minutes later a stewardess with a passenger in tow leans over.

"May I see your seat numbers please?"

The guy on the dock kept our stamped paper, all in Vietnamese anyway. "Uh, we don't have seat numbers."

"You come with me." As we stand up, the other passenger is ushered into our seats. We're led to the front of the cabin and the stewardess points. "You sit there." *Whoa, what the...* It was at this juncture we learned that we'd been sold tickets which allow us to board but didn't actually entitle us to seats. *Oh, crud;*

shades of RAC! Thank you Toto! While everyone else sat in narrow bus-style bucket seats, I spent the next two-and-a-half hours wedged on a slatted wooden bench, slamming, "ka-thunk, ka-thunk," against a curved windowless bulkhead that kept me from sitting upright.

When the stewardess first pointed to the "Group W" bench I threw a minor hissy. This of course caused me to lose considerable face, but it did at least garner Denise an actual seat.

At one point during our crossing, another unfortunate, whose ticket forced her to sit next to the man piloting the boat, jerked in surprise at his sudden movement and accidently back-handed me in the face. *Ah, the joys of travel!*

When we reached the mainland port of Ha Tien, a bus company representative was waiting at the dock with our name on a sign. *Okay, that's better. I guess the ferry thing was an aberration.* A shuttle took us to the bus company office where we were told to again kill an hour-and-a-half until our 12:30 departure.

Ha Tien is interesting in an everyday commercial non-touristy sort of way so we wandered around, poked into the local market, bypassed the smelly fish sellers, and grabbed some noodles at a local café. As boarding time drew near, we strolled back to the bus office. 12:30 came and went. 1:30 came and went.

Eventually, a guy walked up to us. "You go Phnom Penh, come here." The indicated "here" was a slightly grubby twelve passenger van. *Hey, this isn't what our hotel promised!*

"Will it be a big bus?" we'd asked Toto before booking.

"Yes, yes," he'd replied, "big bus, deluxe, fifty-passenger, very comfortable! You like." Clearly, something was amiss.

"Excuse me, where is our bus?"

"You go Phnom Penh that van."

"Is the van going to take us to the bus?"

"No, so sorry Sir, the bus is finish today. Break down. We take you in our van." *Oh, we get it! The bus collided with a huge stack of missing veggie pies which clogged its delicate steering mechanism rendering it unusable. Like the pies, the bus will be back on the menu tomorrow!*

Another question we asked when we bought our tickets; "Do we stay on the same bus the whole way or will we have to change at the border?" "Same bus. Same same whole way." Naturally, at the border we were told to grab our luggage and change vehicles. Evidently, the van we were already in was considered too clean and spacious for Cambodian roads so we were ushered to one that was "full" grubby. The new van also featured a complete lack of luggage space.

In short order, I was bouncing along in the back seat, sitting over a suspension-less rear axle, while shoehorned next to a wall of teetering suitcases and backpacks. So much dust leaked inside from the dirt road that, despite AC and closed windows, we were both forced to tie scarves over our faces to avoid asphyxiation. *Whew! At least I can stretch out my legs.*

At least I could. Adding insult to injury our driver decided to supplement his income by trawling for locals along the road. Two prospective fares looked at our cramped conditions and refused to climb aboard. *Thank you God!* Two others scrambled in and suddenly my knees were up to my chin, pressed tightly against a jump seat. I felt like one of those contortionist yogis who climb into little glass boxes. Denise fared slightly better. Her seat was hard and didn't recline or offer support, but a least it wasn't flanked by a jump seat and a wall-o-luggage. The old adage is, "You get what you pay for." Well, sometimes you don't.

If you ignore our whiney discomforts and the fact that we paid the comfortable-old-person price for a bare-bones-young-person transfer, it was a pretty intriguing day. Van changes aside, the best stuff began at the border. Our crossing point was Xa Xia-Prek Chak, just fifteen minutes up the highway from Ha Tien. As you approach the Vietnamese side of the border you pull up before a large modern building. Squint slightly, and its concrete and glass façade evokes a large department store. Tall gold letters proudly proclaim, "Ha Tien Border Gate." The road splits around a landscaped planter and arrival and departure lanes tunnel through the building.

As we left our van and walked inside, it suddenly struck us that the Ha Tien Border Gate was more about monumental state projects than it was about a working necessity. Interior floors were dirty and the walls needed a good scrubbing. The Gate's windows looked like they were last washed just before installation. A row of shuttered processing counters lined the hall and a lone, obviously bored, civil servant waited to stamp our passports. We wonder whose uncle owns the construction company.

Leave the Vietnam side and things go from quirky to fascinating. We always try to read ahead about the spots we visit, so we know that Vietnam is an economic powerhouse compared to its poorer neighbor. We also know that Cambodia has suffered tough times. Just the same, we didn't expect such an obvious and blatant transition. The pavement literally ends as you cross Cambodia's border and with a wave of the geopolitical wand you step back in time. Not way back, but definitely a few decades.

The Cambodian border area is dusty and the country's official checkpoints are small and shack-like. There's one where you fill out your visa application, another where you fill out a health form, and a third where you pay and get stamped. In the background, vendors, taxi drivers, and tourists mill around while overloaded motorcycles queue up to be processed.

As we rolled up a dirt track toward the main highway (paved but nearly an hour away) we passed through a land of stilt houses and rice farms. Hammocks swing under the houses as people nap and try to stay cool. Children play; women wash and cook; here a cluster of fruit stands, there and old woman in a hammock dangles amid cuts of meat in her "butcher shop." Chickens, cows, pigs, and goats wander the roadside. Front yards tower with yellowed haystacks of rice straw and medieval ox carts await their next load. Outside the houses, huge concrete catchment jugs await the next rain.

If Cambodia's rural scenery isn't enough to hold your interest, there's also its rural traffic. Motorcycles still outnumber cars and trucks, but frequently the motos themselves are outnumbered by bicycles.

Whatever the mix, the motorcycle is still king. In addition to its use as a passenger vehicle the "moto" is Cambodia's ubiquitous beast of burden. This role takes various forms and the governing rules of the road appear, for want of a better word, "lax." Take loading for example. If you can tie it on, strap it on, or juggle it while steering, you're good to go. Cambodian two-wheel jockeys lash pounds and volumes on their bikes that would do proud by any redneck owner of a dual-axle diesel pick-up; everything from mountains of toilet tissue to oversized propane tanks and crates of live pigs. The only practical limit appears to be each rider's ability to keep his mount upright.

Can't fit it all? No problem, add a trailer! Never thought of pulling a trailer with your motorcycle? Take our word for it, the Cambodians have! If it has two wheels and you can hook it onto your bike; it's street legal. Hitches vary considerably. At the high end are commercially manufactured attachments that look, and probably are, safe. Lower on the scale are questionable homemade affairs, baling wire, and our personal favorite, the "muscular wife." In this latter configuration, the trailer is equipped with two handles; ala rickshaw. You place your wife behind you on the moto, have her firmly grasp the handles, and away you go! Some riders, apparently unsure of their spouse's lower arm strength, also add a bar between the two handles and ask the missus sit on it for "security." "Hold on tighter Honey! I can feel the bricks shimmy."

So what can you haul behind a motorcycle? The answer is anything and everything. Cambodian motorcycle trailers come in all sizes. Some are small. Others could easily do service behind a farm tractor. We saw them outfitted as roving stores stacked high with pots, pans, and baskets. We saw them overflowing with ripe melons and buried under preposterous loads of brick. We saw them crammed with lumber and packed with waving people. We even saw a moving "cocktail lounge" with a line of barstools and a counter. To paraphrase from "Treasure of the Sierra Madre," "Trucks? We don't need no stinking trucks! (well, maybe a few)"

A special variation of the motorcycle trailer is the sidecar. If you want to move something from place to place, you put two wheels under it and tow it behind you. If you want to sell the something, you put one wheel under it and hang it off the side. This approach is used for everything from impromptu cafés and bakeries to sundry stores and juice bars. The approach is brilliant! Drive along, find a likely location, pull over, toss out a few tiny plastic chairs, swivel on your seat and you're ready to fire up the grill. We wonder if we could open a chain of those back home.

Day 407 - February 16 - Wednesday

Originally, we thought we'd breeze right though Phnom Penh; now we're glad we didn't. Phnom Penh is pretty darn fascinating. In sharp contrast to the Cambodian countryside, the capital's core feels like it's perched on the cusp of prosperity as though brighter days are just around the corner. Its seductive appeal stems from hustle and bustle that's lively but not gridlock, a riverfront location, and a pleasing abundance of green space.

We nabbed a room at a small genial hotel called the Billabong. It's a bit of a walk from most must-sees, but it makes up for its location with a great swimming pool and garden, both of which offer uber welcome respite from sweltering urban afternoons.

Our first day in town, we walked over to the Royal Palace and Silver Pagoda. Along the way we engaged in a close encounter of the tuk-tuk kind. In a land where motorcycle trailers are common, tuk-tuks rule. In other countries, three-wheeled tuk-tuks tear around hauling passengers. In Cambodia the tuk-tuk is a two-wheeled rickshaw-like conveyance towed by a motorcycle. Cambodian tuk-tuks still tear around hauling passengers but here your driver sits out front on his bike and you sit in the trailer with your friends.

Much to the dismay of most tourists, persistent marketing is the Cambodian tuk-tuk driver's strong suit. They're not pushy, but they're consistent and they're everywhere. In tourist hot spots it's common to get four or five tuk-tuk offers per block. Even shrill cries of, "Hello Sir, Madam, you want massage?" run a distant second. Assembled in packs of varying size; drivers park outside every hotel, every restaurant, and every conceivable tourist attraction. "Hello Sir, Madam, you want tuk-tuk?" Just because you turn down the first guy isn't a deterrent to the driver standing next to him. Sure you just told his buddy that you want to walk, but that was a whole two seconds ago. Hey, you may have changed your mind!

So back to our walk; when persistence fails, some drivers aren't above chicanery to grab a fare. "Hello Sir, Madam, you want tuk-tuk? You go Killing fields?" Cambodia's infamous killing fields of Choeung Ek are fifteen kilometers from central Phnom Penh and an out-and-back fare is the brass ring for the city's tuk-tuk guys.

"No thank you. We're just walking;" our stock response.

"Where you go?" their stock response.

"We're just walking, thank you;" our stock response repeated. And...here comes the creativity.

"You go palace? Palace closed now! King there; is special day. Open 4 PM" This blatant lie, we can see tourists inside and others queued at the ticket booth, is followed by another offer. "You want to go Killing Fields tour? Back at 4 PM."

"Uh, no thanks."

That's the downside. To be fair, tuk-tuks are a great way to get around. When you want or need one, there's always one available. Most of them are comfortable. They go everywhere and if you're on your guard and modestly adept at bargaining, they're cheap. Best of all, tuk-tuks are fun. You have the wind in your hair. You go fast enough to efficiently get from A to B, but you go slow enough to see the things you pass along the way. Tuk-tuks are also occasionally just scary enough to spice up your journey. We love em!

Still under our own steam, we reached the entrance to the Royal Palace and read the rules: "He/She is requested not to:

1. Carry arms and explosives
2. Wear shoes inside the throne room and temple

...

...

4. Be incorrectly dressed.

...

...

7. Touch mural paintings."

Okay, no problem. We're not armed and we aren't planning to touch the murals. Wrong! At the ticket window, the battleaxe behind the counter took one look at Denise's sleeveless top and her large American breasts before declaring her afoul of rule number four. Otherwise modestly dressed in a long skirt, Denise had come prepared to cover her effrontery. She pulled a shawl from her purse and wrapped it around her shoulders and chest. "How about now?"

"No! You must buy t-shirt! Subtext, "I still know they're under there." Since the t-shirts were evidently woven from some type of 24 carat gold thread, we opted for a later visit. Behind us, the ticket-Nazi was giving the next woman in line the same treatment.

Re-attired, we eventually gained entrance to the Palace. The reward for our persistence was: an over-abundance of gilt bric-a-brac, pleasant gardens, classic Khmer rooflines, and inside the Silver Pagoda; lots of Buddha.

The palace made for good sightseeing, but we also walked to many of the city's other close-in sights. The National Museum with its impressive collection of Khmer sculpture and the capital's soaring Art Deco market was especially enjoyable.

Sadly, man's inhumanity to man provides Phnom Penh's most thought provoking "attraction." Today we capped our visit with a stop at the Tuol Sleng Museum. The museum, once a quiet high school, was taken over by Khmer Rouge security forces and turned into an abattoir used to feed the killing fields of Choeung Ek. Known simply as S-21, the detention center "processed" over 17,000 people during its four years of operation. Torture followed by death was the order of the day and only a handful of those who saw its interior survived to tell their tales.

The Tuol Sleng Museum we saw today preserves S-21 much as it appeared on the day it was liberated by Vietnamese troops. It's a horrible and atmospheric place. Metal bunks with leg and hand irons sit in the middle of dirty interrogation rooms. Huge photos on the wall show mutilated corpses that Vietnamese soldiers found chained to the very same bunks. Other buildings are broken into tiny brick or wooden cells; their exteriors covered with nets of barbed wire to prevent despondent prisoners from flinging themselves to their death to escape torture. In the yard stands a high school rope climb, a piece of exercise equipment that was converted into a gallows and torture device under the tyranny of Pol Pot.

Like the Nazis before them, Khmer authorities meticulously documented their atrocities. Simple wooden frames display picture after picture of S-21's unfortunate victims; some depicted both before and after their torture, men, women, and children who disappeared inside the prison's walls. It's a sobering exhibit and one that soon left us drained. In the crazy world of Cambodian politics, trials of those responsible for S-21 continue to this day.

Day 409 - February 18 - Friday - Siem Reap, Cambodia

Yesterday, we took a "Deluxe" bus from Phnom Penh to Siem Reap, home to the world famous ruins of Angkor Wat. This time we got our money's worth. Our fares for the six-and-a-half hour journey came in at $11 each which purchased us comfortable seats in an air conditioned coach with a stewardess, toilet, and boxed meals. Five or six hours is about as long as either of us like to spend on a bus, but a nice lunch stop in Kampong Thom and great scenery, made the drive tolerable. Compared with our last overland trip, this one was the bee's knees. Everything was smooth sailing; well almost.

The "almost" was, surprise, surprise, tuk-tuk weirdness. Siem Reap's bus terminal is located a couple of kilometers west of the town center, so we prearranged a free meet-and-greet transfer to our hotel. When we got off the bus and claimed our bags from underneath, we stepped into the usual scrum of tuk-tuk drivers and touts holding up signs. We spent several minutes searching carefully, but couldn't spot our name. About that time, a driver approached us.

"You need tuk-tuk? What hotel you go?"

"We're okay thanks. We're waiting for someone from the Mekong Angkor Palace Hotel."

"Oh, that's me. Give me your bags."

"Uh, we don't think so!"

"No, no, is okay. I from hotel."

"If you're from the hotel, what's our name?" While he's trying to come up with an answer, another guy butts in.

"Don't worry, he's okay." At this point the first guy produces a sign that reads "Mekong Angkor Palace Hotel."

"See hotel." It's been several minutes and we still haven't seen anyone else holding up our names. *Hmmm, maybe this guy is on the up and up.*

"You're from the hotel and the ride is free?"

"Yes, yes, free. Give me your bags." *Well, we still have to get to the hotel.*

"Okay, let's go."

Of course, at the Mekong Angkor Palace it turns out that the guy is a bummer who wants the hotel to pay him for our fare. We told the hotel that he lied and urged them not to pay, but didn't wait around to see the outcome. As we headed for our room, the tuk-tuk guy hailed me one last time. "Hey mister; how long you here? You need tuk-tuk for tomorrow." *You have got to be shitting me!*

Day 412 - February 21 - Monday

Whenever you see pictures of Angkor it's usually an iconic shot of the Wat's sunset lit towers or the enigmatic stone faces of Bayon. Such pictures look huge and impressive, but believe us when we say they don't come anywhere close to the true grandeur of the Angkor experience. Angkor was more than just a few temples. The word "Angkor" means "Capital City" or "Holy City" and that is just what it was; a sprawling imperial metropolis. Some of its important monuments are many miles away from others and the main complex spreads across a huge area.

Given its shear size the logistics of getting from one Angkor site to another requires thought. Bicycles are a possibility but with afternoon temperatures hovering around 100 degrees, they weren't our first choice. After ruling out group tours and rolling the bones, we decided to splurge for a private guide ($25) and a tuk-tuk ($15). When we finished breakfast, Tom, our guide, and Den, our driver, were waiting in the hotel lobby. We piled into Den's spiffy red chariot and, wind in our hair, putted off down the road that links Siem Reap to the wonders of ancient Angkor.

Entrance fees are collected at a toll plaza just outside the archeological preserve. We opted for $40 three-day passes that seemed reasonably priced considering the attractions that waited for us up the road.

On Tom's suggestion, we rolled straight past Angkor Wat and saved the big enchilada for later in the day; "better light." A short distance later we chugged along beside Angkor Thom's moat, a water feature that encloses three square kilometers, and pulled to a stop before the hoary spectacle of Jayavarman VII's imperial gate. A bridge spans the moat, and acted out along its edges, captured in ancient stone, an endless tug-o-war rages between good and evil; demons on one side, gods on the other. Held tightly in their arms are the scaly stone bodies of two giant seven-headed serpents. In mythology, the tails of these "Naga" wrap around Mount Meru that sits on the back of a giant turtle in the "Sea of Milk." As the gods and demons struggle, the mountain turns back and forth churning the sea to froth and distilling the elixir of life. Towering over the bridge in the guise of Mount Meru stands Angkor Thom's South Gate; giant Mona Lisa faces of stone staring down on any who dare to enter. *Holy Moly! First thing we see and already we're running out of superlatives.*

Next, we hopped back into our tuk-tuk and zipped over to Bayon. *Oh my God!* If the South Gate is awesome, Bayon is mind-numbing and almost surreal. From a distance it looks like a jumble, but as you approach its majesty takes shape and form. Constructed in the late 12th century, thirty-seven of Bayon's towers still reach toward the sky. On most of these, four serene gigantic faces stare toward the cardinal points. Below the faces, the exterior walls are lined with show-stopping bas-reliefs which depict everything from sea battles to daily life. *And, this didn't make the "new seven wonders of the world list?" Somebody screwed up!*

You'd think that these acts would be hard to follow, but the wonders of Angkor go on and on. We visited the huge temple-mountain of Baphoun with its elevated causeway and its giant reclining Buddha, and the impressive laterite and sandstone pyramid of Phimeanakas. We wandered the 300 meter long two-and-a half meter high terrace of elephants where carved pachyderms and Garudas span the heart of Angkor Thom. We walked the Terrace of the Leper King with its deeply carved façade of mythological beings. We explored The Victory Gate, and Ta Prohm where scenes from "Tomb Raider" were filmed and massive fig and silk-cotton trees wrap ruins of the sprawling monastic complex in a rooty embrace.

Sure, these places crawl with tourists, but even the busloads do little to detract from the mystery and grandeur. Angkor is a place so wondrous and so splendid that its majesty spans the ages and transcends the nobility of its creators.

As Tom suggested, we finished our day at the big enchilada, Suryavarman II's 12th century masterpiece, Angkor Wat. You've seen the pictures. It's breathtaking, a three-tiered pyramid crowned by five lotus-like towers that rise more than 200 feet above the ground. It's massive, and it's the only Angkor temple never allowed to fall into ruin. Inside and out the walls are covered with bas-reliefs and other carvings; Hindu mythology, dancing goddesses, and everything in between.

The humidity was high, the temperature higher, and despite the glory we barely managed to haul our hanging jaws and dragging asses from one level to the next. *Okay, that was a full day!*

The next morning, we slept in (8:30) and then headed out again. Our first goal for the day was Banteay Srey located thirty-eight kilometers outside Siem Reap. Along the way we stopped at Pre Rup an architecturally beautiful temple-mountain built in the 10th century. Richly detailed carvings and beautiful false doors got our day off to a good start.

Next, we rolled through small villages and fascinating rural countryside, where roadside production of palm sugar was the name of the game. Almost every home has a cauldron out front, bubbling away atop a wood fired clay oven. Close beside the ovens are row upon row of palm frond shacks selling the finished product.

When Den stopped for gas, Tom bought us a couple of bags of sugar palm fruit to try. These were thick translucent hockey pucks with the texture of jelly fish and a liquid center that tastes a bit like mild coconut. I squirted the first one all over my shirt and Denise tried to gag on hers. Once I got the hang of it, I finished my bag. Denise's sat on the seat for the rest of the day.

Banteay Srey, sometimes called "The Citadel of Women," was built in the 10th century by a Brahmin counselor to a powerful king. It was a time when the Khmer Kingdom was ascendant and the temple reflects this power. Although relatively small in size, Banteay Srey features some of the most beautiful and intricate carvings that we saw at Angkor. The ornate carvings and its pink sandstone walls give it an almost fairyland appeal.

And the hits just keep on coming! After Banteay Srey, we visited East Mebon a ruined temple-mountain with three levels, life-sized elephant sculptures, and five towers; Ta Som with more huge faces, more towers, and root entwined stone doors; Neak Pean, an island temple in the middle of a manmade lake, and Preah Khan a huge monastic complex full of carvings, passages, more tree roots, and photo opportunities. For anyone who ever harbored Indiana Jones fantasies, Angkor is the place!

Day 414 - February 23 - Wednesday

Today, we move on. We're sitting in the Siem Reap airport and our flight isn't scheduled to leave until 2:45 P.M. So how do you kill an hour in Siem Reap between your hotel checkout and your tuk-tuk to the airport? Well, "Doctor Fish" of course! We walked across the street, and stuck our feet into a big glass tank filled with tiny ravenous fish. Immediately, scaly little nibblers swarmed our tootsies, foraged up and down our legs, and wiggled between our toes; all the while munching enthusiastically on our dry skin. The finny scrum looks a like an attack of miniature piranhas and feels really bizarre.

Fish "pedicures," all the rage in Asia, are mostly banned as unsanitary in the U.S. We don't know. The water seemed clean and our feet emerged looking all smooth and healthy. Besides, at only $2 each who can pass up something called "Doctor Fish Massage?"

Chapter 17

THAILAND Redo

Day 415 - February 24 - Thursday - Bangkok, Thailand

We arrived in Bangkok yesterday evening. It's hard to believe, but when we deplaned from Siem Reap it was the fifth time that we either arrived or departed from Suvarnabhumi Airport. The weird part is that after five visits we've only spent one night at an airport hotel. Bangkok is still an unknown.

Both of us exhaled sighs of relief when our bags hit the luggage carrousel. Our scheduled departure from Siem Reap was delayed by three hours so we asked to fly standby on an earlier, also delayed, Bangkok Airways flight. We made the cut for standby seats but our bags were double-iffy. Mine disappeared into the bowels of the Siem Reap luggage system and Denise's was manually pulled from the conveyor. Neither bag was tagged with the numbers we were issued for the standby flight. It was therefore a minor miracle, *thank you Ganesha,* when we and our bags both arrived in Bangkok at the same time.

From baggage claim we made our way to the airport's "Sky Train" terminal. Suvarnabhumi Airport sits about thirty minutes outside of Bangkok and the easiest and cheapest way to get downtown is on the elevated rail link called the BTS, Sky Train. The Sky Train has a station right in the airport and it costs only $1.35 per person for the interesting run, complete with good views of the city.

We got off at Ratchaphrarop station, schlepped our bags into an elevator, descended to street level, and set off in search of our hotel. After several hours of Internet surfing, we'd settled on the Indra Regent. The Indra wasn't our first choice, or our second choice, or even our third, but it had vacancies. After a couple of blocks of walking and fending off tuk-tuk offers we arrived at their lobby.

Indra Regent is a five star hotel, the first of our trip. In practice this means that they have nice rooms and that they also offer a plethora of ridiculously over priced services. They have three restaurants that we can't afford to use. Internet that would leave us broke, and massage that's ten times what we've been paying. On the up side, their Internet booking rate was cheap, the included breakfast buffet is varied (mostly edible), the pool area has plenty of lounge chairs, and the location is surprisingly good. We should also mention that our nondescript room has killer 13th floor (is that allowed?) views out over the city.

We booked three nights at the Indra. Three is a magic number when you hit a new place. Night one, you're tired from travel, so that's a wash. Day one/night two you evaluate your situation, try to get your bearings, and if necessary look for new digs. Day two/night three is a precaution. If day one proves you're in a good place, you extend your stay. If not and you haven't found a new place you keep looking. If you need to move and you manage to book a new place, then day two is a freebie. Otherwise, you keep looking.

The Indra Hotel is comfortable, but it's not our taste. There's nothing to complain about. It's clean, reasonably priced, and well situated. Unfortunately, it's also a boring, milk toast hotel that you could plop down anywhere. We spent today's daylight hours looking for another bed and it was an excellent way to spend them. We did some background research on other places, ate a late breakfast, and then hit the pavement.

Bangkok is a fascinating city and its public transport rocks! We walked for about twenty minutes, through streets packed with market stalls, past upscale malls, and along an elevated pedestrian walkway until we reached the Siam BTS station; then we jumped an elevated train. A fifteen minute ride on the Sky Train put us at the Saphan Taksin station which also happens to be the city's "Central Pier" for boats that ply the Chao Phraya River. For $0.86 each we caught a "tourist" boat for a thirty minute cruise. The "English" commentary was mostly unintelligible, but the scenery was excellent: stylish modern apartment complexes, ancient wats and palaces, and a hodge-podge of fascinating riverside architecture.

At the Phra Arthit pier in the heart of the Banglampoo district we set out on foot to find another hotel. Khao San Street in this area is ground zero for the Bangkok backpacker scene which means plenty of boutique hotels and inexpensive restaurants.

Our second stop was the "New Siam Riverside" hotel. We'd checked it in our guidebook and also on the web and it looked good. Their deluxe rooms feature killer river views but at $75 are too rich for our blood. The standard rooms at $48 are adequate, but a little small and view challenged. Their pool's riverside location is top notch, but there's a shortage of lounge chairs.

We decided to shop around; not one of our better decisions. We visited four more hotels, checked out four more rooms, and walked an exhausting sweat-dripping grand circuit. The mercury reached the boiling point and our stomachs were growling like crazed hyenas before we admitted defeat, tossed in the towel, and accepted that maybe standard rooms at the New Siam Riverside are the bomb after all. Hey... included breakfast and free unlimited Internet! Denise collapsed in a lobby chair while I registered.

Once Denise's body temperature returned to something approaching normal, we slipped across the street and refueled at Ricky's Café; spicy cashew salad, beer, and nachos. Minds and bodies restored; we then returned to the river and caught an "express boat" back to the central pier. Since this ride was "sans" commentary, the fare was only $0.38 each. A different combination of Sky Trains and we landed back within a couple of blocks of the Indra. This was strictly a change-hotels-logistics kind of day, but we did what we set out to do and moving around Bangkok is a blast.

Day 416 - February 25 - Friday

Tomorrow we move to the Banglampoo district so today we pounded the pavement around the Indra. This area screams straight up big city: hustle and more hustle, sidewalks cluttered with stalls, office buildings, apartments, stores, and a traffic tsunami. Pretty much your classic concrete jungle; just the same, after a little prospecting we discovered some hidden gems.

Just as we both reached our melting point, we stepped off the street and into a shady oasis called the "Lettuce Farm Palace." The palace is a collection of five traditional wooden Thai houses set around a quiet semi-enclosed garden complete with ponds and ducks. The compound gets its "Palace" designation because it was once the home of Princess Chumbon of Nakhon Sawan. The name didn't mean anything to us either, but what the heck, royalty is royalty. The "Lettuce Farm" part comes from the site's pre-palace days. The stilt buildings, furnished with antiques and displays of art, are all open and for a small fee, you're free to wander to your heart's content.

Kind of out of context, a separate air-conditioned (*Yes!*) exhibit hall, near the entrance to the compound, houses an outstanding collection of bronze and pottery from a pre-historic settlement named Ban Chiang, that's located in northeast Thailand. Among the treasures are beautiful verdigris covered bracelets and necklaces from 2500 B.C. And, even more amazing, large graceful intact clay pots and urns with subtle artistic designs that were more than 6,000 years old; real head-turner stuff!

Our second gem was the Jim Thompson house. This is another shady compound where we got up close and personal to stunning examples of Thai architecture and Asian art.

Thompson was an American expat who briefly served with a World War II era pre-CIA-agency in Thailand. Afterwards he hung around to call Bangkok home. With a sharp eye for opportunity and an even sharper business sense, he entered the silk trade and eventually built a worldwide clientele anchored by fashion houses in Paris, Milan, and London. As the profits grew, so did Thompson's house. An architect by trade he purchased five traditional Thai stilt homes and reassembled them on his property as a single simple but magnificent wood dwelling. Also, an art collector, Thompson furnished his new home with a small but elegant collection.

In 1967 Thompson went for an afternoon walk in the highlands of western Malaysia. Luckily for the tourist industry and unluckily for Mr. Thompson he mysteriously disappeared, leaving behind one of Bangkok's outstanding homes. We took the guided tour, fondled the wares in the silk shop, still very much a money making concern, and ate lunch on the terrace; all fun worthwhile activities.

A quick Skytrain ride and it was pool time at the Indra.

Day 418 - February 27 - Sunday

Bangkok's public transport rules! Don't get us wrong, we love to walk, but for those times when we can't, it's super-duper nice to be in a sprawling city where at least a few journeys can begin minus the usual drawn-out taxi or tuk-tuk negotiation. Meters are something you find at the end of a rainbow right next to that pot of Leprechaun gold. Yes, taxi negotiations are part of the travel experience, but they're more about frustration than cultural exchange. The first time or two, it's exciting to strike your deal; after that the magic of the give and take abruptly fades. Your goal is to reach a fair price. The taxi guy's is to gouge you for as much as possible.

You tell the driver where you want to go, and then he makes noises that your chosen destination is far away and may be hard to find. Of course he's driven there a million times and knows exactly where it is. You ask, "How much?" Next, the driver either tells you a price that's blatantly too high or asks you what you want to pay. Either way, you respond with a price that's blatantly too low. Let the games begin! He rolls his eyes and either tells you that his first price was fair, or if you started, quotes a ridiculous amount. You come up a little. Oh no, he could never accept that price, but might take you for... He comes down a little. This repartee continues until you reach what you've decided is your final offer. The driver still refuses, so you thank him and walk off. He starts his vehicle and follows you down the street. "Okay, I take you for..." This is still more than you offered, so you thank him again and keep walking. "Okay, I take you for ..." This time he's split the difference. Now, you're quibbling over twelve cents; so you agree to his price and climb in. The cabby flashes you a beatific smile. You wonder how much you just overpaid!

Today, we caught a water taxi, fixed fare, to Bangkok's Chinatown. This was mostly a wander and soak in the atmosphere kind of morning. We did a lot of wandering, but atmosphere was on the lean side. This probably had something to do with the fact that most of Chinatown is closed on Sunday. *Read ahead! Read ahead!* Just the same, the excursion wasn't a total bust.

Looming large, literally, among the sights we saw; the world's biggest "golden" Buddha stole the show. Cast more than 700 years ago during the Sukhothai era, the big guy sits serenely in a purpose built temple and glitters like, well... gold. The statue is twelve feet wide, almost sixteen feet tall, and weighs in at five tons; all of it pure gold!

The really cool part is that he's only strutted his stuff since 1955. To hide the golden Buddha from marauding invaders, he was disguised under a thick coat of plaster and lacquer. In this humble attire he languished in obscurity; his true nature eventually forgotten. So tell us, who forgets five tons of gold? Anyway, centuries later the “plaster” behemoth is being moved; Mister Butter fingers grabs a corner, and suddenly voila, national treasure!

Chapter 18

INDONESIA

Day 422 - March 3 - Thursday - Bali, Indonesia

Our third flight out of Bangkok's Suvarnabhumi airport moved like clockwork, and by 11:40 AM we taxied up to a terminal at Denpasar airport on Bali. Deplaning was fast and smooth. We paid $25 each, collected our on-arrival visas and luggage, and walked through the "Nothing to Declare" line. Outside, we blinked in the bright noonday sun and expectantly sucked in our first warm humid breaths of Bali. *Oh yeah, we're excited to be here!* We began this around the world trip with only a handful of places on our must-see list; Bali made the cut.

While Denise visited the restroom, a friendly taxi guy chatted me up. "Hi, where you from? Oh, America very nice. How long you stay in Bali? You have hotel?" Now, at this point, we didn't have a hotel, but that was definitely something a friendly taxi guy didn't need to know.

"Yes, we're staying at the Dewi Ayu in Ubud." We hadn't made reservations, so this was wishful fantasy, but our son visited Bali a year earlier and he gave both Ubud and the hotel high marks.

"Oh yes," says the friendly taxi guy, "Ubud very quiet, very nice." And, here comes the punch line... "You need taxi?"

"Uh, maybe, how much do you want to take us to Ubud?" By now, you may have noticed that lots of our responses begin with "Uh" or "Hmmm." Just so you know; those are place holders for deer-in-the-headlights moments when our brains scramble frantically for an appropriate response.

Believing that we'd just stepped off the suckers-are-born-every-minute plane, the friendly taxi guy puts on his straight face, "$60 US."

"Hmmm, seems a little high, I think we'll look around."

"No, is very cheap!" delivered emphatically and with a look of concern.

At the official pre-paid taxi counter, we booked the trip for $23. We think taxi drivers from everywhere in the world need special international passports and an official homeland of their own; clearly they're a breed apart.

A pleasant one hour ramble through lush countryside and we unloaded our bags in Ubud. Our luck was running strong and the Dewi Ayu had plenty of vacant rooms. We nearly opted for a $20 per night poolside bungalow with fan, until Nengah, the helpful (and friendly) reception guy, showed us the $31 AC room with a balcony and a jungle river view. *Hey, this is romantic!* Remember, as tourists of a certain age, everyone shows us their most expensive room. In this case, the sales pitch worked.

Day 423 - March 4 - Friday - Ubud, Bali

In Cambodia we picked up a $2 bootleg copy of *The Alchemist* by Paulo Coelho. If you haven't read it, you should. It's a neat little book filled with positive values and uplifting philosophy. At an important plot juncture a young boy is told, "When a person really desires something, all the universe conspires to help that person realize his dream." To paraphrase this tidbit of wisdom and to put it into the context of our personal journey, "luck trumps planning." As we winged our way to Bali, sitting in separate aisle seats, Denise eavesdropped on a conversation from the row ahead. "You'll want a hotel with a pool. They take it seriously. They won't let you leave! If you don't have a pool, you'll be really bored." *Take it seriously, won't let you leave? Okay, what's that about?*

The thing that the Balinese take seriously is "Nyepi," their annual day of silence. With no foreknowledge and even less planning, we'd landed at Denpasar airport two days before Saka New Year; the island's holiest of days.

For the Balinese, Nyepi represents a putting behind them of the past year's troubling aspects and a chance to begin life anew. On the first day of the Saka New Year, everyone hides inside their homes; they light no fires, use no electricity, and observe total silence. Tourists are expected to do the same and special police enforce the 24 hour curfew. This means: stay inside your hotel, no lights, TV, electricity, stoves, or stereos. This is serious stuff! All businesses close. Denpasar airport shuts down, and banks all over the island turn off their ATM's (as panicky tourists with empty wallets rush from one to the next). If you want to eat anything on Nyepi, you must purchase or prepare your meals the day before and store them in your room.

As any seasoned traveler knows; holy days mean festivals! Nyepi is no exception. The day of silence is a time for meditation, reflection, and introspection, but the real reason that everyone stays quiet is so that exorcised demons from the previous year won't hear them and find their way back to earth.

Here comes the luck is better than planning part. Today was "Tawur Kesanga" a day when Balinese gather at crossroad temples (highly supercharged in a supernatural way), pray, and make elaborate offerings to appease their gods and the other powers that reside in their community. The goal of these ceremonies is to harmonize the three worlds of Balinese Hindu belief: "Bhur," the world of lower beings, "Bwah," the world of man, and "Swah," the world of the gods. In the afternoon, the Balinese start to bang pots, set off firecrackers, and make smoke to scare away any evil influences that linger from the past year.

The biggest and most exciting send-offs of evil are the "Ogoh-Ogoh," giant demon puppets; *Oh yeah!* Starting weeks ahead, competing neighborhoods and civic groups vie to see who can build the biggest and scariest creatures. Frames of bamboo, wicker, and wire are given skins of foam and papier-mâché. Fangs, hair, tails, and claws are attached. To ensure that completed "Ogoh-Ogoh" are frightening and suitably sinister they're all painted in gaudy detail and given leering expressions. Competition is fierce!

At about 6 PM under a darkening sky and a steady drizzle we worked our way up Monkey Forest Road to Ubud's soccer field. By the time we arrived, festivities were in full swing. Mounted on bamboo-grid rafts and hoisted on the shoulders of twenty-five or more young men, giant Ogoh-Ogoh were already twirling and gyrating into the street. Percussive music filled the air, and each group tried to outdo the next; shaking and dancing to animate their ghoulish creations. As the parade inched up the road amid an increasing downpour, we slowly followed in its wake. Some demons were so tall that men with bamboo poles had to lift electric wires to allow them to pass.

Ogoh-Ogoh represent dangerous forces and unpredictable passions which threaten to topple the world from its axis. At the crossroads, the monsters were made to whirl and spin; first, to show the creations at their best, but more importantly to confuse the evil spirits they embody. So here we are in a pouring rain, the universe conspiring in our favor, standing shoulder to shoulder with the curious and the devout experiencing some of the best that Bali has on offer. Planning, we don't need no planning; we've got good luck!

Day 424 - March 5 - Saturday

We opened our door this morning and were greeted by a cacophony of jungle sounds: tookie-tookies, chirps, tweets, and chitters welcomed us to the day. Sounds of nature, the occasional crowing of a rooster, and little else; the normal background clatter of cars and motorcycles, hammers and saws, and people about their business, all of it was gone. Nyepi was upon us.

Like most tourist joints, the Dewi Ayu takes the day's strictures with a hefty dose of salt. The electricity stayed on, fans and AC continued to keep guests cool, and our included breakfast still arrived on the balcony table; presumably whipped up by a scofflaw in the kitchen slaving over a demon attracting stove.

Except for an emergency, you're still expected to stay in your hotel and remain reasonably quiet. That doesn't mean we were restricted to our room. Drinks by the pool set a tone for the day. The sun cooperated and guests and staff alike took advantage of the enforced downtime to work on tans, chitchat, and splash around. This was the fourth New Year's Day of our trip: Diwali, Jan 1st, Tet, and Nyepi. Indulging in a little quiet relaxation was a good way to spend it.

A small included breakfast is the only meal Dewi Ayu normally serves, but even with restaurants closed, we didn't go hungry. Lunch, dinner, snacks, and desserts flowed from the cornucopia of our pre-purchased Nyepi "meal boxes." The "boxes," prepared by nearby Café Wayan, were neatly woven straw baskets filled to brimming with all the healthy treats a hungry novice vegetarian might want. Boiled eggs, bread and butter, carrots and sweet pickles, fried mung beans, corn fritters, steamed rice, tempe, peanuts, tofu crackers, croissants with peanut butter, Balinese cakes, condiments, and exotic fruit; everything was tempting and lick-your-banana-leaf yummy. Adding mystery to culinary delight, carefully crafted banana and palm leaf packets transformed every dive into the baskets into a present-opening, childhood-remembering, grab-bag experience. It wasn't exactly playing with our food, but it was high on entertainment value.

Day 428 - March 9 - Wednesday

Ubud gets a mountain of positive press. According to shrewd marketers, if you want to experience the true

Bali up close and personal, Ubud is the place. Elizabeth Gilbert's "Eat, Pray, Love" placed Ubud's blip firmly on Ya-Ya radar, and nearly every guide book and brochure known to man waxes poetic about its warmth and beauty. It's obvious; to us at least, that under the weight of all this loving attention the town is changing.

Ubud is unabashedly a tourist destination. Nearly as many tourists as locals wander its narrow streets and uneven sidewalks, skirting the occasional tiger trap sized hole. It's impossible to venture a block without repeated calls of, "Hello Mister, Taxi? You want transport?" (26 on our last outing) And, don't get us started on the massage and other offers. Soulless modern clothing boutiques are replacing traditional business; Nike, Polo, Quicksilver, and Ralph Lauren in paradise. Snooty galleries and craft stores are rampant. Upscale tourist restaurants stand choc-a-block, boutique hotels are sprouting like mushrooms, and prices are up.

Fortunately, that's not the end of the story. The old Ubud, the quiet traditional community, that has attracted travelers, artists, seekers, and expats for decades, still remains. It's under siege, but it's still here.

Walk anywhere and we immediately encounter small delicately crafted offerings. Tiny palm and bamboo baskets filled with bright flowers and bits of food left on sidewalks, on steps, on ledges, on special display stands, on walls; just about anywhere our eyes alight. Sticks of incense smolder next to the offerings; scented smoke carrying daily messages of supplication and respect. There are literally thousands, maybe tens of thousands, of offerings and they're refreshed every day. Old ones are removed and new ones take their place. Sometimes the new are simply stacked on top of the old.

This tradition stems from the island's earliest history. A holy man called Rsi Markandaya was told by a voice from heaven that worship alone was not enough and that all people must make daily offerings: daily offerings to cleanse the land, daily offerings to appease the gods, and daily offerings to respect their ancestors. Rsi Markandaya and his people heeded the voice; were rewarded with prosperity, and in gratitude dubbed the island "Bali," a name which derives from "wali" or offering.

Wherever they came from and whatever their true significance, the offerings are fun; little splashes of color and peace that provide snacks for monkeys and birds and immediately put smiles on our faces.

As we wander Ubud's streets, we're as likely to see local men dressed in skirt-like sarongs and traditional headscarves as blue jeans and baseball caps. Likewise many women still wear traditional wrap-around skirts and lacy tops, and go about their business with jugs and baskets perched on their heads.

Peek up alleys and into courtyards and you're rewarded with views of private shrines, ornate entrance gates, and carved statuary. Look over a temple wall and chances are you'll spot a quiet ceremony in progress.

Touristic music performances abound, and in the afternoons and evenings, the air pulses to the sound of Gamelan orchestras pounding away on their xylophones, gongs, and drums.

The best thing about Ubud is its location. Sprawl has gobbled neighboring communities (Ubud was once sixteen villages) and encroached on the surrounding area, but Ubud sits in the heart of unspoiled countryside. Our hotel is located on Monkey Forest road, one of Ubud's main drags, yet the back of the property faces a green jungle of banana and palm trees, ferns, and overgrown vines. We stand on our balcony and overlook a babbling stream. Birds and squirrels scamper in the undergrowth and the occasional monkey forages through the treetops.

Day 429 - March 10 - Thursday

We plan to leave Ubud eventually, but so far we lack the motivation. There are lots of things to do here and we've found our stride. Which is to say; we're moving at a leisurely snail's pace. Sleep in a tad, read a little, take breakfast on the balcony then head out for a select activity or two.

On our second day we walked over to "ARMA," the Agung Rai Museum of Art, and breezed through its large galleries. The collection is well regarded and occasional paintings caught our fancy. If put on the spot, we're forced to admit that traditional Balinese painting doesn't seem to be our cup of tea. To our taste, the style is just too busy. Whether the subject is a classic Hindu tale or daily village life every inch of canvas is packed to overflowing; sort of Hieronymus Bosch goes to the tropics. Truth be told, we got better mileage out of the museum grounds; a beautiful park-like setting that includes ponds, a stream, temples, and rice field views.

The next day, we returned to ARMA and took two of their "cultural workshops;" hands-on classes designed to "enrich your experience of Bali's history through a deeper understanding of its arts and culture." I signed up for wood carving and Denise enrolled for offering making. The workshops are one-on-one affairs.

For two hours we sat cross-legged on the floor of an outside pavilion and worked away at our chosen cultural experience; all materials provided. Instruction was pretty much a case of monkey-see, monkey-do.

Holding a block of wood between his feet, my instructor, a nice guy named Wayan, would whittle or chip until he was satisfied, then he'd hand me the block and a knife or chisel. "Now, you do here." According to the ARMA brochure I was being "introduced to some of the basic concepts behind modeling objects in wood." I might have been introduced, but I'm not sure I'd recognize them on the street. "No! You do wrong!"

"Okay, should I do it like this, or like this?"

"Yes." *Hmmm, "Yes" not so definitive; maybe if I turn it around this way.* Wayan watches me fumble then takes the block back and chips away in a different area. When he's again satisfied, and my flaw surreptitiously corrected, the block is returned. "Now, you do here." I suspect that if I was clumsier, he would have just carved the chunk himself, handed me the finished sculpture, and congratulated me on my skill. The upside of the workshop was that my finished "masterpiece" more or less resembles a turtle and I now know that I don't enjoy sitting on the floor while using my feet as Vise-grips.

Offering making, women's work, is a spiritual activity; which means no offensive exposed knees allowed. Modestly wrapped in a loaner sarong Denise sat down, and under watchful tutelage, set out to learn the ins and outs of tiny banana leaf and palm frond creations. Soon she was happily slicing away with a rusty knife and drawing repeated looks of concern from her instructor. "I think she thought I was going to chop off my thumb."

An essential skill for the creation of offerings is an ability to push brittle toothpick-like sticks through resistant pieces of greenery. This is easier said than done and requires a stiff thumbnail or a good thimble. Denise lacked both. In a less traditional workshop she'd have been handed a stapler, but since she was there to "enrich and enhance" she muddled along snapping twigs. At some point during the creation of little square baskets, fan-like trays, tiny palm leaf faces, and flower arranging, Denise is pretty sure that her instructor gave up on her and threw in the towel. "Okay, your two hours are up!"

I walked away from my class with a chunky wooden turtle, but since Denise was making offerings, she was expected to; well... offer them. Her instructor led her to ARMA's on-site temple, helped her arrange her creations, lit incense, and then sprinkled holy water. "Okay, now you drink three times." *Drink! Drink what? That's not bottled! I don't know where that came from. Is that pot clean? I'm not drinking that stuff!* Among other things, Denise learned from her workshop that it is entirely possible to cup your hands, cover your mouth, and do a passable imitation of slurping holy water.

On another day, our selected excursion took us to the Sacred Monkey Forest Sanctuary. Located just down the hill from our hotel, the sanctuary is a small dense patch of jungle; home to three temples and a large population of grey-haired Balinese macaques. The temples are suitably atmospheric and the long-tailed monkeys suitably entertaining. Bananas and cameras in hand, tourists hit the sanctuary by the busload, but it's still a surprisingly peaceful spot to hang out.

To beat the crowds and the heat, we planned to visit bright and early at 9 AM right when the ticket booth opens. With the universe conspiring in our favor, we slept in and didn't arrive until around 10:30; just in time for an elaborate temple procession. We'd stopped to listen to Gamelan musicians and watch greedy monkeys munch sweet potatoes, when up the path came a large group of traditionally dressed boys carrying tall droopy flags and elaborate standard poles. Behind the boys came lines of brightly clad women with tall fanciful offering baskets stacked on their heads. Behind these walked two lines of women holding aloft a white silk runner with gold edges; after them, came men in white carrying large red, orange, and gold parasols; and, under the parasols, two bigger than life-size effigies (gods?). Shambling behind were two large shaggy "elephants" (think two guys in a horse suit). More colorfully dressed men and women brought up the rear carrying long chains of flowers. We have no idea what the procession was for or about, but we're really glad we were there to see it.

On our fourth full day of sightseeing, we headed across town to the Antonio Blanco Renaissance Museum. If you haven't heard of him, Antonio Blanco was an eccentric Spanish artist who came to Bali via the Philippines, took up residence, and styled himself the "Dali of Bali." Blanco wasn't a Salvador Dali and his flamboyant home, now a museum, isn't Figueres but neither fact detracts from the fun of a visit.

You enter the grounds through a lush garden where large parrots, endangered Bali Starlings, and other tropical birds mug on their roosts. When you reach the museum's main building, you're handed a welcome drink and encouraged to admire a giant three-storey sculpture that's formed from Blanco's signature. Based on his art, and random quotes which adorn the gallery's walls, the sculpture was probably sized to match the artist's ego.

The purpose built museum just behind the sculpture is a beautiful stone and marble building that displays Blanco's art to full advantage. Hung on its walls, the fancifully framed collection fills several floors, painting after painting of Antonio's favorite subjects; bare-breasted women and himself. I too have a deep partiality for bare-breasted women and I'm forced to admit Blanco was a major talent in his chosen field. Denise was less sanguine.

We concluded our tour with a look at his more explicit erotica and a stroll through his one-time studio. Blanco was a guy who obviously enjoyed his time in Bali!

Later in the afternoon, we ran smack dab into another run of unsolicited luck. While wandering up a side street, Denise ducked into a small clothing store to try on a dress that caught her eye. The dress didn't fit, but, while she had it on, it caught the eye of a French Canadian woman who'd also entered the store. The dress didn't fit her either, but it did lead to a conversation. In the course of chit-chat, the woman and her husband mentioned a nice walk that they'd taken, and conveniently it began just up the road. A few minutes later, we followed their directions down a lush path and out into the rice paddies that surround Ubud.

What a great way to spend a couple of hours! Bali's rural scenery is breathtaking. Rice fields of indescribable green stretch away into the distance. Palm and banana trees wave overhead. Flowers and blossoms dot the landscape; startling little explosions of color. Ducks squabble and cavort, and everywhere water sings and gurgles. It's a magical trek.

About the time our stomachs began to rumble, we reached Sari Organic, an isolated open-air restaurant, perched on a low commanding knoll. Sitting next to an organic garden that fuels its kitchen, the restaurant serves up outstanding veggie meals and even more outstanding views; couldn't have worked out better if we'd planned it.

Day 430 - March 11 - Friday

Today, we rented two bicycles for the princely sum of $3 each and pedaled off to nearby Bedulu, once the capital of a mighty Balinese kingdom. Traffic was heavy and the road at times white-knuckle narrow. Of course the Balinese drive on the left and we've now switched sides so many times that we never know whether we're coming or going.

There aren't many large trucks, but with virtually no shoulder to the road, each and every one that passes is an experience. They chug up behind you, their throaty roar growing louder and louder, you hold your breath; then suddenly with a honk and a whoosh they sweep past raising goose bumps and leaving bare inches to spare. Helmets would have been nice. Luckily, it wasn't too hot and after about twenty-minutes we reached our first destination sans mishap.

Goa Gajah, better known as Elephant Cave, is an included stop on the lumbering tour bus circuit. It's also a pretty cool place. We locked our bikes to a post, navigated a short gauntlet of souvenir stands, and paid our entrance fees. Since Goa Gajah is a temple complex we also wrapped up in loaner sarongs. Properly attired, we followed a steep concrete path down to the temple's main plaza.

A large pavilion sits at one end of the terrace. At its side, steep stone steps reach down into a pair of sunken pools. Carp wiggle in the shallows and six stone maidens pour never ending streams from mossy urns. Overhead, a giant banyan tree stretches its arms.

Look past the pools and fixed bulging eyes stare back. Goa Gajah's main attraction is a cliff where long dead artists sculpted the living rock into an expressive demon. Fantastic swirls and smaller monkey faces surround its head and beneath its leering gaze, open jaws form a passage into darkness. Inside, Elephant Cave is a musty t-shaped grotto with a small unadorned alter to Shiva. The cave is ho-hum but the entrance is world class.

Spreading out beyond the cave and terrace, the Goa Gajah complex includes other rustic temples, ponds, streams, waterfalls, and a pleasant network of jungle paths.

"It's about a kilometer to that temple, but if you go watch out for snakes. The big ones, the pythons are okay. The small green ones are the ones that are poisonous." We look around; down at our feet. *It's a jungle; everything is green!*

"You know Denise, I don't think I'm interested in walking out to another temple; how about you?"

"No, me neither, I'm good."

Back on our bicycles, we pedaled along searching for a side road that would take us to our next destination. A likely junction, with an excellent "left-over" Ogoh-Ogoh, soon rolled into view, but a confusing lack of signage left us scratching our heads. I held the bikes while Denise walked over to a roadside stand; pointing, "Yeh Pulu?"

"Yes, yes, Yeh Pulu." Yeh Pulu, believed to be a 14th century Hindu hermitage, was "discovered" around 1935. Like Goa Gajah it features an impressive carved cliff face.

Off the main road we began a quiet meander through rural countryside. The ride was appealing, pleasant, and also a little odd. The pleasant and appealing parts were lush surroundings, village life, and a couple of elaborate temples. The odd part was a continuing lack of signage. Yeh Pulu is one of the important attractions in the Ubud area, but there wasn't a single sign to indicate its location. At one fork in the road after another, we stopped and waited for someone to appear. "Yeh Pulu?" The passerby smiles and points, *Okay, Yeh Pulu,* and off we'd go. Sometimes we followed the main flow of the road, other times we branched off. After four or five interactions and as many turns, we reached a ticket booth sitting at the end of a shady lane. Several men sat on its steps.

"Hello, you need guide?"

"No thank you. I think we're fine."

"You should have guide. I am part of local guide organization. Is better with guide. Not easy like Elephant Cave."

"Um, how much do you charge?"

"30,000 rupiah ($3.45)."

"No thanks, we'll just do it on our own."

"Is only $3 not much."

"No, we're good."

"Business very slow, only $3."

"No thank you, we don't need a guide."

"Okay, 20,000 rupiah ($2.30)."

"No thank you."

"Is only $2 not very much money."

"Oh, alright, 20,000 rupiah."

We each paid our 15,000 rupiah entrance fee and with loaner sarongs in hand set out down a lush paved tropical path that leads to the site. Our guide pointed out a few things along the way but it soon became apparent that his knowledge was limited and his presence well short of necessary. What the heck, he was friendly, and like the Egyptian said, $2.30 wouldn't make us broke or him rich.

Instead of leering demons, Yeh Pulu's carvings depict scenes of everyday activity, possibly events from the life of Lord Krishna. Along a low cliff face stretch twenty-five yards of carvings: people on horseback, people hunting, people carrying game on poles across their shoulders, and people grinding food. In one dramatic scene, a hunter clutches the tusk of an attacking boar. Very cool; and we had the place to ourselves.

At the end of the line of carvings there's an altar devoted to Shiva's elephant-headed son Ganesha. A tiny woman, gray-haired and wizened, had positioned herself before the stone pachyderm. She was dressed in tatters and stood all of three foot ten. "She's a priest," whispered our guide.

With a chattering toothless smile, the diminutive priestess waves me over. She indicates that I should bend down so that she can reach me and then presses my palms together in supplication. Still chattering and smiling she pours "holy" water over my hands; then, without warning, she begins to splash the stuff on my face. *Oh crap! Don't do that. All the water around here is filthy.* Apparently unsatisfied with her first attempt, the priestess sloshes on another application. *Oh God, do they have Schistosomiasis in Bali?* Satisfied, that I was properly anointed, the tattered granny pointed to an offering basket cum collection plate at Ganesha's feet. I dug into my wallet and plunked down 5,000 rupiah. The priestess/entrepreneur shook her head. The implication was clear, holy water doesn't grow on trees; Ganesha could never accept such a paltry sum. I explained that 5,000 rupiah was our going rate for fifteen seconds of cultural immersion, and that it was all Ganesha was going to get. While the priestess glared, I slunk away and smeared hand sanitizer on my face.

Day 431 - March 12 - Saturday

Earlier we lamented the changes that tourism inflicts on Ubud. Now we have to own up. We like tourist infrastructure as well as the next wealthy-country hedonists. Eating in Ubud is a gastronomic delight. Over the course of the nine days, we've eaten in sixteen different restaurants. Every meal was delicious and, excluding rounds of drinks, every meal cost well under $20. We're starting to revisit a couple of places, but we're nowhere close to exhausting our options.

As if good food wasn't enough, many restaurants also offer nightly live music; everything from jazz and Cuban Son to rock and reggae. Every hundred yards or so, a different sound throbs into the night air. We wander down the streets until something hits our fancy, then for the price of dinner or a drink we have an evening's entertainment. Yesterday, we skipped the music scene and hit a third floor Italian bistro where we munched gorgonzola penne pasta and watched Marlene Dietrich strut her stuff in a screening of the 1930 classic, "Blue Angel (English subtitles)." When we wandered out, a local wedding celebration was in full swing in the street below.

Day 432 - March 13 - Sunday

Since it's a nice quiet Sunday morning, we think it's a good time for a random rant. As you travel, you run into little annoyances. Some of them come and go with the passing landscape others stick with you like a bad case of head lice. Currency exchange definitely falls into the nit-picky category.

Forget the Euro! Forget the Yen! When it comes to international travel, the U.S. dollar is the undisputed champion of the world. As Americans abroad this comes as both a blessing and a headache. The blessing is that almost anybody anywhere who knows the value of money accepts greenbacks for goods and services. The headache is that the popularity of the dollar leads to a plethora of exchange shenanigans.

In most countries, the deal works something like this; if a price is quoted to you in the local currency, then you are expected to pay in the local currency. If you want to pay with dollars, your money will be accepted, but only at a heinous exchange rate. To avoid this dismal situation, you go to an ATM and you withdraw coin of the realm or you go to a Forex bureau and convert your dollars. Either way you get nicked a couple of percentage points in the process. No one gives you the inter-bank exchange rates listed on the web. Whether they admit it or not, everyone from your home credit union to the little guy behind the counter tacks on some kind of service charge. Now, carrying less money than you started with, you're ready for commerce. Of course, the first time you want to buy something, the vendor has it priced in U.S. dollars. "How much is that in (fill in name of local currency)?" you ask. The amount you're quoted is calculated at an exchange rate that would make a payday loan shark blush. Unless you're carrying, and willing to part with, more bucks, you're up the creek.

When you cross a border, everyone demands that you pay your visa fees in greenbacks. Sometimes, it seems that if what everyone really wants is U.S. dollars, then don't make bones about it, just go the route of Cambodia and make it your de facto currency. In Cambodia the price for everything, everywhere, is quoted in U.S. dollars. All ATM's dispense U.S. dollars and the only time you ever see local currency is when you receive change for less than a buck. It's not as much fun as: lira, baht, rupees, and pounds, but unless you're a dunce, you never get taken on the exchange!

On a related note, while most countries covet your dollars they can get extremely picky when it comes to actually accepting them. "Oh, I'm sorry sir; this bill has a nick in the corner. Do you have another?" "Oh, I'm sorry sir; this bill has an ink mark on it. Do you have another?" Or our personal favorite, "Oh, I'm sorry sir; this bill is five years old. Do you have another with ink that's still fresh?"

Ninety percent of the time currency exchange is reasonable and transparent. The other ten percent the lice are at play!

Day 433 - March 14 - Monday

We started today with tea, fresh fruit, and "jaffles." The Dewi Ayu only serves two breakfasts: tea, fresh fruit, and banana crepes, or tea, fresh fruit, and jaffles; so every other day we eat banana jaffles. For the uninitiated, jaffles, a Balinese breakfast staple, start life as two pieces of buttered white bread. Banana, cheese, or some other filling is placed between the slices and everything gets grilled in a press. After grilling, the jaffle is trimmed into a circle. The result is a round slightly bland pocket of lightly toasted bread. We think jaffles are pretty good, but based on feedback from other tourists they may be an acquired taste. Maybe we're predisposed to like them because Denise's parents introduced us to them years ago under the nom d'guerre, "pudgy pie."

While we quaffed tea and munched away, the sun beamed down and the birds sang. Because we'd arranged a motor-scooter rental for the day, we took this as a particularly good and auspicious omen. There are almost as many places in Ubud to rent a motor scooter as there are places to get a massage or hire a taxi; which is to say that competition is fierce. We arranged ours, new and shiny, through our hotel for the ridiculously low price of $4.70 per day.

After breakfast, we walked up to the reception, filled out minimal paperwork, and were given a quick orientation. "The engine won't start if the kickstand is down." *Okay, good to know.* Next, we tried on helmets which we suspect were offered more in the realm of peace of mind than actual protection. While Denise waited, I thumbed the starter and wobbled down Monkey Forest Road to reacquaint myself with the nuances of scooter operation. A bit of hither and thither later, my confidence was up and my wobble down. She hopped on the back and away we rolled.

Our first stop was a gas station five minutes away. Before we pulled under its overhang we were riding in a light drizzle. The birds still sang, but the sun decided to take the day off and slipped behind a cloud to put his feet up. Our scooter rental was prepaid which meant we either flushed our $4.70 or we went riding in the rain. Misers that we are, we opted for the rain; after all, it's a warm rain.

Wet or dry, Bali is drop dead gorgeous. As we left Ubud, we entered the Bali of postcards. On all sides lush wet countryside sparkled, resplendent in a million shades of green. Small communities looked healthy and unsullied by tourism. Children in uniforms walk to school. People wearing conical hats work in their rice paddies. Giant abandoned Ogoh-Ogoh leer from the roadside. Ancient temples, shrines, and offerings lend serenity to every vista. By the time we reached Tampaksiring, a small town about eighteen kilometers from Ubud, I was wearing a poncho and Denise was hugged up tight against my back.

As the drizzle dwindled, we pulled into a parking area for the UNESCO nominated shrines of Gunung Kwai. Locking our scooter and leaving our helmets under the watchful eye of a "parking attendant," we walked up a short access road and braved the site's semi-obligatory gauntlet of souvenir vendors; "Lady, you want sarong; only 10,000 rupiah!" Just beyond the main entrance and ticket booth, a steep paved path and three hundred stone steps lead down into the lush Pakerisan River Valley and then on to the most impressive ancient site in Bali.

Before we started down, the clouds opened and it began to pour; a hard warm tropical rain with big drops that splashed, splattered, and instantly soaked your clothes. Equipped with only one poncho and no umbrella (my fault, I thought we wouldn't need it!) we took shelter on a tile-roofed platform. As the rain came down in sheets and small streams cascaded from the eaves, other people scuttled in to join us. Soon we were standing with a dozen other tourists, a couple of security guards, and five noisy chickens. Who says they're too dumb to come in out of the rain?

So far, most of the rain we'd encountered in Bali came in brief showers, ones that gust in without warning, drench everything, and presto-change-o disappear; the kind where you dart under an overhang or into a store, wait a moment or two and then go merrily on your way. This shower didn't let up. Eventually, we took advantage of a slight lull and cautiously dashed to a nearby cafe to slurp coffee and wait it out.

Since it was already lunch time, and jaffles don't hold you all that well, the wait was fine with us. If one needs to sit out a rain, Kafe Kawi is as good a place as any. Their food is tasty, their Balinese coffee is strong, and the views from their covered terrace are National Geographic spectacular.

As we pushed back from our plates, Mother Nature decided to close the spigot and make do with an intermittent drizzle. Leaving the café, we tied sacred sashes around our waists, and began the long descent. In places, the stairs were wet, slippery, and coated with slime. We'd both already taken prat-falls outside the café, separately, but at the same spot, so we inched our way down with the exaggerated caution of the vertically challenged.

Despite the rain, the slippery slime, and intrusive tat stands, the walk was fantastic. At every turn we gazed out over rice paddies, jungle, streams, and waterfalls; nature so proud, wonderful, and alive that you want to shout for joy.

At the bottom, carved into sheer stone cliff faces, stand some of Bali's oldest and largest ancient monuments. Gunung Kwai has been described as "Bali's own bit of Angkor." That's a long stretch, but that's not to say that the site isn't unusual and fascinating. Cut into the solid rock on each side of a clear rushing river are ten towering "candi" or shrines. Each of the shrines takes the form of a deeply incised arch-shaped niche well over fifty feet tall. Inside each niche, and carved from the same stone, wait huge monuments; layered geometric alters that bring to mind small Mayan pyramids; more Petra than Angkor.

There are a couple of theories about the exact dedication of the shrines, but no clear agreement. As far as we're concerned the more mysterious the better!

Our other big stop of the day was a sprawling temple complex which surrounds the ancient and holy springs of Tirta Empul. The springs were discovered around 962 AD and were believed to be a powerful font of magical power. Today, the springs, which are still considered holy, bubble up through churning black sand into a large, square, crystal-clear, pool. From this sacred pool, the holy waters pour through a line of stone waterspouts to gush into public bathing pools. We didn't join the devout in the water, but we did rent an umbrella for $0.58 and poked into the temple's nooks and crannies to our hearts' content. We posed for photos, watched Godzilla-sized carp, and ducked another warren of souvenir stalls.

By the time we climbed back on our scooter a thin fog-like mist had replaced the rain and drizzle. We pressed the starter, turned around, and headed back to Ubud; along the way, the mist turned to sunshine. Life is good.

Day 435 - March 16 - Wednesday

Yesterday cooked under a glaring sun, so this morning we made a last minute decision and again rented the scooter. We retraced our ride to Gunung Kwai and Tirta Empul, but this time we kept rolling. We climbed through more lush beautiful countryside, encountered more fearsome Ogoh-Ogoh, whizzed past more famous temples (we've seen a lot), and eventually reached the town of Penelokan perched on the caldera rim of Mount Batur.

Penelokan supports more than its share of persistent vendors and touts, but it makes up for them with spectacular vistas. The huge circle of the volcanic caldera is impressive. The cone of Gunung Batur, at 5,580 feet, rises from its center, lava fields flank the cone's sides, and picturesque Lake Batur nestles against the cone's eastern slopes.

We splurged for a buffet lunch at the upscale, and aptly named, Lakeview Restaurant where we sat on an outside balcony and soaked in wonderful panoramic views. Questionable weather began to blow in as we ate, but for a while we could see Mount Batur's craggy summit and even steam rising from hidden vents (last eruption 1994).

When we rolled away, we continued along the caldera rim intending to take a different road back to Ubud. By returning through Sekardadi rather than Tampaksiring, we were going to make a big loop. About the time we found our turnoff and started down the mountain, the questionable weather caught up with us in earnest. We pulled over and I slipped on the poncho, Denise snuggled up to my back and for a moment, things improved. Then, even more rain pelted down. A few minutes later, when I swung us under the shelter of a partially constructed building, water was coming down in dense sheets and Denise was soaked to the skin.

Standing under what might someday be a large storage shed, we watched as the heaviest rain of our entire trip pummeled the landscape. Water clattered on roofs, erupted from downspouts, ricocheted off the tarmac, and literally roared as it fell. We wrung out Denise's sopping shirt and waited for a half an hour, but the rain just kept falling and falling. Finally, we decided that, like it or not, the deluge wasn't about to stop and we had to get moving.

Over the next hour, we rode through conditions that would have given us pause in our car. Rain pinged noisily on our helmets and visibility ranged between limited and non-existent. Both shoulders of the road were awash with running muddy water that hid wheel-swallowing potholes, and forced us to the center. Lightening flashed, thunder crashed, and at regular intervals shallow muddy streams sluiced across the pavement. In some places waterborne debris littered the road. At one particularly iffy spot, men were working to shore up an irrigation channel that had burst its banks. Cars hogged the clear pavement and oncoming traffic splashed waves of dark muddy water. By the time we reached the Dewi Ayu, I was ready for a stiff drink and Denise's teeth were chattering.

Day 436 - March 17 - Thursday

Today, the sky was blue and the sun was shining, but we didn't do much. We lay around by the pool, ate some good "Mexican" food at Casa Taco, checked our email with free Wi-Fi, and indulged ourselves with long afternoon naps.

By nightfall, we worked up enough energy to hit the town for a little excitement. We walked out the door planning to catch live Reggae at a joint called Benute. We danced there last week and the vibe is good and their happy hour drinks reasonably strong, so it seemed worth a re-do. The universe had other plans. Instead of ending up with two-for-one margaritas, we ended up with classic Balinese "Wayang Kulit;" shadow puppets.

Earlier in the day, I wandered up Gotama Street, a quiet lane that's a throwback to Ubud's earlier days. Most of the traffic is on foot and the street is lined with inexpensive "warung," (eateries), small shops, and assorted home stays. Outside the "Wena Home Stay & Center of Art and Holistic Health," I spotted at poster that advertised, "Shadow Puppet Performance Tonight, 7:30 PM, Dalang (puppet master) Made Winastra." We figured that since happy hour ran until 9 PM and Reggae started at 8:30, we'd take in the puppets and then round out the night with discount drinks and a little Bob Marley.

When we reached the Wena Home Stay we were running a minute or two late and we were concerned that the show might have already started. "Hello, we'd like to see the shadow puppets. Are we late?"

"Shadow puppets, yes, yes. No problem." We paid our entrance fees of 75,000 rupiah each ($8.67), an amount that at the time seemed a tad high, and an older woman led us to the performance area.

Two rows of heavy, straight-backed, wooden chairs, sat on a covered concrete patio facing a small stage. A decorated and slightly shabby performance screen, perhaps six feet wide and four feet high, dominated the front of the stage. We plunked ourselves down in a pair of chairs and looked around in confusion. We were the only spectators.

We waited quietly, and, after a couple of minutes, puppet master Made Winastra appeared, introduced himself, shook our hands, and climbed behind the screen. Moments later, he was joined by a young boy, and another man who crawled through a window in the side of the proscenium. The lights were shut off; then someone lit an oil lamp setting the screen aglow; a flickering yellow orange strobe from the edge of a dream. Live Gamelan music filled the patio, and a large lacy leaf-like image began to flutter and twirl; The Story of Raja Suya, Act One.

Over the next hour Hindu Gods and Demons, kings and commoners, gestured and conversed, joked, struggled and fought; dancing shadows, brought to life by the skillful artistry of Dalang Winastra. Wayang Kulit shows are usually staged within a religious event such as a temple ceremony or a cremation where they last for hours, often running all night. Gods and noblemen speak their parts in Sanskrit, commoners in Balinese. Since this was a short tourist performance, the commoners spoke English. "Hello, Taxi? You want transport?" probably not dialog from an original Mahabharata Epic, but it got a good laugh from the "audience."

Our seats were uncomfortable. We squirmed around and I'll own up to a yawn or two, so it was probably a good thing the show didn't last all night. On the other hand, it's pretty hard to complain when you're watching an on-demand private cultural performance of an art form that sits at the root of everything Balinese from painting and dance to the way people behave in their daily lives. We guess 75,000 rupiah a ticket wasn't such a bad deal after all.

By the time the applause died away and we took a quick peek behind the screen, happy hour was long over and Reggae was winding down. We wandered across the street to a modest little eatery called Dewa Warung and finished the evening with cheap Indonesian chow and good conversation courtesy of a homesick American English teacher (TEFL in Jakarta).

Day 437 - March 18 - Friday

The weather stayed nice yesterday, so this morning we climbed back onto a motor scooter. Roaring (well at least putting) out of Ubud, we headed west following a winding route toward the town of Mengwi.

Roads on Bali are a little odd. Look at any map and you'll see plenty of larger ones that run north and south, up from coastal areas into the volcanic highlands. East to west it's different story. There are plenty of criss-cross connecting roads, but most of the time they don't quite line up. You roll down an east-to-west road until you hit a north-to-south road. You turn onto that road and then you go for a ways, until another east-to-west road finally winds away in the direction you actually want to travel. Most intersections are signed, but more often than not the signs don't list any names that you recognize, much less any names that appear on the map you're holding. All of which makes for round-about routes and lots of direction asking.

In Mengwi, "Pura Taman Ayun" is the town's premier attraction; an elegant, moat-surrounded, temple that dates from 1634. We parked the scooter under a shady tree, crossed the grassy outer courtyard, and then walked a slow circuit of the temple's walled inner courtyard. Just inside the low inner wall, a smaller, lotus choked, secondary moat encircles an open plaza. In the center of the compound, a fascinating assortment of thatched pagoda-like shrines called "meru" reach toward the sky.

Taman Ayun is a pleasant place to stretch, but with the sun beating down and a long ride ahead of us, we hopped back on our scooter. Shortly after leaving the temple, we pulled over and asked a traffic cop for directions. Like traffic cops the world over, he responded with a question of his own. "May I please see your license and registration?" Not exactly the answer we had in mind. Tourists who want to operate a motor vehicle in Bali are required to have an International Driving Permit. This wouldn't have presented a problem except that mine expired three months ago and wasn't endorsed for motorcycles in the first place. Thinking quickly, I helpfully folded the permit open to its identification page, which by a happy coincidence fails to list either its expiration date or endorsements. The cop scrutinized my face and my smiling picture, obviously this was my permit.

"Uh, so Tabanan this way?"

"Yes that way, then turn." While I tried to restrain my glee, he returned the expired permit, and wistfully waved us on our way. We think he was bored and a pay-on-the-spot ticket would have jazzed up his day; much better than giving tourist directions.

Tabanan is a large nondescript town and we rolled straight through. Next, we turned north and struck out along a road that climbs toward the slopes of Mount Batukaru.

Along the way, we stopped to buy gas. Bali has normal gas stations just like everywhere else, but most of these cluster around bigger towns. In villages and the boonies, petrol is the province of resellers. These entrepreneurial folks make a run into town; buy gas at a regular station, and return home to pour it into one liter glass bottles. The glass bottles sit on the shelf in tiny stores, in roadside wooden racks, and in cardboard boxes. Add a minimal mark-up and; Ta da Texaco!

We pulled up in front of a small store with a sign that proudly proclaimed, "Premium," and I stepped inside. "Petrol?" I asked. The proprietress looked at me with a benign expression that people usually reserve for idiots and small children. Clearly, I was speaking gibberish. I tried again, "Petrol," this time pointing to the scooter and the glass bottles of gasoline. Sign language overcame the shortcomings of my pronunciation.

"Ah, petrol!"

Just as in Oregon, gasoline on Bali isn't self-serve. The proprietress picked up one of the glass bottles, a funnel, a wire screen to catch random debris, and poured the fuel into our tank.

"Thank you. How much?"

"Ten one thousands ($1.20)." Luckily, almost everyone on Bali speaks a bit of English. Since we were communicating more or less effectively, Denise also purchased two bags of "janan," homemade snack chips ("ten one hundreds," $0.23 each). One bag contained what looked and felt like pork-rinds, but was actually some kind of puffed tempe with a hint of hot pepper. According to the proprietress the other bag contained "potato chips with sugar." We thought they tasted like corn, but whatever they were; they were definitely drizzled with gooey caramel that stuck to our teeth. *Yum!*

This was our third scooter outing and although they've all had goals and destinations, they've really been about the journey. The countryside in Bali is phenomenal and it's all about the green. It's really hard to do the color justice. There are just too many shades and you too quickly run out of adequate descriptives. Just when you think it couldn't get any better; it does.

Progressively smaller roads led ever upward and by early afternoon we reached the Jatiluwith Rice Fields. The name "Jatiluwith" means "Truly Marvelous" and it's an apt description. Perched on steep slopes; an emerald ocean of rice paddies stair-step into the distance. The

UNESCO nominated terraces are hundreds of years old, and the vistas across them are outstanding; green taken to a whole other level. We stopped at a little café called Krishna Warung and ate a tasty $4 lunch while savoring the view.

Volcanoes attract their own weather and as we finished our meal, the sky darkened and rain began to fall. This time it was a passing shower and we waited it out in the warung. Listening to the rain's staccato music and watching the rice fields sway and dance to its rhythm was almost sublime.

Back in Ubud, our butts numb after five hours on the scooter, we rested a little, cleaned up, and went out to dinner. Another Thursday, another dish of Italian pasta, and another black and white German movie with English subtitles; are we falling into a rut?

Day 446 - March 27 - Sun - Nusa Lembongan, Indonesia

Denise is sitting on the porch of our $18 per night, second-floor, ocean-view, room at Linda's Bungalows on Nusa Lembongan. I'm on the bed with the double doors thrown wide. We're kicked back, relaxing; waiting for a shower to pass so that we can explore.

Our second week and a half in Ubud proved every bit as enjoyable as our first. We continued our pattern, "plan" would imply forethought, do-a-little, rest-a-little; a joyful haze, each day slipping slowly and smoothly into the next. We walked. We visited temples. We walked some more. We again rented a scooter and zipped over to Padangbai where ferries leave for Lombok. We lazed away an afternoon on a beautiful sandy cove called Blue Lagoon. We visited Ubud's Neka Art Museum, the most interesting in town. We listened to more reggae. We ate more pasta and caught another German movie. Toss in a bunch of good meals, a few fattening ice cream cones, the occasional bakery assault, and just like that, another ten days comes and goes.

Yesterday, we wound up our stay in Ubud with a big finish. After breakfast, a van scooped us up from the Dewi Ayu. Fred, from Holland, was already waiting in the passenger seat. Manuela, from Germany, piled in next. Shortly after that, we were joined by a young honeymoon couple from Shanghai China. With our ad hoc international action team assembled, we headed out for a half-day of white-water rafting.

Forty-five minutes of back roads driving through lush countryside, busy with traditional rice harvests, and we rolled up to our destination. The "headquarters" of Payung Rafting consists of a sign-in desk, toilets, and a couple of shelters perched at the lip of a steep ravine. Horace, our river-guide, issued life-vests, helmets, and paddles, and then led us on a long switchback descent down to "Sungai Ayung," Bali's most popular white-water river.

Denise went white-water rafting in Alaska, and we've both floated down the McKenzie in Oregon. The Ayung was a completely new experience. Who'd have thought white-water rafting could be warm?

The other members of our international team were first-timers, i.e. a bit scared and nervous, so Denise and I ended up in the front of the boat. That was fine with us. Up-front is where the fun rushes at you. After our first rapid, we weren't so sure about our choice.

The raft was constructed with a separate inflated rubber floor that was lashed to its sides. At least it was supposed to be lashed to its sides. "Hey, is that open down there? It looks like I could push my foot right through." Right at the very front, eyelets had torn loose; whenever we hit rough water, the bottom popped open and rocks poked through. *Oooo, not good!* After Denise scraped her foot, we convinced Horace to flip the raft around and travel the river ass-backwards. "Why not? It's exactly the same shape on both ends!"

Once we were back in the "front" with a floor that remained closed, everything was hunky-dory. The rapids were all tame class II and III, but they came at us consistently. Our raft plunged and bucked non-stop, shuddering from one to the next. We suspect that Horace's skillful steering had a lot to do with the rollercoaster quality of the ride. "Look, look, monkey!" he'd shout. Then, as we all searched for a non-existent simian our raft would suddenly wham into a huge rock and hurl us laughing and screaming from our seats. In stretches of smooth water we jumped over the side and floated with the current.

The Ayung winds its way down a stony jungle canyon, and the scenery on all sides is magnificent; leaves the size of satellite dishes, huge hanging vines, crashing waterfalls, everywhere you look, an abundance of life.

Unspoiled nature is glorious and the works of man can often seem an intrusion. Every once in a while, however, someone creates something that adds to the whole. As we floated down the Ayung, we suddenly realized that the river's mossy cliff-face was carved into fantastic shapes. Monkeys, some pensive, others mischievous, frolic across the rock; furry grins frozen in stone. Elephants with silent bells around their necks plod sedately. Gods and goddesses act out ancient Hindu tales. Scaly sharp-toothed fish chase each other, bug-eyed demons leer, giant mossy alligators slither; a canvas of stone that stretches for an incredible half a kilometer!

The reliefs appear so at one with their surroundings that you immediately assume they've been there forever. The surprising reality is that the carvings are only ten years old! They're the work of ten craftsmen who labored for three years on bamboo scaffolds; joyful art created for sheer pleasure. We don't know how much they earned for their efforts, but it wasn't enough.

Our raft trip ended with a steep climb out of the canyon and a yummy included lunch.

That evening, the universe again conspired in our favor. We'd languished in Ubud long enough that the Bali Spirit Festival swooped into full swing. Yoga and holistic practices are the festival's beating heart, but each night the focus shifts to world music. We rested up and then headed over to their music venue at the ARMA Museum.

At $25 a pop, one-night tickets were a splurge, but we soon got our money's worth. We caught four bands. All of them were good. Two we really liked. The first was a chanteuse named Saritah who belted out feel-good groove music. The second was the night's headliner, an infectious high-energy outfit from Canada called, Delhi 2 Dublin. Their music melds traditional Indian riffs, global, club beats, Celtic rhythms, Dub Reggae, Electronica, and Hip Hop; pumping, on-your-feet, "Everybody jump!" crowd pleasers.

The main stage was backed by ARMA's massive carved stone gate which together with a little quavering smoke gave the setting a mysterious other-worldly appearance. A second smaller, "traditional," stage rounded out the evening, filling in between acts with Gamelan music and fire dancers; a most excellent show!

When things finally wound down, we grabbed a couple of ice cream cones and wandered back to the Dewi Ayu. It was well after midnight and all the monkeys in Monkey forest were fast asleep.

This morning, we pried ourselves loose from Ubud (imagine the screech of a rusty old nail pulled inch by inch from a warped piece of hardwood) and caught a shuttle bus to the coastal town of Sanur. An hour later, we walked our bags down a sandy beach, waded into the surf and climbed aboard an outrigger equipped "public" boat headed for Nusa Lembongan.

"Public" means wooden bench seats, some random cargo, and a slow passage. Our wind-burnt "captain" was lean and sour-faced. Taking his place behind the wheel, he pulled on a faded yellow souwester-type cap. Between his dour expression and the cap's earflaps, he looked every bit a grizzled New England fisherman who'd lost his way. All he missed was a smoldering pipe.

Our crossing took about an hour and a half and soon we waded ashore. On the Nusa Lembongan beach front, we ignored the offers of touts and porters and set out in search of the Pondok Baruna Bungalows. We didn't have a reservation, but we'd scoped the place on the Web and it looked like a possibility. When we found them, their view rooms were full, and their poolside "garden" rooms too expensive.

Since it was obvious that we needed to do some looking, I stood in the dirt street with our bags while Denise putted away with a tout on a scooter. About the time I began to test drive kidnap scenarios, the tout rode back up holding a note, "Found us a place; bring the bags!"

Day 449 - March 30 - Wednesday

Nusa Lembongan rises from the sea only an hour's boat ride from Bali. Awakening to the sound of crowing roosters, it feels farther apart. The vibe here is an easy mix of rural Indonesia, expat sundowner culture, and surfer funk. The pace of life is relaxed. Accommodations are easy to find and there are plenty of restaurants, but the "boutique" scene has yet to make an appearance. Souvenir shops are few and far between and "galleries" next to non-existent. The people are warm and friendly, and not so jaded by tourism that every interaction is about the money. The air is warm, the water is clear, and idyllic is a word that rolls off our tongues.

And the sunsets, *Oh my Gawd!* The past two evenings we sat on our balcony and watched the sky literally erupt. Above the ocean horizon, dramatic blue-grey clouds billowed, swirled, and built castles in the air. Inside their recesses and along their edges the sun painted bold shades of yellow and orange; flames and coals aglow in an open hearth. It looked like heaven itself was aflame.

Those extravaganzas lasted nearly an hour, but they were only half the panorama! On both nights, the other half of the sky was alive with lightening; electric blue flashes dripping magic and wonder. The seats on our balcony were first row!

Denise has seen her fill of the back of my head and Nusa Lembongan isn't very big, so on our first full day we rented a pair of motor scooters, and we set out in tandem on a circumnavigation.

Tourism helps keep the island afloat, but it runs neck and neck with seaweed production (emulsifier for your cookie dough ice cream). Heading north past the island's lighthouse toward "Paradise Point" and the "Mangrove Forest" we rode through one hamlet after another; seaweed drying on plastic tarps and women tying "starts" onto lines that will eventually be staked into fields under the sea.

Most of the island roads are fair to middling, but broken pavement and potholes are the norm. Near the mangroves, the track we were following devolved into muddy ruts and we decided that we must be headed the wrong way. "The map says this is the main road, but it looks pretty beat up. Maybe they don't use it any more." Of course, it still is the main road and everyone still uses it, but who knew? We backtracked to a crossroads (there are maybe six on the entire island) and cut across to better pavement.

After a few twists and turns and some more bumpity-bumpity road; we arrived at Dream Beach and it was time to park the scooters and change into swim suits. Dream Beach is a small pocket of sand wedged between two rocky headlands. The surf is rough but like the name says; the beach is a dream. We paid $6 each to use lounge chairs and swim in an infinity pool overlooking sand. A splash in the ocean, lunch, a couple of dips in the pool and before we knew it, it was almost four o'clock.

Since there was still plenty of daylight, we hopped back on the scooters and continued around the island, putting toward the Ceningan Bridge. Nusa Lembongan is the small neighbor of another much larger island called Nusa Penida. Wedged into a strait between the two is tiny Ceningan Island, and connecting it to Lembongan is a one-scooter-wide, wood floored, weathered yellow suspension bridge.

Keeping a tight grip on our handlebars and light hands on the throttle, we rumbled across and so racked up our third of Indonesia's 17,000 islands. After the bridge, it was either turn right or turn left. There was no right or wrong and neither track ran far. We chose right and in short order reached the end of the road. Dismounting, we stood on a cliff top and ogled a picturesque pool of churning turquoise water; the beautiful, but unimaginatively named, Blue Lagoon.

Rumble across the yellow bridge again and we're back on Nusa Lembongan. We continued around the island and soon returned to the land of mud and ruts. This time we pressed on, and sure enough, a couple of minutes of perseverance put us on familiar turf and completed our circumnavigation.

Another evening we shared drinks and dinner with a friendly expat Australian surfer-dude who toured us through his beautiful "spared no expense" home and alluded to his hush, hush covert-ops CIA type background. This guy isn't the first alleged ex-spook we've encountered. You always wonder; is it ego, is it reality, or is it something in between; things that make you go *Hmmmm.* Another expat later suggested that James B. (not his real name) had been on Nusa too long. "He's going island; you know, losing his marbles." Oh well, if you're going to scatter your marbles, we can't think of a better place to do it.

This morning, we were loafing when our hotel guy smooth talked us into a snorkeling trip.

"Hey Boss, you want to go snorkeling? I got two people. I can make you a good deal."

"Where are you going?"

"To Under The Wall and Mangrove Reef."

"Uh, how much?"

"Only 100,000 per person ($12) very cheap."

"Okay, why not." Before noon, we're an easy sell.

The 200,000 was well spent. We waded into the surf in front of the hotel's restaurant and climbed into a motor launch with two gals from France. About forty minutes later we jumped into clear green water off Nusa Penida.

Both of us love to snorkel. We didn't see any big fish, but we swam with plenty of small and medium ones; brightly flashing schools of this and that; some with black and yellow stripes, others outlined in electric blue. Angel fish, needle fish, small parrot-looking fish; everything in a constant swirl of motion; the coral below was outstanding; alive, colorful, and diverse. Snorkeling is like peering through an ever changing window into an alien world. No matter how often you do it, the sea always dishes up something new.

Day 450 - March 31 - Thursday - Sanur, Bali

This morning, we caught the "public" boat from Nusa Lembongan back to Bali. We'd planned to take a later "fast" boat named The Perama, but we were tendered an offer we couldn't refuse. While we were eating breakfast, the public boat pulled in just down the beach, something it only does when the tide is right, and a shore representative (tout) began to work the room. Since a ride on The Perama involved lugging our bags a long way down the beach, we figured that convenience might outweigh speed.

"How much do you charge to go to Sanur (Bali)?"

"80,000 each Boss." This was twenty thousand less than the fast boat, but it was also twenty thousand more that we wanted pay for the public experience.

"Uh, no thanks, that's too much. We'll wait."

"How much you want to pay Boss?"

"60,000 each." The tout looks around the tables to where other tourists are forking over the 80K.

"No, is good price."

"Okay, no problem. We'll go on the Perama." A few minutes later, the tables start to thin, and the public guy sidles back over.

In sotto voce, "Okay, is good. You go now."

"So, 60,000 each?"

"Yes, shsss is secret, don't tell." We grabbed our bags and waded aboard. Ah, the power of a bird in the hand.

The crossing was smooth and speed didn't matter since we both nodded and drowsed. When the outriggers crunched sand in Sanur, we deflected a couple of taxi offers and set off down a brick beachfront walk that runs for several kilometers along the shore. The walk was pleasant, but in hind sight we probably should have taken a cab.

Before we reached our hotel, we trundled our bags for nearly an hour and Denise's right foot was giving her fits. Yesterday, after snorkeling she noticed that she'd nicked it on something. She cleaned things up and smeared on some Neosporin, but this morning the scrape was puffy and sore; red around the edges. Adding insult to injury; four steps down the boardwalk she accidently kicked the spot with her other foot making it bleed and pretty much turning her into a gimp.

Day 451 - April 1 - Friday

This is our last day in Indonesia and we planned to spend it poolside. At $42.85 per night the Hotel

Segara Agung is a tad expensive, but it has a nice garden setting and the pool looks inviting. Denise's right foot had other ideas. It woke up grumpy and out of sorts. It was sore, a bit oozy looking, and both the redness and swelling had increased. Since even minor infections can turn nasty in the tropics, we decided that it needed to be looked at sooner rather than later.

Our hotel gave us the name of a doctor and following their directions we made our way over to the Gopa Medical Clinic. The clinic, which is located several blocks from the hotel, is bright, clean, and resembles a small pharmacy with a few chairs for waiting patients. Denise told the receptionist about her foot and was asked to take a seat. "The doctor will be with you shortly."

Three people were already seated, but as promised, the wait was short. The queue moved quickly and after only fifteen minutes, Denise got her turn. The Balinese doctor spoke clear understandable English. First, he checked her blood pressure and then he listened to her heart. Next, he cut away the rough edges of her scrape, picked out grits of sand, flushed the wound with peroxide, and carefully bandaged it. After he finished, he prescribed several days worth of antibiotics and put together a doggie bag of bandages and antibiotic cream for Denise to use until the foot healed; total cost, $40.40 start to finish. When you think what the same service would have cost us in the U.S. you can't help but go, *Hmmmm.*

Tonight a 10 PM we fly to Australia.

Chapter 19

AUSTRALIA

Day 452 - April 2 - Saturday - Mount Victoria, Australia

Aussie! Aussie! Aussie! Oi! Oi! Oi! It's a "footy" thing. If you don't understand it, don't worry, we undoubtedly lost something in the translation. Just because they speak English, doesn't mean that you can understand them.

The timing of our arrival here in Australia, queue Men At Work, was a random event; the precocious love-child of our abiding distaste for long flights and the unpredictable necessity of long term planning. Way back in November we decided that twenty hours in cramped economy seats and the mind numbing culture shock of a sudden return to the U.S. weren't going to cut it. We crossed the Atlantic by ship; why not the Pacific? Tramp steamers and blue water yachts flitted through our dreams, but a garden variety cruise proved more practical. We performed our due diligence, and after a thorough Internet search, we booked a transpacific journey that starts in Sydney and ends in Honolulu.

During the following six months, cheap airfares and the bureaucratic vagaries of visa expiration scheduled our migrations from one country to the next. The unplanned result was that we arrived "Down Under" just two weeks before our cruise; too short to do the country justice; too long to sit on our thumbs and wait. So, what to do? The Unnamed Guidebook told us that Sydney alone is worth two weeks! Distances in Australia are huge and internal flights are expensive. How do you explore a country the size of the continental United States in just fourteen days? We were on the verge of tossing the towel when we stumbled across a suggested week-long auto tour; a veritable "inland odyssey."

"Hey Denise, look at this, this might work: excellent rural museums, fascinating local pubs, historic buildings, Aboriginal art. We can do this!"

"I don't know. It looks like a lot of driving."

"Sure, but it sounds really cool: Australia's oldest inland settlement; armored fossil fish, quirky mining towns. The Outback! You'll see. We'll take it easy. The driving won't be bad. It'll be a blast."

"Well; I have to admit it sounds fun." *Yeah, kangaroos!* At the Sydney airport, we picked up a pre-arranged rental car, channeled the spirits of the "dreamtime," and set out to go "roll-about."

The first thing we noticed about Australians is that they drive on the left. Taken by itself, that's no big deal. We scooted hither and thither around Bali in the "wrong" direction with hardly a scratch to show for it. Why, we're practically left-brain pros. Rental cars it should be noted, however, are much wider than rental scooters and, according to my right-brain paranoia; the lanes of Australian expressways are inexplicably engineered to the width of under-budgeted bike paths. As we pulled out of the parking lot, the Europcar guy warned us, "Be careful!" and helpfully reminded us that "Yanks usually scrape up the left side."

White-knuckled hands firmly clamped on the wheel and an inadequate tourist map flopped on the back seat; we merged (doing it from the right is just plain wrong) onto the Great Western Highway and headed away on our inland odyssey. The rental behemoth (compact) tried repeatedly to drift left, and repeatedly forced Denise to cringe to the right. Through Herculean effort and razor sharp concentration I managed to keep it more or less centered and aimed in the right direction.

Ninety-minutes later, after a minimum of route-selection-bickering, we were out of Sydney's congestion and climbing into the coolness of the Blue Mountains. Our first stop was a recreational gateway community called Glenwood.

Over a late breakfast at the Apple Jazz Kitchen (your basic café): one scrambled egg, one slice of toast, and one cup of coffee each; we learned a second important fact about Australia. It's really expensive! We'd ordered the cheapest items on the menu, but our bill still hit $25.50 without a tip. Of course, it was a Saturday. Still, who's ever seen a menu with two columns; one set of prices for weekdays and another higher set for the weekend? Maybe it's a northern hemisphere bias, but we're not sure we're into it.

Straight from Bali, we expected a modicum of wallet shock, but the U.S. dollar's exchange rate to the Australian dollar lulled us into a false sense of security. Sure the Aussie dollar just broke $1.05 for the first time ever, but the two were still close; "Five cents, big deal!" Then, to the screeching sound of our budget crumbling around us, we discovered that although the exchange rate is nearly one to one, the at home buying power of the Aussie dollar is lower; much lower! Everything in Australia sells for 150 to 200 percent of what it costs in the U.S. Ouch! Maybe it's lucky we've only got two weeks.

Leaving the Apple Jazz Kitchen, we schlepped over to Glenwood's "I." Marked by easy-to-follow blue and yellow signs, accredited information centers throughout Australia greet you; welcoming arms held wide. Volunteers or employees smile, offer advice, help you with accommodations, and load you down with glossy brochures touting the unsurpassed wonders of their given area. Wherever you go, a quick visit to the "I" is darn near obligatory.

We were tired from our overnight flight, so we'd decided to make a short day of it. Our plan was to stay somewhere in the Blue Mountains. "Hi, we hope you can help us with accommodations?"

"Do you have a reservation?" When we replied in the negative, it elicited clucks of concern from the volunteer.

"Oh, I don't know. What with the weekend and the start of the school holiday, we're nearly full up." *Oooh not good!*

"We only need one night."

"All right, let me see what I can do. How much do you want to spend?" We suspected this might be a trick question so we answered cautiously.

"We'd like to keep it around $100." You've heard the expression, "that went over like a fart in church." As it turns out, $100 is the flatulent bottom of the Aussie barrel. In popular recreational areas, it even cavorts with stinky dust bunnies hiding under the barrel.

The helpful volunteer suggested a couple of options, but it was clear from body language that the options weren't ones that she'd actually choose for herself. "The (boring, nondescript) motel in Blackheath has one room left for $129. Would you like them to hold it for you?"

"Uh, can you suggest anywhere else?"

"Well, we don't list all the pubs. They're usually nicer, but they cost a little more. There's a nice one in Blackheath you might try that. It's a little farther along, just at the traffic signal."

We drove the fifty-two kilometers, found the pub, and sidled up to the bar. "Sorry, we're full up." *Okay, that's not promising.* Back in the car, we turned around, passed the boring, nondescript, now full, motel, and backtracked eleven kilometers to the town of Katoomba. Katoomba features the region's largest "I," and a pair of recommended backpacker hostels. The hostels felt shabby and overpriced, but worse still they were already full to capacity.

At the really big "I," our lack of planning again elicits "tsks" of concern. "Oh, you don't have reservations? We've been pre-booked for weeks. You do know that it's the start of the school holiday?" *Are you kidding? We're seniors; we barely know about school holidays at home.* It was about this time that we began to suspect that while conspiring in our favor the universe had forgotten to check its calendar. A popular resort area only two hours outside Australia's largest city might not be the best place to arrive unannounced for the first weekend of Easter vacation!

"Oh, you're in luck. I know a lovely little B&B that still has a room. Would you like for me to give them a call?"

"Uh, how much do they charge?"

"It's quite nice and they only charge $300 per night."

"Splutter, strangle, gasp," and other sounds of being gobsmacked; "Can you suggest anything less expensive?"

"At that price, they include a lovely breakfast."

"I'm afraid it's a little out of our budget."

"Let's see, here's another nice B&B and they're only $280."

"Gag, choke, gack!" After we explain the realities of our budget, the helpful volunteer called a pub seventeen kilometers up the road.

"They have an en-suite room for $149. Would you like them to hold it?" For some odd reason the price suddenly sounded acceptable.

Situated in the town of Mount Victoria, the Hotel Imperial is a popular local watering hole which dates from 1878. In other words; it's an old pub. This is a good time for a brief hemispheric semantic digression. In Australia a "motel" is a business located along a highway where the proprietor rents rooms to people with cars; no confusion there. "Pubs" and "hotels" on the other hand are both bars. In either one, you can wet your whistle and probably order a greasy sausage roll and chips. The weird part to an ignorant American is that neither designation gives you a clue about accommodation. Pubs frequently offer rooms. Hotels sometimes don't! We looked in the back of the Unnamed Guidebook, but couldn't find an English to English translation section; go figure.

Hotel Imperial advertises "Deluxe & Budget" accommodations. Assurances of the big "I" aside, we considered ourselves lucky when the receptionist told us they still actually had a vacancy. The distinction between "Deluxe" and "Budget" hinges on whether a middle-of-the-night pee requires you to walk down the hall. We were considering the $129 per night shared facilities room when the receptionist mentioned that it was directly above the bar. "Since it's Saturday night, we have live music. The other room might be quieter." After determining that the music would run until at least midnight, and encountering a certain evasion as to the actual nature of said music; we bit the bullet and opted to go en-suite.

Hotel rooms were pretty small in 1878, and their toilet facilities were often a pot under your bed. To get around this historical shortcoming, the Imperial had remodeled our room's balcony into a bathroom and a strange little sitting area. This odd arrangement fit perfectly with the room's hodgepodge décor; sort of Motel-6 meets arsenic and old lace. At $149 for a one night stand the Imperial was hands down our most expensive accommodation so far; value, not so much.

We'd spent most of the day looking for somewhere to sleep so by the time we registered, dropped our bags, and squared away, it was late afternoon. Tired, but not ready to hunker down in our slightly dark room, we slid back into the car and went sightseeing.

Despite their name, the Blue Mountains aren't really mountains at all. Instead, they're an ancient sandstone plateau; sculpted by time into a vast landscape of blue hazed valleys, windswept heath, and towering escarpments. On weekends (and school holidays) Sydneyites flock to the area to suck in mountain air, ogle dramatic scenery, and get up close to some of Mother Nature's signature work. Laced with 140 kilometers of walking trails, the World Heritage listed wilderness teems with plant and animal life; hundreds of species of birds, lush pine forests, mammals, reptiles, and eucalyptus varieties galore. Luckily for tired American tourists, one of whom is still plagued by a gimpy foot, it's possible to sample a few of these wonders without venturing far from your car.

Following our third backtrack to Katoomba, we picked up a designated scenic drive and headed for the aptly named "Scenic World." There's plenty of free stuff to do in the Blue Mountains, but we thought this commercial "eco-attraction" seemed like a fun place to start. The Scenic World entrance complex perches on a cliff above the verdant Jamison Valley and offers killer Grand-Canyon-esque (U.S. centric) views of its weathered landscape. The part you pay for is the "world's steepest passenger railway," which plunges down the gorge to a "Jurassic" rainforest, and "Australia's steepest cableway" which hauls you back out again.

We pulled into the attraction's multilevel parking garage and made our way through its semi-obligatory souvenir shop to buy our tickets. At this point, we learned another important Australian fact (#3). Lots of stuff closes early! It was only about 4 PM, sunset was still hours away, but already Scenic World was rolling up its carpets.

If we bought tickets and hustled, we'd have less than an hour to explore. We wasted several of our precious minutes quaffling. Should we? Shouldn't we? The cheapest no frills tickets, train down, and cableway up, cost $22 each. *Arrrgh, decisions!* The next morning, we planned to roll bright and early, so... it was now or never. $44 felt like a stiff price to pay for fifty minutes of eco-tainment, but sometimes it's best not to cheap out. Frugal travelers that we are, we once declined to walk up the Leaning Tower of Pisa to save a buck. Lesson learned; we've kicked ourselves ever since.

Based on a defunct 1800's cable car system, which once hauled coal from a mine far below, the "train" feels more like an amusement park ride than a railway. We climbed into a caged car that suspiciously resembles used carnival equipment. It clattered forward, dove over a lip, and amid delighted rollercoaster squeals we began a near vertical descent. The short ride ended a couple of minutes later and we stepped out into a surprisingly different world.

At the top of the railway, white cockatoos and lorikeets wheel above dense stands of eucalyptus; at its bottom we discovered a rainforest that begs for a dinosaur or two. This is an awesome place. Water drips. Feathery fronds of flowerless (spore producing) plants gently sway. Vines hang, and dappled sunlight filters through a forest canopy that appears untouched by time. Everywhere you look improbable fern trees stretch toward the sky; living fossils that instantly whisk you into the realms of imagination.

We were all, "Yeah! This is great!" Then we noticed the sign. "Blah, blah, blah, last cable car at 4:30, blah, blah, blah, all walks closed, blah, blah, blah, if you miss this car you'll have to hike back, blah, blah, blah, three hours, you losers, etc. (paraphrased)" Scenic World boasts "Australia's longest elevated rainforest boardwalk," but because we started late in the day, most of it was already closed! The only thing we were able to do was walk directly, and quickly, from the railway terminus to the cable car platform. What we saw tantalized. It was probably worth the price of admission, but unfortunately it was definitely a bum's rush experience. Moral of the story; go early.

That night, our dinner at the pub consisted of two beers, one order of greasy fish and chips, and a salad. It set us back $37.50; ouch! We think we're having a déjà vu of British "cuisine."

Day 453 - April 3 - Sunday - Orange, Australia

Today, we planned to escape the Blue Mountains. We didn't want to leave but with the local accommodation industry in a full-on holiday, gouge the yokels, mode we figured we'd be better off somewhere a little farther away from Sydney. As a compromise, we decided that before we cut and ran, we'd catch a little more of the area with a scenic ride on the famous "Zig Zag Railway." The Zig Zag is the area's standout attraction; a narrow-gauge tourist train that follows a former coal route, winds through eucalyptus-covered hills, and chugs across valleys on impressive sandstone viaducts. As luck would have it, an historic steam engine makes the run on weekends and holidays. Promising steep grades, tunnels, and dramatic scenery, and possibly blown cinders, the Zig Zag Railway sounded like just the prescription to get our Blue Mountain visit back on track.

The second train of the day pulls out at 1 PM which we both agreed was perfect. We didn't need to hurry in the morning and after the ride (1.5 hours) we'd still have plenty of time to hit the Great Western Highway and put on a few kilometers. We requested a late checkout, ate a leisurely breakfast (included and much better than dinner), and timed a winding scenic drive so we arrived at the station thirty minutes before departure.

When we pulled into the railway's dirt parking lot we took it as a good omen that there weren't many cars ahead of us. "Hey, it doesn't look very busy. That's good. We shouldn't have any problem getting tickets." We found a shady place to park and wandered toward the station. Then, (déjà vu) we noticed the handwritten sign. "Blah, blah, blah, due to unforeseen circumstances the train will not run today, blah, blah, blah, you losers, etc." *Swell, we just wasted the whole morning waiting for the phantom locomotive!* With a vague feeling that our travel agent needs a stern talking-to, we pointed our rental car, which by the way has now returned to compact proportions, west and resumed our "Inland Odyssey."

The first sizeable city (37,500) we encountered after descending from the Blue Mountains was Bathurst. Described as a place where Victorian buildings "can snap you back to the past," we targeted the town for a possible overnight. At the "I" it was déjà vu all over again. "You don't have reservations?" followed by sounds of concern. "You do realize that this weekend is our annual wine tasting and goat castrating festival (paraphrased). Why, we've been booked for months!"

This unexpected turn of events didn't faze us because we had, *ah hem*, other fish to fry. In addition to the phantom railroad our day's wistful plan called for a three hour side trip to the tiny burg of Canowindra. In 1955 a chance discovery by a road worker unearthed a unique treasure. His bizarre find consisted of an enormous cluster of; you got it, fossilized fish. Not just a couple of fossils, but thousands. Sometime around 360 million years ago a drought dried up their pond and these toothy armored creatures huddled together in a muddy depression and died en mass. Add a little sediment, a lot of time, some serendipitous road construction, and voila you get an internationally acclaimed Age of Fishes Museum! Scads of weird stone fish, what's not to like about that?

Sadly… the Canowindra museum fell afoul of Australia fact number two; "stuff closes early." "You do know it's Sunday?" said the helpful volunteer. "I think they close early on Sunday." Sure enough, if you want to see fossil fish on the Sabbath you have to do it before 2 PM. We were in Bathurst and it was after 1 PM. The drive takes an hour and a half, you do the math. Since accommodation looked sketchy and the Australian Fossil and Mineral Museum (home to the country's only complete Tyrannosaurus Rex skeleton) was also closed, we pushed on.

We didn't push far. Although it was still early afternoon, we decided that today was well and truly shot. We brainstormed a plan for tomorrow and called it quits in the town of Orange. We'd driven a measly seventy-five miles since crawling out of bed. If we're going to finish this odyssey in time to catch our ship in Sydney, we need to do a lot better!

It was a near thing, but we saved the day from total bustdom with the timely collection of another pair of Australia survival facts. The first (#4); if you want reasonable accommodation, get thee to a caravan park! At the "I" in Glenwood we'd grabbed some random brochures. Tucked in among them was one for a campground that offered not only tent and trailer sites, but also something called "en-suite cabins." "I wonder what the cabins are. Maybe we should check them out." As it turns out, en-suite cabins are a feature of all Australian caravan parks and they're a bargain! They're essentially permanently parked trailers (think tiny mobile homes) that come with a full range of self-catering amenities. The one we rented at the Colour City Caravan Park cost us $69 and featured: a kitchen stocked with pots, pans, and dishes, a refrigerator, a stove, microwave, a sitting area, a queen bed, a couple of bunks, and a TV that picked up all three channels. *Sweet!* Sheets and towels cost an extra $14, but we weren't lugging those silk sleep sacks and micro-fiber wonders just for the exercise.

The day's second survival fact (#5; really more of a cultural tidbit) falls into the area of tempered expectations. Small Australian towns are really good at marketing! There's also a corollary; brochures and unnamed travel guides don't necessarily reflect reality. Every Outback town wants your tourist dollar, but most lack the true standout points of interest needed to reel you in. This void is creatively filled with suggested tours, photocopied bits of history, questionable annual festivals, and glossy brochures. Remember, it's the sizzle, not the steak. We're not talking outright fibs, just lots of putting your best foot forward and creative embellishment.

A pleasant walking tour around Orange brought the practice into focus. At the local "I" the helpful volunteer handed us a nice follow-the-dotted-line map that features forty-six carefully marked points of historic interest. After a sunny lunch in the park and a quick visit to a community art gallery with a great textiles exhibit, we set out walking.

European settlement of Orange began around 1823. Regional gold rushes in 1851 led to temporary prosperity and today a few landmark buildings from that era still remain. Our problem was that unless you're an architectural fanatic or a rabid fan of Australian history, the stuff is sort of, well... ho hum. Not to put too fine a point on it, but do we really care that number 23 Goober Street was the birthplace of Jeremiah "Stinky" Fogbottom a village idiot and one time champion lawn bowler (paraphrased)," or that "It was also in this vicinity that the residents of Orange roasted a bullock to celebrate the arrival of the railway in 1877 (verbatim)?" Once we got our expectations in order and stuffed the map in a pocket, the rest of our walk was downright fun.

Day 454 - April 4 - Monday - Cobar, Australia

This morning, the Age of Fishes Museum was still tweaking our imagination so we decided that we'd loop back at the end of our odyssey to give it a second go. Before checking out, we asked the caravan park to reserve us another cabin for a week down the road. "I'm sorry. We're full up for that week. Don't you know? It's our big annual wine and hog goosing festival (paraphrased)." *Arrrgh! Okay, I guess we won't loop back.*

Our drive from Bathurst had branched us off The Great Western Highway and it was now the Mitchell Highway that led us away from Orange. As we traveled northwest the trees grew shorter, the brush scrubbier, and the landscape took on a welcome-to-the-Outback feel.

Two and a half hours behind the wheel and we rolled into the town of Dubbo (39,500); known for its "Uh, umm, yawn..." No, Dubbo is actually known for the Western Plains Zoo, which in all fairness is probably really swell. Unfortunately, we already aced our "Wild Africa" experience and trying to duplicate it in Australia just felt wrong. Instead, we took a mid-morning break over weak coffee and mushy scones; purchased a couple of "veggie pies" for our lunch, and continued down the road.

It might not sound like it, but we're starting to find our stride. Our inland odyssey isn't about attractions. It's about wide open spaces and sparsely populated towns. Australia is a huge country with a relatively small population. Out of a total of 21 million inhabitants almost 19 million live near the coast where they occupy a mere 2.6% of the continent. Our drive is taking us into a harsh land of saltbush plains, arid brown crags, ancient peoples, and serious emptiness. The journey isn't about must-see sights. It's about small pleasures and shared experiences; the sort of journey where you drive with your arm out the window and brake for the giant ball of twine instead of the Magic Kingdom.

Beyond Dubbo, the Mitchell Highway continues northwest for 163, mostly empty, kilometers to the town of Nyngar. Pulling into a city park, we found a shady picnic table, and broke out the veggie pies. At this juncture we learned another important Australia fact. "Veggie" means that there's veggie stuff inside, along with the meat! "For God's sake mate, who'd want a pie with nothing in it but greenies (archetypal reaction)?" When we ordered the pies, there was a menu board that listed: "Meat Pies," "Meat Pies with Potato," "Onion Pies," and "Veggie Pies." We'd figured that if the sign didn't list meat; the pies were vegetarian; our bad. If we fall off the veggie wagon, it's not going to be for questionable mystery meat in goopy brown gravy. The pies reluctantly found their way into the trash and we made a meal of apple slices, rice cakes, and peanut butter. After lunch, we indulged our inner child and played on the swings.

Outside of Nyngar, our road forked again, speed limits increased (70 km/h), and chasing the sun we bombed west. Now we were really on our way. Rock and Roll pumped from our iPod, the Barrier Highway stretched before us, and soon we'd be surrounded by the mysteries of the true Outback. Okay, we'll admit that we're still over-romanticizing and struggling to reign in our expectations. Dreamtime or not, when we tell Australians where we're headed, the common reaction is a roll of the eyes and a look of consternation. Or, as one Sydneyite put it when appraised of our plans; "So what happened mate, you lose a bet?"

We were just about to re-think the wisdom of our choices when we spotted our first Kangaroo sign. By sign, we don't mean tracks or spoor. We're talking about a bright yellow caution triangle. Inside the triangle was the black stylized shape of a kangaroo! Just below the triangle a smaller rectangular sign shouted "NEXT 25KM." Someone (not much of an artist) had painted a bulbous scrotum on the "roo," a questionable addition which had later been modestly covered with a thin splash of white paint. We hardly noticed. This was it! Kangaroo Jack! The big K! We swerved onto the shoulder, jumped out with the camera, and snapped pictures. Sure, it wasn't a real kangaroo, but what the heck; we were excited.

How can a plan that involves marsupials possibly be bad? We know that like "Aliens," kangaroos "mostly come out at night; mostly." That didn't stop us from looking. For the next two hours, we hurtled down the Barrier Highway, relentlessly searching. We strained our eyes toward the horizon, each vying to make the first sighting. Our enthusiasm made the time fly, but despite a succession of yellow roo signs, it failed to result in anything more exciting than a large rodent shaped stump.

By late afternoon we gave up looking for kangaroos. Instead we looked for (and found) a shady parking spot at the Cobar Visitor Center and Museum. Cobar is a productive copper mining town where fortunes wax and wane in tune to the price of minerals and the availability of water. It's also the best place for an overnight before tackling the 300 miles of Barrier Highway leading to Broken Hill.

The visitor center closes early (duh) but thanks to an unexpected time zone change we strolled in with an hour to spare.

In an unrelated aside; speaking as northern-centric people, daylight savings time that requires you to "Fall forward" and "Spring back" just feel wrong!

Inside the visitor center, the volunteer was friendly and helpful. She directed us to the local caravan park, loaded us down with the usual stack of brochures, maps, and flyers, and suggested ways to spend the remainder of our day.

With hardly a grimace, we forked over a $19 entrance fee and wandered through the museum. Interesting folksy exhibits offer up an abundance of information on topics ranging from, town history and mining, to Aboriginal life and local flora and fauna. In a yard next to the building sits the semi-obligatory rural museum collection of old farm equipment, early vehicles, and other cast-offs too large to fit inside. One standout item is an old train car that's fitted out as a doctor's office; a rolling clinic, it once provided the only medical service available to the children of Cobar and other Outback communities.

Next, we headed to a spot called the Fort Bourke Lookout. The attractions there are twofold. First, there's a viewing platform that overlooks the New Cobar Open Cut Gold Mine. The mine is an active enterprise that began by pulling gold out of an open cut. Later it went hard-rock. It's sort of interesting and a little weird to watch huge dump trucks snake their way down into the enormous pit and then disappear into a dusty hole at the bottom (remember, lowered expectations).

The lookout's other draw is the opportunity to gaze across empty flatlands that sweep to the horizon. Our guidebooks and brochures all describe "dusty arid" plains, but from atop the viewpoint the land below looks lush and green and a reservoir sparkles in the distance.

Climate and geography ensure that much of Australia receives minimal rainfall and is therefore blessed with an overabundance of forbidding wasteland. Cobar sits at the eastern edge of the Outback. It's a place so parched that in 1966 a 120 kilometer pipeline was run out from Nyngan to ensure a reliable source of water and end the town's cycles of periodic abandonment. This is not the spot for lush and green. Clearly something was amiss; and that brings us to another Down Under scratch-your-head moment.

A careful reader might notice that we've been schedule-challenged since arriving in Australia. Our timing for nearly everything has been subtly off; wrong day, wrong week, too early, too late, etc. Depending on the sights you want to see, you might also add, wrong year! Around 1992 Australia began to suffer from a severe drought. Reservoirs were depleted, lakes and wetlands dried up; harsh conditions became even harsher. As time passed, the country found itself in the grip of the worst dry spell in a century. This was bad juju for Australians but only increased the Outback's iconic desolation. Then, in late 2010, strong La Niña conditions developed and Australia experienced its wettest spring on record.

If we'd arrived at any time in the past twenty years we would have seen baked arid plains and withered dusty landscapes. Instead, we're looking at a desert in bloom, a green explosion of life. The upshot is that we're getting a view of the Outback that only comes along once every couple of decades. Is this a case of fortuitous timing or just another late arrival? Who knows? It's a bit like catching me in a tuxedo. I look swell, but it's a far cry from my day to day appearance.

Day 455 - April 5 - Tuesday - White Cliffs, Australia

Twenty-five miles outside of Cobar a signpost directed us off the highway and onto an unpaved side road. From the turnoff, another twenty miles of dirt and gravel led us toward the Mount Grenfell Historic Site; home to New South Wales' best collection of Aboriginal rock art. Except for a couple of highway maintenance trucks, full of waving workers and headed in the opposite direction, we had the trek to ourselves.

We rattled across cattle grates and bumped over a few ridges of recently dried mud, but most of the road was well-maintained and the driving easy. A mile or so off the highway we began to see wild goats and the occasional wild pig. "They're not really wild Mate. They're just runaways." Okay then, feral goats and pigs, whatever. The pigs and goats aren't kangaroos and their lineage is questionable, but they entertained us just the same; scampering through the brush and sproinging here and there; all shaggy coats, horns, and corkscrew tails.

At the isolated historic site we found shaded parking, and a nice picnic area with toilets and gas-no-flame grills. We left the car and strolled up a dirt track to the "Ngiyampaa Walkabout," a short trail that leads to the rock art.

Mount Grenfell's big draw card is its art, but long before we saw our first stenciled hand we were already hooked. The natural scenery here is rugged and wonderful; a rolling high desert of red soil and weathered rock formations, yellow and silver grasses; a palette of earthy hues shaded by subtle tones of evergreen and eucalyptus.

We signed in at the trailhead and wound our way up a gully of erosion sculpted stone and hidden waterholes. After about 300 yards, a small sign pointed us to our first cluster of Aboriginal art. "Oh yeah, this is awesome!"

Mount Grenfell is an important spiritual site for the Ngiyampaa Wangaaypuwan people and their art is extensive and varied. Under sheltering rock overhangs generations of artists have created three mystical galleries. More than 1,000 images, ranging from the commonplace to the sublime, crowd the rough walls of cave-like chambers; an overlapping mix of bodies, shapes, and scenes. Depicted in whites and blacks, yellows and red ochre; human figures dance, others gesture with spears or boomerangs. Kangaroos, emus, echidna, and reptiles run slither and jump. Overhead, mysterious symbols twirl in night skies of frozen stone.

Mount Grenfell's art belongs to the Ngiyampaa Wangaaypuwan people, but the images strike a chord which echoes back in time to the beginnings of us all. Standing there it's easy to imagine men and women hunkered next to a flickering fire; a world where humanity's connection with nature hasn't taken a backseat to the latest movie blockbuster or DVD release.

On our way back to the highway, we came upon the previously mentioned road crew hard at work replacing a cattle crossing. This proved a good turn of events on two counts. First, because the road was closed, we'd had Mount Grenfell all to ourselves. Second, and more important, because they'd just started working we were able to creep along the shoulder and ease past. As it turned out, there was more to all that good natured waving on our way in than just an Aussie predilection for a friendly “G’day.” “We tried to flag you down mate. You’re lucky. Another ten minutes and you’d have been stuck all day until we finish.” *Whew, dodged that one.* It looks like the universe is once again conspiring in our favor and thankfully back on schedule.

Returning to the Barrier Highway we flew toward a planned lunch stop in Emmdale seventy-five miles away. The dotted white line dwindled into the distance and grass and saltbush prairie stretched away on both sides. The landscape was too green, but definitely the Outback.

Prodded by yellow triangular signs, we were in the midst of another fruitless kangaroo watch, when large flightless birds suddenly stole the show. “Stop! Stop! You see em? Emus!” Sure enough, there they were; shaggy grey brown feathers, goose-like bills, fuzzy heads, and ridiculously big three-toed feet.

“Get the camera!”

“Stop!”

“Roll down the window!”

“Shssh, you’ll scare them.”

By this time the ostrich-like members of the family Dromaiidae were eying us suspiciously. We slowed down and fumbled with our camera. The emu began to trot. Before you can say, “10x Zoom,” they disappeared into the brush. All of them; all of them that is, except one. Either disoriented or demonstrating its utter contempt for our creeping vehicle, one uber-sized-turkey jumped into the road and made a drumstick pounding, plumage flouncing transit to the other side.

“So why did the emu cross the road?”

"I don't know, but from now on let's keep the camera where we can get at it!"

It turns out that emu are commonplace. Their eggs are said to smell and taste gamey, but if you're whipping up an omelet, one of them equals a dozen chicken eggs! Supposedly, they're better if you leave them on the counter overnight in a porcelain bowl; an assertion we didn't test. By the end of the day we went all the way from "Stop! Stop!" to "Hey (yawn), it's another emu."

Our lunch stop didn't go exactly as planned. Since leaving Cobar, mileage signs kept us appraised of our progress, "Emmdale 159," "Emmdale 84," "Emmdale 15," and so on. When we reached the town limits sign, we pulled into an isolated gas station that also advertised food and accommodation. "I don't know; this looks like a greasy sausage roll and chips kind of place. What do you say, let's head into town and see if we can find something better?" It wasn't until about ten miles down the road that we realized that we'd already driven through town! We'd just visited our first "Outback roadhouse." Emmdale is a blink-and-it's-gone gas and food oasis whose dot on our map roughly equals the town's actual size.

Next stop Wilcannia, 101 kilometers down the road. Wilcannia sits on the banks of the Darling River and once upon a time was Australia's third largest shipping port. In the heady riverboat days of the mid-19th century the town was dubbed the "Queen City of the West." According to one government website; its main street is lined with historic sandstone buildings and a short walk "will transport the visitor back in time to the days when the river was the highway to the Outback."

"Weird, the town looks boarded up. What's with all the storm shutters and barred windows?" "I don't know. Maybe the place was abandoned during the drought."

Nope, nuh-uh! The metal window and door grills are business as usual. If you look hard, the sandstone buildings are still there, but Wilcannia has definitely seen better days. Its population, now around 500 to 700, is mostly Aboriginal, mostly unemployed, and mostly "on the dole." We're told that on days when government checks are issued, liquor sales stop early to prevent the money from evaporating in a drunken haze. Poverty and lack of opportunity have led to the usual shopping list of social ills and Wilcannia's vibrant past is floundering under the assault.

After looking around for a place to eat, we decided to give up and grab some food from a market. We'd almost given up on that option too, when we saw someone enter a store that we'd assumed was closed. The solid door was shut and all the windows were covered by wire screens and wrought iron bars. Past the threshold, the door and windows were backed with roll up steel shutters. Inside a building only slightly less secure than the gold repository at Fort Knox, we perused a few lightly stocked shelves: cans, dry goods, and a rack of cheap plastic kids' toys. Everything was overpriced. After a little half-hearted shopping, we walked out with a diet Coke and a coffee flavored dairy drink for a whopping $8.24.

We later met a tour group of Australian seniors who were supposed to picnic at a Wilcannia park on the banks of the Darling. Instead they found themselves taken to lunch at the local "golf club restaurant." On inspection, their driver felt the park was unsafe. *Sheesh, that's a bummer!* Almost without exception, other small

Australian towns look happy and healthy. Wilcannia needs some serious TLC.

Turning north off the Barrier Highway, we headed down a paved road decorated by occasional large basking lizards; could these be the famous Goanna? A one hour drive to the north and we rolled into the mining town of White Cliffs.

Millions of years ago, the ground under White Cliffs was at the bottom of a shallow sea; a favorite Cretaceous haunt of plesiosaurs, ichthyosaurs, and a bunch of their aquatic buddies; all headed pell-mell for extinction. The ancient seabed also proved conducive to the creation of silica spheres that arranged themselves into interesting close-packed lattices. In the late 1880's a group of curious kangaroo hunters picked up samples, and the opal rush was on! From a population of 30, White Cliffs shot to 5,000. Then... markets dwindled and the opal boom went bust. Bad water caused epidemics. World War I broke out, and that was all she wrote. Today, about 200 hundred of the hardy and the hopeful still call the Cliffs their home.

Opals are nice and all, but they're not what put White Cliffs on our itinerary. It's not the sparkle; it's the weird! The people here grub for opals in one of the harshest (of course now it's green) environments that Australia dishes out. On hot summer days, it's not uncommon for the mercury to hit 50 degrees Celsius. If you're a U.S. citizen like us or just Metric challenged, that's a brain sweltering, egg frying, 122 degrees Fahrenheit! While the sun melts and withers things left outside; underground in the opal mines it's a cool constant 22 degrees (71.6 F). This fact was quickly noted by White Cliffs' early residents. Faced with blast furnace heat, water shortages, and a lack of building materials, many simply burrowed homes into the surrounding hills and stayed underground.

This subterranean trend has continued to the present and according to the brochure, White Cliffs is a place "where most people live underground." The Unnamed Guidebook states (in its usual hyperbole) that "there are few stranger places in Australia." Now we ask you, who could pass that up? Imagine a mega-sized prairie dog hill with grizzled miners popping up ala "Bop-a-Mole" and you have a rough idea of our expectations. Of course, when one is on a giant-ball-of-twine odyssey, expectations rarely match reality.

White Cliffs isn't boring, but it's not the dark side of the moon. Above ground there's: a store, a pub, a school, a few houses, a post office, a motel, a lot of corrugated tin roofs; all the mundane structures you'd expect from a small isolated mining town. There are also plenty of "dugout" homes, but they don't seem all that strange. Most are built into hillsides; sport a normal looking door and a window or two, and none of the dwellers we spotted resembled a troglodyte.

Our first stop was a local National Parks visitor center where we examined the usual natural wonder exhibits and then pumped the friendly (hey, it's a friendly country) ranger for info on what to see and do, and most importantly from our current missed-lunch perspective, where to eat.

White Cliffs features exactly two eateries. One is a long established fixture known as "The Shop," not its real name, just what everyone calls it; a sort of combination fast food counter and convenience store. The community's second "bistro" is a "new" dining experience named the "Red Earth Opal Cafe." The ranger was enthusiastic about the town's cuisine explosion so we headed on over.

The Red Earth Opal is a café/gift shop with an outdoor privy, a small covered patio, and a main dining room that's scooped into a hillside ala dugout (not near as primitive as it sounds). Naturally we ate inside. The place has that small town Americana (Australiana?) feel where you expect the gal behind the counter to chew gum and rock a big laminated plastic name tag that reads, "Blanch." Instead of the mounted animals that you might find in a rural American cafe, the walls here are lined with display cases. Cases full of opals; opals and jewelry for sale to casual diners like us and other specimens whose prices call for the serious collector: pineapple opals, opalized fossils, and more.

Well, actually there was one animal on the wall; a bizarre mummified baby Kangaroo (joey) sitting inside a hole in a bale of hay. The hay bale and the creepy little mummy were mounted into the café's wall behind a piece of Plexiglas. A do it yourself Ripley's Believe It Or Not that made you feel like you'd just pulled aside another bale of hay and ... "Holy crap! Will ya look at this? Jeez!"

The Red Earth Opal's veggie wraps were tasty, under $20, and as part of their full-meal-deal we were given an introduction to the opal digging life and a narrated tour of the café's display cases. We suspect that ulterior motives were at work, but the narration was interesting and, as we've said, we're not ones to look a gift horse in the mouth.

After lunch we set out to follow the "White Cliffs Heritage Trail." Like every small town in Australia, White Cliffs boasts its own self-guided tour. Thrill to the "Bill O'Reilly Oval." Stare awestruck at the local "Postal Services" office. Drink in the majestic wonder of "Hotels (remember bar, not bed), Supplies, and Camel Beer." Allow yourself to be brought to tears by the "Federation Day 1901" marker. Marvel at the technological supremacy of the "Solar Power Station."

Eschewing most of these mundane "wonders," we opted for a bumpy dirt road that wound us through White Cliffs' principle mining area. Along the way the Heritage Trail offers up informational signs. One describes the local discovery of opals, another, the difference between common "potch" and precious opals, a third, different local mining techniques, and so on. The trail rolls past both active and abandoned mines and is moderately interesting in the giant-ball-of-twine sort of way. Holes and hummocks of tailings pock the landscape and stern signs warn of the dangers of open pit mines. "Tread carefully and use common sense." "CHILDREN SHOULD BE SUPERVISED AT ALL TIMES." It wasn't Bop-a-Mole but it wasn't bad.

A couple of times we climbed out of the rental, poked about discarded machinery, and peered into abandoned shafts. Imagine if you will (Rod Serling voice) a hand dug well less than an arm's span wide; a hole that goes straight down into darkness. A rickety ladder runs down one side and a Rube Goldberg contraption that resembles a cheap carnival ride runs down the other. The miner works in a stifling claustrophobic space loading dirt and rocks into a bucket. When the bucket is full, the carnival ride hauls it to the surface and dumps it onto a nearby ever-growing pile of tailings. At some point, the miner quits digging straight down and begins digging sideways. All the dirt and rock still has to be struggled back to the main shaft for extraction. "Shoring, we don't need no stinking shoring!" Supposedly the ground is stable, so no timbers or bracings are used; the miner just digs away and hopes for the best. We don't know if the dictionary mentions opals under "obsession" but it should. This type of mining is clearly a pursuit for the seriously twisted!

If you catch the bug, if the prospecting obsession rubs off, if you find yourself suddenly dreaming of the big score; well then; visitors to White Cliffs are invited to "fossick" for the elusive opal to their heart's content; *Huh?* Here's the deal. Look around you. If you're not standing in the middle of someone's registered claim; then you're welcome to let your eyes glaze over and scrabble through old tailings until the dingos come home or even better until you squeeze your greedy fist around an overlooked treasure. Okay, hold on a minute. Really? How many opal-crazed miners do you think blithely tossed away the good stuff? Naturally we jumped out and scrabbled around. Strangely, our half-hearted efforts failed to produce pay dirt.

You may have noticed that we've not yet settled into our pre-reserved accommodation. That's because we saved the best for last. After completing the Heritage Trail, we headed over to the, drum roll if you please, "world famous White Cliffs Underground Motel." This establishment was about half of the reason that we came to White Cliffs. Purpose built using a special boring (holes not ennui) machine, the Underground Motel is just what the name implies. Oh sure, there's a pool and visible doors and windows on the surface, but like an iceberg, the majority of the motel lies hidden from view. Step past the main lobby and bar, or through a side door, and you find yourself lost in a maze-like warren of giant whitewashed rabbit tunnels. Like the opal mines, the Underground Motel doesn't use any shoring. Repeat after me, "The ground is stable. The ground is stable." The windowless rooms are plain and nondescript, but, hey, how often do you get to sleep in a big cozy hole in the ground?

The motel's warren digs into the side of a hill. We wandered through its tunnels building a mental map, and then made our way up a steep metal stairway which popped us onto a gravelly plant covered "roof." Careful travelers that we are, we timed our ascent to coincide with another magnificent sunset. We scrounged two plastic chairs and sat on the hilltop drinking red Australian wine from plastic bathroom cups. Spread before us in stunning panorama, the Outback sky oozed from yellows to orange, to deep electric orange, to purples and pink. Below it, the landscape crawled slowly from vibrant earthy detail into cool mysterious shadow.

Although the sunset was obviously a private show staged solely for our exclusive benefit, we magnanimously shared its best parts with a revolving group of elderly (older than us) Australian tourists; late-life bus adventurers making the most of their own escorted version of "roll-about." For coastal Aussies, the Outback is every bit as mysterious and wonderful as it is for a couple of curious American tourists. Ranging from their sixties into their sharp and still active eighties the "oldsters" were the motel's only other guests. They were friendly and outgoing and our stay might have been a bit "Bates Motel" without their company.

Did we mention that there are frogs in the toilet? None of the Underground Motel's rooms are en-suite. Remember; underground, dug into a hillside; that means, shared bathroom facilities topside. We arrived at the hotel, got squared away in our room and then I headed for the bathroom. *Oooo la wee, really gotta pee!*

Without going into too much detail, I unzip my convertible pants, and lift the lid, and there they are; two cute little walnut-sized frogs swimming happily in the toilet! *Oh Christ! What am I going to do? I don't want to pee on the little buggers; that's just not right! And, if I flush? Oh my God, what happens to them then?* Confused and under pressure, but not ready to go toilet fishing, I zipped up my pants and stepped back outside. "Hey Denise, there are two frogs in my toilet!" She's in her own bathroom, and has her own concerns. Reluctantly, but faced with limited options, I go back into the bathroom and flick on the light (dark as a tomb without it). Cautiously, I again lift the lid to the only toilet. *Oh thank God, they're gone!* Quickly, I pee, flush, and try to ignore possible consequences. Later, there's only one frog swimming in the toilet. I'm sure it's just a coincidence.

When we first arrived at the Underground Motel, we chatted with the proprietor.

"So how ya liking Australia?"

"We're having a good time; it's a great country. Our only disappointment is that we've driven all the way from Sydney and haven't seen a single kangaroo."

"What, ya haven't seen Skippy yet? Well, you're lucky mate. You run into one and he'll bugger your car good."

"We sure don't want to hit one, but just the same we'd like to see a couple."

"Aw they're all about here mate. Just wait until dusk then drive about 10K out of town. Ya can't miss em."

"Thanks, we'll give it a try."

"No worries." This of course led to the "Great White Cliffs Roo Hunt."

After the sunset dwindled and the toilet frogs disappeared, we slid into the car and crawled down the tarmac scanning the roadside for signs of "Skippy." Dusk slipped into darkness and the pavement gave way to dirt. Ten kilometers turned into twenty. We turned the car so our headlights flooded across the empty scrub. Rocks and bushes stood outlined in stark detail; but no kangaroos. We stopped, turned off the lights, and sat quietly; no kangaroos. We tried different spots; no kangaroos. "Ya can't miss em." Maybe, but we're beginning to suspect that kangaroos are another slick Australian marketing ploy.

Chagrined, we returned to the motel and inquired about dinner.

"Yep, we've got a nice family style spread; only $30 per person."

"We just ate a couple of hours ago and we aren't very hungry (God's own truth). Do you have anything smaller *and less expensive*?"

"Well, you can get a half portion for $15 each."

"Can we split one of those?"

"Why don't you run over to The Shop. They're still open a bit longer if you hurry." *Hmmm, they're already cooking for thirty and labor is expensive in Australia. Maybe $15 doesn't cover the washing overhead for another plate and two forks.*

At any rate, we got the message. We rolled to a stop in front of The Shop where the lights were still burning. Out front, a few people sat at picnic tables doing battle with greasy burgers and fries. Inside, under harsh neon lights, we squinted at the wall board. *Burgers, sausage rolls, meat pies; it's not exactly a vegetarian smorgasbord.*

"I don't know Denise. It doesn't look like there's much here we can eat."

"How about the personal ham and cheese pizza? That sounds okay. We can pick off the ham. What do you think?"

"Yeah, I suppose I could go for some pizza. I'm not really hungry. You get it and I'll just nibble a bite or two." At this point the counter gal strolls up.

"Hi, what can I get you?"

"We'd like one of the Personal Pizzas."

"Okay and what else would you like?"

"That's it, just the pizza."

"It's pretty small, are you sure you don't want something else?"

"No, that'll be fine. We're not very hungry."

Of course when the pizza arrives it's in a cardboard box the size of an anorexic CD case. We're talking a Peppermint-Patty-sized pizza that even a Bagel-Bite wouldn't envy. There was dough, there was sauce, and there was melted orange stuff. There were also microscopic ham bits that Denise removed with tweezers, but we're pretty sure something isn't officially a pizza if it's less than three farb-doodle inches in diameter! Oh well; we were warned. Denise didn't share, but fortunately there was still wine back at the room.

Day 456 - April 6 - Wednesday - Broken Hill, Australia

The morning after our roo hunt and "pizza dinner," we waved goodbye to the "seniors," gassed up in Wilcannia, and put pedal to the metal. Empty miles (kilometers) whizzed by, and just before noon we pulled into the famous Outback town of Broken Hill.

At the Lakeview Caravan Park the owner proudly pointed out that for the first time in years you could actually see a lake in the distance. We checked into our reserved en-suite cabin and then made our way to, you guessed it, the "I" for more brochures.

After looking over the glossy literature and talking to the friendly volunteer we decided that the best way to "experience the times of 'old'" and "capture the true 'guts' of Australia and its people" was on an organized city tour. The fact that half-day tours were currently on sale for half price ($30 pp AUS) may have influenced our decision. We were excited and anxious to explore Broken Hill, but we'd missed the morning tour so we purchased tickets for the next day and left to root out other adventures on our own.

Argent Street is the town's main drag, and to make sure there weren't local attractions that couldn't wait, we gave it a slow up-and-back cruise. Lots of mineral named cross streets: Oxide, Chloride, Sulphide, Bromide, etc; we're definitely in a mining town. Around the start of the twentieth century silver strikes and new found wealth fueled a frenzy of building along Argent Street. If you use your imagination, parts of the broad commercial avenue still exude a strong touch of late-Victorian charm.

On the corner with Sulphide Street stands the Palace Hotel (1889); an impressive if somewhat rundown building that once featured prominently as a location in the Australian hit movie, *The Adventures of Priscilla, Queen of the Desert.* In addition to movie credits, the Palace boasts the state's longest cast-iron verandah. Only moderately interesting in our book, the verandah still managed to snag a National Trust heritage listing.

We settled into Al Fresco's café across the street and to the sprightly tune of $40 US, fueled up on two sandwiches and a beer. Well fed and secure in the knowledge that the best of Broken Hill could wait until tomorrow, we set out for nearby Silverton 25km away.

Like Broken Hill, Silverton was a late 1800's boom town. Unlike its larger neighbor the silver played out and that was all she wrote. Today, Silverton's big claim to fame isn't silver in the ground, but silver on the screen. Dubbed, "The Hollywood of the Outback," Silverton has been the location for numerous productions ranging from *Mad Max II* (*The Road Warrior*, to us American fans) to XXXX beer commercials.

According to our glossy brochure, "Cinematographers are attracted by the clear light, the colonial buildings full of character and haphazardly placed, the wide streets, the famous pub, and the magnificently evocative scenery." "Clear light," okay we'll give 'em that one. It is nice and sunny in Silverton, but "wide streets" and "buildings full of character;" please! It's mostly a ghost town! There are no "streets," just wide dirt tracks. And, "buildings," there are a total of maybe a dozen! We skipped the "Old Goal" museum (American translation, "Old Jail") and the Mad Max2 "museum" with their attendant admission fees and instead poked into the Silverton Hotel (pub) with its memorabilia lined walls. *Yep, that's a picture of Mel Gibson when he was still cool. And, who's that gal? She was in something or other we saw.* Outside we mugged around a whimsical metal sculpture and snapped a few photos next to a replica of Max's V8 Interceptor. We wandered in and out of the local gift shop and café; drove past a couple of outlying buildings, and, well, that was Silverton.

In fairness the "town's" few buildings do have some "character" and the arid scenery probably lends itself to sweeping epics, but without the hustle and bustle of a film crew at work, it's pretty obvious why turn of the century locals picked up their homes and carted them over to Broken Hill.

Speaking of film crews at work, Silverton is in the midst of a long dry spell or more correctly a wet spell. Film-makers are drawn here by the powerful emotional impact of dark red soil set off against clear blue skies; dazzling earthy colors and magical light. At least that's what they usually find. Since the end of the drought, the reds, browns, and tans have all but disappeared under an exuberant carpet of greenery. When you're trying to shoot a Technicolor masterpiece set in a desert wasteland, Silverton's current incarnation doesn't cut it. It's still a dry scrubby looking place, but let's face facts; it's just too darn green. Film-makers will probably return sometime in the future, but for now they're off scouting locations in Arizona and North Africa.

Beyond Silverton we continued along a sealed road that led us to the Mundi Mundi Lookout. Perched atop of a low hill, a gravel parking area opens onto sweeping views across the Mundi Mundi plain; a flat nearly featureless vista that stretches to the far horizon. For most of the last twenty years, this was an otherworldly view of sun-blasted rock and barren soil. What rolled away below on our visit was empty grey-green grassland dotted with occasional darker patches of hardy brush. Australia is proving to be a decidedly odd experience.

After a semi-obligatory picture or two, we backtracked into Broken Hill and immediately headed back out in another direction. This time, we were on our way to The Living Desert Nature Reserve where for a $10 entrance fee we gained access to the site's two advertised attractions, "The Flora and Fauna Sanctuary" and "The Sculpture Symposium." Our quandary was which to visit first. Trails into each area leave the main parking lot, but each promises a different experience. The Sanctuary is ringed with an electric predator fence and provides a protected haven for native kangaroos, an arboretum, wildflowers, and Aboriginal culture displays. The Sculpture Symposium is comprised of twelve sandstone sculptures that jut Stonehenge-esque above the crown of a commanding hilltop.

"So which one do you want to do first?"

"I don't know, maybe the sculptures."

"Yeah, I think so too if there's any kangaroos they'll wait. Let's start with the climb." While not immediately obvious, this was about to prove another case of questionable decision making.

We started along the sculpture trail, and it's an excellent walk. The path works its way through a sandy wash and then quickly winds up the side of the hill. Everywhere we looked the desert was in bloom. The rocks around us were weathered and beautiful and as we climbed higher we were treated to magnificent views of the surrounding country.

At the top of the hill, we reached the Sculpture Symposium itself; a fortuitous blend of outdoor art and creative marketing. Back in 1993 the Broken Hill city council enticed a group of international artists to the area with promises of: a free tent, free food, and all the sandstone they could carve. Each artist picked an appropriate cultural theme, a chunk of rock, and began chipping away. When the twelve huge works, 53 tons in all, were complete, local contactors donated time and equipment to install them on the skyline. Ta Ta! For the cost of some food and camping equipment Broken Hill added an iconic tourist attraction. It was a cool idea. The sculptures are intriguing. The setting couldn't be better, and helpful interpretive signs give insights into the artists and their process. It's a great place to wander. Each sculpture is unique; each one oriented to evoke and compliment the power of the natural surrounding.

The walk down the hill was just as pleasant as the walk up; offering, as good trails do different sights and fresh perspectives around every bend.

When we reached the parking lot, we strolled over to the gate of The Flora and Fauna Sanctuary and were unexpectedly confronted by the flawed logic of our earlier decision. The gate in the electric fence was firmly padlocked! Unwittingly, we'd once again run afoul of Australian survival fact #3; "lots of stuff closes early." Oh well, you can only squeeze so much into each day; and who wants to see a kangaroo anyway?

Day 458 - April 8 - Friday - Gundagai, Australia

We awoke for our second day in Broken Hill brimming with optimism. The sun was shining. The birds were chirping; a perfect morning for a city tour. After reading the glossy brochure, we were pumped! This was it, the high point of our stay Down Under. Our farthest foray into the unknown; a rough and tumble mining town "beyond the Darling River on the edge of sundown...the accessible Outback...a museum without walls..." a place where "distances are huge and the big red kangaroos can cover two hundred kilometers in a night chasing a thunderstorm...a hill that changed a nation." We should have known better, tempered our expectations, and remembered Australian survival fact

#5. Small Australian towns are really good at marketing. Can you say "hyperbole?" Of course you can.

hy·per·bo·le /hīpərbəlē/

n. exaggerated statements or claims not meant to be taken literally.

Don't get us wrong, Broken Hill is a neat place. We like it. The streets are wide and clean. The town history is interesting and "The Hill" has an embarrassment of heritage homes, turn of the century pubs (23 down from 73 in the town's heyday), and assorted historic buildings. In hindsight, we're just not sure that any of that really demands a narrated bus tour.

A mini-van picked us up outside the caravan park and whisked us over to the "I" where we transferred to a full-blown motor coach. Our driver was a good-ole-boy local born-and-bred and for the next three and a half hours he drove us on a circuitous route past anything and everything that a tourist might possibly construe as even remotely interesting. As we meandered, he delivered a lively running commentary. We couldn't understand half of it, but that didn't stop us from enjoying his accent and his liberal application of regional slang. "They dish up bonzer tucker and lolly water." *Now, where'd we put that Australian to English dictionary?*

The tour included: a small one-car-garage-sized corrugated-iron mosque erected in 1891 by Afghan camel drivers. Okay, that gets two stars. A radio station shaped like an old-time radio, complete with round dial-shaped windows, we'll also give the station two stars. The old union hall and an abandoned powerhouse get one star each. The local golf course where lack of water dictated that fairways be made of dirt and "greens" of oiled sand, that gets three stars. The newer traditional (grass) golf course, made possible by a 1950's era 109 kilometer pipeline, that gets zip; likewise all the places where stuff used to be! "If you'll look to your left you'll notice a small park. That's where the public pool used to be until..." Ditto, zip, for the row of "upscale" houses and double zip for all the driver's childhood haunts. The same goes for the giant ant sculpture and the crumbling remains of the local drive-in theater. No scratch that, we'll give the giant ant one star.

The high point of the tour both literally and figuratively was the "Line of Lode," a huge hill of tailings and slag that bisects Broken Hill diagonally from north to south. Formed from the waste of more than a century of continuous mining, the hummock towers over the town; an ever growing pile of rock and dirt that accumulated above the richest deposits of silver, lead, and zinc ever discovered. To date, the coat-hanger shaped load has yielded up over $100 billion in wealth and the mining still continues. At the height of production in the 1950's more than 6,000 men worked underground.

Hard rock mining is a risky profession and it was especially so in the early days when local mines were backbreaking and dangerous. Perched on top of the waste heap, the Miner's Memorial stands as a monument to the more than 900 Broken Hill miners who've lost their lives to: cave-ins, explosions, suffocation, and other assorted carnage. The stark steel building houses a long wall of dark stone. Names of the fallen, their ages, and their causes of death are etched into the wall. The whole structure feels claustrophobic; a design element intended to evoke the feel of life underground. Once you walk past the litany of gruesome deaths, the memorial also offers up outstanding views overlooking the city and surrounding countryside.

We were going to award the memorial four stars, but sadly we had to take one of them back. After several minutes spent soaking in the view and gasping at the recorded mayhem, our driver shooed everyone over to the Line of Load Café. At the café, conveniently located mere steps away, we were given nearly 45 minutes to soak in overpriced lattes and expensive souvenirs! When in due course our tour reached its underwhelming conclusion, we both sighed with relief and clambered off the coach.

Next, we checked out of the caravan park and made our way over to Patton Street. In the glory days of mining, both sides of the Line of Load bustled with activity and Patton was Broken Hill's "other" main street. Today the street is a sleepy backwater. It's also the home to Bell's Milk Bar, the last must-see on our "Silver City" itinerary. Bell's claim to fame is that it's a genuine 1950's soda fountain, a throwback that proudly ignores the passage of time. Homemade syrups, thick milkshakes, old fashioned "spiders" (ice cream sodas) and original décor are the reputed draws. We sat down, ordered "extra thick" $7 apiece chocolate milkshakes, and in so doing learned another Australian survival tip. "Thick" is a culturally relative term. If you think thick means your spoon will stand up in your glass, you're in for a rude awakening. Extra, extra thick might do the trick but we wouldn't bet the farm.

Our straws hit bottom with a slurping sound that marked the beginning of the end of our inland odyssey. We still had another week in Australia but our days were slipping away. If we wanted anything approaching a leisurely trip back to Sydney, it was time to turn around.

The route that we laid out for our odyssey forms a big loop, starting and ending at the Sydney airport, one way out, another way back, no driving anything twice. We spent six days working our way out to Broken Hill, but only two-and-a-half bombing back to the coast. Somehow the faster journey seemed the longer. Maybe it was because we pushed harder. Maybe it was just attitude. The Prince's Coastal Highway and Sydney still waited ahead, but suddenly we found ourselves feeling that Australia was drawing to a close.

By the time we turned our backs on Broken Hill it was well into the afternoon. Because of our late start we only drove as far as Mildura (297km), a thriving (30,000+) agricultural center on the banks of the Murray River. At first, our route took us through windswept scrub and miles of desolate farmland, a landscape struggling to recover from years of drought. As we neared Mildura irrigated orchards and vineyards slowly replaced the emptiness of the Outback. At dusk we crossed the Murray River from New South Wales into Victoria. Our drive ended at the Crossroads Holiday Park with another en-suite cabin, laundry, and another "home cooked" meal. The Outback was behind us.

Our next day, Mildura to Gundagai, was all about the distance; multiple gas stops, bad sandwiches for lunch in the town of Hay, two slices of raisin toast and one coffee at McDonalds in Wagga Wagga; eight hours behind the wheel.

There were more kangaroo signs, wombat signs, and even a koala sign. Sadly, there were no signs of the real thing. If we were asked to hazard a guess, we'd say that we're now eligible for some type of award; if not an award, at least an entry in the Guinness Book of Records. Questionable roadkill aside, we believe that we've just become the first pair of tourists in Australian history to traipse 2,500 kilometers across the "gaffa" (look it up) Outback and fail see a single kangaroo! It wasn't an accomplishment we envisioned when we set out, but you take the laurels that are laid in your path.

It was early evening when we turned off the Hume Highway; our destination, the rural town of Gundagai ("in a pinch, you can stay at a cabin park here"). Gundagai is reputed to possess a "romantic bush appeal" and its main street has been described as "grand." A slow drive up-and-back failed to discover the "grand" or ignite our imaginations. We were worn and frazzled from the day's drive, so instead of sightseeing we turned to the more immediate and mundane concerns of food and lodging.

A conveniently located market reeled us in and we stopped to pick up dinner fixings. You know the sort of stuff; a can of beans and assorted throw-in veggies to make it feel "homemade."

Australian supermarkets and grocery stores (for that matter supermarkets and grocery stores everywhere) are cornucopias of cultural experience. We're not talking big survival rules, just little head-scratchers that remind you that you're far from home. Take parking for instance; in most small Australian towns parallel parking is a newfangled fad that hasn't caught on. When people stop at a market or other business along the main drag they pull in or back their cars up to the curb at an angle. There's something about this type of parking that feels less hectic; a throwback to an earlier era of ice cream socials and band concerts in the park. Maneuver into any slot, and immediately we get a nostalgic "Aw shucks, *Leave it to Beaver*" sort of rush.

Even something as humble as the ubiquitous shopping cart, "trolley" in Australian, can yield an "Ah ha!" tourist moment. In the U.S. you load your shopping cart with goodies and pay for your purchases. Outside the store, you abandon the now unwanted cart in a parking lot where it's either retrieved by a minimum wage worker with acne or a bag lady with shifty eyes. In Australia they've found a better way. The first time we walked up to a row of carts and watched someone feed a two-dollar coin into a slot to free a cart, we were flabbergasted. "No way, I don't believe it! They charge you to use a shopping cart!" As it turns out they don't, but it took a friendly explanation before we understood the system. You feed a one-dollar or two-dollar coin (which by the way is smaller) into a box on the trolley and that unlocks it for use. When you return the cart to the rack and relock it, out pops your coin. Neat, nothing says responsible shopping like, "refundable deposit."

On the slightly more arcane side, there's "Tasty Cheese." Stare into any dairy case and you find rows of the stuff; white waxy looking blocks with nary a hint of explanation for bewildered Yanks. "I don't get it. Is this all they have? Where are the cheddar and the mozzarella? Oh well; maybe we'll just skip the cheese." Forty or fifty years ago the only thing in the case would have been a strange thickened Velveeta-like product with closer ties to the laboratory than the kitchen. Enter cheap generic cheddar that Australians find, well "tasty," and an icon is born. We didn't try it, but we expect it's probably good on toast with a smear of Vegemite.

After filling the larder we went looking for the Gundagai Tourist Park; recommended by the Unnamed Guidebook. The park seemed popular and was located near a public swimming pool, but somehow its $84 (U.S.)

cabins struck us as blah. Luckily, we had an option. Rolling into town, we'd spotted another caravan park's small weathered billboard advertising cabins for $68 AUS ($72 US). After a little scouting we located the place nestled on the banks of the Murrumbidgee River. The cabin was clean and comfy and the river views were serene. In fact, the cabin was in such good condition and located so near the river that it looked suspiciously like it might have been recently washed away and replaced; sweet dreams to the sounds of the murmuring Murrumbidgee.

Day 459 - April 9 - Saturday - Kiama, Australia

Last night was our final en-suite "camping" and by dusk tomorrow we arrive in Sydney. Since we knew that today wouldn't involve very much driving, and since Gundagai is billed as an iconic country town, we decided to slow down and let the region wow us with its giant-ball-of-twine best.

Following a leisurely start, we rolled over to the Prince Alfred Bridge; named for, you guessed it, Prince Alfred. The iron truss span which dates from 1867 is no longer used but in its heyday it was considered a technological wonder. Together with a timbered wooden viaduct that runs across the Murrumbidgee River flood plain, the bridge stretches for more than half a mile. A stones throw away a turn-of-the-century wooden railway trestle also juts across the flood plain. The bridges are mildly interesting, but since they're both closed to entry their entertainment appeal is limited. We spent a few quiet moments enjoying the bucolic scenery, snapped a couple of pictures, and moved on.

Next, we took in commanding views of the surrounding countryside from a high spot called the Mt Parnassus lookout. More bucolic, albeit hazy, snapshots and we were back in our rental wonder, again hurtling down the Hume Highway.

At this point Denise and I have to confess to a smidgen of excitement. Starting yesterday, and many miles back, we began to see signs for the "famous Dog on the Tucker Box." We had no idea what to expect, but we figured it had to be something special. After all, there were plenty of signs. There were small signs. There were official looking signs; you know that brown color which denotes points of interest. There were full-size billboards! "Only 25km to The Dog on the Tucker Box." Clearly, this was an attraction not to be missed!

Eight kilometers outside of Gundagai we pulled off the highway into Snake Gully. Billboards immediately rose to greet us, "Welcome to The Dog on the Tucker Box Tourist Centre." "Coaches Welcome (in case you're traveling with forty-eight of your closest friends)."

We can only assume that, "The Dog on the Tucker Box" is a Australian icon which requires both familiarity and an understanding of cultural context to achieve its full dramatic impact.

"Where is it? I don't see anything?"

"Right there, that's it!" The "it," is a life size, decent but not exceptional, sculpture of a dog sitting on a box.

"Wow, really? Ok, I don't need to get out, do you?"

"No, I'm good." In hindsight we should probably have hit the gift shop for a souvenir patch or at least a refrigerator magnet.

Owing to the intense exhilaration of The Dog on the Tucker Box, we both worked up a considerable appetite; next stop, the Long Track Pantry just down the road in Jugiong. The Pantry is an old general store that's been renovated into a pleasant country café with good coffee and a reasonable menu. We ate a sunny breakfast outside on the porch and promptly forgot the bronze dog.

The distance from Gundagai to Kiama on the coast is only about 185 miles so we took the rest of it at a leisurely touristy pace. Much of our drive followed the Illawarra Highway, an enjoyable byway that turns off the Hume and links to the coast near Shellharbour. The best bits are winding curves, favored by motorcyclists, that snake through the rainforest and eucalyptus stands of Macquarie Pass National Park.

We also feel compelled to mention the town of Robertson, New South Wales; home of "The Big Potato." Yeah! Now there's an attraction we could sink our teeth into. If your local Chamber of Commerce doesn't have a point of interest to market, obviously they should build one. And, if your area grows potatoes, what could be more natural than a tank-truck-sized concrete Russet? Naturally, we hung a U-ey and hopped out for a photo op.

Believe it or not, this wasn't our first "Big Potato." So how does Robertson's Big Russet stack up? Well...compared to the big potato in Idaho Falls (USA), Robertson's spud lacks both "sour cream" and a "pat of butter." On the plus side, Robertson's russet is at least three times as large; hmmm, quality or quantity? We think we have to go for quantity; "sour cream," or not, Robertson's spud gets our big-ball-of-twine nod. If you're going to build a Big Potato, then Paul-Bunyan-size is the only way to go! By the way, that's a native Australian name, "bun'yan." Really, look it up!

The eastern coast around Kiama is beautiful. It's well populated, about 20,000; think Southern California of a bygone era. It's definitely a beach community, but houses are well maintained and reasonably spaced. Like the rest of Australia the area around Kiama is lively but doesn't feel crowded. It reminded me of visits to my grandmother's home in Sunset Beach (CA) back in the 1960's when the coast highway was two lanes and you could wander across without getting squashed or thrown into jail for jaywalking.

Kiama's "I" is located on "Blowhole Point" within spitting distance of the area's favorite attraction, a rocky sea-cave, that under the right conditions, spouts water through a "skylight;" occasionally hurling it 195 feet into the air. Or so we're told. The key to the previous description is the phrase, "under the right conditions." 600,000 visitors a year stop to watch "The Big Blowhole" do its thing. We watched, but didn't see. Once again our timing seems to be on the fritz; something to do with tides and seasonal ocean currents.

After staring at the empty hole for several minutes, crossing our fingers, and wishing really, really hard, we gave up and wandered over to the visitor center. Inside, we were greeted by now familiar looks and sounds of concern. "You don't have reservations? Oh my, we're really busy this time of year. How much would you like to spend?" Options for the spontaneous and budget challenged once again left us with two choices, the boring nondescript motel or the "historic" pub with live rock and roll.

We drove by the motel and quickly opted for the pub. What the heck, we like rock and roll! This decision was just as quickly reversed. After a peek into two of the pub's "historic" (read "old") rooms, we climbed into our car and zoomed back to the not so creatively named "Motel 617." Fortunately the vacancy sign was out, and a mere $127 U.S. secured us a basic place to lay our heads. Motel 617 isn't going to give Motel-6 a run for its money, but at least our room was clean and included: a fridge, a microwave, and a DVD player. There was also a swimming pool, but proximity to the street and an egregious lack of lounge furniture meant that we only noted its existence in passing.

On the plus side, if we accidently locked our key in the room, it wouldn't be a big deal. The 617's helpful management has cut small, 12"x12, hatches into the outside wall of each room. We'll sleep soundly knowing that if a crisis should arrive, the desk guy can open the tiny hatch, stick his hairy arm through the hole, and open our door. We don't know... We might have done it another way; maybe a passkey?

We spent the rest of the day sucking in the sea air and enjoying the ocean vibe. First, we drove to the far end of Kiama and paid a visit to a smaller but more reliable natural attraction called, the "Little Blowhole." In our book a tiny blowhole that actually blows wins hands down over a gigantic one that doesn't. Although also not creatively named, the Little Blowhole rewarded our persistence with one modest gusher after another.

After getting our fill of splashing water, we doodled south along the coast to Gerringong. We parked on the street and a local guidebook pointed us toward lunch at the Perfect Break Café. The Perfect Break is vegetarian oasis tucked in next to the Natural Necessity surf shop. The food is excellent and you can enjoy killer sea views from the surf shop's upstairs dining area. After we ate, we spent a few minutes shooting the breeze with Kent Ladkin, Natural Necessity's owner, a really nice guy who we initially mistook (much to our excitement) for world famous surfer Marco "Occy" Occhilupo. Hey, they both surf, they're both handsome, and they do look a little alike!

From Gerringong it was on to Seven Mile Beach in Gerroa. We walked hand-in-hand along the sand and watched a fiery red sun set majestically over the Crooked River estuary.

Day 463 - April 13 - Wednesday - Sydney, Australia

Tonight will be our fourth night in Sydney and the days left on our journey are disappearing faster than pop-beads at an old school Club Med. Despite the Unnamed Guidebook's admonition that Sydney needs two weeks, we've tried to cram it into 72 hours.

Our drive from Kiama proved longer and less interesting than we expected, and as we all know, there's nothing like unmet expectations to take the wind out of your sails. Because of its "rural nature and lower traffic volumes" we decided to stick to the Prince's Highway, a coast hugging segment of Australia's Highway 1. With the exception of a rugged forest section which winds through the Royal National Park (est. 1879) the route is slow, urban, and congested.

It was late afternoon when we finally hit the Kingsford Smith Airport, dropped our rental car, and wearily made our way to the Sydney Visitors Centre in the international arrivals terminal. When we told the helpful bloke behind the counter that we were looking for a hotel under a hundred dollars, he grimaced and told us that there wasn't anything on offer. Seeing our looks of dismay, he took pity on us and threw us a bone. The bookings desk didn't have anything in our range, but he pointed us to a free computer terminal and told us about a couple of non-visitor-centre places that we could try.

After a bit of Internet searching, we booked four nights at a reasonably nice, reasonably well located hotel called the "Aspire;" $100 AUS ($106.59 U.S.) per night, sight unseen, tax included. A $34 airport shuttle whisked us into town.

The first thing that you notice, at least the first thing that we noticed, about Sydney is the sky. It's clean. It's clear, and it's remarkably blue. After fourteen months on the road, having spent at least some of it in some truly gritty cities, it was a revelation to roll into a national capital as clean and unpolluted as Sydney. If you like modern with a serving of culture, a hint of history, and a dollop of charm, then Sydney's your oyster.

On a recommendation from the Aspire's desk staff, "We'd like something nicer than a McDonald's but nothing fancy," we walked several blocks to the Essen Austrian Café for dinner. The food was first-rate, but in hindsight our budget would have been happier with the Vietnamese takeout down the street. We shared a green salad and a beer, and split a serving of vegetarian spaetzle and forked over $66 U.S.

A misunderstanding over the beer almost pushed our bill to an even higher total. Austria is of course famous for beer and one wall of the Essen sports a huge chalk board listing all of the wondrous beverages on offer. After careful consideration we decided to splurge for a $10 glass of "Falkenbräubergerstädterbladder" or some such brew that we'd never heard of. When the waiter plopped down our "glass" its volume would have put a 32 ounce Big-Gulp to shame.

"Excuse me, we didn't order this."

"You didn't want the Falkenbräubergerstädterbladder?"

"Yes, we want a Falkenbräubergerstädterbladder, but only a glass."

"That is a glass." We have to admit, the waiter had a point. The pony keg sized vessel was clearly made from glass and it did have a handle!

"Uh, but doesn't it come in a smaller size." After further discussion we determined that yes; Falkenbräubergerstädterbladder is available in smaller less manly sizes. Seeing that I was drinking out of my weight class, our waiter agreed to leave the tankard and charge us the lower price. Free beer! I tried mightily to drain the glass but even with Denise's help I ended up slinking away in defeat. Who'd have thought that the day would arrive when I'd walk away from free beer!

Our accommodations at the Aspire Hotel featured an underwhelming view of a wall next door, which might have mattered if we'd spent any time in our room. As things played out, the last three days started early, ended late, and our room was only a place to lay our heads and leave our luggage.

The Aspire, apparently the hotel's third or fourth name, sits on Bulwarra Road in a quiet student district anchored by Ultimo College. For anyone who's interested, Ultimo is south of Darling Harbour; roughly three miles from Sydney Cove and the heart of the city's tourist action.

After a quick included breakfast in the hotel dining room, we headed out to explore. We strolled eastward through the edge of the Haymarket District and into Chinatown where we reached George Street, one of Sydney's main drags. Our plan was to head down to the harbor-front area called "Circular Quay." According to what we'd read the Quay is a good starting place for sightseeing and big views, so we jumped on a free CBD,

Central Business District, shuttle. The free route 555 buses pass by every ten minutes in both directions on a loop that runs from Central Station to Circular Quay along Elizabeth and George streets.

Circular Quay is a bayside transit center where city buses, ferries, and light rail all converge and the 555 deposited us right there at the base of Sydney Cove. This is a great area for gawking and aimless wandering. Facing the water, the iconic Sydney Opera House is on your right and the equally famous harbor bridge towers to your left. Wide harbor-side walkways encourage leisurely strolls and the hustle and bustle of tourists mingles with the scurry of business people and the antics of street performers, all played out to the haunting sound of a digery-doo. Behind you, bright steel and glass skyscrapers declare the city's prosperity, silhouetted against that sky of startling blue. Circular Quay is a people watchers treat, the sort of place where it's easy to pick a seat and simply fritter away your hours.

We gave the harbor its due, but our three day whirlwind schedule kept us on the move. We're nuts for museums, so our first stop was the Museum of Contemporary Art. The MCA is a large waterfront building that hosts an interesting collection of changing exhibits which showcase the up and coming from the mundane to the bizarre. We didn't see the next Rembrandt or the next Picasso, but we had fun and the admission was free.

Next we walked westward into "The Rocks." This small well scrubbed and now preserved historic district was home to Sydney's first European settlement. Once a rough and tumble working class neighborhood where filth, violence, and disease were the norm, its backstreets and colonial buildings are today chock-a-block with the usual array of tourist services, cafes, and boutiques.

Despite rampant commercialism The Rocks is still a good place to poke into nooks and crannies. We visited Cadman's Cottage, a structure that was erected in 1816 as the home for an officer responsible for the harbor's government boats, their operations, and their crews. The cottage is mostly nondescript but its longevity qualifies it as the colonial settlement's third oldest building. Don't ask us about the first two; we didn't get there. Admission to the cottage was free. Are you beginning to see a trend?

Next up was the Rocks Discovery museum, a small converted 1850's warehouse, with simple well done displays that highlight the area's settlement history and The Rocks' pre-colonial aboriginal inhabitants; another freebie.

Toss in a shared tuna sandwich and a couple of lesser stops and the day slipped away. Before we knew it, we found ourselves at a convenience store buying bus tickets back to the hotel. The free 555 shuttle is awesome, but unfortunately the coaches turn into pumpkins at 3:30 PM sharp; 6:00 PM on weekends and for some odd reason 9:00 PM on Thursday. Regular buses in the downtown area (CBD) are Pre-Pay which means you need to purchase your ticket before you climb on board. We wrapped up our evening with Indian food at a joint called Little Haveli.

Day two saw us hop on the Metro Monorail for a quick fifteen minute spin around its short Darling Harbour to the Exhibition Center loop. The single-rail elevated train doesn't go much of anywhere, but who can pass up "the transportation of the future."

After our Jetsons experience, we made our way back toward Circular Quay. Eschewing the 555, we walked into the heart of the city, past Town Hall and the Sydney Tower. Munching chocolate hazelnuts we wandered through the historic Queen Victoria Building; a space that's tucked between George and Pitt streets and now functions as a shopping mall. Continuing toward the harbor and peering at window displays, we wove our way through Sydney's upscale shopping area.

Back in The Rocks, we splurged $8.50 apiece for entrance to the Susannah Place Museum. The museum is a neat little collection of four connected terrace houses built in 1844. The wild thing is that the homes were more-or-less continually occupied until 1990 with only minor concessions to modern convenience. Each of the four homes is intended to evoke a different era of working class life. The interiors are sparse, but peeling wall paper, layered paint, and a few minimal furnishings get the idea across. The kitchens, bathrooms, and laundry facilities (or lacks thereof) were particularly interesting.

"The National Opal Collection" called for another stop. The Collection is unabashedly a high-end opal boutique whose purpose is to exchange shiny baubles and impressive trinkets for cold hard cash. If you're on a budget, the attraction is their free-mini museum which awaits you at the top of an escalator. There's a short video presentation about opal formation and opal mining, and a number of display cases filled with over-the-top opals in the raw, "pineapples" and the like. The best pieces are fossilized bones where the calcium has been replaced by opal. Remember White Cliffs and the shallow Cretaceous sea that dried up millions of years ago? The Collection's showstopper is a nearly complete opalized plesiosaur skeleton that glitters like it was dipped in jewels; dinosaur bling, way cool!

Today, we spent our last full day in Australia plying the waters of Sydney Harbor and exploring nearby Manly. Sydney's natural harbor is about as picturesque as natural harbors come, and there are plenty of sightseeing cruises to help tourists get out and enjoy it. Since we weren't jonesing for a buffet lunch, cocktails, or cheesy commentary, we opted for the public ferry. The Manly Ferry takes thirty minutes to make the scenic run and, at about $7 per person each direction, it isn't a budget buster. We walked on board at Circular Quay under beautiful blue skies and were treated to great harbor views of the opera house, the "Coat Hanger" bridge, and all the harbor's assorted maritime comings and goings.

The community of Manly straddles the northeastern arm of the entrance to Sydney Harbour about seventeen kilometers from the central business district. Our ferry dropped us at a wharf on its western side where the waters are calm and there's a shark netted swimming area. Walking out of the terminal we found ourselves at the start of the "Corso" a pedestrian walk, and shopping gauntlet, which leads across the peninsula to: a long stretch of sand, the open ocean, surfers, and sun worshipers. With no particular agenda, we lazed our way through the afternoon, people watching, picnicking, and sauntering along the seafront boardwalk.

On our way back to the hotel, we stumbled across a hole-in-the-wall takeout pie place and, unlike its Outback counterparts; this one sells actual vegetarian veggie pies. Our favorite is the "veggie tiger," a flaky hockey-puck-sized crust filled with steaming vegetables, served on a piece of wax paper and crowned with a generous scoop of mashed potatoes and "mushy peas;" *Yum!*

We only scratched the surface of Australia, but reservations are telling us it's time to move on. Tomorrow at 3:30 PM we board the "Rhapsody of the Seas" for our cross-Pacific cruise to Hawaii.

Chapter 20

ACROSS THE PACIFIC

Day 467 - April 17 - Sunday - At Sea, South Pacific

Dinner just finished and we're headed into our fourth night onboard the "Rhapsody of the Seas." On our last day in Sydney we were antsy to be on our way, so thankfully the morning flew. We checked out of the Aspire, trundled our bags over to George Street, and again caught the free 555 down to Circular Quay. When we got off the bus is was like, "*OMG...*" the ship was tied up at the pier and the thing looked ginormous huge! It was as if someone snuck an uninspired squat white skyscraper into the harbor while we slept.

We didn't check our luggage, so we swept through security and walked quickly up the gangway. This time no one confiscated our Swiss Army knife, an oversight that left us equipped for mutiny if the need arises. Our stateroom is situated on Deck #3 and located toward the rear of the ship; aft for nautical types. When we opened the door, it looked pretty much like our last stateroom. Hotel décor; decent size, but minus the sea-facing glass wall, the private balcony, and the outside chairs. *Sigh!* You couldn't exactly hear us deflate, but there was a moment. Oh well, it's an outside cabin, and it does have a big window. We tossed our bags on the bed and headed out to investigate what our ship of choice had to offer.

We poked around, located the gym, changed our dinner seating to what we hoped was a better table, and participated in a mandatory lifeboat drill. Before we knew it, night fell and Rhapsody was casting off her dock lines.

The beauty of our exit from Sydney Harbor was an unexpected surprise. Against a dramatic backdrop of clear starry skies buildings towered, their windows all a twinkle like gigantic jewel-covered boxes. Closer to the ship, the opera house hinted at the magic inside; massive clamshells softly illuminated into dream-like arches. Everywhere lights cast shimmering beams across the water; dancing reflections that dappled its dark quiet surface in hues of white and electric blue. The night air was damp and warm and we stood at the rail breathing it in until we reached the gusty expanse of the open sea.

Life on a cruise ship at sea is predictable and you find yourself quickly falling into a routine. Get up. Wander up to breakfast. Go to the gym. Walk a couple of miles around the exercise deck. Drop by the library and check out a book. Stake out chairs by the pool. Play a round of Bingo. Test yourself with morning trivia. Set your clocks forward. Eat lunch. Work on your politically incorrect tan. Listen to the uninspired "Caribbean Sounds" of "Roots Vibrations." Take a ballroom dance class. Eat dinner. Hurry over to the "Broadway Melodies Theater" for the night's "Headliner" extravaganza. Go to bed. Start over.

Fortunately, our table change worked well and we landed with an engaging group of dinner companions. Most of Rhapsody's passengers are Aussies, "Oi! Oi! Oi!," but our table is a mixed bag; two Aussies, two French

Canadians, and another couple from the U.S. Judging from our first few meals, there'll be enough quality conversation to carry us for the duration. On night number two the dress suggestion was "formal attire." In my case that meant that I zipped the legs onto my convertible pants and picked out a less wrinkled t-shirt. *Ah, life is good!*

Day 475 - April 24 - Sunday

We haven't kept up our journal and another eight days have crawled by. "Wait a minute, the 17th to the 24th, that's only a week!" Nope, wrong; day number five was Monday, April 18, 2011. Then, we crossed that imaginary demarcation called the International Date Line, and suddenly "Abracadabra!" day number six was Monday, April 18, 2011 all over again. *Whew, déjà vu, Groundhog Day; who thinks this stuff up?* Pondering the temporal oddities of time-keeping at sea is a fine way to while away your hours, but during the past eight days, the Rhapsody also hit all five of our planned ports of call.

Our first stop was Fiji. *Oh yeah Fiji! How romantic does that sound?* With 300 islands in the archipelago from which to choose, we ended up on Viti Levu, the largest of the bunch and home to seventy percent of the Fijian population. Suva, the republic's capital and largest city is on the east side of the island. We docked at Lautoka which squats on the west side.

Lautoka is a town of about 50,000 that's sometimes dubbed "Sugar City" because it's home to one of the largest sugar mills in the southern hemisphere. Its population is a mix of indigenous islanders who've been there for 3,000 years and descendents of 60,000 indentured laborers that the Colonial British "relocated" from

India in the late 1800's. English, Fijian, and Hindustani are all spoken on the street. Our daily shipboard-newsletter describes Lautoka as a place that "hums with modern day activity."

We suppose a visit to Lautoka dishes up an authentic slice of modern Fijian life. We found it sort of a yawn. Despite a public market, some old colonial homes, and a scattering of 100-year-old banyan trees our overall impression leaned toward nondescript and gritty as opposed to romantic and exotic.

The port is a ten minute drive from town and if you don't fancy the long hot walk, the ship "as a convenience" offers to shuttle you for $10 roundtrip. *Hmmm, $10 times 2,000 passengers; nice convenience, wink, wink!*

Our next stop was Raiatea French Polynesia, "birthplace of the gods." At about 65 square miles and with a population of around 12,000, Raiatea is the second largest of the Society Islands (the biggest is Tahiti). As we approached everything looked promising. The sky was blue and dotted with an appropriate artistic quantity of white fluffy clouds. The island appeared lush and inviting, and the port was right at the edge of town. Our daily shipboard-newsletter, the oracle on such matters, described Raiatea as, "yet to be tapped by tourism." The newsletter also mentioned that the island doesn't have any beaches to speak of. No problem, a boat booked at the "Visitor's Bureau" can whisk you to a nearby "Motu." Motu are small islets resplendent with soft sand and turquoise water. *Okay, sounds good to us, we'll take it!*

When the Rhapsody docked it was noon. We walked down the gangway to the pier and, like everyone else who hadn't booked one of the ship's shore excursions; we made our way into the island's large modern visitor center. Inside, the walls were lined with information and transportation desks. With a nod to the surreal, only two of the counters were open. There was a lone woman at a general information booth and a harried girl with a cell phone at another explaining to a hundred or more, "Motu" ready, tourists that all her boats were full. We have no idea what made all the other counter people disappear; maybe lunch, maybe a random holiday, maybe a shortage of boats, maybe a general lack of interest? Your guess is as good as ours. We looked at the chaos, looked at each other, and decided to settle for a walk. By the way, "yet to be tapped by tourism" means, like Lautoka only smaller and with less selection. If you sailed up to Raiatea in your yacht or hopped off a tramp steamer the island is probably a paradise. Viewed as part of a shuffling Hawaiian-print-clad herd it leaves something to be desired.

Next on our island hopping lineup came the archetypal three-days-and-two-nights, honeymooner, all-inclusive, dream-destination of Bora Bora (actually Pora Pora, since there's no "B" in Tahitian). The Rhapsody threaded its way through the island's barrier reef and churned slowly across turquoise waters of the surrounding lagoon. We could see built-over-the-water bungalows, white sand beaches, crystal clear shallows, and gently waving palms. Throw in the verdant green slopes of Mount Otemanu and we're talking picture postcard perfect. The ship anchored offshore and we tendered in to the tiny port of Vaitape.

As we exited the pier area, we encountered some of the same expectations versus reality disconnect that plagued our first two stops. Our plan was to rent a car and meander around the 22 mile rim road that encircles the island. The reality was that the locals asked, and were getting, $200 USD for a four hour rental. *Ouch!* The idyllic town of Vaitape doesn't offer much in the way of entertainment: a few shops selling souvenirs and jewelry (mostly closed), a couple of small markets, an Internet café, a post office; at this point, we'd add "etc" but there really wasn't any.

"Okay, let's go back to the pier and catch a ride to a beach." When in doubt it's always good to get a smidgen of sand between your toes. Next, we discovered that since it was the start of the Easter weekend, the island's resorts had closed their beaches to cruise-ship day trippers. That left to us with Matira Beach, a public strand of white sand and clear turquoise water that we reached via a 15 minute $5-a-pop ride in "Le Truck;" one of those flatbed-to-rural-bus conversions that seem to be a staple of island life the world over. Except for a public restroom that's seen better days, Matira Beach is short on amenities; no beach chairs, no cold beers. What it does have is location, location, location! Its sand is powdery and soft, the water sparkles, and requisite palms whisper quietly overhead. With the sun beating down, we slathered on sunscreen, spread out our Indian bedspread; that was all she wrote.

Our day wasn't quite what we planned, but we're not complaining. While waiting for our return trip on the Le Truck, a taxi driver asked if we needed a ride back to town. We offered the same fare as the truck and since $10 is better than an empty cab, we rode back in style.

The next morning we again awoke to soaring expectations. Ahead of us lay the iconic and mysterious tropical paradise of Tahiti; our port of call, Papeete, the "alluring cosmopolitan epicenter" of French Polynesia. *Yeah, this is going to be awesome!*

Rhapsody sailed during the night and by 7 AM she was maneuvering up to her appointed dock. The ship's schedule called for us to be in port all day so we didn't see any point in surfing the press of passengers hurrying to get ashore. While people queued and jostled, we ate a relaxed breakfast; later we strolled down the empty gangway.

Leaving the ship we were immediately funneled to a nearby visitor center where a scattering of local vendors sold trinkets and a Polynesian girl in a coconut bra swayed to the beat of a four piece island band. Moving right along, we crossed a busy thoroughfare and dove into the beating heart of the island capital.

To our frustration, the heart was beating pretty darn slowly. On the day before Easter, half of the city was closed! Not that our own hearts were set on strolling through souvenir shops, but there really wasn't much else to do. We walked to Marché Papeete the town's "famous" municipal market, a place that's "always bustling." Admittedly, there were some locals shopping and buying groceries and a smattering of colorful fruit stands, but clearly it was an off day. *Okay, that took all of five minutes.*

After the market, we wandered around taking in the sights. The spirit of Paul Gauguin is invoked everywhere, but we're pretty sure Tahiti has changed since the old boy last wielded his palette. We walked past the pastel colored City Hall, a couple of old churches, and a small park or two, but today, Papeete's main features seem to be heavy traffic and 1960's era concrete buildings, enlivened here and there with a splash of graffiti.

Eventually, we made our way to "Le Musee De La Perle." Like "The National Opal Collection" in Sydney this business houses a small but intriguing private museum;

one that's open to the general public free of charge. Like its Sydney doppelganger, there are also dozens of sparking glass cases full of ulterior motive. Tahiti boasts a few other museums, but the rest are located outside the Papeete limits and are way too far away to walk. We browsed the displays about pearl history and the pearl industry; we peeked into the sparkling cases, fended off a half-hearted sales pitch by a haughty well-dressed saleslady who could smell that we weren't buyers, and then moved on.

Papeete's best attribute is probably its waterfront promenade. This is a modern concrete walkway that stretches for a mile or so along the harbor and buffers you from the city with a wide swath of grass, playgrounds, and landscaping. We'd enjoyed our fill of Papeete's congestion and shuttered stores, so we let the boardwalk escort us back to the ship.

On Easter Sunday we tendered into our final port of call. Moorea is yet another island paradise that looks like it just jumped off a picture postcard. Dramatic peaks jut from startling green hillsides and the island rises like a jewel in its setting from a translucent emerald lagoon. Beyond the edges of a surrounding reef, lap the restless azure waters of the Polynesian sea. Moorea is a seriously beautiful place.

According to our daily shipboard-newsletter the island's beaches are "magnificent expanses of both white and black sand," beaches that "can be rated among the world's finest." What the newsletter failed to mention was that we couldn't reach any of them because the island was closed up tighter than a drum. Hey, at least we weren't in a crowded city. We took a long walk along a coastal road pausing to listen to a Polynesian congregation sing hymns before returning to the ship.

Day 480 - April 29 - Friday - Honolulu, Hawaii

Looking back with 20/20 hindsight, we think that our now long ago cruise from Galveston to Barcelona might have been unusual. Two of our four Atlantic ports of call were interesting. The other two were flat out wonderful, and all of them offered good quality sightseeing within easy walking distance of the ship.

Before each port of call on our current Pacific cruise, our daily shipboard-newsletter warned ominously, "To make the most of your visit to ... (fill in the blank) and the surrounding area we suggest you take one of our organized Shore Excursions." None of those excursions cost less than $100 per person, but perhaps we should have heeded the warning. This cruise line is likely no better or worse than others in this regard, but without those excursions we think we missed out. Maybe we've just been traveling too long and we've reached a point where it takes more to wow us. On the other hand, maybe we're too independent, too cheap, and we've been spoiled by third world bargains.

We're not sure about "traveling too long," but we do know that we've been on this ship too long. Today is day number seventeen. *What were we thinking?* The last three days were all at sea and we're starting to go stir crazy; too much bingo, too much Karaoke, too many trivia tournaments. Sure, we received "special" certificates for "Crossing the Equator" and we made party hats for our waiter's birthday. And... yes, we attended the "famous" midnight chocolate buffet, but our politically incorrect tans have reached well-done and gargantuan buffets and cheesy entertainments have worn tissue thin. After more than a year of independent travel we're moving to a different beat.

As much as we want to get off this ship, we're still far from ready to admit that our travels have drawn to a close. Around noon, under cloudy overcast skies, we stood at the rail staring out at Diamond Head and Waikiki Beach. The Sand Island Coast Guard Base slipped by on our left and before we knew it Rhapsody had tied up next to the Aloha Clock Tower. Honolulu, O'ahu, Hawaii; we guess that if our trip has to end, this is as good a place as any.

EPILOG

If this was an adventure novel, it would end with a car chase, the destruction of an evil wizard, or discovered true love. We have the true love part covered, but this is real life and a long journey's end is every bit as challenging as its beginning.

The United States is a high pressure country that's always in a hurry. We may lack ubiquitous touts and street vendors, but we're still a land of huge expectations and never ending commercialism. Walking out of that port building in Hawaii was as dramatic a change as any foreign border that we crossed. We were, and still are, suffering from severe culture shock. To date, we've purchased a used car, bought auto insurance, paid our taxes, and, now that our COBRA plan has expired, been turned down for health insurance. On the plus side, nearly a year has passed since Zanzibar and Denise's fingernails and toenails are mostly back to normal.

Our first mainland stop after leaving Hawaii was Portland, Oregon to see our son, Austin, and his sweetheart Sally. We spent two weeks camped on a futon in their back room, eating vegan, and re-bonding as a family. After that, we headed up to Bend to house sit for dear friends Claire and Ed; an endeavor which entailed three weeks of petting their two cats, staring at views of the snow covered cascades, watering their plants, and occasionally mowing the lawn; all activities that fit perfectly as we try to wrap our heads around reentry. Next up, we need to decide on a place to live, get our stuff out of storage, and dive in to the future.

We lived our big dream; did we purge the wanderlust from our hearts? Not by a long shot! Our coffers are nearly empty, but we still have itchy feet and other wonderful and exciting cultures await us just down the road. It is a dangerous business going out your door, but allowing yourself to be swept off to who knows where brings you face to face with the sublime. Some adventures end, others wait to begin.

Day 1 – Who Knows Where?

CPSIA information can be obtained
at www.ICGtesting.com
Printed in the USA
BVOW08s1840271016
466217BV00001B/14/P

9 780985 729103